THE RISE AND DEMISE OF GERMAN STATISM

THE RISE AND DEMISE OF GERMAN STATISM

LOYALTY AND POLITICAL MEMBERSHIP

Gregg O. Kvistad

Berghahn Books
Providence • Oxford

Published in 1999 by

Berghahn Books
Editorial offices:
55 John Street, 3rd Floor, New York, NY 10038 USA
3, NewTec Place, Magdalen Road, Oxford, OX4 1RE, UK

Library of Congress Cataloging-in-Publication Data
Kvistad, Gregg Owen.
The rise and demise of German statism : loyalty and political
membership / Gregg O. Kvistad.
    p.   cm.
Includes bibliographical references.
ISBN 1-57181-161-3 (alk. paper)
1. Political participation—Germany—History. 2. Political
parties—Germany—History. 3. Germany—Politics and
government. 4. State, The.   I. Title
JN3770.K83   1999
324.243—dc21   98-41129
                                                            CIP

British Library Cataloguing in Publication Data
A CIP catalogue record for this book is available from
the British Library.

Printed in the United States on acid-free paper

For Amy and the memory
of Rosebud

CONTENTS

PREFACE

I would like to thank the following organizations and institutions for their generous support for various parts of this project: the Fulbright Commission; the Berlin Program for Advanced German and European Studies and the Social Science Research Council; the German Academic Exchange Service (DAAD), and the Office of Internationalization at the University of Denver.

In the process of completing this project, I have incurred intellectual debts from a number of scholars and friends—none of which, of course, translates into responsibility for the lender: Hanna Pitkin, Paul Thomas, Martin Jay, Reinhard Bendix, Peter Katzenstein, Gerard Braunthal, A. James McAdams, David Levine, James Caporaso, Spencer Wellhofer, Claudia Wörmann, Helga Haftendorn, Andrei Markovits, Jeffrey Herf, Uwe Thaysen, Dietmar Schirmer, Martina Sprengel, Beverly Crawford, Peter Merkl, Peter O'Brien, Jeffrey Peck, and Hermann Kurthen. Last, but most, Norbert Finzsch.

I am especially grateful to the staff at the Press Archive at the Social Democratic Party (SPD) headquarters in Bonn, under the able direction of Peter Munkelt. I am also deeply indebted to Klaus-Henning Rosen for providing access to the papers of Willy Brandt at the Friedrich-Ebert-Stiftung in Bonn-Bad Godesberg.

Material from chapters 3, 5, 6, and 7 appeared in different form in: "Between State and Society: Green Political Ideology in the Mid-1980s," *West European Politics* 10, no. 2 (1987): 211–28; "The 'Borrowed Language' of German Unification: State, Society, and Party Identity," *German Politics* 3, no. 2 (1994): 210–25; "Accommodation or 'Cleansing': Germany's State Employees from the Old Regime," *West European Politics* 17, no. 4 (1994): 52–73; "Building Democracy and Changing Institutions: The Professional Civil Service in the Federal Republic of Germany," *Center for German and European Studies, Working Paper 5.31*, University of California, Berkeley, October 1996.

INTRODUCTION

Political Membership, Logics of Appropriateness,
and Political Loyalty in Germany

In the early 1990s, Europe experienced two world-historical events that threatened to sever two of the strongest moorings of postwar West European politics. One planned, the other not, each encouraged the migration and attempted migration of hundreds of thousands of people across Europe; each fundamentally challenged the ability and right of European nation-states to manage population movements across their geographic borders; each provoked consternation among West European publics; and each focused attention on the very definition of membership in a sovereign political community. The dramatic and unexpected collapse of the Iron Curtain in 1989 removed what had been for nearly five decades the most formidable obstacle to relatively free movement across Europe. The West's protests of human rights abuses in the Soviet Bloc for decades had not prepared it for the myriad consequences of ending the division of Europe, a division that had been increasingly regarded as "normalized" via the politics of *détente*, *Ostpolitik*, and *Deutschlandpolitik*.[1] Similarly, the European Community's Maastricht Treaty of 1991, which gave birth to the European Union, less dramatically but no less meaningfully laid down an ambitious blueprint to transform a trade alliance of sovereign nation-states into a monetary, social, and political union. While the Delors regime promoted the step-by-step integration of Europe's monetary, social, and foreign policy, the full ramifications of this process were left for individual nation-states and their political communities to sort out, and then not always tolerantly and universalistically.[2]

Among the many consequences of these events, a frontal challenge to the notion of membership in a political community has been perhaps the most profound. Modern meanings of membership and political community were concretely challenged by migrants and would-be migrants attempting to find new places to live.[3] The end of the Cold War caused many East-Central Europeans to try to act on implicit invitations read in forty years of Western foreign policy, particularly Eastern Germans and East-Central Europeans of German ancestry. The new European Union promised the virtual unimpeded movement and choice of residence and employment to member-states' citizens in Western Europe. As a result, West European publics were disoriented by two relative constants in their political world becoming variable. Reactions in Germany, France, Italy and elsewhere included xenophobic outbursts unprecedented in the postwar era.[4] European governments, in turn, responded in ways reflecting not only the immediate crisis of thousands of noncitizens of one form or another wishing to settle within their national-state borders, but also their own traditional answers to the question of what it meant to be a member of a political community. The European nation-state most affected by these events in the early 1990s was the one that had just become whole, the unified Federal Republic of Germany. A number of political, economic, and social factors combined to make Germany a very attractive magnet for would-be migrants in the early 1990s; some of those same factors made the Federal Republic a very reluctant host.[5]

The question of hosting migrants in the Federal Republic in the early 1990s drew a response that reflected not only the immediate migratory opportunities posed by post-Communism and Maastricht. Germany's response was also informed by a thirty-year debate over the constituent elements of membership in the German political community. This debate involved participants as varied as street demonstrators in the 1960s calling for "more democracy"; political parties, intellectuals, churches, and courts engaged in a divisive battle over entrance requirements for West Germany's professional civil service in the 1970s and early 1980s; leftist ecological activists first founding and then transforming a social movement in the early 1980s into a quite "normal" parliamentary political party; and candle-light marchers, right-wing skinheads, scholars, and politicians from across the political spectrum all weighing in on demands to reform the Federal Republic's asylum, naturalization, and citizenship law in the 1990s. Each of these disparate actors engaged a diffuse democratic challenge to a powerful nineteenth-century German anti-democratic logic of political membership. In most of these cases, what was being challenged was much more coherent and logically consistent than what was challenging. Being challenged was Germany's two-century-old political ideology of statism, a logic of political membership that vertically segmented the realms of state and society and pivoted on the top-down vetting of a political loyalty required for entrance into a variety of venues of German political membership. Challenging was a rejection of that statism informed by a diffuse democratic and horizontalist idea of belonging to and participating in a political community.

The Concept of Membership

A relatively straightforward means of addressing the nature of political membership in modern Europe, which also has the advantage of ease of comparison, is to focus on citizenship law in a nation-state. By definition, citizenship law "excludes," "includes," "separates," "differentiates," "closes," "restricts," "controls," and "regulates."[6] Citizenship is a universalistic category in the sense that, "[to] be defined as a citizen is not to qualify as an insider for a particular instance or type of interaction; it is to be defined in a general, abstract, enduring, and context-independent way as a member of the state."[7] Citizen "insiders" constitute a single legal status, typically entailing residence rights, the right to enter the territory, political rights, social rights, and civil rights, and some obligations like military service. Noncitizen "outsiders," in contrast, are more variegated: all legally "foreigners," some are temporary visitors, some are resident aliens (long- and short-term), some are more ambivalently "denizens," or foreigners with nearly fully guaranteed residence status, many enjoy considerable social rights, and some hold particular political rights. The universality of the category of citizenship across nation-states invites comparison to reveal specific differences and similarities among them. Differences in the particulars of citizenship attribution according to the principles of *jus soli* (law of the soil) and *jus sanguinis* (law of descent) have been the subject of much recent work on Europe.[8]

As horizontal cross-national studies of citizenship policy reveal important differences among nation-states, they reveal rather less about the complicated historical phenomena within particular political communities that contribute to, are buried underneath, or are not addressed by these policies, and that nonetheless remain crucial for defining political membership. Part of the formalism of defining membership by means of legal citizenship status is corrected by studies that incorporate socioeconomic membership in a political community, particularly in the form of the social rights tied to denizen status, or long-term (permanent) residence status.[9] Such studies, drawing on but reformulating T. H. Marshall's classic notion of "social citizenship," argue that formal (political) citizenship is no longer a meaningful indicator of membership status in the political community, either objectively for states as they make socioeconomic policy, or subjectively for noncitizens living in those communities. This "postnational" view of membership, however, counters legalistic formalism with a similarly problematic—from the other direction—abstract and ultimately (for now, at least) false universalism. If national citizenship is too narrow and anachronistic for defining membership in modern European industrial states, postnational citizenship is too broad and premature for defining the same. Until transnational human rights regimes can deploy meaningful sanctions that securely protect the social rights of individuals as opposed to citizens in modern states, national-state citizenship may not be sufficient, but it is certainly not an outmoded means of defining membership in a modern political community.[10]

This study assumes that the nation-state remains the most important context within which to understand political membership in modern Europe through the 1990s. It will attempt, however, to dig beneath common national-state understandings of political membership and present a model that is at once broader and more specific than that used in comparative studies of citizenship law. It will argue that political membership in a community involves participation in a variety of political venues, and each of these memberships is informed by an historical—and evolving—political discourse that serves, in the words of the rhetorician Kenneth Burke, as an "instrument[] for the shaping of human relations." Burke's discussion of constitutions takes him to sublegal instruments "such as we detect in the expression, 'That sort of thing just isn't done.'"[11] The determinants of what "just is" and "just isn't" done in a political community are embedded in historical traditions of discourse that, if deciphered, help make clear who is a member in a political community, what kind of a member that person is, and why that attribution has been made. Such discourses are constituted by sets of more or less sophisticated concepts, with normative and descriptive values, that are linked together in propositions of greater and less formality, consistency, and staying power. James March and Johan Olsen have called these political discourses "logics of appropriateness." These logics are typically implicit, shared codes of action and recognition by which members in a political community more or less explicitly abide, but that, at the same time, are typically not fully and systematically articulated anywhere: in a constitution, a set of laws, or in particular policies. Specific laws and policies may revealingly reflect parts of that logic in a political community, but they usually do not depict that logic in its entirety. As March and Olsen write,

> From this perspective, the polity embodies a political community, and the identities and capabilities of individuals cannot be seen as established apart from, or prior to, their membership and position in the community.... The role of civil servants is defined by shared assumptions about what is due to occupants of other roles, like those of an elected leader or a citizen. The political community is based on a shared history, shared interpretation and common understanding embodied in rules for appropriate behavior. The rules provide criteria for what is worth striving for, and for what is accounted as good reasons for action.... The language is one of the duties and rights associated with specific role relationships.[12]

Broad structural and cross-nationally comparative phenomena like economic systems (e.g., advanced industrial capitalism) and political systems (e.g., liberal-democratic parliamentarism) are thus not the subjects of these logics of appropriateness.[13]

Just as political logics of appropriateness are spatially specific, they are also temporally specific. Political communities are constantly engaged in reproducing, challenging, and reshaping these logics—sometimes in a revolutionary and dramatic fashion, but usually gradually and even then nonlinearly. As Terence Ball, James Farr, and Russell Hanson write, conceptual change in the practice of politics is usually slow and complicated: "Although critical and creative, conceptual change has a profoundly conservative aspect as well. For it never occurs *de novo* or *ex nihilo*. Almost always occurring with reference to relatively settled and stable linguistic conventions, conceptual change tends to be piecemeal and gradual, sometimes proceeding at an almost glacial pace."[14] Sometimes the glacier of conceptual change in politics seems even to reverse itself, particularly in times of existential political threat, and a logic that appeared to be dying out is (briefly) reinvigorated.

As a result, invoking such a logic for understanding political membership makes meaningful cross-national comparison very difficult, and then not necessarily more useful than a cross-temporal investigation. The old comparativist saw about not being able to see at all without seeing differences is not violated by an historical treatment of the evolving articulation, consolidation, and ultimate demise, within one national-state context, of a political logic of membership over the course of two centuries.[15]

Membership in a political community is thus both objectively (from the perspective of the community) and subjectively (from the perspective of the individual) a more variegated construct than what national-state legal instruments typically reveal. Legal citizenship in a community may be a "general, enduring, and context-independent" status relative to noncitizen "outsiders," but that status reveals nothing about the particular roles and identities of "insider" citizens, or how those in turn might even inform a community's understanding of the nature of "outsiders." Indeed, it will be shown that Germany's historical logic of appropriateness for "insider" political membership directly informed the rules and legal institutions that differentiated citizen "insiders" from foreign "outsiders": for decades the political sorting device used to determine whether aliens could become naturalized German citizens incorporated some of the exact (and much older) language used to determine which German citizens could become German state civil servants. To discuss what March and Olsen call the "identities and capabilities" of the members of a political community that are "based on a shared history, shared interpretation and common understanding embodied in rules for appropriate behavior" meaningfully, a national-state perspective is still arguably required. This study addresses important episodes in the articulation, consolidation, and demise of Germany's statist logic of political membership from a period bounded on one end by the promulgation of the Prussian General Code in 1794, and on the other by unified federal Germany's reform of naturalization law two centuries later. It will be argued that German statism as a political logic of membership was first articulated in late eighteenth-century Prussia; it consolidated in the German states in first half of the nineteenth century and survived intact the revolution of 1848; it was challenged more profoundly in the early Weimar years and was fractured, but still survived Germany's first democracy as an appropriate political discourse; and finally, it appeared as part of an early anti-Nazi legitimation effort in the early years of the Federal Republic and informed a variety of venues of political membership only ultimately to collapse after a divisive series of political battles beginning in the 1960s.

Types of Political Membership

Political membership ranges from an ascribed "natural" status inherited at birth to a highly prescribed "rational" linkage that requires the will of the would-be member, a demonstration of adequate qualification, and an explicit acceptance on the part of the political community. What is referred to as "natural" membership here is elsewhere called "ascribed" or "attributed" status; similarly, "rational" membership here is referred to elsewhere as "acquired" or "achieved" status.[16] "Natural" membership in the modern nation-state is a typical linkage, and most people are attributed it at birth in the form of citizenship, though according to widely differing criteria. The term "natural" has been chosen not to suggest biologically determined, correct, and/or immutable, but to differentiate it from willful action, on the parts of both would-be members (e.g., naturalization applicants) and membership gatekeepers (e.g., nation-states) determining the adequacy of potential membership. Citizenship is one of the only natural political memberships in this sense. Some people are citizens of a political community because one or more biological parents (or ancestors) were citizens, which is more or less the definition of *jus sanguinis*, or the law of descent, and others are citizens because of the territory on which they were born, which is more or less the principle of *jus soli*, or law of the soil. In neither case does a person have control over the natural citizenship attributed by virtue of birth. Likewise, gate-keeping state officials do not have the formal volition to select who is or is not an adequate candidate to receive this status of natural membership. Citizenship law is certainly amendable by political authorities, but its "general, abstract, enduring, and context-independent" features formally prevent the law from being applied in a discriminatory manner within a population (which is of course not to suggest that the law itself does not discriminate).

As studies of citizenship and immigration reveal, the attribution of natural membership in the form of citizenship can tell us a great deal about the self-definition of a political community. A community that relies on *jus soli*, for instance, is arguably more open to the prospect of integrating and/or assimilating diverse populations within its territorial borders than one relying on *jus sanguinis*. A community that relies more on *jus sanguinis* than *jus soli*, in contrast, may alternatively view itself as a more homogeneous entity where integration and assimilation are regarded either undesirable or impossible. But studying natural political membership via citizenship law tells us very little about how political actors more traditionally understand political life within a community. Rules for natural political membership reveal how a political community projects its identity relative to other such communities, but they reveal little about particular role relationships and rules for appropriate behavior among the actors within that community. Role relationships and the sublegal rules for appropriate behavior in a political community become important when the purely accidental sorting of natural membership is challenged by people who wish to become members of another community or to acquire a different status in the political community into which they were naturally born. Then membership ceases to be a natural status and becomes a "rational," "chosen," or "selected" status. Dealing with how to define the various "rational" memberships in a political community forces that community to be explicit and self-conscious about who can qualify as a member and why.

The most common form of rational membership in a political community is naturalized citizenship. Natural*ized* citizenship is acquired by a person rationally, as in intentionally, attempting to become for a wide variety of reasons a member of a political community into which he or she was not naturally born. Such action is intentional in two ways: first, reasons always exist (though not always treated as valid) for a person to attempt to acquire a different (or added) membership from the one provided naturally at birth; second, that action is always controlled by a discretionary, though ideally not arbitrary, instance of political authority—even when that authority removes discretion regarding individual cases from the acquisition of the new rational status. Choosing to seek rational membership in a political community is thus a necessary but not sufficient condition for a person to acquire that new status. A person must also meet the requirements established by the political community he or she seeks to enter.[17] It is at this point where traditional understandings of politics in a political community matter a great deal, in particular, the discourse of political membership that the community has constructed and reconstructed over time. At issue is not only the general identity of the community—

e.g., blood-based, homogeneous, and relatively closed; or territory-based, diverse, and relatively integrative—but also the particular roles and identities that a community assigns to individuals occupying different statuses and institutions over time. In the criteria for acquiring rational political membership in a community, what March and Olsen call the "shared history, shared interpretation and common understanding embodied in rules for appropriate behavior," in short, the "logic of appropriateness" of political membership, is revealed.

Rational Political Membership

The logic of appropriateness for rational membership in a political community is relevant for many more people than just alien "outsiders" attempting to become naturalized citizen "insiders." Naturalized citizenship may be the easiest rational membership to imagine, but others are equally common if we expand the notion of membership in a political community beyond that which is controlled by obvious legal institutions concerning foreigners. Other political actors informed by the logic of appropriateness for membership include ordinary citizens attempting to acquire a political status different from their current status: citizens attempting to enter the ranks of the civil service, the armed forces, the judiciary, a political party, or even an interest group. These actors are attempting to alter or add to their existing political role definitions, definitions that involve "insider" and "outsider" assignments within the political community. Specific logics of appropriateness for this kind of political membership in a community are somewhat more subtly defined than the legal differentiation of citizen "insider" from alien "outsider." Specific rules for inclusion in and exclusion from membership venues within a political community reveal, with some degree of differentiation, definitions of legitimate political agency and legitimate political action, the status accorded to different political role assignments, who occupies what roles in which institutions, and how these institutions and their role inhabitants relate to one another. In part because of their complexity, these definitions beg to be considered vertically, over time, for a particular political community.[18] This study will depict how a logic of political membership arose in Germany in the early nineteenth century and finally became inappropriate in the Federal Republic beginning in the 1960s.

Murray Edelman's classic discussion of "meanings" behind both "referential" and "condensational" (emotional) political symbols is informative for purposes here. The meanings, he writes, "are not in the symbols. They are in society and therefore in men. Political symbols bring out in concentrated form those particular meanings and emotions which the members of a group create and reinforce in each other."[19] Yet such meanings—including the logic of appropriateness for membership in a political community—are constantly evolving and not simply created and then reinforced. They are sometimes shocked by events into dramatic revision, but most often they shift in subtle ways, reflecting the ongoing conversation and struggle that political actors and commentators experience with the terms of this logic and its posited relationships. According to Kenneth Dyson, "Language is part of the social and political structure; it reveals the politics of a society. Hence analysis of political discourse will indicate how the political world is perceived, and a diachronic analysis of concepts can be helpful in uncovering long-term structural changes by showing how words acquire new meanings in the context of such changes."[20] The diachronic analysis of these meanings reveals eminently political processes. It reveals relative settlements of political participants and commentators, both explicit and implicit, about what matters and how, and how those settlements are constantly subject to challenge and change. Dyson argues that a logic of political membership is "connected in an intimate, complex and internal way with [political] conduct, shaped by and shaping it, manipulated by and imprisoning the political actor whose political world is defined in its terms."[21] Yet logics of membership are revised as meanings shift, and those political revisions reflect a plethora of complicated sources. While every nation-state has an identifiable logic of appropriateness for political membership, some of those particular logics are more easily traceable than others. In terms suggested above, acquiring rational political membership in a political community—such as naturalized citizenship, civil service employment, or membership in a political party—demands that a community determine the requirements for entrance, more or less formally and explicitly. Those requirements, in turn, are likely to be more formal, consistent, and explicit in so-called state-societies—of which Germany is a paradigmatic case. In such societies, "The concept of the state ... is articulated as a body of values, powers, procedures and offices and represents a concern for logic and order in collective arrangements."[22] The requirements for rational political membership in communities with more "rationalistic" traditions of political discourse or "policy styles" are somewhat easier to decipher than such logics in more informal and pragmatic contexts.[23] A more rationalistic discursive context places value on clear role definitions that are consistent with identifiable principles; a less formal context values, in contrast, more fluid, pragmatic, and at least apparently open-ended processes. Less rationalistic contexts do not have less "logic," so to speak, but they tend to be harder to penetrate analytically.

State, Society, and German Political Membership

This study will address the "shared interpretation and common understanding" of what it has historically meant to be a member of the German political community, and how the traditional German logic of appropriateness for addressing this issue—with its vertical separation of the realms of state and society and its central concept of political loyalty—began ultimately to unravel in the Federal Republic. The roots of modern Germany's logic of political membership reach back to the end of the eighteenth century and the promulgation of the Prussian General Code in 1794. This code established a *Gesetzesstaat*, or lawful state, a precursor to the more familiar *Rechtsstaat*, or rule of law state, and it contributed to the legalization, institutionalization, and depersonalization of modern Prussian politics.[24] It also declared rules for the inclusion of what we have called rational members of the Prussian political community. Those members were not foreigners who would become Prussian subjects—indeed, the Code did not even differentiate between foreigners and Prussian subjects—but rather Prussian subjects who would become loyal Prussian *Diener des Staates*, or servants of the state, behind Frederick the Great who placed himself as Prussia's "first" state servant.[25] Modern German political membership thus began with rational membership in a state organization, not with rational membership in a citizenry or in a state's body of subjects, or even with a natural membership into which a person, according to rules of citizenship or subjecthood, was born. Before it had legal citizens or even differentiated subjects—natural or rational—Germany had state civil servants.

The Prussian General Code's positing of state civil servants as Germany's first rational political members was informed by the German *Staatslehre*, or state theory, of the seventeenth and eighteenth centuries. According to Hans Maier, the German Staatslehre of the mid-seventeenth century simply assumed—and did not strive to demonstrate or construct—the state's existence; and state theory at that time amounted to little more than a descriptive account of the "state activity of civil servants."[26] Assuming the primacy of the state in the German tradition was matched, with very different consequences, in Anglo-American liberalism with a similarly abstract and problematic assumption of a solitary individual. By the eighteenth century, German Staatslehre had also accommodated a notion of the individual, but not one with positive political proclivities. Instead, it theorized an apolitical, private, and "spiritually autonomous" realm of "state-free individuality." Eighteenth-century German theory completely separated the province of "state-free individuals," or subjects, from what it called a "free state." A "free state" was composed of, but not composed by, subjects who enjoyed a realm of "state-free individuality." Indeed, the opposite was the case: the state was seen as "forming," but not being "formed by," its subjects.[27] Hence, according to Rogers Brubaker, the Prussian General Code's "emphasis ... on the state, not on membership [of Prussian subjects]."[28] The Prussian state did, however, have members in the early nineteenth century. The state was not "formed by" those members, but it was materially constituted by them; and those who constituted the state were at one time ordinary Prussian subjects. How one became a state servant from being a mere state subject—how one acquired rational political membership—was one of the most important political questions that appeared in *Vormärz* Prussia.

The "emphasis on the state" in the Prussian General Code and the old Staatslehre's assumption of a "state-free individuality" combined to inform the nineteenth-century German political ideology's hierarchical dichotomization of state and society. This extraordinary powerful and pliable conceptual pairing in German political ideology posited a political state of civil servants existing on a plane above, and acting for, an essentially nonpolitical society of subjects (later citizens). The dichotomization received its richest theoretical treatment in Hegel's *Philosophy of Right*, in 1820, and since then has informed and been the subject of countless discussions and applications in modern German politics.[29] This study will invoke that pairing once more, arguing that state and society survived well into the late twentieth century as meaningful referents in German politics, specifically for informing the duties and rights associated with particular role relationships in the traditional logic of German political membership. Subsumed within that dichotomy is the key political element of traditional German political membership: a powerful concern for political trustworthiness based on a hierarchical differentiation of political loyalty. Historically, more positive and demonstrable political loyalty has been required of rational members, like German state actors, and little, if any, from natural members of German society, like ordinary citizens. As suggested, however, the status of rational political membership appears in various venues in a political community. When non-Germans have sought naturalization, or German natural citizens have sought membership in a political party, or political groupings have sought the status of political party, criteria for rational membership in the political community are invoked again—and again, these criteria in Germany have historically involved concerns for the positive and demonstrable political loyalty of the would-be members. Germany's initial and lasting "emphasis on the state" that prompted this overwhelming concern for the testable political loyalty of would-be rational members in various political venues started to unravel in the 1960s when German citizens began to demonstrate an unequivocal unwillingness to accept their derivative status relative to the German state.

The German state/society conceptual pairing thus has a long and complicated history. Its main features include a "state" that is posited as a realm of hortatory politics occupied by civil servants who are duty-bound and legally obliged to pursue what is understood as society's general or universal interest. That interest in the nineteenth century was equivalent to the "idea of the state," which usually meant the institutional preservation of the political regime, not the program of the government of the day. The state and its agents were located above the partisan politics and conflict of society and thereby purportedly able to define and act on a universalistic public good. Civil servants were to be loyal, expert, politically reliable, and moral agents for the rest of society. They were to protect ordinary citizens from the conflict produced by their self-interested pursuit of particularistic ends, and they were to serve as exemplary political actors for society's members to respect and try to emulate. The state's idea, however, was virtually but not completely embodied in these Diener des Staates. Their loyal service to the state was categorically impossible to suffice, for the idea of the state remained definitionally dissociated from real persons. At best, a contingent "loyalty to an impersonal, secular political entity, the well-being or power of which, presumably, meant the common well-being" was to be adopted.[30] That entailed a rational political membership, closely controlled by a political gatekeeper, in an institution dedicated to forming, and not being formed by, subjects or citizens located in the nonpolitical and lower realm of society.

Society (later civil society) has been understood historically in the German tradition as a nonpolitical—or at best inadequately political—realm relative to the hortatory state. Of the two elements in this conceptual dichotomy, society was more derivative of state in the German tradition than state of society, and, at least in the nineteenth century, society remained distinctly undertheorized. The concept appeared initially as a private and spiritual realm of individual *Bildung*, and was, as industrialization proceeded, transformed into the notion of civil society, connoting primarily market-economic activity. In civil society, people were regarded as acting in a self- or group-interested manner usually for particularistic and/or material gain. These activities were regarded as conflict-laden, divisive, and potentially threatening to public order; civil society was, in short, home to individual self-interest, not loyalty to the idea of the German state. While natural members of society might not thereby violate the definition of a universalistic public good, they certainly could not be positively relied upon to define it or to uphold it. For that, rational members of Germany's political community—state civil servants—were needed, and they were required to be unquestionably loyal.[31] Similarly, whenever society itself became the site of rational political membership, e.g., with naturalization or with participation in a political party, the constituent elements of such membership, such as reliable political loyalty, were borrowed from the realm of the state and inserted into what otherwise was treated as a particularistic realm of conflict and divisiveness.

The key elements of this dichotomization were thus twofold: first, the state was the realm of politically loyal state servants relative to the politically unreliable realm of civil society and its citizens; second, whenever rational political membership was at stake anywhere in the German political community, political loyalty surfaced as a central means of differentiation. If we are to understand German political membership, then, we must understand the meaning of political loyalty. Before treating the more applied meaning of the term in Germany's specific logic of political membership, a brief general treatment of the concept is required.

Rational Political Membership and Loyalty

Loyalty is easily dismissible as anachronistic in a modern, let alone postmodern political context. Already in 1924, Josiah Royce wrote in his classic, *The Philosophy of Loyalty*, "We ... have been forgetting loyalty. We have been neglecting to cultivate it in our social order. We have been making light of it. We have not been training ourselves for it. Hence we, indeed, often sadly miss it in our social environment."[32] The particulars of Royce's treatment are often rejected in modern treatments of the concept, but not his *pladoyer* to preserve loyalty as an important public and private virtue. Many philosophical discussions of loyalty place the concept—not unlike the Germans have, historically in their logic of political membership—as a constituent element of political and other types of community. In those discussions, loyalty is typically understood as an objectified concept, something that cannot be spoken of without an object toward which a person is loyal. In contrast to duty, its close relative, which if adopted—at least according to Kant—indicates an ability to transcend all objectified and empirical reality, we have trouble thinking of a loyal person without asking loyal to what? or loyal to whom? Kant argues that "everything ... empirical is ... highly injurious to the purity of morals"; we typically do not speak of a person who is indifferently and non-empirically loyal.[33] Indeed, it is loyalty's embodiedness in an object that makes it so attractive to some modern commentators, especially those troubled by the postmodern sensibility. Resembling Hegel's idea of ethical life, or *Sittlichkeit*, loyalty is frequently understood as contributing to fully developed personhood, or, in Hegel's words, "liberation from the indeterminate subjectivity which, never reaching reality of the objective determinacy of action, remains self-enclosed and devoid of actuality."[34]

Modern commentators also adopt an Aristotelian assumption of the fundamentally social/political nature of human existence and suggest that loyalty's object determinateness is literally constitutive of individual persons. Herbert Bloch argues that "a man devoid of loyalties ... is impossible, an incongruity in thought.... For the immediate assumption of man, a social being, is the obverse fact of community, a heterogeneous mass of loyalties coming to rest in the individual."[35] Others argue that these loyalties, which are natural to humans as social beings, develop at the same time into strongly held attachments and aversions to the objects of loyalty. George Fletcher links loyalty's objectification to the generation of strong attitudes in a person. Loyalty, Fletcher argues, "generate[s] *partialities* ..., loves and hates, dispositions to trust and distrust. In the realm of loyalty, inequality reigns: Outsiders cannot claim equal treatment with those who are the objects of loyal attachment."[36] Royce similarly defines loyalty as "*The willing and practical and thoroughgoing devotion of a person to a cause*.... Instances of loyalty are: The devotion of a patriot to his country, when this devotion leads him actually to live and perhaps to die for his country; the devotion of a martyr to his religion; the devotion of a ship's captain to the requirements of his office."[37] Another commentator suggests that such strongly held attachments and aversions provide the "solace of human existence."[38]

The consequences of understanding loyalty as a naturally appearing objectified partiality in human beings who are naturally social/political actors must be considered more closely. According to this understanding, only some people and entities qualify as objects of loyal devotion for a particular person; most do not. Fletcher writes, "Loyalty to the group and its purposes provides the basis ... for counting some people in and others out, for believing that insiders count for more and outsiders for less." "Insiders" get special treatment relative to "outsiders," and loyalty within the "insider" group, Fletcher continues, "enables individuals to grasp the humanity of their fellow citizens and to treat them as bearers of equal rights."[39] Loyalty thus leads us to treat some people, but by no means all, as ends in themselves, as mutual embodiers of a Kantian universalism. Treating "outsiders" differently —indeed, as bearers of different rights—is certainly contrary to Kant's demand to act as though "*my maxim should become a universal law*."[40] But most theorists of loyalty posit a context-bounded domain of action that essentially rejects the universality, but not the validity, of the Kantian noumenal actor. Loyalists can still transcend the ego, but within boundaries that define particular zones of categorical action. Those zones constitute what Fletcher calls "our natural limits of sympathy."[41] Only within the zone defined by these "natural limits" can persons treat one another in a manner that at all resembles the imperative to act on a universal rule. Outside of that zone, loyalists are apt to see competitors and "others" who "count for less."

Returning to our concepts of natural and rational membership, this understanding of loyalty appears to link it with natural membership in a community, or one into which a person is born or at least does not somehow rationally choose. "Natural limits of sympathy" are said to define boundaries to a person's loyal ties. Fletcher argues that the loyalist is a "self acting in harmony with its personal history." That history is not only social, but also non-rationally contingent: "The person who reflects about his loyalties should realize that things might have been different.... We do not choose our historical selves in any direct and immediate sense. We are born into a particular culture, acquire a mother tongue, receive exposure to certain political and religious ideas, learn a national history—all without significant choices on our part."[42] Those cultural, linguistic, political, and religious attachments of loyalty are thus not the products of rational choice, but rather of the natural accident of birth. Natural accidents of birth produce natural memberships constituted by strongly held loyal attachments to "insiders" and aversions to "outsiders." Yet this latter attribute of loyalty —aversion to outsiders—is generally recognized as problematic by most theorists of loyalty. Confronted with this problem, Fletcher is unwilling to invoke what he calls "the impartial moral theories of the Enlightenment speak[ing] to the universal human condition,... designed to transcend our emotional links to individuals and countries and to generate objective, universally shared reasons for our actions."[43] Instead of transcendence, Fletcher pleads for balance: "For all the virtues of loyalty to community and nation, the countervailing vices of xenophobia and racism put us on guard. The moral challenge for every devotee of a cause is to find the proper balance of loyalty and independent moral judgment."[44] We must, he argues, live and struggle with "the pangs of conscience triggered by allegedly excessive loyalty."[45]

Fletcher's response to loyalty's dualism is rooted in conceptualizing loyalty as an attribute of natural—and only natural—membership in a community. Loyalties appear in relationships of membership that are not rationally chosen by the loyalist. The accident of birth determines the objects to which a person is loyal, whether that be a nation-state, a religion, or even a baseball team. Missing in Fletcher's account is any discussion of *how* loyalties in natural memberships actually develop. They must "develop," since Fletcher does not ascribe particular loyal partialities to processes of biological inheritance. Loyalties develop, of course, as products of years of complex socialization—by exposure, by more or less explicit education, and by socially sanctioned processes of individual adaptation. If such socialization processes were present, there would seem to be nothing about loyalty as such that would prohibit it also from developing in relationships of what we have called rational membership, where the venue in which a person seeks membership is somehow rationally selected and not determined at birth. Loyalty would thus not be a concomitant of a natural membership, as Fletcher suggests, as much as a result of a complex socialization process. That is not to say initial loyalties may not be different from subsequent loyalties. It is only to argue that loyalty should not be understood as inhering only in a relationship of natural membership.

In addition, Fletcher's response to the risks of what we might call predatory loyalty is constructed on an abstract and static understanding of social interaction. In failing to acknowledge socialization processes that produce loyalties in venues of both natural and rational membership, Fletcher similarly posits a dualistic enjoyment of the particularism of one's specific loyalties, on the one hand, while trying to avoid devaluing—if not worse— "outsiders," on the other. The fact that the mere presence of "outsiders" to the objectification of one's loyalty may change the way one thinks about, and even defines, "insiders" and "outsiders" does not enter into his analysis. The same socialization processes that produce loyalties also produce profound challenges to static bimodal frames of social reference. Since the meanings of "insiders" and "outsiders" are social constructions and not natural facts, those meanings are modified by political and social interaction. That is not to suggest that "insider" and "outsider" frames of social reference are irrelevant; it is only to argue that socialization processes in heterogeneous environments combine with political action to allow "outsider" challengers to alter and extend, over time, the very meaning of "insider" status in a community, and perhaps even—as in Germany in the last thirty years—to discount the relevance of a top-down vetted loyalty for rational membership in that community.

Loyalty as Josiah Royce understands it, however, is ultimately not naturalistic. Royce argues that loyalists must explicitly choose their objects; they are neither born into binding ties, nor do they stumble into them. He writes, "His devotion is his own. He chooses it, or, at all events, approves it."[46] Royce instructs: "You must find, then, a cause that is really worthy of the sort of devotion that the soldiers, rushing cheerfully to certain death, have felt for their clan or for their country.... This cause must be indeed rational"; and, "There is only one way to be an ethical individual. That is to choose your cause, and then to serve it"; and finally, "*Decide, knowingly if you can, ignorantly if you must, but in any case decide, and have no fear.*"[47] Royce, unlike Fletcher, thus understands loyalty as entailing a conscious selection of a good and worthy object from among the bad and unworthy. He apparently fears that wrong choices will be made and an "outsider" to a specific relationship of loyalty will be harmed as a result. Royce's response to this risk is not Fletcher's, which calls on people to temper loyalty with moral judgment and to balance and offset loyalty with moral choice. Refusing to harbor any such dualism, Royce invents a meta-object toward which loyalty must ultimately be directed. He argues, "a cause is good, not only for me, but for mankind, in so far as it is essentially a *loyalty to loyalty*, that is, is an aid and a furtherance of loyalty in my fellows."[48] Royce concludes that it is necessary to *"Be loyal to loyalty."*[49] A loyalist's relationship to that meta-object is partial, but ultimately only in the service of universality, which, in turn, makes loyalty safe for the "outsider." Royce thereby invokes exactly the "impartial moral theories of the Enlightenment" that Fletcher rejects. As Royce concludes, *"all lesser loyalties … and all serving of imperfect or of evil causes, are but fragmentary forms of the service of the cause of universal loyalty."*[50] Fletcher's abstract dualism, balancing loyalty's partialities and aversions, is replaced by an abstract transcendence that negates the defining feature of loyalty with which this discussion began: its embodiedness in a particular object. In the process, "loyalty to loyalty" essentially becomes "duty to duty" and, with Kant, inimical to "everything that is empirical."

Loyalty and Germany's Logic of Political Membership

For purposes here, Royce's rescue of loyalty from inhering only in relationships of natural membership is important. It allows loyalty to appear in venues of rational membership. Yet Royce's denaturalization of loyalty is beset by a problematic negation of the very dangers of excessive or predatory loyalty that Fletcher attempts to address in his plea for balance. Royce's transcendent solution to these dangers moves the discussion from the realm of embodied loyalty to the realm of abstract duty, and that essentially defines away the problem.

A useful alternative for our discussion of historical Germany's loyalty-laden logic of political membership is to combine the rational and socialization attributes of Royce's analysis with the objectified partiality found in Fletcher's treatment. Loyalty is not a primordial particularism that nonrationally binds people to objects of their devotion. People acquire loyalties by means of socialization processes. At the same time, objects of loyalty are particularistically social and political if they are anything at all. Those objects range from athletic teams to nation-states, and they provide, as Hegel writes, a "liberation from indeterminate subjectivity." To these attributes should be added the evolving dynamism of the socialization process itself that produces these loyalties. The objects of loyalty and the meanings of loyalist "insider" and nonloyal "outsider" are social and political constructs that are constantly undergoing reproduction, reevaluation, and adjustment. They are not the static phenomena that Fletcher suggests. Finally, all theorists of loyalty treat the concept as a "bottom-up" attribute embodied by individuals forming a relationship with the object of loyalty. Socialization agents obviously play a central role in developing that relationship, but loyalties are nonetheless developed by individuals interacting with those agents. For that reason, theorists repeatedly stress the humanness and deep intimacy of loyalty. Loyalty develops from within, as an authentic disposition, in interaction with a person's social and political environment. The vetting of this disposition from above, by a bureaucratic institution, would seem to violate that intimacy, perhaps even destroy it. In fact, loyalty may not be authentically testable or authentically positively demonstrated without it transforming into another attribute—perhaps conformism, or its opposite, defiance.

Germany's history of controlling the acquisition of rational membership in various political venues by means of a top-down vetting of adequately demonstrated political loyalty produced, until the 1960s, a closed and politically homogeneous realm of political "insiderism." By the mid-1960s, the political logic of appropriateness defining the realm of politically loyal insiders began systematically to be challenged by a political-cultural revolution occurring within West German society. The stasis of the vertical dichotomization of a hortatory state above a politically unreliable society began to be rejected on the street, in academic scholarship, and in political debate. Over a period of three decades of contentious political and policy battle, Germany's statist logic of political membership, with top-down vetted loyalty as its centerpiece, gradually became inappropriate. In the process, loyalty was not itself consciously rejected as an inappropriate political value, only so-called loyalty as a top-down tested attribute for the acquisition of rational political membership. Consistent with Royce, this transformation in Germany suggested that loyalty could also inhere in a venue of rational membership; consistent with Fletcher, this transformation did not reject loyalty's objectification in concrete particular objects. Inconsistent with Fletcher, however, the transformation that began in Germany in the 1960s demonstrated that loyalist "insiders" and nonloyal "outsiders" are evolving statuses that are socially and politically constructed, as is the process of socialization that produces loyalty in people to begin with. Beginning in the 1960s, Germany's logic of political membership was in flux: "outsiders" were challenging "insiders," denying that it was legitimate to require the demonstration of a top-down loyalty for entrance into realms of rational membership; "insiders" themselves finally began to acknowledge, in the late 1980s, that "outsiders" might be better conceptualized as potential "insiders" whose potential membership status, including their potential loyalty, needed to be cultivated and developed by social and political institutions of socialization, and not as eternal "outsiders" for whom the aversion of "insiders" had somehow to be balanced by moral judgment.

Loyalty was a central constitutive concept in Germany's traditional logic of appropriateness for political membership for nearly two centuries. It occupied that role as a result of the power of German statism as a logic of political membership. This logic contained a vertically dichotomous distribution of political power and political legitimacy. What appeared in the rationalistic membership realm of the German state, a realm to which entrance was controlled by an administrative test of an applicant's positive political loyalty, was, according to this traditional logic of appropriateness, literally more significant for German political life than what appeared in German society. Only when the ascribed power and role relationships in this logic of appropriateness became inappropriate, that is, only when the vertical dichotomization of state and society—and its attendant specific attributes, including the centrality of tested political loyalty for determining rational political membership—became anachronistic in German political discourse, did the nature of legitimate political membership change in Germany. Less controlled from above, less sanctioned by formalistic criteria, less institutionalized, political membership in Germany became, starting in the 1960s, in short, more democratic. The story of this difficult political transformation will be addressed in what follows.

Why Not Nazi Germany?

This discussion of the rise and demise of Germany's statist logic of political membership will not treat Nazi Germany as a case. Given the cross-temporal national-state perspective that has been defended in these preliminary remarks, it is perhaps necessary to explain why. The statist logic of German political membership is a discourse about political inclusion and political exclusion, and the stakes of political inclusion and political exclusion were never higher in German political history than during the Nazi era. Political inclusion in Germany between 1933 and 1945 meant participation in, and at least protection by, a genocidal regime; political exclusion meant at least persecution, often imprisonment, and frequently extermination. Then why not include the Nazi era? In addressing this question, there is no intention to enter the debate over whether Germany's twelve years of Nazi rule should generally be regarded as exceptional or typical in German political development. That question periodically arises and abates in German historiography, but here is not the place to address it. Specifically, there are two main reasons for not treating this period of German history in the current discussion of political membership. The first is the political context of the Nazi era relative to the contexts of the cases treated here, and the second is the nature of "natural" and "rational" political membership and how membership was defined in Germany between 1933 and 1945.

First, the Nazi era was not, as is every other case in this study, an era of popular political mobilization in which the constraining boundaries of a political logic of membership were broadly challenged "from below." Hitler's seizure of power in January 1933 did not follow on the heels of a broad democratic movement by the German citizenry to expand and deepen their repertoire of political power. Precisely that kind of mobilization occurred in the Prussian Vormärz, the first historical case of this study; in the early years of the Weimar Republic, the second case; and in the Federal Republic of Germany beginning in the 1960s, the third case. The actors in these three historical cases were as different as politically marginalized liberal commercial elites in Vormärz Prussia, politically marginalized Social Democrats and Communists in Weimar, and politically marginalized students and leftists in the Federal Republic. But the general context of their actions was the same: a progressive and democratizing challenge to a logic of political membership that had excluded them from the realm of legitimate political agency. No such challenge existed in the Nazi era.

Second, the Nazi understanding of political membership between 1933 and 1945 destroyed any meaningful differentiation between the two main constructs informing this study: "natural" and "rational" political membership. While no mass popular mobilization challenged the terms of the statist logic of political membership in the Nazi era, the Nazi regime did precisely that. But it did so not in the manner of the democratizing mobilizations of the Vormärz, the early Weimar years, and the Federal Republic beginning in the 1960s, all of which were political attempts to redefine and liberalize the German understanding of rational political membership. Rather, the Nazis completely corrupted any meaningful differentiation between natural political membership, into which a person is born and unproblematically retains, and rational political membership, which a person seeks and a regime—or other authoritative entity—awards. The overt, irrational, and unpredictable manipulation of political discourse, which is a hallmark of a totalitarian regime, was practiced by the Nazis from the day they seized power.

The discourse of German statism, rooted in the Prussian General Code of 1794, rested on a vertical dichotomy between a "higher" and rationalistic state of professional civil servants able to decipher a universalistic political good, above a "lower" society of citizens and subjects engaged only by particularistic, self-interested, and definitionally non-political concerns. Hitler's racist attempt to "Aryanize" the German civil service in April 1933, barely two months after seizing power, introduced a category utterly foreign to the German statist tradition of political membership.[51] That tradition was built on ascriptions of "universalistic" and "particularistic" political dispositions, ascriptions made with regard to the location a person inhabited—either the state or (civil) society—and not alleged "naturalistic" biological facts. The Nazi regime further challenged traditional German statism by a party-politicization of the civil service in 1936, when membership in the Nazi Party was required for German civil servants.[52] While the party-politicization of the German civil service was not unprecedented in the nineteenth century, no German regime had ever been dominated by a totalitarian political party like the NSDAP. This fact was reinforced in 1937, when German civil service law was formally amended to demand civil servant loyalty to Adolf Hitler "until death."[53] With that stipulation, the traditional principle of serving the German state and not a particular individual, a principle enshrined in the Prussian General Code of 1794, was completely negated. That appeared two years after the Nuremberg Laws of 1935 removed the civil, political, and social rights of Jews in Germany. The Nuremberg Laws thereby did not just break with Germany's statist logic of political membership; they also broke with any semblance of a meaningful definition of natural and rational political membership. "Natural" members of the German political community, people who had been born as German citizens in accordance with the principle of *jus sanguinis*, were "rationally"—as in intentionally, according to government policy—excluded from that "natural" membership status on the basis of their identity. They were not just excluded from that status; they were ultimately killed on account of it. In sum, the political context of Nazi Germany did not include a powerful mass attempt to expand the contours of rational political membership in Germany. The Nazi regime's manipulation of political discourse also rendered not just German statism, but the terms of any internally consistent discourse of political membership, literally meaningless. For these two main reasons, this study will not systematically discuss the Nazi case.

Notes

1. A. James McAdams, *Germany Divided: From the Wall to Reunification* (Princeton: Princeton University Press, 1993).
2. Herbert Kitschelt, *The Radical Right in Western Europe* (Ann Arbor: The University of Michigan Press, 1995), 129–35; George Ross, "After Maastricht: Hard Choices for Europe," *World Policy Journal* 9, no. 3 (1992): 487–513.
3. Tomas Hammar, *Democracy and the Nation-State: Aliens, Denizens, and Citizens in a World of Internal Migration* (Aldershot: Avebury, 1990), 30–33; see however, Yasemin Nuhoglu Soysal, *Limits of Citizenship: Migrants and Postnational Membership in Europe* (Chicago: The University of Chicago Press, 1994), 163–67, for a critique of legal citizenship as an indicator of membership in post-Cold War Europe.
4. Hans-Georg Betz, *Radical Right-Wing Populism in Western Europe* (New York: St. Martin's Press, 1994), 69–106.
5. Timothy Garton Ash, *In Europe's Name: Germany and the Divided Continent* (New York: Random House, 1993).
6. Rogers Brubaker, *Citizenship and Nationhood in France and Germany* (Cambridge: Harvard University Press, 1992), ix–xi; Hammar, *Democracy and the Nation-State*, 29.

7. Brubaker, *Citizenship and Nationhood*, 21, 29.
8. Reinhard Bendix, *Nation-Building and Citizenship* (Berkeley: University of California Press, 1977), 89–126.
9. Joseph H. Carens, "Membership and Morality: Admission to Citizenship in Liberal Democratic States," in *Immigration and the Politics of Citizenship in Europe and North America*, ed. William Rogers Brubaker (Lanham: University Press of America, 1989), 31–49.
10. See J. M. Barbalet, *Citizenship: Rights, Struggle, and Class Inequality* (Minneapolis: University of Minnesota Press, 1988), 67–72.
11. Kenneth Burke, *A Grammar of Motives* (Berkeley: University of California Press, 1969), 341–42.
12. James P. March and Johan P. Olsen, *Rediscovering Institutions: The Organizational Basis of Politics* (New York: The Free Press, 1989), 160–61.
13. Cf., Gary P. Freeman, "Modes of Immigration Politics in Liberal Democratic States," *International Migration Review* 29, no. 4 (1995): 881–902.
14. Terence Ball, James Farr, and Russell L. Hanson, "Editors' Introduction," in *Political Innovation and Conceptual Change*, eds. Ball, Farr, and Hanson (Cambridge: Cambridge University Press, 1989), 3.
15. Herbert Kitschelt, *The Logic of Party Formations* (Ithaca: Cornell University Press, 1989).
16. William Rogers Brubaker, "Citizenship and Naturalization: Policies and Results," in *Immigration*, ed. Brubaker, 101.
17. Max Weber, "Political Communities," *Economy and Society*, ed. Guenter Roth and Claus Wittich, 2 vols. (Berkeley: University of California Press, 1978), 2: 911ff.
18. Exceptions to the verticalist perspective are Brubaker's *Citizenship and Nationhood in France and Germany*, which treats the historical traditions of formal citizenship in France and Germany, and Kenneth Dyson's *The State Tradition in Western Europe* (New York: Oxford University Press, 1980), which comparatively treats the concept of the state in Europe.
19. Murray Edelman, *The Symbolic Uses of Politics* (Urbana: University of Illinois Press, 1964), 6–11.
20. Dyson, *State Tradition*, 1–2.
21. Ibid., 2–3.
22. Ibid., 270.
23. See Kenneth Dyson, "West Germany: The Search for a Rationalist Consensus," in *Policy Styles in Western Europe*, ed. Jeremy Richardson (London: George Allen & Unwin, 1982), 17–46; Kenneth Dyson, "The Ambiguous Politics of Western Germany: Politicization in 'State' Society," *European Journal of Political Research* 7 (1979): 375–96.
24. Ernst Rudolf Huber, *Deutsche Verfassungsgeschichte Seit 1789*, vol. 2, *Der Kampf um Einheit und Freiheit 1830 bis 1850* (Stuttgart: W. Kohlhammer Verlag, 1968), 16–19; Kurt G. A. Jeserich, "Die Entstehung des öffentlichen Dienstes, 1800–1871," in *Deutsche Verwaltungsgeschichte*, ed. K. Jeserich, H. Pohl, and G. C. v. Unruh, vol. 2, *Vom Reichsdeputationshauptschluß bis zur Auflösung des Deutschen Bundes* (Stuttgart: Deutsche Verlags-Anstalt, 1983), 304–05. All translations are those of the author unless otherwise noted.
25. Hans Rosenberg, *Bureaucracy, Aristocracy and Autocracy: The Prussian Experience, 1660–1815* (Boston: Beacon Press, 1966), 178–91.
26. Hans Maier, "Ältere deutsche Staatslehre und westliche politische Tradition," *Recht und Staat*, 1966, no. 321:20.

27. Ibid., 21.
28. Brubaker, *Citizenship and Nationhood*, 63.
29. G.W.F. Hegel, *Philosophy of Right*, trans. T. M. Knox (London: Oxford University Press, 1967). For modern synthetic historical and theoretical accounts of this dichotomization in German politics, see Dyson, *State Tradition*; Reinhard Bendix, John Bendix, and Norman Furniss, "Reflections on Modern Western States and Civil Societies," *Research in Political Sociology* 3 (1987): 1–38; Jane Caplan, *Government without Administration* (Oxford: Oxford University Press, 1988), 1–13.
30. Liah Greenfeld, *Nationalism: Five Roads to Modernity* (Cambridge: Harvard University Press, 1992), 286.
31. John Schaar offers a striking contrast to this traditional German logic of political membership: "The system belongs to the citizens. It is theirs; and at the moment an elite 'saves' it for them, at that moment it dies," in Schaar, *Legitimacy in the Modern State* (New Brunswick: Transaction Books, 1981), 296.
32. Josiah Royce, *The Philosophy of Loyalty* (New York: Macmillan, 1924), 114.
33. Immanuel Kant, *Groundwork of the Metaphysics of Morals*, trans. H. J. Patton (New York: Harper and Row, 1964), 93.
34. Hegel, *Philosophy of Right*, 107.
35. Herbert Bloch, *The Concept of Our Changing Loyalties: An Introductory Study into the Nature of the Social Individual* (New York: Columbia University Press, 1934), 39.
36. George P. Fletcher, *Loyalty: An Essay on the Morality of Relationships* (New York: Oxford University Press, 1993), 7 [Fletcher's italics].
37. Royce, *Philosophy*, 17 [Royce's italics].
38. Andrew R. Cecil, *Equality, Tolerance, and Loyalty: Virtues Serving the Common Purpose of Democracy* (Dallas: The University of Texas Press, 1990), 217.
39. Fletcher, *Loyalty*, 21.
40. Kant, *Groundwork*, 70 [Kant's italics].
41. Fletcher, *Loyalty*, 21.
42. Ibid., 9, 17.
43. Ibid., 165.
44. Ibid., 35.
45. Ibid., 164.
46. Royce, *Loyalty*, 17.
47. Ibid., 46–47, 56, 98, 110, 196 [Royce's italics].
48. Ibid., 118 [Royce's italics].
49. Ibid., 151, 187, 200 [Royce's italics].
50. Ibid., 375 [Royce's italics].
51. "Gesetz zur Wiederherstellung des Berufsbeamtentums," in *Die politische Treuepflicht: Rechtsquellen zur Geschichte des deutschen Berufsbeamtentums*, ed. Edmund Brandt (Karlsruhe: C. F. Müller Juristischer Verlag, 1976), 110.
52. Martin Broszat, *The Hitler State: The Foundation and Development of the Internal Structure of the Third Reich* (London: Longman, 1981), 242.
53. "Deutsches Beamtengesetz vom 26. Januar 1937," in *Die politische Treuepflicht*, ed. Brandt, 127–28.

One

STATE BUREAUCRATS BEFORE SOCIETAL CITIZENS

The Articulation and Consolidation of German Statism in the Early Nineteenth Century

The statist logic of political membership in Germany consolidated in Prussia in the first half of the nineteenth century. Two important events bracketed this period and helped to determine the logic's content. The first was the promulgation of the Prussian General Code in 1794. The second was the German revolution of 1848. The Prussian General Code laid the institutional framework that informed this logic, while Prussian society's mobilization and attempt at revolution a half-century later provided the political rationale for that logic's consolidation. The logic of German political membership that appeared in the Vormärz hinged on an institutional articulation of the Prussian state, on the one hand, and a popular mobilization of Prussian subjects, or *Staatsmitglieder* (members of the state) acknowledging that articulation, on the other. This political logic defined not Prussian territorial "insiders" from territorial "outsiders"—which appeared only after the institution of state citizenship in 1842—but rather vertically segmented layers of legitimate political participation and their inhabitants within the Prussian political community. The fundamental principles of this logic of membership, with its central place for reliable political loyalty, informed both the sorting of German citizens into "legitimate" and "illegitimate" political agents and—later—the processes by which foreign "outsiders" became naturalized German "insiders." Ironically for the nation-state whose "naturalistic" ethno-cultural definition of citizenship is much debated in the 1990s, the roots of Germany's original logic of political membership lie in what we have called "rational" and not "natural" membership. German political membership was first articulated as a rational status that a person must seek and for which he had to qualify.

The German State as Idea and Institution

Sixteenth- and seventeenth-century Western political theory, particularly French, Italian, and English, broke with the Middle Ages by incorporating two powerful and potentially emancipatory political literatures: the "reason of state" (*Staatsräson*) literature, which treated the state as an independent institution with its own rationale; and the early-modern natural rights literature, which posited individuals with a freedom independent of and prior to the institutions of organized political authority. Neither of these literatures had much resonance in the German *Staatslehre* (state theory) of the time. Rejecting the amoral "realism" of the Staatsräson argument, German theory understood the state as an ethical and moral entity linked to the church. German state theory also broke with the natural rights doctrine by means of an *a priori* assumption of the existence of the state. While other Europeans elaborated rights, laws, and states of nature for prepolitical individuals, German theorists concentrated on *Staatsverwaltungslehre*, or state administration theory, which has been characterized as a descriptive "state practice of civil servants."[1] When early-modern natural rights theory was integrated into German Staatslehre at the end of the eighteenth century, a distinctly German accommodation was apparent: the natural rights idea of a "state-free individuality" was posited as entirely nonpolitical. "State-free individuality" had nothing to do with the political construction of a "free state." Other Western treatments introduced "state-free individuality" as a precursor to a "free state," denoting a polity constituted by free citizens. But the German understanding retained a denotation of privacy, locating "state-free individuality" within an already-existing state order. "Free individuals," according to German Staatslehre at the end of the eighteenth century, enjoyed a private "spiritual autonomy" from the state in society, but not the political right freely to constitute a state. German Staatslehre thus remained immune to early modernism's effort to dislodge the political and ethical preeminence of the state relative to the individual. Through the first half of the nineteenth century, the individual in German political theory continued to be "formed by" and did not "form" the German state.[2] Even when natural rights (*Grundrechte*) began to appear in German liberal theory in the early nineteenth century, they were not seen as natural freedoms valid prior to the state, but rather as freedoms guaranteed by a well-functioning state.[3] The prominence of the German idea of the state was codified in the Prussian General Code (*Allgemeines Landrecht für die Preußischen Staaten*) of 1794.

The Prussian General Code created a *Gesetzesstaat*, or state of laws, which largely legalized, depersonalized, and made relatively transparent the actions of the Prussian administration and judiciary. While still distant from the celebrated *Rechtsstaat* of the nineteenth century—with that state's separation and limitation of political power and involvement of a representative body in lawmaking—the Code charted new and important territory by explicitly placing the state "above" all persons in Prussia, including the monarch.[4] In fact, the Code did not even mention the Prussian monarch; it referred to him only as a legal personality standing in relation to the state, as an *Oberhaupt*, or chief or head, of state.[5] This literal disembodiment of political authority was captured in Frederick the Great's claim—prior to the promulgation of the Code—that he was only the Prussian state's "first servant."[6] The General Code provided a means of checking state power, but not by the more direct and pragmatic means of locating ultimate political sovereignty in the hands of the people.[7] Political power, rather, was to be checked by the state itself, which was not identical to, or even embodied by, any person or institution.

Reinhart Koselleck, the leading historian of the Prussian Vormärz, argues that in the absence of a Prussian religious, ethnic, linguistic, legal, or even geographical unity, a Prussian *Geist*, or spirit, served as the only viable integrating and unifying force of the Prussian state.[8] Though "spirit" is not a prominent category in Western political theory, it does capture the most important feature of the Code's peculiar legalization of politics. The ultimate authority that all Prussians were now to serve, including the monarch, was a disembodied idea. This idea was an abstraction that emanated from, incorporated, and yet transcended all of the particularity that appeared in the Prussian political community. The abstraction of Prussian Geist differentiated the Prussian state from all other political formations. Individual Prussians, including the monarch, were subject to that Geist, not sovereign over it. In spatial terms, the Prussian General Code vertically elevated and abstracted the state's integrating moment above all actors in Prussia, which meant that no member of the Prussian community, whether the monarch or the landless peasant, could ever fully embody political sovereignty. The Prussian state was sovereign, and that state was an abstract idea that was at the same time filled with peculiarly Prussian content. As such, the Geist of the Prussian state served as a potential check on any exercise of concrete political power. That obviously did not prevent ascriptions of rather "low" content to the Prussian state, especially in the 1830s and 1840s, but the power and versatility of positing an abstract idea as ultimately sovereign was to prove very meaningful in German political discourse for the next two centuries.

Concretely some Prussians were deemed closer to the Geist of the Prussian state than others were. Frederick the Great and his royal successors were the self-proclaimed closest. State civil servants were right beneath them. What had been "royal servants," became after 1794 with the promulgation of the Code "servants of the state" (*Diener des Staates*) and "professional officials of the state" (*Beamten des Staates*).[9] Practically, the head of state, or *Staatsoberhaupt*, remained the person to whom Prussian state civil servants formally owed their loyalty. According to the Code, "Military personnel and civil servants are especially intended to support the further the security, the good order, and the prosperity of the state…. In addition to holding the general duties of the subject, they are responsible for being loyal and obedient servants of the chief of state."[10] In this none-too-clear document, which Tocqueville called a "monstrous thing" of contradictions, the state servant was said to owe political loyalty to the head of state, who concretely checked that loyalty's adequacy. But the state servant's real object of service was the idea of the state, not the political whim of the monarch.[11] Both the monarch, as "first servant," and bureaucratic "servants of the state" served the Geist of the Prussian state; they did not embody it, define it, or control it. For state servants in this period, Gillis argues, "inner attachment to an objectified rational order, to the idea of 'the' sovereign state, was infinitely more rewarding, uplifting, assuring, and promising than submission to an eccentric monocrat."[12]

The existential inability for any person fully to embody the abstract Geist of the Prussian state in the Vormärz was of singular importance for the early articulation of the statist logic of German political membership. It meant that some Prussians could be "closer" to the politically sovereign state than others, but even they would only ever be "*Träger*," or bearers, of the state's Geist.[13] They could never be unequivocal embodiers of the state's sovereignty. The "*Dienst an sich*," or service for itself, that was demanded of Prussian civil servants in the early nineteenth century did differentiate state civil servants from all other members of Prussian society; but the ethical requirement to provide "service for itself" also differentiated state actors from the Prussian state.[14] In turn, service to the Geist of the Prussian state was a political good for the community, but not a good that the community had any direct hand in defining. This differentiation of state actor from state idea, and state actor from ordinary subject implied, according to Greenfeld, "dissociation and fostered the development of loyalty to an impersonal, secular political entity, the well-being or power of which, presumably, meant the common well-being."[15] The unbridgeable dissociation of each person from sovereign political authority allowed the creation of a political sorting device to determine legitimate proximity to that sovereignty. The sorting device Prussia instituted was a determination of a person's political loyalty to the Geist of the Prussian state. If a person wished to become a servant of the Prussian state, he or she needed to demonstrate an intense loyalty to Prussian Geist. Demonstration of that loyalty allowed a vertical differentiation of the Prussian state servant from the ordinary Prussian subject acting on myriad—and, in the Vormärz, categorically nonpolitical—particular interests.

The institution of political loyalty as a device to differentiate Prussians politically was profoundly invasive. Koselleck notes that "what was understood as the concept of Geist for the entire state, was understood as *Gesinnung* [conviction] for the concrete individual."[16] An individual could accommodate Geist only by means of a conscious identification with the idea of the Prussian state, but that identification could never be a complete embodiment. Contained within the demanded Gesinnung of the Prussian state civil servant was a politically useful and ever-present *Verdacht*, or suspicion, about its adequacy.[17] However onerous for the individual state servant, the existential inability for anyone, including the monarch, to embody the state's authority did constitute a reformist turn of the Prussian General Code. The civil servant's conviction to the Geist of the Prussian state could be only more or less adequate, and therein lay the rationale for its constant testing and monitoring. It could never be unquestionably present. Rational membership in the Prussian political community thus became the first formal modern iteration of German political membership. Political membership in the early eighteenth century required a rational and loyal identification with the Geist of the Prussian state. The General Code alluded to entrance and retention criteria for Diener des Staates in the Prussian state. These were more fully detailed in the Stein-Hardenberg Reform Era between 1807 and 1819. The identity of Prussian Mitglieder des Staates, or ordinary subjects of the Prussian state, were, in contrast, rather an afterthought. The General Code did not even differentiate between "residence" and "membership" for Prussian Mitglieder. Resident foreigners on Prussian soil were treated as Prussian Staatsmitglieder along with native-born Prussians. That is, natural membership in the Prussian political community—a status with which one is born and does not require demonstration—was not codified in any differentiated form in a period when the rational membership status of state civil servants was a political priority. Prussian Staatsmitglieder, or ordinary Prussian subjects, were ascribed their status by their mere existence within a geographical area governed by the Prussian state; Prussian state servants, in contrast, rationally and consciously sought their status by attempting, with proper Gesinnung, to serve the Geist of the Prussian state. This difference is crucial for understanding the nature of German political membership. On the one hand, the lack of horizontal differentiation between foreign and native-born Prussian state members in the Prussian General Code indicated that "the emphasis was on the state, not on membership."[18] On the other hand, this *Verstaatlichung*, or statification, of Prussian political life surely did not mean ignoring individual members of the Prussian state. Indeed, the point was to differentiate between ordinary Staatsmitglieder inhabiting the realm of society and Staatsmitglieder who wished to become Staatsdiener and thereby enter the realm of the state. The emphasis in Prussian political discourse in the early nineteenth century was on the Prussian state; but it was also on the civil service members of that state. The Prussian state was served "rationally" and not "naturally" by those who would be its servants, and that service was to be judged as more or less adequate according to the criterion of a testable political loyalty. An adequate and demonstrable political loyalty to the Geist of the Prussian state differentiated Prussian Diener des Staates from ordinary Prussian Mitglieder des Staates.

The need to delineate territorial inclusion and exclusion criteria for ordinary Prussian subjects did not arise until decades later, in 1842, when interstate relations in Europe and the migratory practices of the poor pushed Prussia to codify more precisely the respective statuses of "subject" and "foreigner." At that time, "the state ... appeared (and was legally defined) as a membership association; it was no longer merely a territorial organization."[19] But by then the Prussian state civil service had already been a "membership association" for nearly a half-century. It was a rational and not natural form of political membership association, but a membership association nonetheless. Prussia's state civil servants occupied a very specific political membership status in this period. They were not chosen merely on the basis of territorial domicile. As the Code stated, "in addition to holding the general duties of the subject, they are responsible for being loyal and obedient servants of the head of state." This "addition" of political responsibility differentiated them from, and elevated them above, ordinary natural Prussian subjects. Prussian Diener des Staates in the early nineteenth century were thus also Mitglieder des Staates. But far more important for those state civil servants, for Prussian politics at the time, and for understanding the centrality of political loyalty in the idea of German political membership in the next two centuries were the explicit and restrictive rules for inclusion experienced by those civil servants, not Prussia's relative lack of concern for differentiating natural subjects from foreigners.

The Early Institutional Determinants of Prussian Political Membership

As the Prussian Reform Era was a period of institution building, it also became an era of turning ordinary Prussian Staatsmitglieder into Prussian Staatsdiener. Prussian politics in the early nineteenth century was highly interested in the personal and political status of subjects who would become members of the new state service.[20] Technical competence, rationality, and political reliability became the new bywords of the Prussian reformed bureaucracy in the early nineteenth century. These characteristics, all related to Prussian Geist, had to be concretized in individuals wishing to become and remain state civil servants. Friedrich Freiherr vom und zum Stein and Karl August Fürst von Hardenberg were early nineteenth-century Prussia's foremost bureaucratic reformers. They argued in

1818 that the desired "freedom through administration"—and not through revolution, as had been experienced in France—could be achieved only if Prussia were "governed by salaried, educated, non-self-interested, propertyless bureaucrats. These four words [*besoldeten, buchgelehrten, interessenlosen, ohne Eigentum*] contain the spirit [Geist] of our ... government machine."[21]

What "non-self-interested" practically meant for would-be state servants in the Prussian Reform Era was not neutrality, but rather the full loyal conviction to serve the Geist of the Prussian state. The connotation of "neutrality" as "disinterest" has never characterized the German civil servant. Hans Rosenberg writes that in Prussia in the Reform Era, "'The career open to talent' came to mean career open not to the vocationally most competent, if politically neutral or lukewarm, but to the politically talented with the 'right opinions.' ... More decisive [for standards of selection] than professional qualifications were the political leanings, views, and convictions they had."[22] Prussian Reform Era political ideology, grounded in the General Code of 1794, identified the object toward which "right opinions" were demanded that were not, at least ideally, synonymous with any person's or group's particular interests. Even if this ideology were anywhere fully realized in practice—and some scholars have generously analogized the Prussian state bureaucracy at this time to Plato's guardian class and Hegel's general estate[23]—particular interests in Prussian society would, of course, be served in the process, but only derivatively and not intentionally. The proper object of service was the Geist of the Prussian state, an entity that by definition transcended and incorporated all of the multiple particularities that constituted Prussia at this time. The versatility of German statism's demand for loyal service to an integrating abstraction "above" all societal particularity allowed it to survive the most profound regime changes and political upheavals in the next two centuries.

The appearance of German statism as a logic of political membership in the Vormärz entailed more than the codification of the roles and duties of state civil servants. The codification addressed the status of the political "insider," but not the identity of the "outsider," who the Prussian General Code left as a more or less derivative actor. The derivative status of the "outsider" was instead elaborated in a concrete political struggle in the Vormärz over what Koselleck calls the "social-political pre-eminence of the civil service estate" in Prussia.[24] In 1794, the Prussian Legal Code retained the traditional estate, or *Stand*, differentiation of Prussian society. The nobles, the burgers, and the peasants acquired a state-sanctioned legal status. The Code divided the burger estate into three different categories and also created a *Staatsstand*, or state estate, of Prussian state servants.[25] The Code thereby linked individual rights and obligations to estate membership. In so doing, it expressed the political sovereignty of the Prussian state over the estate-organized Prussian society. It also indicated the political conventionality, and not "naturalness," of an estate-ordered society. Estates were retained in 1794 as an act of the sovereign Prussian state, not according to a "natural" order said to be sanctioned by God.[26] This bifurcation of Prussian public life into a sovereign state realm, on the one hand, and a derivative estate-affiliated society, on the other, became more complex by the middle of the nineteenth century. But the legal differentiation was clearly drawn between a political entity that organized Prussian public life and societal entities that were so organized. The Prussian Emancipation Edict of 1807 somewhat complicated, but did not remove, this differentiation.

The Edict stated that the landed property owned by the Prussian nobility could be bought by nontitled commoners, and that Prussian subjects could freely engage in occupations of their choice. These progressive reforms complicated the political and economic significance of estates in Reform Era Prussia, but they certainly did not remove their importance. In 1815, the German Federal Principles of the Confederation of German States codified their continued existence with the acknowledgment of *Landständen*, or provincial estates, in all German states.[27] That same year Frederick William III promised a written constitution for Prussia and representative institutions at both the provincial and state levels. Eight years later, in 1823, the promised constitution had long been forgotten, but a royal edict established *Landtagen*, or provincial diets, on a modified but still significant estate principle.[28] This half-measure of political reform creating provincial representative bodies in Prussia in 1823 was of singular importance for the consolidation of statism as a logic of German political membership. For it appeared after the Emancipation Edict of 1807, a measure that separated property from people, but not property or people from estates.

With the establishment of provincial assemblies in 1823, Prussian subjects enjoyed political significance only by means of their membership in one of the estates that were now allowed provincial, but not state-wide, political representation. The main qualification to enter the provincial diets was explicitly economic. Eligibility for election to the provincial diets hinged on ownership of land in the province for at least ten years, or inheritance of land from a person who had owned it for that period; membership in the Christian church; age of at least thirty years; and possession of an "irreproachable reputation." Frederick William's decree that "landownership is the condition for membership in an estate," and the subsequent creation of provincial representative bodies based entirely on the estate principle, meant that the political life of Prussian society—though not of the Prussian state—was entirely subordinated to the ownership of landed property. The Emancipation Edict may have progressively broken the economic monopoly of the Prussian landed nobility, but the creation of estate-based provincial diets sixteen years later sanctioned the continued economic monopolization of Prussian society's politics by landed-property owners.[29]

In a context where Prussia's Geist was owed loyal and dutiful service by "salaried, educated, non-self-interested, and property-less" bureaucrats, the landed-property qualification for the political representation of Prussian society had a profound impact. The landed-property qualification for estate representation not only separated landed-property owners who were members of, or represented by, the provincial diet from the landed propertyless (be they poor workers or rich bankers). It also separated provincial assemblies of property owners from the Reform Era bureaucratic ideal of the propertyless state bureaucrat serving Prussia's universalistic Geist. The creation of the provincial diets based on land ownership in 1823 essentially dichotomized a universalistic politics practiced by state bureaucrats, on the one hand, and a particularistic economic activity practiced by societal landowners in representative bodies, on the other. Non-self-interested and loyal service to a universalistic idea of the Prussian state was set against self-interested action to enhance material gain and protect particular rights. Left out of Prussia's institutional arrangement altogether in 1823 were the socially and economically most vibrant and potentially destabilizing sectors of Prussian society: the nonpropertied rural and urban poor, bankers, industrialists, merchants, academics, intellectuals, doctors, and lawyers—in short, any person who was not a state servant and/or lacked the necessary landed property to receive estate representation.[30] These half-measure accommodations of the Prussian nobility, with the retention of the landed-estate principle for the provincial Landtagen, institutionally arrayed the economic particularism of provincial diets against the putative political universality of the bureaucratic state service. In the process,

Prussia's property-based estates became derogatorily known as "economic interest representations," and the Prussian state civil service ideologically secured, according to Koselleck, a place "in front of" and "above" the provincial estates.[31] Nowhere yet on Prussia's political institutional map were the forces that made Frederick William IV bare his head some two decades later for a procession passing by the royal palace in Berlin honoring the revolutionary fighters who had recently died.

"Rational" Political Membership in a Mobilized Society

The Prussian Reform Era lasted between 1807 and 1819. The Prussian Vormärz, or "pre-March," referring to the revolutionary activities that occurred in March 1848, lasted roughly between 1820 and 1848. The term Vormärz suggests "view[ing] the era as a prelude, a preparation for the revolutionary days of March 1848, and suggests the irrepressible force of social change."[32] While Prussian political actors at the time obviously did not view themselves as participants in a "prelude," the term does capture the instability of the period's institutional arrangement. The provincial assemblies were essentially anachronistic even before they convened. They were partial accommodations that satisfied neither the Prussian nobility nor the owners of nonlanded property, among others, who were excluded from them. The very existence of the institutional arrangement hinged on the ability of the Prussian state and its civil servants to integrate, serve, and—not least—contain Prussian society between 1820 and 1848. Such tasks required more political skill than the Prussian state or any Prussian government possessed. The temptation to put state civil servants to work for conservative party-political ends proved too powerful for Prussian governments to resist.[33]

Prussia's Reform Era, between 1807 and 1819, was a "revolution from above" that established the bureaucracy as the most progressive, rational, and enlightened organized force in Prussian politics.[34] Progressive Prussian reformers, consistent with old German Staatslehre, argued that freedom could be served better by a rational and efficient administration than by a written constitution. Though this logic regarded it impossible for anyone fully to embody the Prussian state's Geist, it was championed by government ministers and partly realized by the personnel policies of the Prussian civil service in this period.[35] Until about 1819, the reformed civil service had a mediating and integrating effect on the growing social contradiction between the nobility and burger estates. By the end of the Reform Era, the Prussian bureaucracy was a powerful political institution whose members saw themselves as servants and protectors of the Geist of the Prussian state. According to Wunder, "In the belief of service for the 'common good,' the civil service saw itself way above a society following only individual or group interests.... All criticisms from society were rejected as egoistic special interests. Their own group interest [the civil servants'] was not recognized, for it was part of the ruling state legal order."[36] This identity was posited not merely by the bureaucrats. The state civil service was, Berdahl argues, "commonly viewed by the public as the guardian of the public interest, elevated above the conflicting interests of the other Stände."[37] The broad political perception of the Prussian state service as a reliable political elite for realizing the "common good" through its service to the Geist of the Prussian state marked the appearance of a logic of "rational" political membership in early nineteenth-century Germany. The logic was based on an ideology that posited a political state of dutiful and loyal bureaucrats serving Prussian Geist, on the one hand, existing "in front of" or "above" an inadequately political and self-interested economic society organized in representative diets (or not at all), on the other.

Insofar as the Prussian civil service was ideally codified as a "Diener" (servant) or "Träger" (carrier or caretaker) of the Geist of the Prussian state, individual bureaucrats were conceptualized as better and worse "servants" and "carriers" of that entity. This made the performance of even the best bureaucrats always, by definition, a policy concern. To encourage civil servants responsibly to serve "the security, the good order, and the well-being [*Wohlstand*]" of Prussia, a "special loyalty and obedience" to the head of state was demanded, and that created an "elitist consciousness ... of a mythical tie to the dynasty."[38] This was joined by complete security against material hardship—for retirement and for dependents after the civil servant's death—provided by a non-contributory pension.[39] To extract optimal service to the Prussian state's Geist, Reform Era ideology thus offered reward, and not the threat of punishment or penalty, as most commensurate.[40] The impact of this personnel policy, however, affected not only civil servants. Caplan writes, "The creation of a non-contractual civil-service status was in some respects a deliberate anachronism in an increasingly capitalist society for which freedom of contract was a cardinal virtue, and it emphasized the unique status of the civil servant as the executive arm of the sovereign."[41] That "unique status" came under increasing fire in the Vormärz as the once-proud independent bureaucracy became a party-political and tractable instrument for regulating and containing Prussian society's growing political mobilization.

As early nineteenth-century Prussian political ideology elevated an abstract Geist above Prussian society as the object toward which loyal and dutiful service was due, state civil servants in the Vormärz had a difficult time approximating what was ideally demanded of them, and Prussian governments succumbed to the ready temptation to degrade the ideology to serve their own party-political interests. Landed nobles, encouraged by a monarchy searching for reliable conservatives in an increasingly volatile political and social context, pressed into the ranks of the Prussian civil service between 1820 and 1845, when the percentage of nobles in the Prussian provincial administration increased from twenty-five to thirty-three percent. Hardenberg's ideal of "non-self-interested and propertyless" bureaucrats became increasingly challenged by the institution's "*Aristokratisierung*."[42] From a Reform Era institutional ideal of progressive, if paternalistic, social reform, the Prussian bureaucracy developed between 1819 and 1848 into a reactionary and often inexpert institution of self-interested privilege. Service to the Geist of the Prussian state had descended to service to the political whim of the government of the day.

Already in 1814, Theodor Schmalz, professor of law at the University of Berlin, began a campaign that accused some of his colleagues of "Jacobinism" and "demagogically" inciting university fraternities in the name of German nationalism. This unleashed a *Demagogenverfolgung* (persecution of demagogues) directed against moderately liberal university professors, all of whom were Prussian state employees.[43] The Carlsbad Decrees of 1819 also targeted the university—including students, who were subject to expulsion if active in liberal and nationalist fraternities, and state-employed academics, who were to be fired if they compromised the "maintenance of ethical life and good order."[44] Around this time, the construct "intellectual state subversion" surfaced in Prussia.[45] In 1822, Frederick William issued a decree that prohibited paying "promoters of demagogic intrigues" with Prussian state money and demanded the "tighter drawing of the bands of discipline" of state civil servants in "this unsettled period."[46] The Prussian Culture Ministry was informed that academic appointments in the next five years could be made only after checking with the Interior Ministry and the police on the applicant's "political reliability."[47] Four years later the political noose tightened around Prussian administrative state servants, as "inadequate service and moral defects" were codified as career-ending offenses.[48] These policies were meant to secure a conservative bulwark against the rising threat of a politically mobilized, yet disenfranchised, Prussian society. A progressive institution of political Gesinnung, or conviction, had been reduced by the 1830s to a beleaguered institution of blind *Gehorsam*, or obedience, to what Koselleck called an "artificially-educated characterlessness."[49]

The "aristocratization" and instrumentalization of the civil service in Vormärz Prussia proceeded in tandem with the political mobilization of the disenfranchised of Prussian society, a huge group that included all persons who were not state civil servants and/or who lacked the landed property necessary for representation in the provincial diets.[50] The creation of land-based provincial assemblies legally sanctioned an "economic" realm in Prussia differentiated from the state or "political" realm inhabited by civil servants. It also statically defined an economic realm according to landed-property ownership in a context undergoing extremely rapid economic change. Having neither the hortatory political voice of the state civil service nor even the "lower" voice of "economic" estates, these disenfranchised interests challenged Prussia's political-institutional arrangement. As the Prussian bureaucracy was made a pliable political instrument of a conservative government in the Vormärz, Prussian society produced nascent political organizations that breached the boundaries of formal Prussian estate society.[51] Many of those organizations were informed by the tenets of early German liberalism.

German Liberalism and the Statist Logic of Political Membership

Liberalism appeared as a political movement in West and Central Europe in the late eighteenth and early nineteenth centuries. Its broad vision included a society of spiritually developed, materially secure, and self-responsible individuals; a representative constitutional state; and a catalogue of guaranteed political and civil rights.[52] German liberalism differentiated itself from other European variants of the ideology in this period with the positive role it reserved for the state in German political, economic, and social life. According to Rudolf Vierhaus, "The 'liberalism' of Hardenberg and his bureaucrats was governmental. It included Staatsräson-thinking; enthusiasm for modernization; an ear for public opinion in order to make the politics of reformed renewal useful; anti-traditional pragmatism and opposition to revolution; administrative competence; good education and a sense of propriety; and an inclination toward tutelage."[53] The liberalism of the Reform Era did not address individual political and civil liberties from state control. It instead adopted the position of the old German Staatslehre that the state was the primary, and beneficent, actor in any properly constructed political community. Indeed, Sheehan argues that the problem for the majority of German liberals in the Vormärz was not state power, as such, but rather how to reconcile their hatred for official and monarchical despotism with their belief in state power as the only possible instrument for fulfilling their ideals.[54] This belief led German liberalism to the construct of a Rechtsstaat.

A transcendent Rechtsstaat, or constitutional law state, which went beyond the Gesetzesstaat, or legal state, of the Prussian General Code and acted according to "the norms of rational law," would halt governmental arbitrariness and help to modernize German public life.[55] The rational Rechtsstaat had representative political institutions, it promoted political emancipation (though not unrestricted), and it assisted in the moral transformation of subjects into citizens. The negation of the Rechtsstaat, according to the liberals Rotteck and Welcker writing in the *Staatslexikon* of 1834, was "anarchy," a term denoting two political pathologies: the perverted rule of a despotic and arbitrary political authority, and the absence of a functioning political authority in a society that was not self-regulating.[56] The ideal state, according to early nineteenth-century German liberalism, was an ethical entity that simultaneously served the *Gemeinwesen*, or common being, of the community, and acted as a caretaking *Anstalt*, or (therapeutic) institution, for German society. Franz Bahl, a liberal businessman, wrote in 1842, "Who does not wish the state well?... We all want it to be great, mighty, powerful, and rational. We all have no other wish than to be absorbed into the state, and to devote our strength to it."[57] As an entity "above" all particularistic interests and persons, the state, according to the liberal Friedrich Dahlmann, was "sacred" and fully sovereign.[58] German liberalism rejected the ideas of *Fürstensouveränität* (princely sovereignty) and *Volkssouveränität* (peoples' sovereignty) as particularistic and illegitimate. Only *Staatssouveränität* (state sovereignty) would guarantee rational political rule, and only a fully developed Rechtsstaat could execute this Staatssouveränität and be, according to Dahlmann, the "magic spear that heals and wounds."[59] With this imagery Dahlmann clarified that the proper liberal state was a political actor—through its expert and loyal civil service—for promoting the social, economic, and moral well-being of German society. That state, liberals argued, did not exist in Prussia after 1830. In its place was an anarchic, "aristocratized," and conservatively politicized *Bureaukratie* that impeded the development of Prussian society.

The most eloquent critique of Bureaukratie was written in 1846 by Robert von Mohl, a German liberal who had set his sights on becoming the "Adam Smith of state administration."[60] While the specific variant of Mohl's liberalism is somewhat disputed, his attack on the Prussian bureaucracy in the Vormärz is generally regarded as a classic of German liberal ideology.[61] Mohl grounded his critique on a definition of a rational Rechtsstaat, which was to "regulate the common life of the people in such a way as to support and promote every member in the freest and most all-round possible exercise and use of his powers.... Freedom of the citizen is the supreme principle under such a view of life... Hence, support by the state can only be of a negative kind, clearing away the obstacles whose removal would be beyond the powers of an individual."[62] At the same time, Mohl continued, "the administration can and must act as soon as it has convinced itself of the suitability of a measure; and it may be only to its renown when, with the right insight, it is ahead of the sensibility of the citizens."[63] Mohl thereby clarified what he meant by state "support of a negative kind." The "negative" actions of the state were hardly related to what Anglo-American liberalism has defined as "negative freedom," or freedom from state control. The properly ordered state was a positive political institution endowed with a "higher" rationality and intelligence than that of ordinary citizens. The removal of "obstacles" to society's development, for Mohl, was not simply the removal of state administrative and regulatory impediments to economic development. The "negative" support of the state must also remove societal "obstacles" that rapidly developing economic systems themselves create. Mohl argued that rapid economic transformation in the Vormärz had posed the "social question" in Prussia very sharply, especially for the fourth estate, and that it would be nothing short of "barbarism," he wrote, to shrink the state's supportive activities.[64] The problem, according to Mohl, was not the state or state activity, but rather, "nothing other than the exaggeration of the idea of the state, executed by numerous, and, in part, very mediocre members of an organism of professional civil servants."[65] These "mediocre members" were labeled *Bureaukraten* in contrast to the Reform Era Staatsdiener who, before 1820, had won the respect of much of Prussian society. Bureaukratie, Mohl argued, was not synonymous with "government as such"; or with "too much governing [*vielregieren*]"; or even with "absolute government."[66] These distinctions were crucial for German liberalism, and for Mohl, who joined his colleague Karl Heinzen in worrying that if Bureaukratie were not fixed, the liberal *Bureaukratiekritik* could descend to a broader, dangerous, and anarchic *Staatskritik*.[67] Bureaukratie for Mohl was a problem of excess and misunderstanding that could be repaired within the "current existing state."[68] The solution was to reform and reorder, not to remove. Because of "mediocre minds," "ethical indifference," and "purely formal," "unkind," and "*ungebildete* behavior" resulting in a "spiritless practice," the civil service "no longer"—in contrast to the early nineteenth century—had an "ethical influence" over the people.[69] It was necessary only to rid the civil service of rude, coarse, insensitive, ignorant, loud, and insolent Bureaukraten who "lacked judgment" and had service to themselves as their primary goal.[70] Replacing them with genuine "statesmen" would change an "unspiritual atmosphere" (*ungeistige Atmosphäre*) that "suffocates," "buries," and "flattens" instead of promotes the "development of individual life purposes." Mohl called for a "spiritual breeze blowing through the institution from above" to remove an insolent "civil service regime" and encourage proper "political thinking."[71] The alternative of parliament as a location of "political thinking," as some of his more radical colleagues supported, was for Mohl, "out of proportion to the current problem."[72] The "current problem" required not the democratic elevation of "societal" political forces, but rather a renewal of the state civil service to allow the institution to reacquire its original Reform Era identity.[73]

German liberalism's fear of anarchy was, however, two-sided. Liberalism's critique of the deformed Prussian Bureaukratie was joined by a rejection of the other more familiar anarchic site Rotteck and Welcker warned against in their *Staatslexikon*. Most German liberals in the Vormärz viewed society as a non-self-regulating realm that needed to be "acted on" by a properly institutionalized state. Society required Staatssouveränität for self-preservation, to guarantee good order and protect individual basic rights. Freedom was realizable through good administration, not the dangerous French notion of Volkssouveränität, or popular sovereignty, that was radicalizing the fourth estate.[74] State sovereignty needed to be located not in the Bureaukratie of the Vormärz, but in a rational Rechtsstaat that provided the assistance and ethical influence to curb society's natural tendency to anarchy.[75] Running throughout early nineteenth-century German liberalism was thus a clearly defined dichotomization of state and society, a dichotomization that some regard as having impeded the development of constitutionalism in this period.[76] German liberalism at this time elaborated different role assignments for the inhabitants of state and society; in the process, German liberalism rendered the state/society dichotomy serviceable for German political discourse for the next century-and-a-half. German liberals regarded society as a realm that required the state's activities as an *Anstalt*, or a therapeutic institution. The liberal Karl von Rotteck argued that the most important task of the properly ordered state was to transform particularistic subjects into informed and obedient—but not sovereign—"state-citizens," or Staatsbürger.[77] We are thereby reminded of Franz Bahl's desire to be "absorbed" by the state.[78] As 1848 approached, however, the ability of the state successfully to create Staatsbürger was challenged by the presence of what German liberals identified as Bureaukratie, on the one hand, and by the mobilization of what liberals regarded as a societal "mob," on the other.

Conceptualizing society as a dangerous and potentially anarchic realm marked a clear break from German liberalism's early nineteenth-century undifferentiated view of society as inhabited by a moderate and prosperous *Mittelstand*, or middle class. The early stages of German industrialization in the 1830s began to wrench apart this image and the early liberal assumption of an unproblematic harmony between the realms of state and society. Hegel's systematic theorization of *bürgerliche Gesellschaft* in *Philosophy of Right* marked a quite radical shift in the meaning of "society" in the Vormärz.[79] Society became bürgerliche Gesellschaft, or civil society, and it was regarded as an economic realm standing in a sharply antagonistic relationship to the state.[80] Civil society connoted self-interest, particularism, a "negation" of the "state" and the "political," and at best, a completely "governed [but not governing] body of the people."[81] The state became an ordering power situated above an economic, volatile, chaotic, anarchic, and potentially dangerous civil society.[82] More concretely, a well-ordered state was, for many moderate German liberals, all that stood between them and a civil society of radicalized workers, artisans, and peasants.[83] The fear of civil society, for German liberals in the Vormärz, increased the attraction of the state. Civil society was seen as dominated by special interests, selfish motives, dependence, spiritual degradation, atomization, unenlightenment, and the *Pöbel*, or the people, as liberals derisively referred to the uneducated and unpropertied urban and rural poor.[84] As the liberal Friedrich Dahlmann had earlier warned of the "depraved clamor of the mob, which ignorantly runs after every immediate advantage," David Hansemann despaired in 1840 of the "dangerous" realm of civil society with its "strong increase in the democratic element."[85] Especially terrifying was the insurrection of workers in the countryside that many liberals saw as a "Frankensteinian monster" on the loose.[86] In short, being shut out of the landed provincial diets did not inspire nonpropertied German liberals politically to ally with disenfranchised Pöbel. The Pöbel were driven by "particularism," which Rotteck's *Staatslexikon* defined in 1843 as a political consciousness "deficient in Gemeingeist," or concern for the common good.[87] Instead, German liberals in the Vormärz politically situated themselves between the dangerous Pöbel of civil society, on the one hand, and the civil service of the properly functioning Prussian Rechtsstaat, on the other.[88] But this was not an equidistant positioning.

Liberals placed themselves much closer to a properly functioning state than to the threatening Pöbel of civil society. German liberals wanted to be "absorbed" by the state but protected from civil society. German liberals nonetheless found it difficult to locate a concrete home for their oppositional stance. In 1843, Karl Rosenkranz wrote that *Partei*, or party, denoted "partiality" and the inability ever to "inherit the mantle of the state." "Party" was associated with conflict and particularism and was thus inconsistent with the universalistic, transformative, and protective mission of the state. Instead of parties, German liberals saw themselves in this period belonging to *Vereine*, or unions, and *Assoziationen* that were *Meinungsgemeinschaften*, or communities of belief, and *Gesinnungsgemeinschaften*, or communities of conscience.[89] These entities connoted collective cooperation and integration with a state that retained the role of sovereign political agency. German liberals wanted a state at mid-century that resembled the Reform Era ideal but was competent to act on society's massive needs in a rapidly changing economic and social context. Necessary for constructing that state were professionally expert and politically reliable Staatsdiener serving not a reactionary political agenda, but rather the Geist of an economically and socially dynamic Germany in the middle of the nineteenth century. Germany's statist logic of political membership was thus not challenged by Germany's most progressive and organized force of political opposition in the Vormärz. It was, rather, glossed, extended, and refined by the discursive efforts of German liberals wedging themselves between a terrifying civil society and a mollifying protective state.

The Revolution of 1848 and the Consolidation of German Statism

Between February and October 1848, Prussia's King Frederick William IV was a busy man. He literally doffed his hat to the fallen heroes of the German revolution; he promised a "truly popular liberal administration" with civil and political liberties for all Prussians; he appointed two governments with liberal ministers—one including the liberal figure David Hansemann; he dismissed a subsequent government under the leadership of an army general for failing to declare a state of siege; and he appointed a "battle cabinet" (*Kampfkabinett*) to "defeat the March revolution decisively and victoriously."[90] An important instrument for defeating the revolution was the logic of rational political membership that German liberalism in the Vormärz had helped to articulate. The logic was deployed against a mobilization of Prussian society that had challenged the "social-political pre-eminence of the civil service estate" by arguing that the German state required, in the words of the liberal Robert von Mohl, only "spiritual renewal," not dismantling or the relocation of power into a democratic institution. Renewal was not, in any case, on Frederick William's agenda in the autumn of 1848, except in the sense of consolidating the political preeminence of the state civil service to prevent anything like a revolution "from below" from ever occurring again.

The liberal Auerswald-Hansemann government appointed after March 1848, viewed the civil service as performing important and "influential political activity."[91] A ministerial decree in July 1848, ostensibly directed at curbing the political activity of reactionary civil servants in the countryside, called for securing the "power and strength of the state organs" in the "difficult situation of the present."[92] The new government had lifted press restrictions, guaranteed the right of peaceful assembly and organization, and formally destroyed the estate system, but it did not view the institution of the Prussian civil service as antithetical to its goals. Indeed, the liberal Auerswald-Hansemann government fell because it refused to support a National Assembly bill calling for military officers to distance themselves from "all reactionary efforts" in order to "realize a constitutional condition of legality."[93] The first application of the July civil service decree was not to reactionaries in the countryside, but rather to leftist officials in Berlin.[94] In the moment of truth, German liberals in power were unwilling in the summer of 1848 even to risk antagonizing an institution they regarded as existentially vital for German politics. They were unwilling to endorse a policy that was little more than a concrete expression of the Bureaukratiekritik anchoring their oppositional program in the Vormärz. Tolerating reactionary *Landräte* in the countryside was preferable to the risk of weakening the civil service institution by means of reform—even if that reform were entirely consistent with the Reform Era ideal of the well-functioning German state. In the process, the German professional civil service was projected as an existentially vital—and non-regime-specific—institution for saving German politics from the anarchy, conflict, and self-interest of German civil society. Not only German conservatives believed this in the middle of the nineteenth century. In 1848, German liberals in power acted on it.

By October 1848, the counterrevolution in Prussia was in full swing. Frederick William added a chapter to Germany's tradition of "revolution from above" by dictating a constitution to circumvent the draft constitution being laboriously worked on in the National Assembly. His constitution nominally guaranteed a catalogue of liberal freedoms, but it left the monarch in complete control of the armed forces, provided him with an absolute veto over all governmental bills, gave him broad discretion to issue emergency decrees, and commanded civil servants to "swear loyalty and obedience to the king and [his] constitution."[95] Hamerow observed that the octroyed document "establish[ed] royal domination under the guise of popular rule."[96] With the estate system no longer viable in Prussia at the end of 1848, the state civil service was increasingly seen as the only effective institution for the political containment of a mobilized Prussian society.[97] The new interior minister, Manteuffel, warned in the spring of 1849: "The government cannot carry on successfully when its subordinate officials do not with all honesty guarantee their strongest support. All those who do not believe they can do this would do well to resign voluntarily; where this is not done, it will be the duty of the ministry, in the interest of the country, to remove in a lawful manner those who fulfill their duties lackadaisically or grudgingly, as well as those who awaken distrust where, through education and understanding, trust should have been created."[98] The new political role of Prussian state civil servants had thereby begun to consolidate.

With the nominal guarantee of civil and political rights for all Prussian subjects appearing in the octroyed constitution, the singular hold on Prussia-wide political activity by professional civil servants was formally broken. Though this political opening was not substantial—and the three-class voting system without a secret ballot introduced in May 1849 narrowed it further—formal political rights and thus formal political roles in Prussia had measurably shifted.[99] This shift, in turn, was accompanied by a refinement of the German statist logic of political membership: the new logic differentiated between types of political activity in a formally broadened political sphere, not just between political activity in the state and economic activity in civil society. While the expansion of the Prussian political sphere was modest and formal, it was significant enough discursively to introduce a vertical segmentation of political agency into two separate domains. A "higher," politically legitimate, and hortatory domain of politics was assigned to the state, a region populated by rational members of the political community—politically loyal civil servants. A "lower," politically illegitimate, and derogatory domain of politics was assigned to civil society, a region populated by natural members of the political community—ordinary Prussian citizens belonging to political associations, clubs, and nascent political parties.

Conclusion

The definition of a distinctly rational realm of political membership in 1848 was not new in German political discourse. New was the vertical segmentation of a formally expanded Prussia-wide political realm into legitimate and illegitimate domains. What had been the only political realm in the Prussian Vormärz—the Prussian state with its loyal civil servants—became a higher segment of the political realm after Frederick William's minor concessions to the 1848 revolution. Prior to the revolution, the Prussian civil service constituted a state estate that alone occupied the Prussian "political" realm and was set against the "economic" provincial estates located in civil society. While Frederick William insisted that the Prussia-wide United Diet constituted from the provincial diets in 1847 was not a parliamentary body, this institution combined with formally guaranteed political and civil liberties—however adumbrated—to challenge the political monopoly in Prussia of the state civil service.[100]

The state civil service was then discursively reconceptualized as a "legitimate" political agent standing above the "illegitimate" mobilized interests of political actors in Prussian civil society. These mobilized interests and nascent political parties had become "political," but, according to the postrevolutionary statist logic of political membership, not legitimately political. Their ascribed conflict-ladenness, particularism, and self-interestedness made them the rough analogue of the "economic" actors of Vormärz Prussian statism. The postrevolutionary differentiation between types of politics—and not between "politics" and "economics"—required a similar differentiation between types of political actors. The "rational" membership status of Prussian state civil servants was thereby given its strongest *raison d'être* to date. Prussian Staatsdiener were differentiated from ordinary Prussian Staatsmitglieder not just categorically, as inhabiting the realm of the state and not the realm of civil society, but now also politically, as inhabiting a realm existentially vital for preserving the political order.

As German liberalism in the Vormärz demonstrated, this logic of political membership was not in any sense definitionally absolutist in nature. Rational political membership had become not just different from natural political membership; it had also become the means for saving postrevolutionary Prussia from the anarchy said to inhere in civil society. The Prussian state had been challenged from below by ordinary Prussians exploring various iterations of self-governance. The logic that articulated the roles and relationships of rational political membership in Prussia had become a political logic, but a logic that was extraordinarily versatile and not inextricably tied to any particular political regime. The logic identified politically reliable and loyal members of the German community and the ways to create them; it also identified politically dangerous members of that community and the ways to contain them. The difference between reliable political agency and dangerous political agency turned on the agent's proximity to the universalism of the German state. Ideologically, at least, that state could be the state of Vormärz German liberalism, of post-1848 Prussian reaction, or, as we shall now see as we turn to the Weimar Republic, of Germany's first liberal democracy.

Notes

1. Hans Maier, "Ältere deutsche Staatslehre und westliche politische Tradition," *Recht und Staat*, 1966, no. 321:9. *Staatsräson* appeared first in the early seventeenth century in Prussia, but with considerable confusion. See Werner Conze, "Ständegesellschaft und Staat," in *Geschichtliche Grundbegriffe: Historisches Lexikon zur politisch-sozialen Sprache in Deutschland*, ed. Werner Brunner, Werner Conze, and Reinhart Koselleck, vol. 6, *St-Vert* (Stuttgart: Klett-Cotta, 1990) 12–17.
2. Maier, "Ältere deutsche Staatslehre," 21.
3. Günter Birtsch, "Gemäßigter Liberalismus und Grundrechte: Zur Traditionsbestimmtheit des deutschen Liberalismus von 1848–1849," in *Liberalismus in der Gesellschaft des deutschen Vormärz*, ed. Wolfgang Schieder (Göttingen: Vandenhoeck & Ruprecht, 1983), 26–7.
4. Ernst Rudolf Huber, *Deutsche Verfassungsgeschichte seit 1789*, vol. 2, *Der Kampf um Einheit und Freiheit, 1830 bis 1850* (Stuttgart: W. Kohlhammer Verlag, 1968), 16–19.
5. Kurt G. A. Jeserich, "Die Entstehung des öffentlichen Dienstes, 1800–1871," in *Deutsche Verwaltungsgeschichte*, ed. K. Jeserich, H. Pohl, and G.C. von Unruh, vol. 2, *Vom Reichsdeputationshauptschluß bis zur Auflösung des Deutschen Bundes* (Stuttgart: Deutsche Verlags-Anstalt, 1983), 305.
6. Jeserich, "Die Entstehung," 306; Harold-Jürgen Rejewski, *Die Pflicht zur politischen Treue im preußischen Beamtenrecht (1850–1918)* (Berlin: Duncker & Humblot, 1973), 14.
7. Reinhard Bendix, *Nation-Building and Citizenship* (New York: John Wiley & Sons, 1967), 122.
8. Reinhart Koselleck, *Preußen zwischen Reform und Revolution: Allgemeines Landrechts, Verwaltung, und soziale Frage von 1791 bis 1848* (Stuttgart: Ernst Klett Verlag, 1967), 398–400.
9. Hans Rosenberg, *Bureaucracy, Aristocracy, and Autocracy: The Prussian Experience, 1660–1815* (Boston: Beacon Press, 1966), 191.
10. "Allgemeines Landrecht für die Preußischen Staaten. Vom 5. Februar 1794," in *Die politische Treuepflicht*, ed. Edmund Brandt (Karlsruhe: C. F. Müller Juristischer Verlag, 1976), 39.
11. See John R. Gillis, *The Prussian Bureaucracy in Crisis: 1840–1860* (Stanford: Stanford University Press, 1971), 5; Rogers Brubaker, *Citizenship and Nationhood in France and Germany* (Cambridge: Harvard University Press, 1992), 57.
12. Gillis, *Prussian Bureaucracy*, 6.
13. Koselleck, *Preußen*, 399.

14. Huber, *Deutsche Verfassungsgeschichte*, vol. 2, *Der Kampf*, 22; Hans Hatten-hauer, *Handbuch des öffentlichen Dienstes*, ed. Walter Wiese, vol. 1, *Geschichte des Beamtentums* (Cologne: Carl Heymans Verlag, 1980), 154.
15. Leah Greenfeld, *Nationalism: Five Roads to Modernity* (Cambridge: Harvard University Press, 1992), 286.
16. Koselleck, *Preußen*, 402.
17. Ibid., 402–5.
18. Brubaker, *Citizenship*, 63.
19. Ibid., 70–71.
20. Ibid., 63.
21. Quoted in Bernd Wunder, *Geschichte der Bürokratie in Deutschland* (Frankfurt am M.: Suhrkamp, 1986), 7; see also Jeserich, "Die Entstehung," 310.
22. Rosenberg, *Bureaucracy*, 213.
23. See Erich Angermann, *Robert von Mohl: Leben und Werke, Ein altliberalen Staats-gelehrten* (Neuwied: Hermann Luchterhand Verlag, 1962), 86; Gillis, *Prussian Bureaucracy*, 16.
24. Koselleck, *Preußen*, 342–343, 381–384, 387, 447.
25. Robert Berdahl, *The Politics of the Prussian Nobility: The Development of a Con-servative Ideology, 1770–1848* (Princeton: Princeton University Press, 1988), 104; Brubaker, *Citizenship*, 59–60.
26. At the same time, the Code limited its own reach by applying the subsidiary principle—it was to operate only when provincial law was unclear or nonex-istent. See Berdahl, *Prussian Nobility*, 102–3.
27. Wunder, *Bürokratie*, 26; Brubaker, *Citizenship*, 61; Berdahl, *Prussian Nobility*, 203.
28. Berdahl, *Prussian Nobility*, 182–85.
29. Ibid., 201–3.
30. Koselleck, *Preußen*, 337–41, 348–49, 352, 431, 446; Hattenhauer, *Geschichte des Beamtentums*, 206–7; Wolfgang Hardtwig, *Vormärz: Der monarchische Staat und das Bürgertum* (Munich: Deutscher Taschenbuch Verlag, 1985), 64.
31. Koselleck, *Preußen*, 342–44, 379.
32. Berdahl, *Prussian Nobility*, 182.
33. Koselleck, *Preußen*, 344.
34. Rosenberg, *Bureaucracy*, 203; Wunder, *Bürokratie*, 23.
35. Karl Marx's critique of Hegel's *Philosophy of Right* on this point is sharp, but is neither something that Prussian reformers did not already know nor did not support. See Karl Marx, "Contribution to the Critique of Hegel's Philoso-phy of Law," in Karl Marx and Friedrich Engels, *Collected Works* (New York: International Publishers, 1975), 3: 3–129; Jeserich, "Die Entstehung," 310; Gillis, *Prussian Bureaucracy*, 16.
36. Wunder, *Bürokratie*, 67.
37. Berdahl, *Prussian Nobility*, 312.
38. "Allgemeines Landrecht," in *Die politische Treuepflicht*, ed. Brandt, 39; Hatten-hauer, *Geschichte des Beamtentums*, 242; Greenfeld, *Nationalism*, 286.
39. Bendix, *Nation-Building*, 122.
40. Wunder, *Bürokratie*, 27–33; Gillis, *Prussian Bureaucracy*, 27; Angermann, *Mohl*, 79.
41. Jane Caplan, *Government without Administration: State and Civil Service in Weimar and Nazi Germany* (New York: Oxford University Press, 1988), 4.
42. Koselleck, *Preußen*, 434–37.
43. Walter Simon, *The Failure of the Prussian Reform Movement* (Ithaca: Cornell Uni-versity Press, 1955), 117–19; Hardtwig, *Vormärz*, 41–2; Rejewski, *Die Pflicht*, 30.

44. Wunder, *Bürokratie*, 61; Hardtwig, *Vormärz*, 38.
45. Ernst Rudolf Huber, "Zur Geschichte der politischen Polizei im 19. Jahrhundert," in *Nationalstaat und Verfassungsstaat*, ed. Ernst Rudolf Huber (Stuttgart: W. Kohlhammer Verlag, 1965), 147–50.
46. "Allerhöchste Kabinettsorder vom 12. April 1822, betreffend das Verfahren bei Amtsentsetzung der Geistlichen und Jugendlehrer wie auch anderer Staatsbeamten," in *Die politische Treuepflicht*, ed. Brandt, 40–44.
47. Rejewski, *Die Pflicht*, 30.
48. Ibid., 19–20.
49. Koselleck, *Preußen*, 413.
50. Ibid., 355–56.
51. Ibid., 342–43, 381–84, 387, 447.
52. Lothar Gall, "Liberalismus und 'bürgerliche Gesellschaft': Zu Charakter und Entwicklung der liberalen Bewegung in Deutschland," in *Liberalismus*, ed. Lothar Gall (Cologne: Kiepenheuer & Witsch, 1976), 162.
53. Rudolf Vierhaus, "Liberalismus, Beamtenstand und konstitutionelles System," in *Liberalismus in der Gesellschaft*, ed. Schieder, 39–54.
54. James J. Sheehan, *German Liberalism in the Nineteenth Century* (Chicago: University of Chicago Press, 1978), 39–43.
55. Karl-Georg Faber, "Strukturprobleme des deutschen Liberalismus im 19. Jahrhundert," *Der Staat* 14 (1975): 214; Dirk Blasius, "Bürgerliches Recht und bürgerliche Identität: Zu einem Problemzusammenhang in der deutschen Geschichte des 19. Jahrhunderts," in *Vom Staat des Ancien Regimes zum modernen Parteienstaat*, ed. Helmut Berding et al. (Munich: R. Oldenburg Verlag, 1974), 214–16.
56. Peter Christian Ludz, "Anarchie," in *Geschichtliche Grundbegriffe*, ed. Brunner, Conze, and Koselleck, vol. 1, *A-D*, 69–70; Blasius, "Bürgerliches Recht," 216; Huber, *Deutsche Verfassungsgeschichte*, 322.
57. Quoted in Sheehan, *German Liberalism*, 43.
58. Quoted in Hardtwig, *Vormärz*, 194.
59. Huber, *Deutsche Verfassungsgeschichte*, 377; Dahlmann quoted in Sheehan, *German Liberalism*, 39.
60. Angermann, *Mohl*, 102–59.
61. Ulrich Scheuner, "Der Rechtsstaat und die Soziale Verantwortung des Staates: Das wissenschaftliche Lebenswerk von Robert von Mohl," *Der Staat* 18 (1979): 5; Michael Stolleis, "Verwaltungslehre und Verwaltungswissenschaft, 1803–1866," in *Deutsche Verwaltungsgeschichte*, ed. Jeserich, Pohl, and Unruh, vol. 2, *Vom Reichsdeputationshauptschluß bis zur Auflösung des Deutschen Bundes*, 69; Jeserich, "Die Entstehung," 315.
62. Quoted in Erich Angermann, "Germany's 'Peculiar Institution': The Beamtentum," in *Oceans Apart? Comparing Germany and the United States: Studies in Commemoration of the 150th Anniversary of the Birth of Carl Schurz*, ed. Erich Angermann and Marie-Luise Frings (Stuttgart: Klett-Cotta, 1981), 89.
63. Quoted in Angermann, "Germany's 'Peculiar Institution,'" 90.
64. Robert von Mohl, *Politische Schriften*, ed. Klaus von Beyme (Cologne: Westdeutscher Verlag, 1966), 297.
65. Quoted in Vierhaus, "Liberalismus," 41.
66. Mohl, *Politische Schriften*, 278–79.
67. Hattenhauer, *Geschichte des Beamtentums*, 216.
68. Mohl, *Politische Schriften*, 287–88.

69. Ibid., 285–86, 295, 297, 303.
70. Ibid., 279, 282, 285, 291, 293–94, 300, 304.
71. Ibid., 282–83, 291, 303–05.
72. Ibid., 302.
73. Jeserich, "Die Entstehung," 315.
74. Birtsch, "Gemäßigter," 26–27.
75. James J. Sheehan, "Liberalism and Society in Germany, 1815–1848," *Journal of Modern History* 45, no. 4 (1973): 598.
76. Ernst-Wolfgang Böckenförde, "Die Einheit von nationaler und konstitutioneller politische Bewegung im deutschen Frühliberalismus," in *Moderne deutsche Verfassungsgeschichte (1815–1918)*, ed. Ernst-Wolfgang Böckenförde (Cologne: Kiepenheuer & Witsch, 1972), 33.
77. Stolleis, "Verwaltungslehre," 67.
78. Sheehan, *German Liberalism*, 43.
79. Manfred Riedel, "Gesellschaft, bürgerliche," in *Geschichtliche Grundbegriffe*, ed. Brunner, Conze, and Koselleck, vol. 2, *E-G*, 775.
80. Gall, "Liberalismus," 177.
81. Riedel, "Gesellschaft," 777–79.
82. Birtsch, "Gemäßigter," 38.
83. Sheehan, *German Liberalism*, 47; Birtsch, "Gemaßigter," 36.
84. Sheehan, *German Liberalism*, 16–32; Hardtwig, *Vormärz*, 145; David Blackbourn, "The Discreet Charm of the Bourgeoisie: Reappraising German History in the Nineteenth Century," in David Blackbourn and Geoff Eley, *The Peculiarities of German History: Bourgeois Society and the Politics of Nineteenth-Century Germany* (Oxford: Oxford University Press, 1984), 257; Sheehan, "Liberalism," 602–03; Riedel, "Gesellschaft," 777; Huber, *Deutsche Verfassungsgeschichte*, 389.
85. Friedrich Dahlmann, "Ein Wort über Verfassung," in *Western Liberalism*, ed. E.K. Bramsted and K. J. Melhuish, (London: Longman, 1978), 461; David Hansemann, "Memorandum on Prussia's Position and Politics," in *Western Liberalism*, ed. Bramsted and Melhuish, 338.
86. Theodore S. Hamerow, *Restoration, Revolution, and Reaction: Economics and Politics in Germany, 1815–1871* (Princeton: Princeton University Press, 1958), 108; Faber, "Strukturprobleme," 221.
87. Quoted in Irmgard Viet-Brause, "Partikularismus," in *Geschichtliche Grundbegriffe*, ed. Brunner, Conze, and Koselleck, vol. 4, *Mi-Pre*, 741.
88. Berdahl, *Prussian Nobility*, 311–13.
89. Koselleck, *Preußen*, 344, 367, 369; Sheehan, *German Liberalism*, 17–18; Klaus von Beyme, "Partei, Faktion," in *Geschichtliche Grundbegriffe*, ed. Brunner, Conze, and Koselleck, vol. 4, *Mi-Pre*, 677, 703; Hardtwig, *Vormärz*, 138–39.
90. Huber, *Deutsche Verfassungsgeschichte*, 576–77, 740–48; A. J. P. Taylor, "1848: The Year of German Liberalism," in *1848: A Turning Point*, ed. Melvin Kranzberg (Boston: D. C. Heath, 1959), 27–28; Theodore Hamerow, "Die Wahlen zum Frankfurter Parlament," in *Moderne deutsche Verfassungsgeschichte*, ed. Böckenförde, 218–19; Ernst Rudolf Huber, *Dokumente zur deutschen Verfassungsgeschichte* (Stuttgart: W. Kohlhammer Verlag, 1978), vol. 1, *Deutsche Verfassungdokumente 1803–1850*, 456.
91. Fritz Hartung, "Studien zur Geschichte der preußischen Verwaltung," in *Staatsbildende Kräfte der Neuzeit: Gesammelte Aufsätze*, ed. Fritz Hartung (Berlin: Duncker & Humblot, 1961), 312.

92. "Zirkularverfügung an sämtliche Königlichen Regierungspräsidenten, betreffend die Wirksamkeit für das dermalige Regierungssystem, vom 15. Juli 1848," in *Die Treuepflicht*, ed. Brandt, 53–54.

93. "Anti-Reaktions-Beschluß der preußischen Nationalversammlung, vom 9. August 1848," in *Dokumente zur deutschen Verfassungsgeschichte*, ed. Huber, 457–58.

94. Gillis, *Prussian Bureaucracy*, 103, 112–14; Hartung, "Studien," 312.

95. Rejewski, *Die Pflicht*, 54.

96. Hamerow, *Restoration*, 187.

97. Karl Griewank, "Ursachen und Folgen des Scheiterns der deutschen Revolution von 1848," in *Moderne deutsche Verfassungsgeschichte*, ed. Böckenförde, 55.

98. Quoted in Gillis, *Prussian Bureaucracy*, 137.

99. Gillis, *Prussian Bureaucracy*, 135–36.

100. Berdahl, *Prussian Nobility*, 335.

Two

"THE MOST DEMOCRATIC DEMOCRACY IN THE WORLD"

German Statism Survives the Weimar Republic

The consolidation of German statism as a logic of political membership in the first half of the nineteenth century secured a vertical segmentation of loyal German political agency. Located at the top of that vertical segmentation was the state civil service. The identity of this institution was articulated by the Prussian General Code in 1794 and elaborated in the Prussian Reform Era between 1807 and 1819. It posited a politically loyal body serving the universalistic Geist of the Prussian state located above all of society's—and later "civil" society's—diverse particularism. Individual Prussian civil servants were tested to ensure that their Gesinnung, or conscience, matched as closely as possible the Geist, or spirit, of the Prussian state. In the early nineteenth century, "natural" membership accorded all other Prussians a spatially "lower" political role and an inability to "carry" the universalism of the Prussian state. In the 1830s, modernization and industrialization began the differentiation of those natural Prussian subjects into unenfranchised workers and peasants, unenfranchised landless professional and nascent commercial elites, and provincial diet-represented landed-property owners. To contain this differentiation that would become a political mobilization in the Vormärz, conservative Prussian governments resorted to an overt conservative politicization of the state civil service. This reciprocally fueled

German liberalism's reformist political agenda in the Vormärz. Nonlanded liberals reacted by linking their self-differentiation from the "anarchism" of mobilized rural and urban workers to a critique of "Bureaukratie" and a call to return the Prussian state to its Reform Era universalistic roots. In the process, German liberalism did not reject the vertical differentiation of legitimate and loyal political agency. Instead, it attempted to shore up that logic's differentiation, "re-universalize" the Prussian bureaucracy, and create a reliable bulwark for defense against the "democratic excess" of the urban and rural working poor. The statist logic of German political membership thereby consolidated. Its roots were absolutist, but its applicability was not regime specific.

The flexibility of Germany's statist logic of political membership was demonstrated some seventy years later, in the early years of the Weimar Republic. An extraordinarily different context from the absolutism or constitutional monarchism of the nineteenth century, the Weimar Republic was characterized by its first interior minister as "the most democratic democracy in the world."[1] Between 1918 and 1922, however, Weimar experienced the power of German statism as a logic of political membership as the new regime suffered profound challenges from across the political spectrum. Formed in the wake of war defeat, the Weimar Republic in its early years was home to a vicious debate over who qualified as a legitimate political actor and according to what criteria. The central referent for that question was a refurbished and updated German statism that no longer had room for a monarch, but that retained an important role for civil servants and the military vis-à-vis ordinary citizens and political parties in Germany's young democracy.

Germany's First Democracy

Nineteenth-century German socialism did not foresee that a social democratic regime would be appointed by a German prince whose hand was guided by war-weary generals searching for forces with whom to share—and ultimately assign—responsibility for Germany's defeat in the First World War.[2] On 9 November 1918, Friedrich Ebert was appointed chancellor, the kaiser abdicated, a new government was formed, and Ebert sent a note to Germany's civil servants appealing for cooperation. That note was the first chapter in what many regard as Weimar's civil service debacle, a policy arena that contained, according to Arthur Rosenberg, the "question of life and death for German democracy."[3] Studies in public administration suggest two different ideal-typical responses that the new Weimar regime could have provided to this question: the "accommodate" response, which recognized the technical indispensability of old state actors for governing the new order; or the "cleanse" response, which recognized the political will, of governments and citizens, to rid the new order of loyalists of the old.[4]

Neither response fit well into the German political context in 1918. The "accommodate" response was not particularly fitting because it isolated technical expertise as an institutional imperative, and German civil servants had never historically been only technical experts for keeping the state's machinery functioning. The role of the German civil servant as *Beamter*, or officeholder, differed from both the French *fonctionnaire*, who had specific functions to discharge within the complex of public power, and the Anglo-American public servant or clerk, who had to carry out particular tasks that the law assigned. In turn, the "cleanse" response was also problematic, for the German *Amt* occupant had always enjoyed a "special relationship" politically both to the German state and to the German citizen.[5] The Reform Era ideal of the state civil servant, which had endured no revision or even substantial challenge prior to 1918, saw a civil servant's "rational" loyalty to the Geist of the German state as necessary for serving ordinary "natural" citizens in German society. With the ideal-type of the German civil servant serving a state Geist, and not a party government, the political "cleanse" option for the new Weimar government was impeded by the very powerful ideology, if not concrete reality, that civil servants were loyal political actors "above" party politics. Instead, the new Weimar regime combined both the technical and the political concerns of these two options in response to the political challenges it faced—challenges both from actors of the old regime and from actors of the new. In the process, the statist logic of political membership became a political sorting device not just for nineteenth-century enlightened monarchs, reformist bureaucrats, and German liberals, but also for twentieth-century German democrats between 1918 and 1922 to use in their attempt to preserve the Weimar Republic.

The Wilhelmine era, from 1890 to 1918, saw the growth of the German bureaucracy into an immensely powerful and conservative political institution. While Bismarck had used the bureaucracy as a "passive instrument for his personal rule," his departure in 1890 saw the shift in power from the chancellor's office to a "refeudalized" institution of bureaucratic policymakers.[6] In the years before the war, state secretaries in government ministries became "quasi-ministers" making policy without parliamentary control.[7] Between 1875 and 1907, state employment had increased threefold.[8] The growth in power and numbers of state actors in this period made the Wilhelmine state, according to Geoff Eley, "its own constituency, whose primary purpose was to rally the loyalties of the state's own personnel: not just the higher grades of civil servants, but also the clerical workers, teachers, clergy, uniformed working class of railwaymen, postmen and foresters, and conscripts to the Army and Navy."[9] By the first decade of the new century, the German state had acquired the legal capacity directly to reward and discipline roughly eleven percent of the German workforce.[10] A good part of that capacity was directed toward what Chancellor Caprivi described to civil servants in 1899 as "the most serious question of our time"—which was "the struggle against Social Democracy." Caprivi called on officials to embody "loyalty, the unimpeded fulfillment of duty, and discipline" in the struggle against the "*Umsturzpartei*," or party of destruction, as he termed the Social Democratic Party of Germany.[11] But the campaign against the SPD was not simply a party-politicized anti-socialism, of which there was plenty in the Wilhelmine years. Informing the campaign was a deep political logic of membership that located German Social Democrats as anarchic threats in the realm of society. Against this threat, loyal German state bureaucrats serving the universalistic idea of the state had to be mobilized. Germany's Social Democrats adopted virtually the same political discourse—redirected at forces to their left—as they unexpectedly came to power in November 1918.

On 9 November, only hours after being appointed chancellor of the German Reich, Friedrich Ebert came face-to-face with a homogeneous civil service with a "common estate- and state-consciousness."[12] He said, "I know that it will be difficult for many of you to work with the new men who have taken over the leadership of the Reich, but I appeal to your love of the people," a people who were, he said, facing "anarchy" and were on the verge of "civil war." These dangers could be avoided "only if all administrators and civil servants in town and country lend a helping hand."[13] Ebert thereby stated to the conservative Wilhelmine civil service that its members were indispensable political actors in the new Weimar

Republic. They were indispensable not as partisan political actors, but rather as servants of the state whose duty it was to protect German society from disorder and anarchy. Regardless of the other roles they may have had in mind in November 1918, German civil servants could identify with this role, and they were evidently reassured by the Social Democrats' appeal to it. When the new transitional government—the Council of People's Commissioners, or Rat des Volksbeauftragten—explicitly guaranteed on 12 November and again on 15 November an unlimited freedom of speech and organization, and a continuation of current salaries and pensions for all German state civil servants, the six largest civil service organizations in the country, with a total of 1.5 million members, agreed to "place [themselves] at the disposal" of the current government and thereby to serve the "common good." Not only was the civil service not "cleansed" in the process, but with the guarantee of free speech and association, the new Social Democratic government was offering German state employees political rights they had never before enjoyed.[14] The Social Democratic government did this, however, not mainly because they were committed civil libertarians—though a liberalism did inform their actions in this period—but because they believed that the professional civil service, whose formal political identity was an "above-party" universalism, was essential for governance and stability. If they had chosen to "cleanse" the bureaucracy of Wilhelmine anti-republicans, of whom there were many, they would themselves have been susceptible to the charge of politicizing the institution.[15]

In these early days, the new German government's only substantively republican civil service policy was to assign political "assistants" (Beigeordneten) to the most senior bureaucrats in the ministries. These "assistants," who were demanded by leftist Independent Socialists and the council movement in order to ensure the "republican" nature of the bureaucrats' service, were initially received with great bitterness by the old Wilhelmine officials.[16] That was until many political assistants revealed they were less interested in "controlling" the ministers and state secretaries to whom they were assigned than in protecting "their" officials from the political meddling of the workers' and soldiers' councils. Abetted by majority Social Democrats, many assistants strove to secure "the least complicated conduct of official bureaucratic functions."[17] This outcome, though politically incompatible with the powerful anti-republicanism harbored by many Wilhelmine bureaucratic holdovers, was compatible with the statist logic of political membership. It was also compatible with what the new German government believed was necessary for protecting the new German Republic: a professional state civil service ideally serving a universal good that existed "above" the conflict and anarchy of a non-self-regulating German society. Political "assistants" from that society were, according to the statist logic of membership, definitionally particularistic in their concerns. The power of that logic of political membership not only made senior Wilhelmine civil servants see the "assistants" that way, but made the "assistants" see themselves that way, as well.

In the spring of 1919, the newly formed German Civil Service Federation (DBB)—with support from the right-wing German National People's Party and the right-wing press—demanded a meeting with the constitution-drafting committee of the National Assembly. That meeting produced an agreement to incorporate into the Weimar constitution a guarantee of the existence of the "German professional civil service," a guarantee that Hugo Preuss, author of the first draft of the constitution, had never contemplated. By the time the constitution was approved in August 1919, civil servants had their "duly-acquired rights" (*wohlerworbene Rechte*) made constitutionally inviolable; their role was defined as "serving the whole [*Gesamtheit*] and not a party"(which was the document's only mention of political party, and it was negative); their "freedom of political belief and assembly" was guaranteed; and their loyalty to the Weimar constitution was required.[18]

Germany's statist logic of political membership thereby acquired a constitutional foothold in Germany's first democracy.[19] First, the protection of "duly-acquired rights" formalized an implicit and organic link to Germany's past—not the democratic-republican past of the 1848 revolution, but rather the statist past of the Prussian General Code and Reform Era. Second, "serving the whole" was a modern restatement of nineteenth-century service to the universalistic Geist of the Prussian state. Third, the explicit slight of political parties reaffirmed German statism's definition of parties as particularistic and of dubious political legitimacy. Fourth, the provision of a set of newly acquired rights, in the form of freedoms of political belief, assembly, and organization expanded the civil servant's political role to include full and free rights of citizenship. Finally, political loyalty, required for Germany's rational political membership in the nineteenth century, was still required, but its object—soon to be disputed—became the Weimar constitution. Rudolf Wissel, economics minister of the first government, commented at the time, "we have no real program ... in place of one form of military and bureaucratic government another has been introduced, and the principles of the new government do not differ essentially from those of the old regime."[20] Reinhard Rürup, a modern observer, concurred, concluding that the constitution writers could not "get loose of the hypostatization [*Überhöhung*] of the nineteenth-century state."[21]

The continued power of that hypostatization was revealed in a political battle during the summer of 1919 over the precise meaning of the Weimar civil servant's required "loyalty" to the Weimar constitution. This one arguably republican attribute of the civil servant's role definition was contested by the DBB, which maintained that the constitutional declaration of the new regime as a "Republic" was only a "statement of fact" (*Tatsachenfeststellung*) and not a "legal prescription" (*Rechtsvorschrift*) that mandated "loyalty" to the Republic as such.[22] The Weimar government ultimately agreed with that assessment and declared that the civil servants' loyalty entailed only an obligation to secure the "maintenance" (*Wahrung*) of the constitution and not loyalty to the Republic. At the end of 1919, the government repeated that the loyalty demanded of the civil servant meant only the need to "observe the provisions of the constitution loyally." Out of context, the challenge of the DBB and the government's response might be viewed as evidence of a liberalized political discourse and a diminution of the German civil servant's political role. That certainly was not the intent of the DBB and its right-wing supporters. Their concern to differentiate the precise object of political loyalty away from the Republic was essentially a ploy to delegitimize the new political order; it signaled that political loyalty was to be withheld from the Republic as an illegitimate "state-form."[23]

Challenges to Germany's First Democracy and Statist Political Membership

Three political crises occurring between March 1920 and June 1922—an attempted coup and two political assassinations—revealed in sharp detail that Germany's nineteenth-century statist logic of political membership not only survived the Weimar constitution, but also survived as a discursively "appropriate" instrument for the new regime's effort to maintain political order. The Kapp Putsch occurred in March 1920 as an effort to create what the putsch leaders, Generals Kapp and Lüttwitz, called a "government of order, freedom, and action" to replace the "party-regime" of the Weimar Republic.[24] The putschists controlled Berlin for five days while the government hid outside of the city. The army, under the command of General von Seekt, refused to intervene because, Seekt said, "*Reichswehr* does not fire on *Reichswehr*."[25] The Republic's civil servants generally did not join the coup attempt, but evidently less out of loyalty to the Republic than because of the coup leaders' ineptness and dilettante behavior.[26] Though civil servants preserved a "facade of loyalty," Jasper concludes that Kapp's desire to rid Germany of "political party domination" found "internal sympathy" within the ministerial bureaucracy.[27] To put down the coup attempt, the Weimar government found itself turning to the forces of societal disorder that nineteenth-century German statism had warned against: urban workers who, with the support of the SPD and the USPD, called for a general strike.[28] But as the workers organized and the coup began to fizzle, the government became much more ambivalent about endorsing the workers' demands beyond providing lip service. First and foremost, according to Rudolf Olden, the workers wanted to "detach the leaders of the Social Democrats from the dangerous coalition with reactionary civil servants and army officers."[29] Indeed, the second of eight demands the strikers issued—superseded only by the call for the putsch leaders to be punished—was to purge the German civil service of "counterrevolutionaries."[30]

Although higher civil servants had not even actively supported the coup attempt, the political power of the civil service and its legitimating statist logic of political membership were powerful enough to crystallize as a primary target for German workers mobilizing to save the new Republic. After the Social Democratic chancellor, Gustav Bauer, agreed in principle on 20 March to the strikers' demand to "cleanse" the Weimar bureaucracy of its conservative Wilhelmine holdovers—an agreement that was never implemented—the labor action began to wind down.[31] When the workers in the Ruhr refused to return to work, however, President Ebert, also a Social Democrat, called out Reichswehr and Free Corps troops—the very same forces that had refused to protect the Republic two months before—to put down the strike.[32] Ebert thereby benefited from his previous unwillingness to "republicanize" the military, a policy he regarded as a "dangerous experiment."[33]

Prussia's interior minister, Carl Severing, subsequently pursued what he called the "implementation of a self-evident necessity"—

to "clean up one province after the other, until we have a civil service corps that is prepared to work with the Prussian government to make Prussia into a democracy and the Prussians into democrats"—and he met with substantial resistance, some from within the SPD. The "System-Severing," as it was denounced, was criticized as doling out jobs to Severing's unqualified party friends.[34] Severing's refusal to regard Communist Party membership as automatically disqualifying a person for state employment in Prussia contributed to the uproar. But Severing also shied away from more radical measures. He refused to endorse an Anglo-American-style independent civil service commission for the new Republic, he rejected a proposal to require a "Socialist conviction" for senior appointments, and he would not touch the Prussian judiciary, which was not exactly a bastion of republicanism in the early 1920s.[35]

Five years later, Severing's "system," whatever it was, had produced only fifty-eight Social Democrats among four-hundred-twenty-three Prussian *Landräte*, or provincial commissioners. Severing himself could count only thirteen reliably "republican" higher officials in his own Interior Ministry of sixty-five state employees.[36] In response to this first major political crisis, Bauer's March promise to rid the new regime of its anti-republican Wilhelmine holdovers was never implemented, workers in the Ruhr who were not appeased had their action put down by the very state forces that the workers were striking to have removed, and when Severing tried a modest civil service reform in Prussia, he was mocked and rebuffed. The statist logic of political membership suffered its first serious political challenge in Weimar, and it survived virtually unscathed.

On 26 August 1921, two right-wing Free Corps soldiers assassinated Matthias Erzberger, a retired Zentrum party leader who had served in the SPD-Zentrum coalition government in 1919–1920. This second grave crisis for the new Republic was openly applauded in the anti-republican and anti-Semitic press, where Erzberger had been vilified as a "lily-livered, muckraking picture of misery" for his part in concluding the Versailles Peace Treaty.[37] Three presidential emergency decrees and three bills to amend standing law appeared directly in response to Erzberger's murder. The presidential decrees forbade the public wearing of military uniforms by former soldiers, empowered the interior minister to ban printed material encouraging or applauding acts of violence or that held in contempt any state institution or organ in a manner that endangered domestic peace, and explicitly reiterated state protection for all "persons in public life."[38] In parliament, Independent Social Democrats proposed, on penalty of termination and loss of pension, to "forbid civil servants from representing monarchical views in public or manifesting those views in the exercise of their official duties."

In December, four months after Erzberger's murder, the federal government greeted the proposal with stony silence. In January, the Social Democratic interior minister, Köster, proposed a watered-down version of what his leftist colleagues had suggested and called on civil servants to "defend the existing state form from every sort of attack and to intervene on behalf of the reputation of the Reich and Länder governments." Only a few Social Democratic Länder governments supported that proposal, it was actively rejected by many Reich ministers, and the Wirth government let the initiative die before it reached the Reichstag.[39] As was the case with the Kapp Putsch, when anti-republican state civil servants had neither engineered nor generally supported the insurgency, anti-republican civil servants had not murdered Matthias Erzberger. But as was also the case after the putsch, anti-republican civil servants were again targeted by defenders of the Republic. And again, according to Jasper, the flurry of government activity subsequent to Erzberger's murder was mainly for show, calculated to appease the Left but not to contain the Right. To avoid another general strike, Jasper writes, "all of the measures of the Reich government at this time were tactically determined.... The task of the Reich government was seen to be to keep the huge working class movement in orderly control... The decrees for the defense of the republic were primarily a means to prevent a second revolution."[40] Preventing a "second revolution" required at least the appearance that the Wirth government was clamping down on what was called "right-wing bolshevism."[41] By the end of 1921, the Weimar government had once more "defended the Republic" not by removing anti-republican state civil servants from office, but by preempting an uncontrolled left-wing reaction to a right-wing political murder. A "second revolution" had been prevented, and there was no reason to risk a civil service policy that would not only alienate the Right, but also—according to the logic of German statism—possibly undermine the regime's ability to contain the threat of another political mobilization of German society in the future.

That threat presented itself about six months later, when the Weimar regime faced its third major political crisis in a little over two years. On 24 June 1922, two right-wing nationalists assassinated Walter Rathenau, a centrist German Democratic Party member who was foreign minister in the Wirth government. This third catastrophic event in the Republic's short history kicked the Wirth government into action once more. Again, civil servants had not killed Rathenau, and again, the politics of civil servants were targeted by a chorus of leftist and left-center voices. Three decrees for the "defense of the Republic" were issued within six days. They included press restrictions, the power to ban political meetings that called for overthrowing the "republican state-form," and the death penalty for anyone advocating the assassination of a government minister.[42] These measures and Wirth's speech in parliament the day after Rathenau was killed—ending with the infamous phrase, "*dieser Feind steht rechts*," or "this enemy is on the right"—indicated to some a resolve at last to confront the right-wing threat.[43] A proposal to amend German civil service law was finally successful. Five days after Rathenau's murder, the Reichstag heard the demand to "cleanse" the bureaucracy of anti-republican civil servants. This time action was taken and it was made illegal for state civil servants to utter "malicious and provocative" statements "in public" that called for the "reconstitution of the monarchy," or that "opposed the Republic." It was also demanded that civil servants "distance [themselves] from all active participation in efforts to change the republican state-form, even when those efforts remain with the bounds of constitutional legality."[44]

By formally removing the unprecedented political rights granted to Weimar's civil service and returning to the nineteenth-century demand for "full-person" (during both work and nonwork hours) loyalty, the amendment addressed what many Germans had identified as the new Republic's greatest institutional weakness. The German Left, whose forces had mobilized twice within a little over two years to save the Republic, were also emboldened by Wirth's rhetoric about where the Feind stood on the Weimar political spectrum. But, once more, the actual implementation of the laws against that Feind was modest at best. According to Hans Fenske, "The law concerning the duties of civil servants to defend the Republic remained largely just on paper… The law actually amounted to a gesture to the public, nothing more."[45] It removed a few Prussian higher officials but otherwise did very little.[46] Again, the main target of the government's actions appears to have been the leftist societal mobilization that Social Democrats like Severing were increasingly warning about, not the right-wing coup leaders, murderers, and their supporters who had generated those mobilizations in the first place.[47] At the same time, the lack of a systematic implementation of these measures to protect the Republic remained largely consistent with Germany's statist logic of political membership. Society was anarchic, and the German state had to maintain its ability to contain it. The government's gestures were just meaningful enough to the German public to reduce the threat of further social unrest. As Charles Maier has observed, Weimar governments felt forced to contain social tensions on conservative terms or not contain them at all.[48] The political rationale for that position, which was more or less consistent with Germany's statist logic of political membership, was revealed in the party-political and intellectual discourse in Germany in this period.

Party-Political Discourse and German Statism

The German Social Democratic Party was thrust into power by the events of 9 November 1918, when Friedrich Ebert, the party leader, was appointed chancellor. Prior to 1922, the party provided the regime's first president, three of five chancellors, and many cabinet ministers. As a party thus standing on the "floor of the Republic," however wobbly, and providing many of its personnel, the SPD is a logical place to search for a counter-discourse to the statist logic of political membership inherited from the nineteenth century. That search turns up very little. By the end of the First World War, commentators agree that German Social Democracy had considerably "grown into" the Wilhelmine political order and become more or less *staatserhaltend*, or state-maintaining. This was indicated by the party's renunciation of revolution and endorsement of parliamentarism, the bureaucratization of the party's organization, and the party's overwhelming fear of "Bolshevik" or "Russian" conditions developing in Germany.[49] These were joined by the SPD's elevation of the values of expertise and professional experience to a level equal to, if not above, its own perceived legitimacy to govern Germany. By the time the SPD assumed political power in late 1918, it was, according to Hans-Ulrich Wehler, "trapped by powerful continuities in German history" that led it to "perceive the liberating discontinuity of the revolution mainly as a threat."[50]

German statism not only posited revolution as a threat, but it also identified the need for a strong and reliable state to contain that threat. The threat for Caprivi had been the SPD, as the "party of destruction"; when the "party of destruction" assumed power in 1918, the threat became the leftist Independent Social Democrats and Spartacists.[51] A month prior to being named chancellor, Ebert said that "revolutions come" when "the people progress" and reforms do not follow; "take a look at Russia and be warned," he concluded.[52] At the same time, Ebert admonished German workers to avoid "Bolshevik chaos" and "Russian conditions."[53] On 4 November, the SPD's executive board demanded that German workers ignore the Spartacist call for a general strike, maintain "quiet blood and discipline," and not be captivated by "slogans of confusion."[54] Two days prior to being named chancellor, Ebert stated, "I hate revolution like sin."[55] On 9 November, Chancellor Ebert's first public statement included as its last sentence, "I beg of you urgently, leave the streets and maintain quiet and order."[56] On the next day, Ebert formed an "alliance" with General Wilhelm Groener, chief of staff of the Supreme Army Command. Groener's memoirs recount, "the officer corps expected from the government a fight against bolshevism and is prepared to be employed for that end. Ebert accepted my offer of alliance. From then on, we spoke every evening."[57] On that same day, General Field Marshal von Hindenburg, who was later to become president, called on his troops to "save Germany from great danger" and to "prevent the spread of terroristic Bolshevism" and "the threat of civil war." Hindenburg ordered the army to "work together with" Ebert, whom he called the "leader of the moderate Social Democratic Party."[58] In January, the SPD party organ, *Vorwärts*, went so far as to place recruitment advertisements for Free Corps troops that read, "Who will defend us from bolshevism and terror?" and "Machine-gunners: only German men whose heart is on the right side need apply."[59]

Clearly, what united the SPD with anti-republican bureaucrats and soldiers in the early days of the new regime was rooted more deeply in German political discourse than the fear that had recently been deposited by the Russian revolution.[60] "Bolshevism" connoted the nineteenth-century image of disorder and anarchy in a mobilized society no longer contained by a strong German state. A political logic of appropriateness had consolidated in the nineteenth century that not only counseled against the reform, or "cleansing," of the German civil service, army, and judiciary in the early Weimar years; it also allowed the SPD and the *Ordnungskräfte*, or forces of order, of the old regime literally to understand one another in this period of political uncertainty. One observer's conclusion that Ebert had "no choice" but to collaborate with the army and bureaucracy is, of course, logically wrong.[61] Abstract choices abounded for the SPD, but none made more sense to the party leadership, and to many ordinary Germans, than the one suggested by Germany's statist logic of political membership. To regard the SPD's actions here as evidence of an "historical error" is to miss the point.[62] The party's choice was perfectly understandable, if profoundly tragic, within the old German logic of political membership. In the early Weimar years, that logic was what might be called derivatively anti-republican; the SPD's attraction to it was not based on its explicit anti-republican content, but on the high value the logic placed on expertise and "rational" political reliability. "Of fateful significance for the Weimar Republic," Karl-Dietrich Bracher wrote, was that for many Germans, "good administration was regarded as the best politics."[63] Germany's "good administration" was validated by no less an observer than Max Weber, who wrote in 1917, that Germany's state bureaucracy was superior to all others on measures of integrity, education, conscientiousness, and intelligence—which, Weber also argued, did not also make bureaucrats good political actors.[64] But that caveat was not shared by many other Germans in this period, including the party leadership of the SPD.[65]

At the end of November 1918, Friedrich Ebert waxed eloquent about the bureaucracy he inherited from the old regime:

> The Reich machine is a somewhat complicated apparatus.... After we assumed political power, we had the responsibility to see to it that the Reich machine did not break apart.... And that was not easy. We used all of our powers, working day and night, to prevent a downfall [*Niedergang*] and collapse [*Zusammenbruch*]. We could not have done this alone; for that we needed the experienced assistance of the professionals [*Fachleute*]. If we had fired the experienced Reich officials, if we had been forced to fill these positions with persons who lacked the necessary knowledge and experience, then we would have been, in a few days, at the end of our ropes [*am Ende unseres Lateins gewesen*].[66]

Ebert's praise went beyond acknowledging the functionality of the civil service. He was close to stating that "the Reich machine" would have collapsed had it been taken over by Social Democrats like himself, and collapse was unthinkable. In 1925, the Social Democrat Philip Scheidemann wrote in his memoirs that Ebert was unable to "loosen himself from the pre-revolutionary idea-world" and wanted "no experiments"; "we turned naturally to the professionals," Scheidemann wrote.[67] The "expertise" argument used by the Right against the SPD was thus completely serviceable for the SPD's own campaign against the Left.

While the value the SPD placed on order and expertise in the early Weimar years was consistent with Germany's statist logic of political membership, another of the party's apparent values, personal liberty, was not. The liberalism of SPD ideology in this period was not dominant, but it did partly inform the new government's early overture to the Wilhelmine bureaucracy guaranteeing unlimited freedom of speech and organization. An article in 1918 in the party organ, *Vorwärts*, criticized what was called the "all-healing power of the police and military" and noted that while Germany was still "far behind English liberalism," "civil liberty is such a good thing" that "we must accept a bit of discomfort."[68] This was obviously not a ringing endorsement of liberalism—and it was echoed by Helmut Schmidt some sixty years later—but it was an acknowledgement, and the SPD put it to use in its attack on the Spartacists, who were charged with advocating limits on the freedoms of speech and press.[69] The SPD's early support for civil and political liberties for Wilhelmine civil service holdovers was informed by its desire to "liberate civil servants from the economic and philosophical constraints of the authoritarian state."[70] But the party was also driven by the fear of losing the state's capacity to contain what the party saw as a threateningly anarchic German society. By 1922, when the SPD revised—on paper—its magnanimous view of the Wilhelmine civil service holdovers as victims of the German authoritarian state, the party was using those holdovers as important political actors to contain a much more threatening, in its eyes, revolutionary German society.[71] In Weimar's early years, that society consisted of a number of new claimants on political power.

To the left of the SPD in the early Weimar years stood the USPD, or Independent Social Democrats, and the Spartacus Union, which had been on the left within the USPD and then broke off to form the KPD, or Communist Party of Germany. Ownership of the so-called surprise of the revolution, the short-lived workers' and soldiers' councils, was claimed by the USPD and the KPD.[72] In early November 1918, the council movement called for the disaggregation of the German state bureaucracy into popularly elected workers' and soldiers' councils. The SPD responded that the new regime could govern only if the old administration were not disturbed by what it called the "interference" of "unqualified persons" in the councils.[73] But not just the councils' "unqualified persons" threatened the new regime; the council movement provided an alternative—however ill-defined—to Germany's entire institutional order and thereby the gravest threat to Germany's nineteenth-century statist logic of political membership. The council movement sprang up spontaneously in Germany during the first two weeks in November 1918, when, Wolfgang Mommsen somewhat broadly concluded, "the traditional political institutions had completely vanished."[74] Had those institutions indeed vanished, the story being told here would be quite different. Instead, the councils, as the "creation and essence of the German revolution," briefly challenged Germany's political institutions, including the civil service and political parties, but they certainly did not succeed in replacing them.[75]

On 9 November, the Berlin workers' and soldiers' councils had declared that "the German people has power in its own hands," and "the foundation of the government's entire legislative, administrative, and judicial power rests only in the hands of representatives of the workers and soldiers."[76] Under Ebert, the SPD immediately dismissed the substance of the councils' demand to "cleanse" the bureaucracy.[77] But the Spartacists explained that this was not to mean a "new manning of political posts from above, but rather a new organization of politics from below," with the "election of workers' and soldiers' councils throughout Germany, in whose hands only legislative and administrative power must lie."[78] Ernst Däumig, a USPD member of the Vollzugsrat, argued on 18 November that the inherited Wilhelmine administration had to be dealt with "according to revolutionary law.... Executive power cannot return to a form of absolutism ... we demand a state form that organically grows from the foundation of the revolution."[79] But a month later, at a political gathering in Berlin, Däumig had seen nothing of that sort:

> The German Revolution trusts itself cursedly little; the subject- and corporal-mentality [*Untertanen- und Korporalgeist*], an inheritance of decades, sits deeply within it. This mentality cannot be defeated through an election and political leaflets thrown at the masses every two or three years, but only by a heart-felt and powerful attempt to maintain the constant political activity of the German people, and that can happen only through the council system... How are you to teach a people the widest possible self-administration ... if you simply send delegates to some parliament who let fly with the usual speeches and

party quarrels, but do not change a thing for the people outside?...
What now exists is a compromise between revolution and the old system.... The old state machine with all of the people who worked in it
before is still present.[80]

The councils were promoted as "schools in which the German citizen could win the political experience so vitally necessary to the
new democracy."[81] The council movement thereby reconceptualized society as a realm whose political interests were to be mediated by organizations of workers and soldiers, not political parties
and parliament. Däumig's critique of political parties, though
from the Left, was not unfamiliar German political discourse. His
quarreling and speech-making parliamentarians were also attacked in this period by the right-wing legal theorist Carl Schmitt,
as will be shown shortly. In any case, by mid-December 1918, the
council movement had sunk into "political meaninglessness."[82]
Not unlike the "Round Table" movement in East Germany in
1989–1990, the council movement in Weimar was an intellectually
coherent and understandable response to the regime it was rejecting, but not a well-articulated political alternative to it. Support
for the council movement, according to Sebastian Haffner, was
largely "instinctive."[83] It called for a radical system of citizen self-
governance in a completely new institutional arrangement when
Germany in 1918 had very few citizens. In contrast to the Greens,
sixty years later in the Federal Republic, the council movement in
Weimar was an intellectual, but not viable political, alternative to
the new institutional order, and it disappeared just as quickly as it
had appeared.

To the right of the SPD in the early Weimar years, political parties ranged from the liberal-moderate DDP, or German Democratic Party, to the right-wing DNVP, or German National People's
Party. None of these parties contributed to a critical dialogue with
the inherited statist logic of German political membership. On the
moderate end, the DDP, with its liberalism, "stood on the floor of
the republican state-form"; it was deeply disturbed by the "disor-
ders of violent revolution"; it woodenly invited into the party "all
men and women who are today not remaining inactive, but who
acknowledge the new facts and wish to express their rights to participate"; it adopted the nineteenth-century state/society dichotomization as a "*Selbstverständlichkeit*," or matter-of-course;
and it viewed the "expert" professional civil service as the "backbone" of Germany's new Republic.[84] On the other end, the radical

right-wing DNVP supported the Kapp Putsch in 1920; it drove the insertion of the "duly-acquired rights of the German professional civil service" into the constitutional draft; it pressed the issue of loyalty to the "republican state-form" required of civil servants and received the response from the SPD-led government that only loyalty to the constitution was required; and it rejected the half-hearted attempts at "cleansing" the civil service, especially in Prussia, as "*Gesinnungsschnüffelei*," or snooping into personal beliefs.[85] A powerful concern of the Right in this period was to protect the functioning capacity of a conservative professional civil service to contain the threat of a politically mobilized civil society. While this position was shared with the SPD, right-wing parties did not—like the SPD—view "rational" political membership in the early Weimar years as the means to protect the Republic as much as the means to preserve the capacity, at some point, to undermine the Republic.

Intellectual Discourse and German Statism

About a year before the council movement unsuccessfully challenged Germany's statist logic of membership, the social theorist Max Weber issued his own challenge to this surviving political ideology. It appeared in a series of newspaper articles Weber wrote for the *Frankfurter Zeitung* in 1917. Weber's critique of Wilhelmine politics in these articles held Bismarck responsible for inhibiting the development of parliamentary democracy in Germany. Weber found Bismarck's shadow to be long and dark, leaving Germany governed by pretentious bureaucratic parvenus responsible for catastrophic domestic and foreign policy failures. Yet Weber believed it was possible to modify Germany's institutional arrangement by taking advantage of the approaching war defeat. For Weber, what was required was quite straightforward: "We are dealing here with simple questions of techniques for formulating national policies."[86] Those techniques involved strengthening the parliament, controlling the bureaucracy, separating their respective competencies, and developing genuine political leaders. Nowhere in Germany did genuine political leaders exist to check the political pretensions of the professional bureaucracy. The bureaucracy had been allowed to follow its own "irresistible" course and to "turn all problems of politics into problems of administration."[87]

Weber's critique somewhat resembled Robert von Mohl's Bureaukratiekritik of the 1840s. Neither rejected the professional bureaucracy as such, and each demanded only that it function according to its proper role. For Mohl, however, that role was enlightened and expert bureaucratic governance requiring a "cleansing" of incompetent officials. For Weber, the role was enlightened and expert administrative implementation requiring the empowerment of parliament to act as a governing body. Weber thus challenged the statist logic of political membership by elevating parliament to the position of governance and relegating the bureaucracy to implementation. Yet he saw the bureaucracy's iron grip on information as indispensable for an increasingly complex society. Germany's "rational" political members in the state bureaucracy would be demoted to administrative servants of a parliamentary will, but their need to be dutiful, expert, and politically reliable would not be altered.[88] At the same time, Weber also placed a very high value on political—and not mere administrative—expertise, though political expertise had to be properly located: he called for the long-term development of a "corps of professional parliamentarians" who viewed politics as a vocation and not as periodic service to the community.[89]

Weber's intellectual challenge to Germany's statist logic of political membership thus involved a rearrangement of institutional competence, but not the demotion of the traditional statist values of expertise and professionalism. Politics remained for Weber an essentially hortatory activity practiced by professionals above a society of ordinary citizens.[90] Those professionals worked in parliament and were thus closer to citizens than the bureaucrats of German statism. But Weber was little interested in empowering ordinary citizens as sovereign political actors in Germany in 1917. Consistent with German statism, Weber viewed German citizens with considerable disdain. They were plagued by "emotional cowardice," on the one hand, and "irrationality" and "blind fury," on the other.[91] The former characterized the bourgeoisie, whom he admonished to "stand at last on their own political feet," and the latter characterized the proletariat, whom he alternatively saw as capable of "mob rule."[92] At the same time, Weber recognized that his "small group" of "cool and clear-minded" parliamentarians with "clear responsibilities" could be put into power only by the electorate. He admonished German citizens to "wake up," be "rational," and "show discipline" by putting the new parliamentary elites into office.[93] Weber traded bureaucratic expertise for parliamentary expertise, but political expertise of the statist logic of political membership as such lost no ground to the untutored ways of democratic citizenship.

Hermann Heller, a self-described "politically engaged" legal theorist, targeted not the institutional competencies of the new Weimar order, but rather what he saw as its political-cultural promise. Heller was intrigued by the opportunities and challenges provided in Weimar's constitution, which he viewed as an "expression of real-existing social power relations" in Weimar society.[94] Heller believed that the constitution sanctioned a *sozialer Rechtsstaat*, or social-constitutional law state, which he saw as the means for producing a non-antagonistic, peaceful, and lawful social-economic balance between the German working class and bourgeoisie.[95] He viewed the sozialer Rechtsstaat as much advanced relative to liberal parliamentarism, which, he argued, would ultimately allow the ruling class to control political parties, the press, and schools, and thereby form a "dictatorship" over the working class.[96] A sozialer Rechtsstaat, in contrast, would emancipate the lower classes from poverty and misery by means of a "national culture community" based on a *"Wir-Bewußtsein,"* or collective consciousness.[97] The heart of Heller's sozialer Rechtsstaat was thus not an institutional configuration, but rather a homogeneous Rousseauian general will produced by citizens and transcending the material antagonisms and contradictions inherent in modern society.[98]

Heller's emphasis on the homogeneity of the political community rejected the traditional statist segmentation of an expert professional political class above a politically unreliable society of citizens, which was a value that Weber clearly shared. But Heller's "national culture community" was consistent with retained German statism's other idea of a singular societal will or public interest, a will that was articulated in Vormärz Prussia by professional civil servants. Heller acknowledged the need for an "especially trusted" civil service, but his attack on the state/society dichotomy of traditional German political discourse was waged from below.[99] He argued that it was impossible to discuss "'the' state" or "the state as such" because the "state never rises above the societal waters"; its power lay in a legitimate law-making parliament that would decipher the content of the societal *Willensverband*, or community of will.[100] The state bureaucracy was nothing more than an institution for "implementing" what the parliament produced in its "leading" role.[101] The state bureaucracy required only a depoliticization, which Heller understood as the prohibition of active civil servants from sitting in parliament.[102] Heller thus demoted "rational" bureaucratic members of Germany's political community to the status of implementing German society's interest, not deciphering it or articulating it, as in Reform Era Prussia. In the process, according to one sympathetic critic, Heller "actually assumed that the professional bureaucracy would develop no political dynamic of its own in opposition to Weimar's parliamentary democracy."[103] While Weber's call for institutional reform was accompanied by his acknowledgement of the difficulty of realizing that, Heller appears to have had little appreciation of the enormity of the political-cultural reform for which he was calling. Somewhat like the council movement in 1918, Heller more or less abstractly posited a very radical alternative to the German statist tradition, more as if that tradition were simply an intellectual body of ideas than a deeply held political logic of appropriateness. Next to that tradition, Heller recast German citizens as heroic Rousseauian democrats, informed by a Wir-Bewußtsein and coming together in a "national culture community." Sympathetic critics have called Heller's alternative, which appeared in a discursive context where German citizens/subjects had been cast as non- or anti-political actors for nearly a century, "unrealistic" and built on a confusion of "norms" with "social reality."[104] According to Ilse Staff, Heller "neither adequately analyzed nor theoretically worked out the fact of Germany's bureaucratic absolutism."[105] Without a more thorough appreciation of the power of the statist political discourse that had dominated German politics since the Vormärz, Heller's self-described "engaged" commentary, informed by what he called "the totality of the concrete-historical reality of society," was an interesting intellectual exercise, but it was also politically inconsequential.[106]

Carl Schmitt, in contrast to Hermann Heller, became one of the most influential German political and legal theorists of the twentieth century. This very problematic and complex "theorist for the [Third] Reich" was an unrelenting critic of the Weimar regime.[107] Schmitt's critique of Weimar was a disturbingly brilliant combination of theorization, observation, conceptual analysis, and polemic. Unlike Weber and Heller, Schmitt neither wanted to preserve the new Weimar regime nor offered any recommendations to contribute to its survival. He argued that political theory in the last century-and-one-half was informed by a "triumphal march of democracy"; but Weimar, like other "liberal-democratic" and "parliamentary-democratic" regimes, was constructed on an irreconcilable conceptual contradiction.[108] The contradiction pitted genuine democracy, on the one hand, which required a homogeneity of political membership, "perhaps the eradication of heterogeneity," and was consistent with "dictatorship," against liberalism, on the other, which characterized Weimar and involved heterogeneity, pluralism, discussion, and compromise.[109] Schmitt's critique of liberal and parliamentary democracy rested on the nineteenth-century statist denigration of civil society as a realm of conflict and particularism. Schmitt, according to Schwab, was intent on "rescuing the German state of his time from the encroachments of civil society ... Schmitt ... believed that the Weimar state—and particularly, the president, the officialdom, and the Reichswehr—constituted a sphere of objective reason in comparison with the egoism of pluralistic groups."[110] The institutional manifestation of civil society, according to Schmitt, was parliament, which he derisively called a "plurality of organized social power-complexes."[111] Arguments supportive of parliamentarism, he asserted, rested on the false "belief in government by discussion" and mistakenly understood parliament as a "state organ."[112] On this score, Schmitt acknowledged that he joined "the long German tradition" of viewing parliamentary governance as the "government of amateurs."[113]

Above "amateurs" were genuinely sovereign state actors, who, for Schmitt, were distinguished less by their expertise than by their Hobbesian capacity to act decisively. "Sovereign," Schmitt wrote, "is he who decides on the exception."[114] In the so-called modern democracies of Europe, Schmitt argued, citizens were at best capable of ascribing sovereign decision-making capacity to a single authority. That single authority was located in the state.[115] The sovereign state, as a "sphere of objective reason," was populated by a variety of actors, including the military and the bureaucracy. But the most important actor, for Schmitt, was the single personality. In Weimar that was the President.[116] The single personality in the sovereign state was existentially incapable of experiencing the conflict, discord, discussion, and compromise that problematically informed civil society. The sovereign state actor's authority was most strikingly manifested in what Schmitt called the "pre-normal" or "abnormal" political context that required "distinguish[ing] friend from enemy.[117] Again, the key for Schmitt was not the expertise or rationality of the single personality, as it was for traditional German statism, but rather the unambiguous and conflict-free capacity to decide. Neither long study nor the "rational" entrance into a political community qualified a person to wield the decision-making capacity crucial for a regime's survival. Schmitt assigned political sovereignty only on the basis of location—in a singular state actor situated above the anarchy of society.[118]

Carl Schmitt thus tilted traditional German statism a few degrees, but he by no means discarded it. Schmitt layered some Hobbesian elements on top of it, but nothing was allowed to threaten the sovereignty of a unitary state above an anarchic and pluralistic civil society of ordinary citizens. While Schmitt kept ordinary citizens distant from political sovereignty, he also refused to endow the professional civil service with any semblance of that role. Schmitt, like Weber, was critical of a bureaucracy that had fallen "prey to ever-changing parliamentary majorities, and no longer stood above society but between the different classes." For Schmitt, the professional civil service was an institution that, at best, functioned only in a "normal" political context. Unlike Weber, Schmitt did not call for institutional reform in Weimar, or political-cultural reform, as did Heller, but rather for the elevation of a single sovereign personality who would be capable of "deciding on the exception," and, as a state actor, fend off societal "encroachments" on his competence.[119] Schmitt's project was thus not to offer an alternative political discourse to the statism of the nineteenth century; it was, rather, to sharpen the terms of that discourse and put it to work to rationalize and attempt to legitimize political dictatorship.[120]

Conclusion

Not the abdication of the kaiser, or the promulgation of a democratic-republican constitution, or the institutionalization of a parliamentary regime prevented Weimar Germany's political actors and intellectual elites from continuing to find "rational" members of Germany's political community, particularly state civil servants, more trustworthy and legitimate political actors than "natural" German citizens. During the important first five years of Germany's first democracy, the statist logic of political membership that consolidated in the nineteenth century easily survived as an appropriate discourse for the new regime's political actors. Minor challenges to that discourse were mounted, but none serious enough and accompanied by a viable political—and not just intellectual—alternative to replace Germany's statist logic of political membership. In the process, German statism was domesticated and made serviceable for German democracy. Party discourse across the political landscape in the early Weimar years provided no sustained programmatic alternative to this logic. Nowhere do we find a sustained challenge to the dichotomization of state and society and the accompanying hypostatization of German state civil servants as protective and hortatory political actors "above" ordinary German citizens. The power of German statism in this period of crisis was as immense as the weakness of the republican political vision that would subvert it. The SPD stressed the overriding values of political order and bureaucratic expertise; the liberalism it embodied served only to coddle Wilhelmine civil servants whom the party regarded as necessary for the Republic's survival. On the left, only the short-lived council movement provided a sharp critique of German statism, but it was more an intuitive negation of that logic of political membership than a politically meaningful alternative to it. On the right, responses ranged from concerns about violence and personal security to outright reactionary efforts to reconstitute the old regime.

Representative voices within Weimar's intellectual elite similarly failed to provide a viable critique of and political alternative to the powerful political discourse of nineteenth-century German statism. Max Weber, Hermann Heller, and Carl Schmitt are good representatives of "intellectual republican," "heart-felt republican," and "anti-republican" political discourse in Weimar in this period. Combined, their work reveals how powerful the German statist logic of political membership remained in the crucial early years of the Germany's first democracy. None engaged a concrete rejection of the role assignments of that discourse and consciously sought to provide alternatives to those assignments. Max Weber and Carl Schmitt each, in different ways, retained the pivotal state/society dichotomization of that logic, while Hermann Heller simply ignored its historical political-cultural presence. Weber and Schmitt each located political agency in an arena "above" ordinary citizens, though in different institutions, while Heller again abstractly posited Rousseauian citizens acting in accord with a homogeneous collective consciousness.

The survival of Germany's statist logic of political membership in the early Weimar years was German democracy's tragedy. German statism proved capable of accommodating formally democratic citizens, but only by relegating those citizens to a "lower" realm of civil society in which their most political act was voting for representatives to act for them in a political body—parliament—that was still discursively arrayed "below" the German state and its "rational" political members. In the process, German statism remained politically appropriate for far too many leaders, parties, and ordinary citizens for the Weimar Republic successfully to have consolidated in its crucial first five years. At the same time, these are "mistakes" or "lost opportunities"—as some have judged the politics of the early Weimar years[121]—only from within a completely decontextualized discourse of normative democratic theory. These developments were perfectly understandable, which is not to say preferable, within the particular discursive context of German politics in the early 1920s.

Notes

1. Quoted in Rupert Emerson, *State and Sovereignty in Modern Germany* (New Haven: Yale University Press, 1928), 231.
2. A. J. Ryder, *The German Revolution of 1918: A Study of German Socialism in War and Revolt* (Cambridge: Cambridge University Press, 1967), 13–15.
3. Arthur Rosenberg, *A History of the German Republic*, trans. Ian F. D. Morrow and L. Marie Sieveking (London: Methuen and Co., 1936), 22.
4. See George J. Szablowski and Hans-Ulrich Derlien, "East European Transitions, Elites, Bureaucracies, and the European Community," *Governance: An International Journal of Policy and Administration* 6, no. 3 (1993): 304–24, and other articles in this special issue of *Governance*, which is titled *Regime Transitions, Elites, and Bureaucracies in Eastern Europe*.
5. Nevil Johnson, *State and Government in the Federal Republic of Germany: The Executive at Work*, 2nd ed. (Oxford: Pergamon Press, 1983), 21.
6. Gary Bonham, "State Autonomy or Class Domination: Approaches to Administrative Politics in Wilhelmine Germany," *World Politics* 35, no. 4 (1983): 631–651; Rudolf Morsey, "Zur Beamtenpolitik des Reiches von Bismarck bis Brüning," in *Demokratie und Verwaltung: 25 Jahre Hochschule für Verwaltungswissenschaften Speyer* (Berlin: Duncker & Humblot, 1972), 106; Bernd Wunder, *Geschichte der Bürokratie in Deutschland* (Frankfurt: Suhrkamp, 1986), 95; Jane Caplan, "'The Imaginary Universality of Particular Interests': The 'Tradition' of the Civil Service in German History," *Social History* 4, no. 2 (1979): 316.
7. Wolfgang Elben, *Das Problem der Kontinuität in der deutschen Revolution: Die Politik der Staatssekretäre und der militärischen Führung vom November 1918 bis Februar 1919* (Düsseldorf: Droste Verlag, 1965), 35.
8. Wunder, *Geschichte der Bürokratie*, 83.
9. Geoff Eley, *Reshaping the German Right: Radical Nationalism and Political Change after Bismarck* (New Haven: Yale University Press, 1980), 216.

10. Wunder, *Geschichte*, 72, 78–83; Harro-Jürgen Rejewski, *Die Pflicht zur politischen Treue im preußischen Beamtenrecht, 1850–1918* (Berlin: Duncker & Humblot, 1973), 112.

11. "Verwarnung an die Beamten des Reiches und Preußens, 25. März 1899," in *Die politische Treuepflicht*, ed. Edmund Brandt (Karlsruhe: C. F. Müller Juristischer Verlag, 1976), 84–85.

12. Gotthard Jasper, *Der Schutz der Republik: Studien zur staatlichen Sicherung der Demokratie in der Weimarer Republik* (Tübingen: J. C. B. Mohr, 1963), 211.

13. "Aufruf Eberts an die Behörden und Beamten vom 9.11.1918," in *Die deutsche Revolution, 1918–1919*, ed. Gerhard A. Ritter and Susanne Miller (Frankfurt: Fischer, 1983), 80.

14. Wunder, *Geschichte*, 111; Hans Hattenhauer, *Handbuch des öffentlichen Dienstes*, ed. Walter Wiese, vol. 1, *Geschichte des Beamtentums* (Cologne: Carl Heymans Verlag, 1980), 298; Morsey, "Zur Beamtenpolitik," 109.

15. Gotthard Jasper, "Wer schützt die Republik?" in *Weimar ist kein Argument, oder Brachten Radikale im öffentlichen Dienst Hitler an die Macht?* ed. Freimut Duve and Wolfgang Kopitzsch (Reinbek bei Hamburg: Rowohlt, 1976), 143.

16. "Antwort des Vorstandes der USPD an den Vorstand der SPD vom 10.11.1918," in *Die deutsche Revolution*, ed. Ritter and Miller, 90.

17. Morsey, "Zur Beamtenpolitik," 110; Dietrich Orlow, *Weimar Prussia 1918–1925: The Unlikely Rock of Democracy* (Pittsburgh: University of Pittsburgh Press, 1986), 125; Volker Rittberger, "Revolution and Pseudo-Democratization: The Formation of the Weimar Republic," in *Crisis, Choice and Change: Historical Studies in Political Development*, ed. Gabriel Almond, Scott Flanagan, and Robert Mundt (Boston: Little, Brown, 1973), 341.

18. See Articles 129, 130, and 176, "Verfassung des Deutschen Reiches (Weimarer Verfassung)," in *Deutsche Verfassungen*, ed. Rudolf Schuster (Munich: Wilhelm Goldmann Verlag, 1978), 121, 130.

19. Theodor Eschenburg, *Die improvisierte Demokratie: Gesammelte Aufsätze zur Weimarer Republik* (Munich: R. Piper & Co., Verlag, 1963), 55.

20. Quoted in Rosenberg, *History of the German Republic*, 125–26.

21. Reinhard Rürup, "Entwurf einer demokratischen Republik? Entstehung und Grundlagen der Weimarer Verfassung," in *Fünfzig Jahre deutsche Republik: Entstehung-Scheitern-Neubeginn*, ed. F.A. Krummacher (Frankfurt: Norddeutsche Verlagsanstalt O. Gödel, 1969), 105.

22. Wolfgang Runge, "Die alte Oberklasse—die neue Beamtenschaft," in *Weimar ist kein Argument*, ed. Duve and Kopitzsch, 52.

23. Wunder, *Geschichte*, 118; Wolfgang Runge, *Politik und Beamtentum im Parteienstaat: Die Demokratisierung der politischen Beamten in Preußen zwischen 1918 und 1933* (Stuttgart: Ernst Klett Verlag, 1965), 42.

24. Jasper, *Der Schutz*, 26.

25. W. M. Knight-Patterson, *Germany: From Defeat to Conquest, 1913–1933* (London: George Allen and Unwin, 1945), 279.

26. Jasper, *Der Schutz*, 31–32; Rosenberg, *History of the German Republic*, 136; Orlow, *Weimar Prussia*, 130; Sebastian Haffner, *Failure of a Revolution*, trans. Georg Rapp (New York: Library Press, 1973), 186; Rittberger, "Revolution," 359.

27. Jasper, *Der Schutz*, 32.

28. Jasper, *Der Schutz*, 26; Ryder, *German Revolution*, 242.

29. Rudolf Olden, *The History of Liberty in Germany* (London: Victor Gollancz, 1946), 156.

30. Ryder, *German Revolution*, 242.
31. Hattenhauer, *Geschichte des Beamtentums*, 338.
32. Horst Möller, *Weimar: Die unvollendete Demokratie* (Munich: Deutscher Taschenbuch Verlag, 1985), 146.
33. Jasper, *Der Schutz*, 29–30.
34. Ibid., 225.
35. Runge, *Politik und Beamtentum*, 51–52, 82–83; Orlow, *Weimar Prussia*, 132, 222–23.
36. Jasper, *Der Schutz*, 225–26; Herbert Jacob, *German Administration since Bismarck: Central Authority versus Local Planning* (New Haven: Yale University Press, 1963), 98.
37. Erich Eyck, *A History of the Weimar Republic*, 2 vols. (New York: John Wiley & Sons, Inc., 1967), 1: 189; Dietrich Strothman, "Hitler's Aufstieg –'Versagen' der Demokraten?" in *Fünfzig Jahre*, ed. Krummacher, 116–17; Haffner, *Failure of a Revolution*, 40–41.
38. Jasper, *Der Schutz*, 45–46.
39. Ibid., 38, 49, 53–56.
40. Ibid., 37.
41. Ibid., 125.
42. Ibid., 58, 293–300.
43. Möller, *Weimar*, 152.
44. "Gesetz über die Pflichten der Beamten zum Schutze der Republik, vom 21. Juli 1922," in *Die politische Treuepflicht*, ed. Brandt, 100; Hattenhauer, *Geschichte des Beamtentums*, 340; Wunder, *Geschichte*, 119.
45. Hans Fenske, "Monarchisches Beamtentum und demokratischer Staat: Zum Problem der Bürokratie in der Weimarer Republik," in *Demokratie und Verwaltung. 25 Jahre Hochschule für Verwaltungswissenschaft Speyer* (Berlin: Duncker & Humblot, 1972), 132.
46. Orlow, *Weimar Prussia*, 232; Jasper, *Schutz*, 213.
47. Jasper, *Der Schutz*, 64; Hattenhauer, *Geschichte des Beamtentums*, 339.
48. Charles Maier, *Recasting Bourgeois Europe: Stabilization in France, Germany and Italy in the Decade after World War I* (Princeton: Princeton University Press, 1975), 385–86.
49. Ryder, *German Revolution*, 24–25; Elben, *Das Problem der Kontinuität*, 13–14; Karl-Heinz Janßen, "Die ungewohlte Revolution," in *Fünfzig Jahre*, ed. Krummacher, 35.
50. Hans-Ulrich Wehler, *The German Empire: 1871–1918* (Leamington Spa: Berg Publishers, 1985), 226.
51. Ryder, *German Revolution*, 72–97.
52. Quoted in Möller, *Weimar*, 14–15.
53. Ryder, *German Revolution*, 138; Susanne Miller, "Die Entscheidung für die parlamentarische Demokratie," in *Fünfzig Jahre*, ed. Krummacher, 75–76.
54. "Aufruf des Vorstandes der Sozialdemokratischen Partei Deutschlands vom 4.11.1918," in *Die deutsche Revolution*, ed. Ritter and Miller, 52–53.
55. Quoted in Knight-Patterson, *Germany*, 215.
56. "Aufruf Eberts an die deutschen Bürger vom 9.11.1918," in *Die deutsche Revolution*, ed. Ritter and Miller, 79–80.
57. "General Groener über sein Bündnis mit Ebert vom 10.11.1918," in *Die deutsche Revolution*, ed. Ritter and Miller, 98–99.
58. "Befehl des Generalfeldmarschalls von Hindenburg an das deutsche Feldheer vom 10.11.1918," in *Die deutsche Revolution*, ed. Ritter and Miller, 99–100.

59. "Werbung für die Freikorps im Zentralorgan der SPD," in *Die deutsche Revolution*, ed. Ritter and Miller, 195.
60. Miller, "Die Entscheidung," 80.
61. Hattenhauer, *Geschichte des Beamtentums*, 299, 306.
62. See Eschenburg, *Die improvisierte Demokratie*, 46.
63. Karl-Dietrich Bracher, *The German Dilemma: The Throes of Political Emancipation* (London: Weidenfeld & Nicholson, 1974), 18–19.
64. Max Weber, "Parliament and Government in a Reconstructed Germany," *Economy and Society*, 2 vols., ed. Guenther Roth and Claus Wittich (Berkeley: University of California Press, 1978), 2: 1405.
65. Morsey, "Zur Beamtenpolitik," 108; Lothar Albertin, *Liberalismus und Demokratie am Anfang der Weimarer Republik* (Düsseldorf: Droste Verlag, 1972), 36.
66. "Rede Eberts auf der Reichskonferenz der Ministerpräsidenten der deutschen Staaten vom 25.11.1918," in *Die deutsche Revolution*, ed. Ritter and Miller, 395.
67. Quoted in Rittberger, "Revolution and Pseudo-Democratization," 349; Elben, *Das Problem der Kontinuität*, 163–64.
68. "'Massen Heraus! Hoch die Sozialdemokratie!' Der 'Vorwärts' über den Sinn der Demonstrationen vom 8.12.1918," in *Die deutsche Revolution*, ed. Ritter and Miller, 130.
69. "Aufruf der Reichsregierung an die Bevölkerung Berlins vom 8.1.1919," in *Die deutsche Revolution*, ed. Ritter and Miller, 184.
70. Wunder, *Geschichte*, 110, 117.
71. Ibid., 123.
72. Ryder, *German Revolution*, 76, 148, 231–32.
73. "Erlaß der Reichsregierung vom 11.11.1918," in *Die deutsche Revolution*, ed. Ritter and Miller, 100; "Richtlinien des Vollzugsrats für die Arbeiter- und Soldatenräte vom 23.11.1918," in *Die deutsche Revolution*, ed. Ritter and Miller, 119; Rittberger, "Revolution and Pseudo-Democratization," 341; Elben, *Das Problem der Kontinuität*, 34.
74. Wolfgang Mommsen, "The German Revolution 1918–1920: Political Revolution and Social Protest Movement," in *Social Change and Political Development in Weimar Germany*, ed. Richard Bessel and E. J. Feuchtwanger (London: Croom Helm, 1982), 24.
75. Haffner, *Failure of a Revolution*, 167.
76. "Aufruf des Berliner provisorischen Arbeiter- und Soldatenrats, Delegiertie zu wählen, 9.11.1918," in *Die deutsche Revolution*, ed. Ritter and Miller, 81–82.
77. Wunder, *Geschichte der Bürokratie*, 121–22.
78. "Aufruf der Spartakusgruppe an die Arbeiter und Soldaten Berlins vom 10.11.1918," in *Die deutsche Revolution*, ed. Ritter and Miller, 82; Wunder, *Geschichte*, 110.
79. "Protokoll der gemeinsamen Sitzung von Vollzugsrat und Rat der Volksbeauftragten am 18.11.1918," in *Die deutsche Revolution*, ed. Ritter and Miller, 115–16.
80. "Rede des Vollzugsratsmitglied Ernst Däumig—Berlin auf dem Rätekongress über Nationalversammlung oder Rätesystem, 19.12.1918," in *Die deutsche Revolution*, ed. Ritter and Miller, 382–83.
81. Emerson, *State and Sovereignty*, 226.
82. Mommsen, "German Revolution," 31; Elben, *Das Problem der Kontinuität*, 22; Wunder, *Geschichte der Bürokratie*, 110.
83. Haffner, *Failure of a Revolution*, 107–08.

84. Lothar Albertin, "German Liberalism and the Foundation of the Weimar Republic: Missed Opportunity?" in *German Democracy and the Triumph of Hitler,* ed. Anthony Nicholls and Erich Matthais (London: George Allen and Unwin, 1971), 30–32; "Aufruf zur Gründung einer demokratischen Partei vom 16.11.1918," in *Die deutsche Revolution,* ed. Ritter and Miller, 311–13; Gordon Craig, *Germany: 1866–1945* (New York: Oxford University Press, 1978), 502; Jürgen C. Hess, "Wandlungen im Staatsverständnis des Linksliberalismus der Weimarer Republik 1930–1933," in *Wirtschaftskrise und liberale Demokratie: Das Ende der Weimarer Republik und die gegenwärtige Situation,* ed. Karl Holl (Göttingen: Vandenhoeck und Ruprecht, 1978), 50, 53–54, 77; Runge, *Politik und Beamtentum,* 36.

85. Walter H. Kaufmann, *Monarchism in the Weimar Republic* (New York: Bookman Associates, 1953), 54–55, 62, 87–88; Hattenhauer, *Geschichte des Beamtentums,* 309; Runge, *Politik und Beamtentum,* 40–43.

86. Weber, "Parliament and Government," 1383.

87. Weber, "Parliament and Government," 1403; Reinhard Bendix, *Max Weber: An Intellectual Portrait* (Garden City: Doubleday, 1962), 426–45; Wolfgang J. Mommsen, *Max Weber and German Politics: 1890–1920,* trans. Michael S. Steinberg (Chicago: The University of Chicago Press, 1984), 40, 169; Karl Loewenstein, *Max Weber's Political Ideas in the Perspective of Our Time* (Amherst: The University of Massachusetts Press, 1966), 31–32.

88. Weber, "Parliament and Government," 1426.

89. Ibid.

90. Bernhard Blanke, "Theorien zum Verhältnis von Staat und Gesellschaft zum Problem der Legitimation politischer Herrschaft in der bürgerlichen Gesellschaft," in *Kritik der Politischen Wissenschaft I: Analysen von Politik und Ökonomie in der bürgerlichen Gesellschaft,* ed. Bernhard Blanke, Ulrich Jürgens, and Hans Kastendick (Frankfurt: Campus Verlag, 1975), 158.

91. Weber, "Parliament and Government," 1459–61.

92. Quoted in Mommsen, *Max Weber,* 304; Weber, "Parliament and Government," 1459–61.

93. Weber, "Parliament and Government," 1439, 1460.

94. Hermann Heller, "Freiheit und Form in der Reichsverfassung," in *Gesammelten Schriften,* 3 vols. (Leiden: A.W. Sijthoff, 1971), 2: 375.

95. Wolfgang Luthardt, "Staat, Demokratie, Arbeiterbewegung: Hermann Hellers Analysen im Kontext der zeitgenössischen sozialdemokratischen Diskussion," in *Staatslehre in der Weimarer Republik: Hermann Heller zu ehren,* ed. Christoph Müller and Ilse Staff (Frankfurt: Suhrkamp, 1985), 89–90.

96. Hermann Heller, "Das Berufsbeamtentum in der deutschen Demokratie," in *Gesammelten Schriften,* 2: 384; Ilse Staff, "Staatslehre in der Weimarer Republik," in *Staatslehre in der Weimarer Republik,* ed. Müller and Staff, 10.

97. Wolfgang Schluchter, "Hermann Heller: Ein wissenschaftliches und politisches Portrait," in *Staatslehre in der Weimarer Republik,* ed. Müller and Staff, 36; Eike Hennig, "Nationalismus, Sozialismus, und die 'Form aus Leben': Hermann Hellers politische Hoffnung auf soziale Integration und staatliche Einheit," in *Staatslehre in der Weimarer Republik,* ed. Müller and Staff, 102; Pasquale Pasquino, "Politische Einheit, Demokratie und Pluralismus: Bemerkungen zu Carl Schmitt, Hermann Heller und Ernst Fraenkel," in *Staatslehre in der Weimarer Republik,* ed. Müller and Staff, 122.

98. Schluchter, "Hermann Heller," 38.

99. Heller, "Das Berufsbeamtentum," 390; Hermann Heller, *Staatslehre* (Tübingen: J. C. B. Mohr, 1983), 148, 280.
100. Heller, "Freiheit und Form," 377.
101. Heller, *Staatslehre*, 232–33.
102. Heller, "Das Berufsbeamtentum," 388.
103. Luthardt, "Staat, Demokratie," 96–97.
104. Hennig, "Nationalismus, Sozialismus," 103.
105. Staff, "Staatslehre in der Weimarer Republik," 22.
106. Heller, *Staatslehre*, 126.
107. Joseph Bendersky, *Carl Schmitt: Theorist for the Reich* (Princeton: Princeton University Press, 1983), 96; George Schwab, *The Challenge of the Exception: An Introduction to the Political Ideas of Carl Schmitt between 1921 and 1936* (Berlin: Duncker & Humblot, 1970) 149–50.
108. Carl Schmitt, *The Crisis of Parliamentary Democracy* (Cambridge: The MIT Press, 1985), 22; Ellen Kennedy, "Introduction," in Schmitt, *Crisis*, xx.
109. Schmitt, *The Crisis of Parliamentary Democracy*, 8–13.
110. Schwab, *The Challenge of the Exception*, 28.
111. Quoted in Angelo Bolaffi, "Verfassungskrise und Sozialdemokratie. Hermann Heller und die Kritiker der Weimarer Verfassung am Vorabend der Krise der Republik," in *Staatslehre in der Weimarer Republik*, ed. Müller and Staff, 64.
112. Schmitt, *The Crisis of Parliamentary Democracy*, 3–8; Blanke, "Theorien zum Verhältnis," 158.
113. Schmitt, *The Crisis of Parliamentary Democracy*, 19.
114. Carl Schmitt, *Political Theology: Four Chapters on the Concept of Sovereignty* (Cambridge: The MIT Press, 1985), 5.
115. Schmitt, *The Crisis of Parliamentary Democracy*, 8–13.
116. See Jürgen Meinck, *Weimarer Staatslehre und Nationalsozialismus: Eine Studie zum Problem der Kontinuität im staatsrechtlichen Denken in Deutschland, 1928 bis 1936* (Frankfurt: Campus Verlag, 1978), 109.
117. Schmitt, *Political Theology*, 30–33; Schwab, *The Challenge of the Exception*, 52–57.
118. Schwab, *The Challenge of the Exception*, 57.
119. Ibid., 10.
120. Kennedy, "Introduction," in Schmitt, *Crisis*, xxx, xxxviii; Bendersky, *Carl Schmitt*, 33.
121. See Mommsen, "German Revolution," 31.

Three

THE INSTITUTIONAL POLITICS OF POSTWAR WEST GERMANY

The *Parteienstaat*, the Professional Civil Service, and the Political Mobilizations of the 1960s and 1970s

I t has thus far been argued that a German statist logic of political membership first consolidated in Vormärz Prussia with the development of a nascent mass politics. Seventy years later that logic was challenged, but largely survived, the tragic experience of the Weimar Republic. German statism dichotomized the realms of state and society, positing the state as a site of hortatory political agency in which the public interest could be discerned and implemented above a society of antipolitical particularism and anarchy. Only in the state realm, populated primarily by civil servants and protected from the vicissitudes of the market for the satisfaction of needs, could the universal good of the entire community and not the partial good of individuals or groups be articulated and properly pursued. In the abstract, the statist logic of political membership is ill suited and arguably inappropriate for informing the politics of modern liberal democracies. Modern liberal democracies locate political power in representative legislative institutions, the membership of which is determined by popular elections, not in state bureaucracies. Yet it is possible for statist traditions to continue to serve as powerful legacies for modern liberal democracies, not as singular determinants of institutional arrangements and policy outcomes but as constituent elements of those phenomena.

Kenneth Dyson has called such legacy-laden liberal political orders "state-societies," and they include Germany and France.[1] Here it will be argued that the statist logic of political membership survived, though in diminished form, the institutionalization of politics in the postwar Federal Republic. This occurred despite the conscious striving of West German political elites to exorcise not only Hitler's legacy, but also that of the statist tradition of the nineteenth century.

Democracy and Its Institutions in the Federal Republic

After the Second World War, Western Germany under Allied tutelage had no option but to adopt some form of Western-style liberal democracy. But Western German political elites, especially local and regional party leaders, appear to have been willing participants in the process of political transformation between 1945 and 1949.[2] The constitution ratified in May 1949, marking the birth of Germany's second democracy, was a German affair. It has been called a home-grown "reactive" document looking backwards not only to the disasters of Nazism and the failed Weimar Republic, but further, according to Peter Graf Kielmansegg, to the more amorphous and problematic German above-parties ideology of the authoritarian state.[3] The new institutional order in the Federal Republic secured a prominent place for rehabilitated political parties—both as agents of societal interest representation and as participants in the exercise of state power. Plebiscites and the direct election of the German head of state, regarded as two of the most problematic institutional artifacts of Weimar Republic, were rejected, and Article 21 of the Basic Law defined for political parties the role of "forming the political will of the people."[4] Political parties, the pejorative "societal" actors of the 1848 revolution and the early Weimar years, were thus constitutionally elevated in the new regime to a role that had been largely occupied by civil servants in Germany's traditional statist logic of political membership. This chapter will address the Federal Republic's attempt to transcend the statist logic of political membership by means of the political-institutional arrangement mapped out by the Federal Republic's Basic Law in 1949. It will argue, however, that transcending Germany's statist inheritance was not simply an issue of institutional design. Though ultimately successful, that transcendence more complexly involved a political transformation within German society, a transformation informed by an antistatist counter-discourse of political membership that began to appear in the 1960s. This chapter will first treat the institutional identities of the Federal Republic's political parties and professional civil service, both of which had specific roles and capacities ascribed by Germany's nineteenth-century statist logic of political membership.

The collapse of the Weimar Republic had a profound impact on the Federal Republic's institutional founding. As Kurt Sontheimer argued, "Other comparative cases from the standpoint of democratic orders are not available in German history." In the early postwar period, the political debate in Western Germany was suffused by the "fear ... that, what happened to the republic of Weimar could happen once more."[5] According to Dolf Sternberger, writing in 1949, "In hundreds of political, state, and constitutional discussions, one witnesses so often a sensitive and fearful ... fixation: what must be done in order to avoid the 'mistakes of the past?' This question appears much more frequently than the more natural and healthy question: what must be done in order to make it good?"[6] The attempt to avoid these "mistakes" left the Federal Republic's political elites engaged in a broad discussion of the new regime's institutional order. In their effort to remake German politics, West German policymakers first determined that political institutions and their composition were relatively more pliable than the German public's political attitudes, which were found to be of questionable democratic vintage. According to Bracher, "Historical experience has led to institutional arrangements [in the Federal Republic] the object of which is to prevent any return to the more obvious structural weaknesses of the Weimar Republic."[7] Very quickly a consensus developed among Western German political elites that Weimar's demise was due to the regime's institutional "value-neutrality," weakness, and resulting inability to defend itself from its "enemies."[8] In response, the Federal Republic's founders envisioned what Kommers has called an "objective order of values" that was to inform all aspects of German political institutions and their activity. Expressed as the "unity of the [Federal Republic's] Constitution as a logical-teleological entity," the regime's "framers are said to have arranged these values in a hierarchical order, the most important of which is a 'free democratic basic order' crowned by the principle of 'human dignity' ... These principles, or values, are 'objective' because they have an independent reality under the Constitution. As a consequence, all organs of government must affirmatively enforce these values."[9] In short, all institutions in the Federal Republic were to be "value-laden." In contrast to Weimar, which was celebrated as the "the most democratic constitution in the world" but criticized by Western German elites as too liberally and tolerantly open to the subversion of its "enemies," the Federal Republic's institutions would be governed by a metalegal requirement to defend the "free democratic basic order." The two primary institutions relevant for this were political parties and the state civil service.

The Parteienstaat and the Federal Republic's Democracy

After 1945, the "vertical" pull of German statism that had historically relegated political parties to the status of politically illegitimate purveyors of particularistic interests was said to have dissipated and been replaced by a constitutionally sanctioned pluralistic "horizontal" calculation of party advantage.[10] Some have seen this encouraged by the postwar power vacuum in Western Germany left by the collapse of the civil service and the military, and by the ability of political parties to "create the impression, whether or not true, that they were persecuted from the beginning [of the Nazi era]."[11] The rehabilitated hortatory role for Western Germany's political parties was buttressed by the rapid consolidation of a two-and-one-half party system, which, by the second federal election in 1953, had already awarded the CDU/CSU, the SPD, and the F.D.P. a combined 84 percent of the vote. In addition, the Federal Republic's new 5 percent hurdle, which prohibited parliamentary representation for minor parties receiving less than five-percent of the national vote (or not winning three mandates outright), combined with the transformation of Western German political parties in the 1950s and 1960s, led by the CDU, into pragmatic, broadly based agents of multiple interest intermediation and mass integration, to further this transformation process.

By the mid-1960s, large Western German parties had even become models for a European party-type, the "catch-all party," conceptualized by Otto Kirchheimer. Unlike the divisive and particularistic parties of Germany's past, the "catch-all party," or *Volkspartei*—which the CDU became under the early tutelage of Adenauer and the SPD after its Godesberg Program in 1959—was marked by a reduction in the party's ideological baggage, a strengthening of top leadership groups, and a de-emphasis on class and denominational clientele.[12] The business of West Germany's new political parties by the early 1960s was to attract voters, win elections, and pragmatically govern. The effectiveness of the regime's political parties was argued to have removed the rationale for other institutions in the Federal Republic to appeal to an ultimate political value residing "above parties."[13]

As this development proceeded, Western German politicians and commentators rescued the term *Parteienstaat*, or party-state, from its Weimar usage, when it connoted ineffective and divisive parliamentary wrangling, to apply now to the Federal Republic's new positive role for political parties.[14] Yet this redefinition of West German parties as constituent elements of the Federal Republic's rehabilitated Parteienstaat occurred against the backdrop of Germany's pre-democratic dichotomization of state and society and the positing of parties as societal agents of particularistic interest representation. This legacy provided a unique institutional context—not shared by "stateless-societies"—against which West German party political elites were forced to direct their rehabilitating efforts. The result was a new Parteienstaat for the Federal Republic that essentially bridged and accommodated the two parts of the traditional German political dichotomy of state and society, but that did not completely leave that dichotomy behind. The bridging involved redefining the nature of membership in and relationships between political parties and the state civil service. Not only did party success in policy making right after the war demonstrate to senior civil servants that the Federal Republic's political parties were legitimate political actors, but party membership was frequently sought to demonstrate that postwar Germans desiring entrance into the civil service had the requisite democratic value commitment.[15] The rehabilitation of the Parteienstaat in the Federal Republic meant, in other words, that successful "rational" political membership in the German professional civil service after the war hinged partly on membership in the political parties that nineteenth-century German statism had previously rejected as societal agents of conflict and particularism. So dramatic was this evident institutional shift that some commentators argued in the 1960s that the German state had completely "dissolved" into German society. While the state/society dichotomy was important for understanding nineteenth-century German politics, they suggested it had become completely "obsolete" and "inappropriate" for the modern Federal Republic.[16]

This rather hopefully expressed Western-liberal "normalization" of postwar German politics via the Parteienstaat, however, quite seriously overstated the obvious. The Federal Republic was indeed a liberal democratic regime built on much firmer foundations, with better institutions and constitutional safeguards, than the ill-fated Weimar Republic. But it was not a regime marked in all regards by a "zero hour" or totally clean slate. Surely, the total defeat of the Hitler regime in 1945 and the subsequent occupation of Germany by the Allied powers created a more conducive context for Federal Republic's founding and democratic consolidation than what Weimar experienced. That did not translate, however, into a completely new political discourse for the new regime with completely new institutional role assignments and value attachments. Clear vestiges of old German political discourses and practices were discernible within the Federal Republic's much-vaunted Parteienstaat. Observers noted the retention of "statist" elements in the Federal Republic's political parties, calling them "heirs to state norms" and "institutional reference points of the state" in postwar Germany.[17] In turn, political parties in the new Parteienstaat were seen as the new "bearers" of the German state. That necessitated a "new interpretation" of society as a realm no longer controlled and contained by the state, as in traditional German statism, but rather as a realm occupied by "those forces within [society] which have successfully established a claim to embody the state in virtue of their ability to express the political will of the majority."[18]

The traditional role of the German state had thus not completely disappeared in the Federal Republic but rather had been partly incorporated in the catch-all parties of the Parteienstaat. Indeed, it has been argued that the "political will" that these parties formed, in keeping with Article 21 of the Basic Law, reflected the will of "party elites who speak the moralistic language and adopt the didactic style of leadership of the state tradition of authority." The Federal Republic's political parties thus embodied—and certainly not problematically, according to many commentators—a moral sense of mission, a shared responsibility for the whole, and a high-minded view of politics as a collaborative effort among qualified elites.[19] The term Parteienstaat still retained, after all, the word Staat. The Federal Republic's professional civil service had a quite different historical legacy to sort out.

The Professional Civil Service and the Federal Republic's Democracy

Unlike political parties, which had been denigrated by German statism as agents of particularism and conflict, the state civil service was identified in this tradition as the most important institution for defining and acting on Germany's public interest. But now that catch-all political parties functioning in the Federal Republic's Parteienstaat were "forming the will" of the German people, the role of the German civil service had to be redefined. As the new regime's foremost "rational" political membership institution, however, that redefinition did not involve a transformation into a pragmatic Anglo-American institution of neutral public administration. The Federal Republic's professional civil service retained a central role in upholding the new regime's "objective order of values." The lingering power of the statist logic of political membership continued to suggest after 1945 that the institution of the professional civil service, as such, had always been "the most secure support of the state," and that remained true for the new West German democratic state as well.[20] That sentiment was reflected in the explicit mention of the professional civil service in Article 33 of the Federal Republic's constitution, which stated, "Civil service law is to be regulated under the consideration [*Berücksichtigung*] of the traditional principles [*hergebrachte Grundsätze*] of the professional civil service." The performance of the civil service during Weimar and the Nazi period, however, suggested to a few members of constitution-drafting Parliamentary Council that the institution had indeed been—but problematically—a "secure support of the state," and that led them to join the Allies in questioning the wisdom of constitutionally securing the "traditional" civil service in Germany's new democracy.[21]

But those voices were outnumbered by the many defenders of the institution who pointed both to the functional requirements of the modern state and to the proud tradition of the German professional civil service, a tradition grossly violated, it was argued, but not destroyed by Hitler's genocidal regime.[22] The belief that Hitler violated, instrumentalized, and perhaps even victimized Germany's professional civil service and its proud tradition helped to promote what observers have called the "complete failure" of the de-Nazification of the institution by 1948.[23] Between 1945 and 1948, 53,000 officials lost their positions; by 1951, all but 1,004 of those officials were reinstated.[24] By 1955, approximately two-thirds of the German civil servants in the Federal Republic occupied offices that were roughly the same as what they held in Hitler's administrative state.[25] The traditional German statist identity of the civil service was powerful enough in the early years of the Federal Republic to allow Nazi practice to be rationalized away as institutionally aberrant. When the Allies challenged the retention of the institution, West German political elites—including Social Democrats—virtually unanimously closed ranks around the need to preserve the German professional civil service and its "traditional principles." Germany's postwar political elites shared, in other words, a political logic of appropriateness that insured the retention of a politically powerful, protective role for the Federal Republic's professional civil service. West German political elites shared a peculiar political discourse at this time that caused them, according to Wunder, to receive the Allies' demand for civil service reform with "complete incomprehension." West German political elites utterly rejected Allied proposals to neutralize the institution politically, to eradicate the special status of Beamten, or to establish a civil service commission with independent personnel officers.[26]

Observers have argued that the Parliamentary Council and other West German political elites who defended the professional civil service were not attempting to link the West German bureaucracy to "reaction and traditionalism," but rather to preserve the "core of the structural principles of the German civil service" that they saw as necessary for the "functioning of the state."[27] Identifying the "core of the structural principles" of this institution has required reaching well before 1949. In an exercise that has proven difficult for German legal scholars, these principles have been identified as reaching "at least as far back as the Weimar constitution," which evidently includes the Nazi period, but not to the absolutist or constitutional monarchies of the nineteenth century; others make direct reference to tenth-century feudal law, the Prussian General Code of 1794, Bavarian law of 1805, Imperial law of 1873, and Weimar law of 1919.[28] Justices of the Federal Constitutional Court cited legal commentary published in 1876, 1885, 1928, 1930, 1956, and 1967 in a discussion of the institution's traditional principles. In that ruling, the Court argued that, according to the traditional principles of the civil service, "if the civil service is not dependable, then society and the state are 'lost' in critical situations."[29] A later civil service reform commission in the Federal Republic found that the traditional principles posited some rights for the individual civil servant, such as free speech and free assembly, but referred primarily to the civil servant's duty of political loyalty, including the requirement loyally to "intervene on behalf of the state and its constitutional order at all times." The civil service relationship, the commission concluded, involved the "entire personality" of the civil servant.[30] The most important "rational" political institution for protecting the Federal Republic's free democratic basic order was thus grounded on "traditional principles" that predated by decades, if not centuries, the advent of democratic politics on German territory. By early 1952, the Allies had given up their efforts to effect a substantial reform of the civil service, the traditional nineteenth-century logic of political membership of which the Federal Republic had inherited and whose political elites had strenuously defended.[31]

The preservation of the German professional civil service in the Federal Republic nevertheless existed in tension with another aspect of the value-ladenness of the new democratic political order: the individual fundamental rights located in the first nineteen articles of the Basic Law dedicated to protecting the "dignity of man." The collision was not realized until the early 1970s, but the potential was inherent in the constitution's simultaneous inclusion of a predemocratic institution wholly dedicated to the upholding of the political order, on the one hand, and the prominence of a catalogue of democratic rights and liberties for individual citizens, on the other. Those rights included protections of free speech, equal treatment, and assembly, as well as prohibitions of discrimination by sex, origin, race, language, belief, religion, or political perspective. According to Carl Friedrich, writing in 1949, the appearance and location of these fundamental rights in the constitution marked an important break with Germany's past: "Man is thereby put above the state, and all state authorities are specifically enjoined to respect and to protect the dignity of man."[32]

The preservation of the professional civil service and its traditional principles in the Federal Republic, however, modified Friedrich's essentially accurate description. "Man is put above the state" only if "man" were not part of the state. If a person were part of the West German state, that is, employed in the state civil service, then the person enjoyed a *Sonderstatus*, or special status, relative to an ordinary German citizen. That status, according to both Federal Constitutional Court decisions and much legal commentary, relativized the catalogue of civil and political protections accorded German citizens who happened to be civil servants.[33]

Intervening between German civil servants, as "rational" members of the German political community, and the fundamental rights of German citizens as "natural" members of the community, were the "traditional principles" of the German professional civil service appearing in Article 33 of the Basic Law.

The rationale for the continued applicability of these traditional principles and their precedence for German civil servants relative to their fundamental civil and political liberties as German citizens, appeared in the statist logic of political membership that still remained appropriate for West Germany's political elites in the 1950s and early 1960s. That logic identified the German state and its actors as existentially crucial for protecting against the inherent anarchy of German society. Without the guarantee of civil servants' political loyalty at all times, the state could not reliably protect the "dignity of man," which was, it was argued, the most fundamental political value of the new order. When the political loyalty of civil servants became a contentious issue in the Federal Republic in the early 1970s, the first nineteen articles of the Basic Law were often invoked by critics rejecting the civil service loyalty requirement. But the battle that developed in this period over civil servants' political loyalty was informed less by the private rights/ civil libertarian discourse familiar in "stateless societies" like the United States, than by a critique of the hortatory political role of state civil servants "above" a society of ordinary citizens.[34]

The "Militancy" of the Federal Republic's Democracy

The Federal Republic's political order thus combined a liberal-democratic institution of party governance with a preliberal institution of bureaucratic political agency. Article 21 of the Basic Law gave political parties in the Federal Republic the right and duty to form the political will of the people, while Article 33 reserved for the professional civil service a protective and exclusive political role vis-à-vis German society. Party governance via the Parteienstaat was said at least to bridge—if not to transcend —the nineteenth-century German dichotomy of state and society. But bureaucratic political agency, sustained in the Federal Republic by a surviving statist logic political membership, retained a clear dichotomy between the rights and duties of state actors, on the one hand, and the rights and duties of citizens, on the other. This unique combination of liberal party politics and preliberal bureaucratic politics in the Federal Republic has been captured in the political construct of "militant democracy," or what is referred to in German political and legal commentary as *streitbare Demokratie, wehrhafte Demokratie, wertgebundete Demokratie,* and *militante Demokratie.*[35]

Very distant from a Rousseauian notion of radical popular sovereignty, militant democracy in the Federal Republic reflected long-standing tensions within German liberalism as well as concerns about the "normalcy" of German political development. Some German commentators boasted in the 1970s that the Federal Republic was one of the "most liberal" orders in the world, while others warned against the "unenlightened liberalism" of the Anglo-American tradition.[36] Some argued that militant democracy was present in virtually all liberal state forms, while others argued the militant democracy was a "specifically German affair" because of Germany's past and its international security exposure.[37] None of these particular views disputed the legitimacy of the construct, but its precise meaning was difficult to ascertain in the Federal Republic, even for its defenders.[38] What is clear, however, is that militant democracy—involving the Parteienstaat and the professional civil service—became an important tool for determining rational political membership in the effort to protect the new regime's "objective order of values."

Militant democracy posed rules for inclusion and exclusion in the Federal Republic's rational political community. Included were those forces who would either positively uphold, or who would not threaten, the Federal Republic's free democratic basic order. Excluded were political actors deemed to threaten the free democratic basic order—not only those with threatening substantive political agendas, but also ordinary citizens who attempted to act outside of the Federal Republic's sanctioned political institutions. Article 21 of the Basic Law stated that, "Parties which, by reason of their aims or the behavior of their adherents, seek to impair or abolish the free democratic basic order or endanger the existence of the Federal Republic of German, shall be unconstitutional." It also stated that, "Political parties shall form the political will of the people." The Parteienstaat of the militant democracy thus preserved a powerful controlling instance on the political organization of German society, both substantively and procedurally. Rules for rational political membership within society were thereby adduced, and those rules reflected the statist ideology that the Federal Republic's democracy had inherited. Militant democracy was intended as an institutional means for saving German democracy, and not a nondemocratic regime, from its enemies; as such, it mandated exclusion from politics in the Federal Republic if rules for society's democratic political organization were violated. That exclusion was determined by the decision of state authorities and not—which a "militant democracy" might be taken to imply—a mobilized citizenry.

In the early 1950s, Germany's professional state civil service and its traditional principles were invoked to respond to what Richard Löwenthal called the "deep impact that a wide anti-Communist and anti-Soviet current had during the regime's formative years."[39] The early Cold War in this period rationalized vigilance about the possible infiltration of West German political institutions—particularly political parties and the state civil service—by East German and Soviet-sponsored functionaries.[40] The Communist threat was regarded by West German elites to be much more menacing in the early 1950s than the Nazi "small-fry" who had been reinstated into the civil service; indeed, it was suggested that the expertise of the old officials would be useful for consolidating the new Federal Republic.[41] Adenauer issued a decree in September 1950 that built not only on the constitutional requirement implicit in Article 33 for civil servants to uphold the free democratic basic order, but also on recent federal and Land civil service laws calling for civil servants to "acknowledge" (*bekennen*) the democratic state order at all times.[42] Adenauer listed thirteen organizations, ten of which were Communist or leftist in orientation, "the support of which is inconsistent with official duties." The decree's anti-Communist colors were further revealed by the statement that "especially serious offenses to duty" are those committed by civil servants who support the "resolutions of the Third Party Convention of the Communist [East German] Social Unity Party and the so-called 'National Congress.'"[43] Adenauer's decree, which was part of a broad effort to secure the Federal Republic in the Western alliance, appeared within a domestic context of political apathy if not outright fear of politics. His explicit demand on the political loyalty of West German civil servants met with virtually no critical reaction in either the German public or legal commentary.[44] This was to change dramatically by the 1970s.

The first systematic usage of the term streitbare Demokratie, or militant democracy, appeared in the 1956 Federal Constitutional Court decision banning the KPD, or Communist Party of Germany. Coming four years after the banning of the SRP, the right-wing

Socialist Reich Party, the Court argued, "The Basic Law represents a conscious effort to achieve a synthesis between the principle of tolerance with respect to all political ideas and certain inalienable values of the political system. Article 21 (2) does not contradict any basic principle of the Constitution; it expresses the conviction ... based on concrete historical experience, that the state could no longer afford to maintain an attitude of neutrality toward political parties. [The Basic Law] has in this sense created a 'militant democracy,' a constitutional [value] decision that is binding on the Federal Constitutional Court."[45] Protecting the "inalienable values of the political system" was the paramount goal of militant democracy. The Court argued that, "if limitations on the political freedom of opponents [*Gegner*] of the political order are necessary for this defense, then so be it."[46] Militant democracy thereby legitimized the "rational" exclusion of even "natural" members of Germany's political community, i.e., German citizens. As long as German citizens did not, by their individual actions or participation in a political party, endanger the free democratic basic order, their fundamental political and civil liberties prominently guaranteed in the first nineteen articles of the Basic Law were secure. This so-called enlightened German position differed from what Roman Herzog saw as the naive and "simplified worldview" in "America and also in Europe" that posits "only the state ... endangers freedom."[47] Eckart Bulla similarly argued that "'reason of state' [*Staatsräson*'] and spheres of freedom for citizens are not constitutionally opposite ends of a continuum."[48] At the same time, the Federal Republic's militant democracy accorded ordinary citizens and political parties more freedom of political belief and action than state civil servants. Political parties were not allowed to endanger the Federal Republic's free democratic basic order; state civil servants, however, had to guarantee a positive willingness actively to uphold the free democratic basic order at all times.

This difference has been captured in the statist logic of political membership that locates in civil servants the main "rational" capacity to protect against the political anarchy inherent in German society. Ludwig Raiser has argued that "the principle of militant democracy ... requires civil service loyalty to the constitution."[49] Martin Kriele has somewhat more pointedly suggested that the most important question to ask in the Federal Republic's militant democracy is, "In which direction will the civil servant shoot?"[50] Consistent with traditional German statism, the "rationality" of the state civil servant's membership in the Federal Republic was thus heightened relative both to the "rationality" of political party participation in the construction of the will of German people, and to the "naturalness" of ordinary citizens engaging in legal political activity. Civil servants were assigned a special constitutional obligation not just to avoid endangering the free democratic basic order, as required of political parties in the Federal Republic, but also to demonstrate a positive willingness and capacity to defend that order at all times. Institutionally, the role of the Federal Republic's professional civil service thus remained informed by the nineteenth-century idea that the state must protect German society from its inherent anarchistic self-destructiveness. The Federal Republic renamed this basic institutional arrangement a militant democracy, thereby nominally, and in object, "democratizing" the traditional statist logic of political membership, but statism as a political logic of membership by no means disappeared from the new democratic order.

Residual Statism Collides with a Mobilized Citizenry

The institutions of postwar West Germany may have been informed by elements of nineteenth-century German statism, but they were nonetheless the products of a conscious attempt by political elites to establish the means by which democracy could take root and successfully consolidate on German territory. Entrance into much of the political order was controlled by "rational" membership criteria, by performance requirements that, if met, sanctioned participation, but if unmet, rationalized exclusion. State employees in the professional civil service had the role of positively protecting the free democratic basic order from its enemies at all times; catch-all political parties had the role of forming the political will of the German public consistent with the free democratic basic order; and ordinary citizens had the role of not endangering the free democratic basic order with acts hostile to the constitution. Nonperformance of these roles—which were hierarchically arranged in order of existential importance for the survival of the democratic regime, and, not accidentally, arranged in a manner consistent with nineteenth-century German statism—earned exclusion, in some form or another, from the Federal Republic's political community. This was exclusion, however, with the preservation of democracy on German soil as its goal and rationale. Estimable in the eyes of the Allies and the rest of the world watching Germany's second experiment in democracy, it nonetheless collided, beginning in the 1960s, with the "revolutionary" democratization and mobilization of the lowest factor in the Federal Republic's "rational" institutional arrangement: the German citizenry.[51]

Karl Jaspers, the noted philosopher, published a book in the spring of 1966, titled, *Wohin treibt die Bundesrepublik?*, or *Where Is the Federal Republic Going?* Jaspers's provocative thesis was that the country was spiraling from a "party oligarchy" to an "authoritarian state" and would end in a new "dictatorship."[52] Jaspers's polemic was bad social science, but it became an immediate bestseller in the Federal Republic, which had just left the Adenauer era behind.[53] The book argued that responsibility for the prevention of dictatorship in the Federal Republic rested not with institutions—the Parteienstaat and the Berufsbeamtentum that constituted the militant democracy. "It depends" instead, according to Jaspers, "decisively on the people ... even the best institutions do nothing when the people fail to use them."[54] He criticized West Germans for having "respect for the government as such; ... a need to honor the state in the form of representative politicians as replacements for the emperor and the king; the feelings of being a subject [*Untertan*] in relation to authority in all of its forms, down to the last counter of the bureaucratic clerk's office; a readiness for blind obedience; the trust that the government will make it right;... In short: state consciousness is for us frequently subject consciousness, not the democratic consciousness of free citizens."[55] Jaspers's polemic directly identified and challenged the statist logic of membership that had survived the Federal Republic's political institutionalization. Whereas West Germany's political elites had structured the new regime's institutions to preserve democracy through "rational" means, Jaspers called on German citizens to mobilize themselves to protect democracy. Jaspers demanded a "real revolution," which, he claimed, had to be led by "free citizens" who "do not want power, but rather [want to] convince," and who act "from below and are non-violent."[56]

Jaspers's call to action in 1966 in the Federal Republic coincided with the formation of the "Grand Coalition" government, a move that catapulted the post-Godesberg reformed SPD into governmental responsibility and left the small middle-class F.D.P. as the only parliamentary opposition in the Bundestag. Many intellectuals, left-wing Social Democrats, and trade unionists regarded the new government with considerable unease and began to explore other avenues of political representation, especially as the government began parliamentary deliberations of proposed "Emergency Laws" in 1967.

Not only was the Grand Coalition led by a chancellor who was a former member of the Nazi Party, and, according to the author Günter Grass, "had already once acted against all reason and served criminals," but it was also debating the reinstitution of emergency laws that reminded many of the infamous Article 48 of the Weimar Constitution, which allowed governance virtually by emergency decree in the early 1930s.[57] Coming together in what they called an "extraparliamentary opposition," or APO (*Außerparlamentarische Opposition*), these new activists in the Federal Republic rejected both the "economic miracle" and Ludwig Erhard's corporatist call for a "formed society" (*formierte Gesellschaft*) constructed by the West German state.[58] Overlapping with the activism of the APO in the late 1960s in the Federal Republic was the mobilization of West German university students.[59] The early days of the student movement saw the demand to "open up" West German institutions. According the Jürgen Habermas, writing at the time, "The worldview of these students is shaped by the impression that social institutions have coalesced into a relatively closed, conflict-free and self-regulating, yet violent apparatus. Enlightenment and opposition can be provided only by uncorrupted individuals on the margins of the apparatus. Whoever assumes a function within it, however unimportant, becomes integrated and neutralized."[60]

Though the worldview of mobilized students in the Federal Republic in the late 1960s was diffuse and not settled on a conscious rejection of Germany's traditional statist logic of political membership, a counter-discourse of democratic political emancipation "from below" did begin to appear in this period. In 1967, after the Berlin police killed a student at a demonstration protesting a visit by the Shah of Iran, Rudi Dutschke, the intellectual force behind the West German student movement argued, "We are no longer represented by the institutions in this system. Therefore, these institutions are not an expression of our interests. Therefore, we must take a position against these institutions ... Our only chance for a genuine democratization from below is not from within the established organizations, but only from within the centers of action that we have created, which really produce actions, and actions are the only requirement for democratization from below."[61] A noted historian described the mobilization of 1967–1968 as producing in the minds of many West Germans a sense that, unlike at the beginning of the Federal Republic, "now one stood before a genuine 'hour zero.'"[62]

Occurring simultaneously with Jaspers's call for a "revolution in the way of thinking" were two related developments directly impinging upon the state's control of political membership in the Federal Republic. First, the Communist Party of Germany, or KPD, that had been banned by the Federal Constitutional Court in 1956 as antithetical to the value order of the Federal Republic and outside of the bounds of the Parteienstaat, was refounded in 1968 as the DKP, or German Communist Party. Second, in the late 1960s and early 1970s, a violent leftist terrorism appeared on the West German scene that first targeted property and then people, particularly political and economic elites.[63] Unlike the mass of "silent revolutionaries" growing in the Federal Republic at this time, who were beginning to organize in various interest groups and "citizens' initiatives," the DKP and terrorist groups were interested in an active confrontation with the institutional order of the Federal Republic and were suspected of having—and later proved to have had—financial and logistical support from the GDR and the Soviet Union.[64]

Throughout the 1970s and early 1980s, these developments were perceived as substantial threats to the institutional order of the Federal Republic. Similar to the Spartacus Union and council movement fifty years earlier, which were subject to a strong anti-socialist ideology in the early Weimar years, the DKP and terrorists in the Federal Republic in the late 1960s and early 1970s were subject to a strong Cold War ideology of anti-communism. But in the Federal Republic in this period, as in the early years of the Weimar Republic, these political oppositional forces were also subject to the much older and more powerful political tradition of German statism, a tradition that regarded the realm of "natural" political membership in German society as anarchic and politically dangerous. Indeed, in early 1969, Chancellor Kurt Kiesinger stated, "Communism is not the danger ... The real danger to our present society and order are not Communists and their agents; the real danger, that grows from the depths of a people that has a difficult history to overcome, is nihilism and anarchism. If we do not deal with these by the necessary means, then one day they could become dangerous for us."[65] Kiesinger's invocation of the familiar political threat of civil society, where the "depths of the people" produce "nihilism and anarchism," carried with it the implicit invocation of the strong and reliable German state, the role of which was to contain these threats to the Federal Republic's free democratic basic order.

The Reassertion of Institutions in the Face of Popular Mobilization

Willy Brandt, a Social Democrat, became chancellor of the Federal Republic in the autumn of 1969. Regarded a *Machtwechsel*, implying regime change, and not just a *Regierungswechsel*, or change of government, Brandt's government came to power only months after Gustav Heinemann, another Social Democrat, was chosen to be federal president. Heinemann was said to represent the "absolute antipode of the state understanding of the CDU/CSU."[66] The federal president's inaugural address to parliament contained words, he said, that "some will not want to hear," especially those who "continue to cling to the authoritarian state [*Obrigkeitsstaat*] that was for a long enough time our misfortune to have." He stated, "we stand only at the beginning of the first really free period of our history. Free democracy must finally be the life element of our society…. Not less, but rather more democracy—that is our requirement, that is the main goal which we all, and especially the youth, have prescribed."[67] With German society's mobilization in the 1960s, Heinemann saw a "spring breeze" wafting through the Federal Republic's institutions, earning him the title of "radical in the civil service" from the author Heinrich Böll.[68] Willy Brandt's first speech before parliament four months later echoed Heinemann's new political discourse. He stated, "we wish to dare more democracy … each citizen will have the possibility of participating in the reform of state and society." Brandt concluded: "In a democracy, government can only be successful if it is supported by the democratic engagement of the citizenry. We have as little need for blind assent as our people have need for stilted dignity and grand sovereign distance…. We stand not at the end of our democracy; we are, rather, only now really beginning.[69] In an earlier interview, Brandt argued that democracy was less an "organizational form of the state," than a "principle that must influence and inform the entire societal being of the people."[70]

The election of new federal political leaders with a self-proclaimed new "democratic" political discourse, following on the heels of the most intense political mobilization of German society since the Weimar Republic, appeared directly to challenge the statist logic of political membership that had survived the Federal Republic's founding. The "rationalism" of state institutions—including the militant democracy constituted by the Berufsbeamtentum and the Parteienstaat—that, in the Federal Republic, was to exclude the participation and influence of nondemocratic political forces, was challenged by a discourse of "more democracy" and an unprecedented call for the political mobilization of German citizens "from below." On the streets and now in federal government offices, a seachange appeared to be occurring in the Federal Republic at the end of the 1960s that would displace or at least diminish the political centrality of state institutions, particularly the professional civil service and perhaps also the parties of the Parteienstaat. But the politics of the Federal Republic in this period was much more complicated than the rhetoric its new leaders.

Two days after Brandt's inaugural address to parliament, his foreign minister, Walter Scheel, met the Soviet ambassador in Bonn to discuss a possible treaty based on the mutual renunciation of force. Within the next three months, the Brandt government established further bilateral talks with Poland and East Germany on the normalization of relations. This extraordinarily rapid "third cycle" of the Federal Republic's Ostpolitik resulted in separate signed treaties with Moscow and Warsaw in 1970.[71] Willy Brandt's call for "more democracy" at home was put on the back burner while his government engaged in the boldest foreign policy initiative in the Federal Republic's history. Yet critical observers, especially from the very agitated CDU/CSU, posited a link between the leftist societal mobilization that SPD rhetoric was calling for at home with the normalization of relations with East Germany's patron state, the Soviet Union. Arnulf Baring attempted to capture the mood of the right-wing of the CDU/CSU with this sketch of the SPD leadership: "Had not Willy Brandt already once turned his back on Germany and adopted a foreign citizenship? Had not Herbert Wehner, that old Communist, as everyone knew, worked in Moscow in the 1930s for the Comintern? That sounded secretive, yes, it seemed threatening.... And now Egon Bahr [Brandt's negotiator], again in Moscow, had for months been shut behind closed doors in conference with the Soviet Foreign Minister, and, from what one heard, not even the Foreign Office in Bonn had learned exactly what was discussed by the two men."[72]

These images of "leftist" foreign policy intrigue merged with attributions of Social Democratic "sympathizing" with anti-institutional politics and leftist terrorism that had begun to erupt in the Federal Republic in the summer of 1970.[73] The Social Democratic federal president and chancellor both endorsed an "engagement of the citizenry" and following the "prescriptions" of the Federal Republic's politically mobilized students. German statism's generalized indictment of noninstitutional politics in German society made it difficult in this period—especially for people uninterested in doing so to begin with—to distinguish between legitimate leftist politics and violent leftist terrorism. Both activities had forsaken the protective institutions of the Federal Republic's militant democracy and replaced them with direct action. Furthermore, the SPD's rebellious youth organization, the Jusos, not only supported the party's Ostpolitik, but also called for collaboration between the SPD and the DKP.[74] Though the DKP was founded in 1968, while the CDU was the dominant federal government party, and its presence was not immediately challenged by the Christian Democrats, the CDU asked the SPD in June 1971 what it planned to do about the DKP, hinting that it might begin constitutional banning proceedings against the party.[75] The Social Democrats were put on the defensive.

At this time, Willy Brandt attempted, with checkered success, to distinguish between a primitive anti-communism that would prevent forward movement in Ostpolitik, and the SPD's rejection of the DKP's repeated offers—and Jusos's endorsement—of political collaboration.[76] This took the form of an explicit Social Democratic *Abgrenzungsbeschluß*, or demarcation decree, written by Richard Löwenthal and issued by the party leadership in November 1971. It stated: "Free democracy on one side, Communist party dictatorship on the other: no policy of peace and no foreign policy of *rapprochement* can overcome the contradictions between these systems.... A reduction in conflict between states requires that every state respect the domestic order of others.... Social Democracy accepts once more the challenge of defending this order without compromise against the false teachings of Communism."[77] Foreign policy "normalization" with neighboring communist states, including East Germany, would thus be joined by a continued domestic "containment" of Communist influence within the Federal Republic. Militant democracy required keeping an eye on the DKP and its electoral strength and holding the possibility of banning (via Article 21 of the Basic Law) at the ready. Not actually banning the DKP unless absolutely necessary, however, was argued to serve democracy's consolidation in the Federal Republic, because elections were more effective weapons against political extremism than court verdicts. But it was also suggested in this period—denied by Willy Brandt in 1976, but partly affirmed by him in 1986—that not actually banning the DKP served the interests of the government's Ostpolitik.[78] Willy Brandt allegedly told the Soviet leader, Leonid Brezhnev, in September 1971 that, to facilitate Ostpolitik, his Social Democratic government would not pursue a banning of the DKP.[79] In any case, the Parteienstaat was challenged by the appearance of the DKP in the late 1960s, and militant democracy had the formal institutional means to remove it from the political landscape. But political parties in the Federal Republic, to remain legal, only had to avoid endangering the free democratic basic order. The civil service, in contrast, the foremost "rational" institution in the Federal Republic for protecting the free democratic basic order as an "objective order of values," had to guarantee a loyal willingness positively to uphold that order at all times.

In a political context of continued doubt about the Social Democrats' anti-Communist credentials, skillfully nurtured by the CDU/CSU, the Brandt government issued a second Abgrenzungsbeschluß in early 1972, this one directed at the professional civil service. In January 1971, the CDU leader, Rainer Barzel, called for amending the Basic Law explicitly to prohibit the employment of "active Communists for teaching our children."[80] While many at the time thought the traditional principles appearing in Article 33 adequately defined the protective role for German state civil servants, this signaled a move to provide a more explicit institutional means to contain the Communist threat. Seven months later, in July, the SPD-led Bremen government denied a tenured professorship to a DKP member on political grounds.[81] Four months later, the SPD-led Hamburg government issued a decree banning political activity in "right- and left-radical" groups for Land civil servants, especially those involved in the "educational realm, and then especially if the person in question is particularly active in such a group."[82]

Following on the heels of these moves in Bremen and Hamburg, the second federal-level Abgrenzungsbeschluß appeared on 28 January 1972. The so-called *Radikalenerlaß*, or the Radicals Decree, mandated the consistent implementation of standing civil service law to prohibit the employment of people who were "hostile to the constitution" (*verfassungsfeindlich*) and unable to "guarantee" a readiness to uphold the Federal Republic's free democratic basic order at all times.[83] Issued by the Länder minister presidents and the federal chancellor, the Radikalenerlaß, or "Basic Principles Regarding the Question of Anti-Constitutional Elements in the Civil Service," required German state employees to: 1) guarantee a willingness positively to intervene on behalf of the free democratic basic order at all times; 2) avoid membership and all activity in organizations that pursued goals "hostile to the constitution" (*verfassungsfeindlich*), which would establish doubts about that guarantee; and, 3) demonstrate a positive attachment (*Bekenntnis*) to the free democratic basic order with one's entire conduct.[84] The stated intentions of the drafters of the Radicals Decree were simple and direct: to make consistent the implementation of standing civil service law in the Länder and at the federal level in the face of new applicants to the Berufsbeamtentum of the Federal Republic's value-laden militant democracy.[85] But the Decree's appearance in the agitated political context of the early 1970s was neither accidental nor simply an effort to make bureaucratic procedure consistent. Indeed, it has been suggested that if student activist Rudi Dutschke had never uttered his infamous call to "march through the institutions" of the Federal Republic, the Radicals Decree never would have appeared.[86] Thus began the most contested, and for some participants the most traumatic, political debate that the Federal Republic had yet experienced.

The legal and political wrangling over the Radicals Decree in the 1970s and early 1980s is legendary and filled volumes of commentary. Most fundamentally, the battle addressed the attempt to establish the means by which the "special status" of the civil servant vis-à-vis the ordinary West German citizen could be determined and adequately required and measured. This struck at the very heart of the "rational" statist logic of political membership inherited by the Federal Republic and at least implicitly contained in the traditional principles of the civil service in Article 33 of the constitution. The civil servant's "special status" called for an "especially intensive" degree of political loyalty relative to that of an ordinary citizen, and that suggested to many that civil servants were more important political actors than citizens in the Federal Republic's democracy.[87] The debate also addressed the nature of the object of the civil servant's required political action. While "free democratic basic order" served as a useful general construct to refer to the political order of the Federal Republic, it proved to be problematically vague to be of much help in sorting the particular beliefs and actions of German civil servants that were required and allowed from those that were not. [88]

The debate over the Radicals Decree challenged Carl Friedrich's characterization of the Federal Republic as a political order that put "man" before the "state," at least with regard to civil servants. The prominence of the civil and political liberties front loaded in the Basic Law helped to generate a broad discussion of the intensity and breadth the state civil servant's required political loyalty relative to that person's civil and political rights as a citizen.[89] In addition, the designation of some beliefs and actions of civil servants as "hostile to the constitution," or verfassungsfeindlich, not only generated concern about reintroducing from the Weimar and Nazi years the Schmittian concept of domestic political "enemy" (*Feind*). It also produced a battle over the difference between that designation and "unconstitutional," or *verfassungswidrig*, which could be legally assigned only by action of the Federal Constitutional Court.[90] Each of these disputes revealed, in broad terms, an unsettling of the statist logic of political membership in the Federal Republic, a logic that survived the Federal Republic's institutional founding in 1949, but was profoundly challenged by the political mobilization of German society in the 1960s and 1970s.

A Constitutional Court decision in 1975 attempted to clarify the legal issues at stake in the controversy over the Radicals Decree, concluding that the traditional principles of the civil service, including the loyalty demand, superseded the citizen freedoms of political belief and expression for the individual civil servant.[91] But that decision, legally controversial, did hardly anything to end the political conflict over the Decree. In the 1970s, the SPD, F.D.P., and CDU/CSU engaged in endless polemics and sometimes serious legislative efforts—all failed—to resolve their differences over the Radicals Decree and its implementation. These party-political battles turned on a variety of questions: whether party membership (e.g., in the DKP) or an "individual case test" would indicate the civil servant's required political loyalty;[92] whether a functional security differentiation among roles in the civil service would rationalize a differentiated political loyalty for civil servants;[93] whether all applicants to the civil service should undergo a political "automatic check" with the Office for the Protection of the Constitution;[94] and, self-referentially, how the continuing controversy over the Radicals Decree was affecting the general political climate in the Federal Republic.[95]

Reformers found it difficult to exit from the Decree's strictures without being accused of violating constitutional law or engaging in a fundamental institutional overhaul that few party leaders were interested in undertaking. Regret and frustration beset particularly the SPD, with Willy Brandt acknowledging in 1976 the collapse of the appropriateness of the statist logic of political membership in the Federal Republic, at least with regard to that logic's most "rational" and protective state institution, the civil service. He stated, "What I mean is the following: one always proceeded from the idea of the civil service as totally unified and homogeneous. But that is absolutely not the case… A somewhat differentiated way of looking at things is appropriate here."[96] Ten years later Brandt lamented that he "had not imagined that the Decree would have the effect that it did."[97] By the time the SPD was forced out of government in 1982 and Helmut Kohl of the CDU took over as federal chancellor, much of the party-political debate over the Decree had become tactical. Somewhat liberalized implementations of the Decree were invoked by some Länder during the 1970s and early 1980s, and by the federal government in 1979, but most of these were regarded as only "refinements" or "corrections," and they were handily criticized by the political opposition.[98] By the end of the 1980s, the Decree had produced over three-hundred-fifty organizations in the Federal Republic dedicated to its removal.[99]

Conclusion

Constructed on the "traditional principles of the professional civil service" appearing in Article 33 of the Basic Law, the Radicals Decree was, essentially, "no new law," as Federal Chancellor Willy Brandt argued in 1972. Minutes of meetings of the federal coalition party leaders and the federal cabinet on 17 January and 19 January 1972, indicate neither strong support for nor misgivings about the content of the Decree. Brandt's Chancellor's Office did not participate in the formulation of the Decree, and Brandt himself later claimed he could not recall what happened at these meetings.[100] The Decree's most immediate context was constituted by the pragmatic desire of the coalition partners for continued success in détente, by the SPD's willingness to demonstrate its anti-Communist credentials at home without derailing its Ostpolitik, and by the opposition's effort to make the government parties pay for its foreign policy. These were quite mundane beginnings for a policy debate that became, over the next nearly two decades, the most divisive political battle that the Federal Republic had experienced.[101] But the innocuousness of the beginnings of the Radicals Decree is precisely part of what made this political fight so momentous in the Federal Republic. The battle was ultimately not over the civil service, as such, or even over the government's new foreign policy. It was, instead, over the relative appropriateness of a logic of political membership that informed the political discourse not only of West Germany's political elites, but also of ordinary West German citizens. This logic had consolidated in nineteenth-century Prussia, it had been weakly and unsuccessfully challenged in the Weimar Republic, and it had been pragmatically deployed in the Federal Republic's institutional founding in 1949.

By the late 1960s, however, that logic had begun to lose its hegemonic position in West German political discourse. Brandt's "no new law" appeared in a newly transformed political context—constituted by an unprecedented popular mobilization of citizens in German society, a new Social Democratic government rhetorically promising "more democracy," and an attempt to "normalize" relations with Communist Eastern Europe. The "no new law" thus was no longer politically appropriate in the Federal Republic. The nineteenth-century idea of a state institution politically protecting and acting for an unreliable and particularistic German citizenry located in an "anti-political" society was rejected by Germans on the street, by the proliferation of interest groups and citizens' initiatives, and by political and social commentary throughout the Federal Republic.[102] It is to the discursive unsettling of the German statist logic of political membership that we now turn.

Notes

1. Kenneth H. F. Dyson, *The State Tradition in Western Europe: A Study of an Idea and Institution* (New York: Oxford University Press, 1980), 243–50.
2. Peter Merkl, *The Origin of the West German Republic* (New York: Oxford University Press, 1963), 3–22.
3. Peter Graf Kielmansegg, "The Basic Law—Response to the Past or Design for the Future?" in *Forty Years of the Grundgesetz*, Occasional Paper no. 1, ed. Hartmut Lehmann and Kenneth Ledford (Washington, D.C.: German Historical Institute, 1989).

4. Donald P. Kommers, *The Constitutional Jurisprudence of the Federal Republic of Germany* (Durham: Duke University Press, 1989), 39–40.

5. Kurt Sontheimer, *Die verunsicherte Republik: Die Bundesrepublik nach 30 Jahren* (Munich: R. Piper Verlag, 1979), 7.

6. Dolf Sternberger, "Demokratie der Furcht order Demokratie der Courage?" *Die Wandlung* 4, no.1 (1949): 8.

7. Karl Dietrich Bracher, *The German Dilemma: The Relationship of State and Democracy* (New York: Praeger, 1975), 50.

8. Ernst-Rainer Hönes, "Beamte als Verfassungsfeinde? *Der Öffentliche Dienst,* no. 12, (1972): 222; Hermann Borgs-Maciejewski, "Radikale im öffentlichen Dienst," *Aus Politik und Zeitgeschichte, Beilage zur Wochenzeitung Das Parlament,* 1973, no. 27: 9; Egon Plümer "Mitgliedschaft von Beamten und Beamtenanwärtern in verfassungfeindlichen Parteien," *Neue Juristische Wochenschrift,* 1973, no. 1–2: 5; Hella Mandt, "Grenzen politischer Toleranz in der offenen Gesellschaft: Zum Verfassungsgrundsatz der streitbaren Demokratie,"*Aus Politik und Zeitgeschichte, Beilage zur Wochenzeitung Das Parlament,* no. 1–2, (1972): 4; Eckhart Bulla, "Die Lehre von der streitbaren Demokratie: Versuch einer kritischen Analyse unter besonderer Berücksichtigung der Rechtssprechung des Bundesverfassungsgerichts," *Archiv des Öffentlichen Rechts* 98 (1973): 343; Friedrich Fuchs and Eckhard Jesse, "Der Streit um die 'streitbare Demokratie': Zur Kontroverse um des Beschäftigung von Extremisten im öffentlichen Dienst," *Aus Politik und Zeitgeschichte, Beilage zur Wochenzeitung Das Parlament,* 1978, no. 3: 18; Andreas von Schoeler, "Liberalismus und Extremismus," *Liberal,* 1978, no. 4: 277.

9. Kommers, *The Constitutional Jurisprudence,* 53–54.

10. David Southern, "Germany," in *Government and Administration in Western Europe,* ed. R. Ridley (New York: St. Martin's Press, 1979), 54.

11. Eckhard Jesse, "Parteien in Deutschland," in *Parteien in der Bundesrepublik Deutschland,* ed. Heinrich Oberreuter and Alf Mintzel (Munich: Olzug, 1990), note 103; Merkl, *The Origin,* 83; Kenneth Dyson, "Party Government and Party State," in *Party Government and Political Culture in Western Germany,* ed. Herbert Döring and Gordon Smith (New York: St. Martin's Press, 1982), 84.

12. Otto Kirchheimer, "The Transformation of the Western European Party Systems," in *Political Parties and Political Development,* ed. Joseph LaPalombara and Myron Weiner (Princeton: Princeton University Press, 1966), 190–91.

13. M. Rainer Lepsius, "Institutional Structures and Political Culture," in *Party Government and Political Culture,* ed. Döring and Smith, 118.

14. Kenneth H. F. Dyson, *Party, State, and Bureaucracy in Western Germany* (Beverly Hills: Sage, 1977), 6–7, 10.

15. Nevil Johnson, *State and Government in the Federal Republic of Germany: The Executive at Work,* 2nd ed. (Oxford: Pergamon Press, 1983), 187; John Herz, "Political Views of the West German Civil Service," in *West German Leadership and Foreign Policy,* ed. H. Speier and W. P. Davison (Evanston, Ill.: Row, Peterson, 1957), 106.

16. Dyson, *Party, State, and Bureaucracy,* 11; Klaus von Beyme, *Das politische System der Bundesrepublik Deutschland nach der Vereinigung* (Munich: R. Piper Verlag, 1991), 138, 152.

17. Dyson, "Party Government and Party State," 88–90.

18. Dyson, *Party, State, and Bureaucracy*, 6–10; Nevil Johnson, "Parties and the Conditions of Political Leadership," in *Party Government and Political Culture*, ed. Döring and Smith, 160.

19. Dyson, "Party Government and Party State," 87–98.

20. Hönes, "Beamte als Verfassungsfeinde?" 223.

21. Ibid.

22. Martin Broszat, *The Hitler State: The Foundation and Development of the Internal Structure of the Third Reich* (London: Longman, 1981), 257–58.

23. See, however, Merkl, *The Origin*, 83, 177.

24. Herbert Jacob, *German Administration since Bismarck: Central Authority versus Local Autonomy* (New Haven: Yale University Press, 1963), 10, 158.

25. Peter Katzenstein, *Policy and Politics in West Germany: The Growth of a Semi-sovereign State* (Philadelphia: Temple University Press, 1987), 256–57.

26. Bernd Wunder, *Geschichte der Bürokratie* (Frankfurt am M.: Suhrkamp, 1986), 153–55.

27. Konrad Kruis, "Berufsbeamtentum—Ärgernis oder Forderung der freiheitlichen rechts- und sozialstaatlichen Demokratie?" *Politische Studien*, 1979, no. 3: 189–201.

28. Klaus Stern, *Das Staatsrecht der Bundesrepublik Deutschland* (Munich: C. H. Beck'sche Verlagsbuchhandlung, 1977), 1: 270; Ulrich Battis, "Rechtssprechung zur Radikalen-Frage," *Juristische Arbeitsblätter*, 1979, no. 2: 73; Anke Warbeck, "Die hergebrachten Grundsätze des Berufsbeamtentums im Wandel der Zeiten und ihre Bedeutung," *Recht im Amt* 37, no. 6 (1990): 296.

29. "No. 16," in *Entscheidungen des Bundesverfassungsgerichts* (Tübingen: J. C. B. Mohr, 1975), 39: 374.

30. See Stern, *Das Staatsrecht*, 270–71.

31. Wunder, *Geschichte*, 162–63.

32. Carl J. Friedrich, "Rebuilding the German Constitution, II," *American Political Science Review* 43, no. 4 (1949): 707–08.

33. Stern, *Das Staatsrecht*, 270, 285–86; Borgs-Maciejewski, "Radikale im öffentlichen Dienst," 9; Gottfried Arndt, "Zur Vereinbarkeit der Mitgliedschaft in nicht verfassungsfeindlichen Parteien und Vereinigungen mit Beschäftigung im öffentlichen Dienst," *Zeitschrift für Beamtenrecht*, 1974, no. 4: 123–24; Egon Plümer, "Mitgliedschaft von Beamten und Beamtenanwärtern," 6; Hönes, "Beamte als Verfassungsfeinde?" 224; Ulrich Matz, "Extremisten im öffentlichen Dienst," *Die Öffentliche Verwaltung*, 1978, no. 13–14: 468; Carl Hermann Ule, *Die Grundrechte: Handbuch der Theories und Praxis der Grundrechte* (Berlin: Duncker & Humblot, 1962), 573; "No. 16," *Entscheidungen des Bundesverfassungsgerichts*, 39: 350–51.

34. Gregg O. Kvistad, "Civil Liberties and German State Employees," *German Politics and Society*, no. 19, (1990): 14–26.

35. Mandt, "Grenzen politischer Toleranz," 16; Johannes Lameyer, *Streitbare Demokratie: Eine verfassungshermeneutische Untersuchung* (Berlin: Duncker & Humblot, 1978), 173.

36. E. von Löwenstern, "Kein Überwachungsstaat," *Die Welt*, 12 October 1978; Martin Kriele, "Die Gewähr der Verfassungstreue," *Frankfurter Allgemeine Zeitung*, 25 October 1978.

37. Hartmut Maurer, "Das Verbot politischen Parteien," *Archiv des Öffentlichen Rechts* 96 (1971): 206–207; Peter Graf Kielmansegg, "Ist streitbare Demokratie

möglich?" *Frankfurter Allgemeine Zeitung*, 25 May 1978; Matz, "Extremisten im öffentlichen Dienst," 466.

38. For a critique, see Martin Kutscha, *Verfassung und "streitbare Demokratie"* (Cologne: Pahl-Rugenstein Verlag, 1979).

39. Quoted in Sontheimer, *Die verunsicherte Republik*, 19.

40. Merkl, *The Origin*, 105–08.

41. Gerard Braunthal, *Political Loyalty and Public Service in West Germany: The 1972 Decree against Radicals and Its Consequences* (Amherst: The University of Massachusetts Press, 1990), 15; Merkl, *The Origin*, 3; Jacob, *German Administration*, 158.

42. Reinhard Böttcher, *Die politische Treuepflicht der Beamten und Soldaten und die Grundrechte der Kommunikation* (Berlin: Duncker & Humblot, 1967), 30.

43. "Beschluß der Bundesregierung vom 19. September 1950," in *Die politische Treuepflicht*, ed. Edmund Brandt (Karlsruhe: C. F. Müller Juristischer Verlag, 1976), 138–39.

44. Sontheimer, *Die verunsicherte Republik*, 18–19; Fuchs and Jesse, "Der Streit um die 'streitbare Demokratie,'" 26; Wunder, *Geschichte*, 156.

45. Quoted in Kommers, *The Constitutional Jurisprudence*, 228.

46. Quoted in Klaus Stern, *Zur Verfassungstreue der Beamten* (Munich: Verlag Franz Vahlen, 1974), 11.

47. Roman Herzog, "Recht und Schutz des Einzelnens," *Die Politische Meinung*, no. 166, (1976): 8.

48. Bulla, "Die Lehre von der streitbaren Demokratie," 341.

49. Ludwig Raiser, "Der 'Radikalen-Erlaß': Prüfstein eines demokratischen Rechts-staates?" *Zeitschrift für Evangelische Ethik*, 1979, no. 2: 116.

50. Martin Kriele, "Der rechtliche Spielraum einer Liberalisierung der Einstellung-spraxis im öffentlichen Dienst," *Neue Juristische Wochenschrift*, 1979, no. 1–2: 4.

51. For the use of the term "revolution" to characterize these events, see Dennis L. Bark and David R. Gress, *A History of West Germany* (Oxford: Basil Blackwell, 1989), vol. 1, *From Shadow to Substance, 1945–1963*, xxxi-l.

52. Karl Jaspers, *Wohin treibt die Bundesrepublik?* 2nd ed. (Munich: R. Piper Verlag, 1988).

53. Kurt Sontheimer, "Einführung zur Neuausgabe, 1988," in Jaspers, *Wohin treibt die Bundesrepublik?* i.

54. Jaspers, *Wohin treibt die Bundesrepublik?* 141.

55. Ibid., 146.

56. Ibid., 185–86.

57. Arnulf Baring, *Machtwechsel: Die Ära Brandt-Scheel* (Stuttgart: Deutsche Verlags-Anstalt, 1982), 39–40; Klaus Hildebrand, *Geschichte der Bundesrepublik Deutschland* (Stuttgart: Deutsche Verlags-Anstalt, 1984) vol. 4, *Von Erhard zur Großen Koalition*, 369.

58. Eckhard Jesse, *Die Demokratie der Bundesrepublik Deutschland*, 7th ed. (Berlin: Colloquium Verlag, 1986), 29.

59. Wilfried Röhrich, *Die Demokratie des Westdeutschen: Geschichte und politisches Klima einer Republik* (Munich: Verlag C. H. Beck, 1988), 77–78.

60. Jürgen Habermas, *Toward a Rational Society*, trans. Jeremy Shapiro (Boston: Beacon Press, 1970), 25.

61. Quoted in Baring, *Machtwechsel*, 84.

62. Baring, *Machtwechsel*, 363.

63. On the shift in attitudes in the Federal Republic beginning in the late 1960s, see Ronald Inglehart, *The Silent Revolution: Changing Styles among Western*

Publics (Princeton: Princeton University Press, 1977); Ronald Inglehart, "New Perspectives on Political Change," *Comparative Political Studies* 17, no. 4: 485–532; David Conradt, "Changing German Political Culture," in *The Civic Culture Revisited*, ed. Gabriel Almond and Sidney Verba (Boston: Little, Brown, 1980), 212–72; Kendall Baker, Russell Dalton, and Kai Hildebrandt, *Germany Transformed: Political Culture and the New Politics* (Cambridge: Harvard University Press, 1981).

64. Hildebrand, *Von Erhard zur Großen Koalition*, 372–73.
65. Quoted in Hildebrand, *Von Erhard zur Großen Koalition*, 374.
66. Hildebrand, *Von Erhard zur Großen Koalition*, 399.
67. Gustav Heinemann, "Ansprache vor dem Deutschen Bundestag und dem Bundesrat in Bonn, 1. Juli 1969," in Gustav Heinemann, *Präsidiale Reden* (Frankfurt: Suhrkamp Verlag, 1975), 25–32.
68. Wolfgang Jäger, "Die Innenpolitik der sozial-liberalen Koalition, 1969–1974," in Karl Dietrich Bracher, Wolfgang Jäger, and Werner Link, *Geschichte der Bundesrepublik*, vol. 5/I, *Republik im Wandel: Die Ära Brandt 1969–1974* (Stuttgart: Deutsche Verlagsanstalt, 1986), 159.
69. Willy Brandt, "Regierungserklärung vor dem Bundestag am 28. Oktober 1969," *Reden und Interviews*, (Bonn: Presse- und Informationsamt der Bundesregierung, 1971), 1: 13–30.
70. Quoted in Jäger, "Die Innenpolitik der sozial-liberalen Koalition," 25.
71. Baring, *Machtwechsel*, 251–53; Gordon Smith, *Democracy in West Germany: Parties and Politics in the Federal Republic* (New York: Holmes and Meier, 1979), 172–73.
72. Baring, *Machtwechsel*, 89.
73. Ibid., 382.
74. Michael Balfour, *West Germany: A Contemporary History* (New York: St. Martin's Press, 1982), 241.
75. Baring, *Machtwechsel*, 389.
76. Franz Osterroth and Dieter Schuster, *Chronik der deutschen Sozialdemokratie*, 2nd ed. vol. 3, *Nach dem Zweiten Weltkrieg* (Berlin: Verlag J. H. W. Dietz, Nachf., 1978), 419–504.
77. Quoted in Baring, *Machtwechsel*, 358.
78. Willy Brandt and Helmut Schmidt, *Deutschland 1976—Zwei Sozialdemokraten im Gespräch* (Reinbek bei Hamburg: Rowohlt, 1976), 48; Willy Brandt, *"…wir sind nicht zu Helden geboren…": Ein Gespräch über Deutschland mit Birgit Kraatz* (Zurich: Diogenes Verlag, 1986), 132.
79. Baring, *Machtwechsel*, 394.
80. Quoted in Helmut Gollwitzer, "Stellungnahme," *Wortlaut und Kritik der verfassungswidrigen Januarbeschlüße* (Cologne: Pahl-Rugenstein Verlag, 1972), 31.
81. See Komitee für Grundrechte und Demokratie, ed., *Ohne Zweifel für den Staat* (Reinbek bei Hamburg: Rowohlt, 1982), 43.
82. "Grundsätzliche Entscheidung des (Hamburger) Senats, 23.11.1971," in *Die politische Treuepflicht*, ed. Brandt, 162.
83. Braunthal, *Political Loyalty and Public Service*, 29–30.
84. See Erhard Denninger, ed., *Freiheitliche demokratische Grundordnung* (Frankfurt: Suhrkamp, 1977), 2: 518–19.
85. Brandt and Schmidt, *Deutschland 1976*, 48; see also Peter Graf Kielmansegg, "Von der Notwendigkeit und den Schwierigkeiten streitbarer Demokratie,"

in *Verfassungsfeinde als Beamte?* ed. Wulf Schönbohm (Munich: Günter Olzog Verlag, 1979), 52–53.

86. Sontheimer, *Die verunsicherte Republik*, 27.

87. See, for example, Helmut Lecheler, "Die Treuepflicht des Beamten—Leerformel oder Zentrum der Beamtenpflichten?" *Zeitschrift für Beamtenrecht*, 1972, no. 8: 232; Hönes, "Beamte als Verfassungsfeinde?" 224; Matz, "Extremisten im öffentlichen Dienst," 468; Hans-Walter Scheerbarth and Heinz Höffken, *Beamtenrecht: Lehr- und Handbuch*, 3rd ed. (Siegburg: Verlag Reckinger, 1979), 113; Klaus Stern, *Zur Verfassungstreue der Beamten* (Munich: Verlag Franz Vahlen, 1974), 20; Hans-Dietrich Weiss, "Die Verfassungstreuepflicht des Beamten im Spiegel der Rechtssprechung—eine Dokumentation zum 'Radikalen-Problem,'" *Zeitschrift für Beamtenrecht*, 1974, no. 3: 81; Otthein Rammstedt, "Zur Vermessung des Beamten," *Frankfurter Hefte*, 1975, no. 10: 5; Kriele, "Der rechtlichen Spielraum," 1; Borgs-Maciejewski, "Radikale im öffentlichen Dienst," 20–21; Erich Heimeshoff, "Bemerkungen zur Extremisten-Problematik," *Deutsche Richterzeitung*, 1979, no. 3: 81.

88. See, for example, Jürgen Habermas, "'Verteufelung kritischen Denkens'—Briefwechsel zwischen Kurt Sontheimer und Jürgen Habermas," *Süddeutsche Zeitung*, 26–27 November 1977; Helmut Ridder, "'Berufsverbot'? Nein, Demokratieverbot," *Das Argument*, 1975, no. 7–8: 581; Helmut Krüger, "Verzicht auf die Gewähr der Verfassungstreue?" *Zeitschrift für Rechtspolitik*, 1978, no. 12: 74; Peter Frisch, *Extremistenbeschluß* (Opladen: Heggen-Verlag, 1975), 79–80; Richard Löwenthal, "Wer ist ein Verfassungsfeind?" *Die Zeit*, 23 June 1972.

89. See, for example, Bernhard Blanke, "'Staatsräson' und demokratischen Rechtsstaat," *Leviathan*, 1975, no. 2: 154; Ernst Martin, "Extremistenbeschluß und demokratische Verfassung," *Aus Politik und Zeitgeschichte, Beilage zur Wochenzeitung Das Parlament*, 1973, no. 50: 8–12; Kurt Frederking, "Das außerdienstliche Verhalten des Beamten aus beamtenrechtlicher Sicht," *Die Polizei*, 1980, no. 2: 61; Wulf Damkowski, "Radikale im öffentlichen Dienst," *Recht im Amt*, 1976, no. 1: 6; Karl-Otto Konow, "Grenzen der schriftstellerischen Betätigung der Beamten," *Zeitschrift für Beamtenrecht*, 1972, no. 1: 49; Georg Berner, "'Radikalenerlaß' und Rechtssprechung," *Politische Studien*, no. 233, (1977): 290; Johannes Gerlach, *Radikalenfrage und Privatrecht: Zur politischen Freiheit in der Gesellschaft* (Tübingen: J. C. B. Mohr, 1978), 25–26; Bulla, "Die Lehre von der streitbaren Demokratie," 351; Klaus Stern, *Zur Verfassungstreue*, 19.

90. See Thomas Ellwein, *Das Regierungssytem der Bundesrepublik Deutschland*, 4th ed. (Opladen: Westdeutscher Verlag, 1977), 467; Habermas, "'Verteufelung kritischen Denkens'; Ridder, "'Berufsverbot'? Nein, Demokratieverbot," 581; Krüger, "Verzicht auf die Gewähr der Verfassungstreue?" 274; Frisch, *Extremistenbeschluß*, 79–80; Löwenthal, "Wer ist ein Verfassungsfeind?"; Schoeler, "Liberalismus und Extremismus," 278.

91. "No. 16," *Entscheidungen des Bundesverfassungsgerichts*, 39: 350–51, 366–67.

92. See, for example, Hans Koschnick, ed., *Der Abschied vom Extremistenbeschluß* (Bonn: Verlag Neuer Gesellschaft, 1979); *24. Bundesparteitag der Christlich Demokratischen Union Deutschlands, Niederschrift, Hannover, 24.-26. Mai 1976* (Bonn: Christlich Demokratischen Union Deutschlands, 1976), 204–05.

93. See, for example, Klaus-Henning Rosen, "Ärgernis und Mahnung: Seit Zehn Jahren wirkt der Ministerpräsidentenbeschluß," *Sozialdemokratischen Pressedienst 37*, no. 17 (1982): 5; "Beschluß E 12, Verfassungstreue im öffentlichen Dienst," in *27. Bundesparteitag der Christlich Demokratischen Union Deutschlands,*

Niederschrift, Kiel, 25.-27. März 1979 (Bonn: Christlich Demokratischen Union Deutschlands, 1979).

94. See, for example, "No. 42: Protokoll über die Sitzung des Parteivorstandes am 29. Mai 1978," *Sitzungen des Parteivorstandes [SPD] Protokolle, 1978* (Bonn-Bad Godesberg: Friedrich-Ebert-Stiftung, 1978), 6–7; Hans Klein, "'Eine verantwortungslose Politik,' 138. Sitzung des 8. Bundestages am 15. Februar 1979," *Das Parlament*, 24 February 1979.

95. See, for example, Karl Liedtke, *Informationen der Sozialdemokratischen Bundestagsfraktion*, 1979, no. 184: 1; 26. *Bundesparteitag der Christlich Demokratischen Union Deutschlands, Niederschrift, Ludwigshafen, 23.-25. Oktober 1978* (Bonn: Christlich Demokratischen Union Deutschlands, 1978), 72.

96. Brandt and Schmidt, *Deutschland 1976*, 49–50.

97. Brandt, *"...wir sind nicht..."*, 131–32.

98. Braunthal, *Political Loyalty and Public Service*, 93–137.

99. See "Die GEW will Extremisten den Zugang zum Staatsdienst öffnen," *Frankfurter Allgemeine Zeitung*, 14 October 1978.

100. Letter from Willy Brandt to Klaus-Henning Rosen, 30 November 1977, in Papers of Willy Brandt, File No. 16, "Extremisten: Einzelfälle/8 (151–170)," Bonn-Bad Godesberg: Friedrich-Ebert-Stiftung; Letter from Klaus-Henning Rosen to Willy Brandt, January 1978 (but evidently meaning January 1979), in Papers of Willy Brandt, File No. 13, "Extremisten: Bestandsaufnahme (Material), (II)," Bonn-Bad Godesberg: Friedrich-Ebert-Stiftung.

101. "Demokratie und Sicherheit: Interview des Bundeskanzlers," *Bulletin*,1972, no. 55:773; Kielmansegg, "The Basic Law—Response to the Past or Design for the Future?"

102. P. C. Mayer-Tasch, *Die Bürgerinitiativbewegung* (Reinbek bei Hamburg: Rowohlt, 1976), 13–15; Jürgen Habermas, ed., *Observations on "The Spiritual Situation of the Age"* (Cambridge: The MIT Press, 1985).

Four

GERMAN STATISM AND WEST GERMAN POLITICAL PARTY AND INTELLECTUAL DISCOURSE IN THE 1970S

Describing the demise of a political logic of appropriateness within a community, let alone measuring that, is a less precise activity than many social scientists might desire. Supporting the claim that a political logic of membership is no longer hegemonic does not take the form of marshaling data that unambiguously confirm or refute an hypothesis. While political culture studies go some distance in detailing confirmable "culture shifts" in modern societies, individual attitudinal measurements of elites and masses in political culture studies do not supply all of the nouns and verbs or grammar of a particular political discourse under siege in a political community.[1] Political culture characteristics like "post-materialism" and an "elite-challenging style of politics" are clusters of attitudes relating to individual self-perceptions of political efficacy, and they do constitute part of what we have termed a logic of political membership. But those clusters, decipherable in Western industrial societies generally in the mid-1970s, do not reveal in any detail the intersubjectively shared definitions of the roles of various members of a particular political community. Similarly, discourses of political membership that are "appropriate" in some Western industrial states are relatively meaningless in others: in the "state society" of the Federal Republic, for instance, an "elite-challenging" politics directed against the traditional hortatory role of state civil servants would be quite different from such a politics in a "stateless society" like the United States.[2] To describe the fate of German statism as a logic of political membership in the Federal Republic in the 1970s, this chapter will turn to two different types of political discourse in the period: political debate among the main party actors, including the SPD, the CDU/CSU, and the F.D.P.; and selected political commentary from within West Germany's intelligentsia, including liberal, conservative, and left-radical perspectives.

Political Party Debate and German Statism in the 1970s

Political party debate in the Federal Republic in the 1970s that addressed the discourse of German statism was largely articulated within the bitter party conflict over the Radicals Decree. As argued above, however, the 1972 Decree was not solely responsible for putting German statism on the Federal Republic's political agenda in this period. By the mid-1960s, West Germany's political discourse began a profound questioning of the Federal Republic's political-institutional arrangement and ideological inheritances from the past. Party discussion of German statism in the 1970s thus transcended the specifics of the Radicals Decree, but the particular components of the Decree—its explicit dichotomization of state and society, its differentiation between the political roles of state civil servants and ordinary citizens, and its grounding on "traditional principles" reaching back well before the appearance of democracy in Germany—provided excellent material for discussing the "appropriateness" of the statist logic of political membership in the Federal Republic in the 1970s. By discussing German statism via the Radicals Decree debate, however, many issues tangential to the Decree itself were raised in that debate, and they contributed to the Decree's wildly inconsistent implementation.[3]

The SPD

No political party had more difficulty in sorting out the political-ideological transformations occurring in Federal Republic in the 1960s and 1970s than the SPD, or *Sozialdemokratische Partei Deutschlands*. Similarly, no party was more divided than the SPD by the furious domestic political debate over the Radicals Decree in this period. And no politician was more traumatized by these phenomena than Willy Brandt, the young charismatic federal chancellor who, upon his election in 1969, called for "more democracy" and the political "engagement of the citizenry." The SPD found itself simultaneously encouraging this political-ideological transformation in the Federal Republic in the early 1970s, and yet lacking the necessary conceptual tools to guide and provide that transformation with substantive and logically consistent content. For example, Willy Brandt approvingly quoted Federal President Gustav Heinemann in a speech in 1971, claiming that the "state is 'all of us and every one of us individually'" and warning against "state deification." Moments later Brandt also warned against the "infiltration of forces" from within the West German society that would "endanger the existence of the state," thereby suggesting that "the state" was not literally "all" West Germans. In the same speech, Brandt argued that "democracy cannot assume a fundamental separation of state and society," yet immediately thereafter he referred eight different times to "state," on the one hand, and "society," on the other, as distinct and apparently separable entities.[4]

The concept of the state was very troubling for the Social Democrats when they came to power in 1969. For one, the SPD wanted to shed the authoritarian trappings of the old German state and to "engage" the Federal Republic's citizenry politically, though that meant different things for different Social Democrats. For another, the party wanted to preserve the welfare state as a positive and necessary political institution for the Federal Republic in the 1970s. And for yet another, the SPD attempted to do both of these without clearly coming to terms with the state/society dichotomy that West German political discourse had inherited from the nineteenth century. Willy Brandt's idea of the state in the early 1970s was informed by his call to "democratize" the institution. Brandt pleaded for "more democracy in state and society" and "co-responsibility" on the part of West German citizens who were to have a "direct concern for the common good" and thereby help determine "the best path to take."[5] Exactly what Brandt meant by democratizing state and society was not clear, but his invocation of these paired terms was familiar to his West German listeners. Brandt's language challenged the old German statist tradition of positing state experts as concerned with the public good and ordinary citizens as, at best, nonpolitical private self-interest seekers. He amplified this challenge in early 1973: "We need people who will think critically with us, decide with us, and assume responsibility.... It is the unpolitical citizen who tends to bow before authority [*Obrigkeit*]. We want the citizen [*Bürger*] and not the *bourgeois*. Ideologically, we have moved closer to the Anglo-Saxon citizen, the French *citoyen*. And perhaps we can even say that the Federal Republic has become in that sense more "Western"—even in a period of Ostpolitik."[6]

Brandt's self-conscious concern for German political identity thus rejected the unpolitical role of the nineteenth-century middle-class bourgeois, yet he did not clearly define what a "Western" politicized citizenship could mean in the German context. Brandt urged West German citizens not to "bow" to institutionalized political authority in the Federal Republic. But did that mean taking to the streets, as urged by Karl Jaspers? Or did it mean acting as confident, but relatively apolitical, modern welfare-state clients, a familiar role in Social Democratic discourse in the 1960s? Or did it mean a kind of participatory republican citizenship that stood between the revolutionary citoyen and the relatively passive and obedient bourgeois? With the German authoritarian state looming large as a negative political referent for Brandt and other critical voices in the SPD, it was difficult to articulate a positive and substantively clear role for the new "co-responsible" West German citizen.

Brandt also argued that the SPD would "not shy away from" upholding "the value of the German state [*Würde des Staates*]." That meant not treating it as an "all-powerful idol [*Götze*]" or as a "watering can" for special party projects, both of which he accused the CDU/CSU of doing. Brandt's rejection of these identities of the German state touched precisely on the two different identities associated with the realms of state and society in traditional German statism. Brandt rejected both the "all-powerful idol" image associated with the universalistic German state, and the "watering can" image of particularistic interest seeking associated with German society. Brandt thus implicitly rejected both values of the traditional dichotomy without consistently rejecting the dichotomy itself. Instead, Brandt's state in the 1970s resembled a welfare institution in its broadest sense: the state was to "guarantee civil liberty" and engage in a "sober self-limitation in the service of security for its citizens." German Social Democracy, he argued, "never made the state into an inhuman abstraction. It saw in the state an instrument for the community that got its value from service to the citizenry and the individual."[7] This state, however, did not provide an obvious location for the German citoyen. Brandt's plea for a "balanced and relaxed relationship to the state" in fact resembled more the role of the bourgeois than the citoyen.[8] Nearly two centuries of the derogation of citizenship in German political discourse made Brandt's effort to articulate clear and positive notions of the state and citizen very difficult. Yet Brandt had his finger on the Federal Republic's increasing dissatisfaction with German statism as an appropriate logic of political membership in the 1970s.

That dissatisfaction was sharpened in the 1970s in the political debate over the Radicals Decree. On the one hand, as signatory to it, Brandt regarded the Decree in 1972 as "no new law," squarely resting on existing civil service law and ultimately on Article 33 of the Basic Law, and simply embodying the axiom that "democracy must protect itself from its enemies."[9] On the other hand, by early 1973, Brandt had began to express serious misgivings about the Decree, both in terms of its inconsistent implementation in the Länder and what he somewhat euphemistically referred to as its "imprecision."[10] Two years later he was complaining about the "snooping," "climate of fear," "hypocrisy," and "slipping from liberality and the principles of free democracy" that the Decree had produced in West Germany's political culture.[11] By 1976, two years out of office, Brandt declared that he had made a "mistake" by supporting the 1972 Decree, and he complained of the "grotesque developments" that had occurred in its wake. He stated that he was wrong to view "the civil service as totally unified and homogeneous."[12]

Brandt thus questioned the image of a unified and homogeneous institution of politically loyal and reliable state civil servants arrayed above a nonpolitical society of particularistic German citizens. Brandt's torment over the Radicals Decree continued until the end of the decade. He struggled not only with his own self-described mistaken support for the Decree that had so polarized West German society, but also with the biting criticism of foreigners whom he respected. Dutch and Danish Socialists chastised him for tolerating "rights abuses" in the Federal Republic, and the French Socialist leader, François Mitterrand, established a French "Committee for the Protection of Civil and Professional Rights in the Federal Republic of Germany" in 1976, two months after Brandt had personally explained the Decree to him and pleaded for his understanding of the problems it was creating for the SPD.[13]

The most troubling development for Brandt, however, was the "Third International Russell Tribunal on the Situation of Human

Rights in the Federal Republic of Germany" convened in 1978. The Tribunal had previously investigated torture, assassination, and murder in Latin America and Southeast Asia, and Brandt could not abide the parallel drawn between these acts and the Federal Republic's civil service policy. He declared the Tribunal "not welcome" in West Germany and forbade SPD members from any form of participation in it.[14] As the Russell Tribunal convened in the Federal Republic, Brandt was exploring with party colleagues a differentiation in the level of political loyalty required of German state civil servants according to the security risk of their positions. This option was greeted critically by some Social Democrats because of the major institutional reform it implied.[15] Brandt nonetheless received support from the Social Democratic mayor of Hamburg, Hans-Ulrich Klose, who wrote in a public letter to Brandt that the Decree had caused "part of our youth to develop an elitist understanding of politics according to the slogan, politicians are there to lead and people to obey... The spirit of the German authoritarian state, which we thought was eradicated long ago, is appearing once more."[16] The SPD sensed that the statist logic of political membership was no longer fully appropriate in the Federal Republic by the end of the 1970s, but the party—even its most "democratic" former chancellor—had difficulty in producing anything like a substantive alternative political discourse. Brandt concluded his public pronouncements on the Decree in a speech to parliament in 1980, when he acknowledged his "co-responsibility" for the Decree, called it an example of "bureaucratic idiocy," and criticized it as "punishing the youth for asking whether something could not be made better."[17]

Brandt's Social Democratic successor to the chancellor's office, Helmut Schmidt, shared neither Brandt's exuberance in calling for "more democracy" nor his pathos when the rhetoric did not easily translate into institutional reform. Pragmatic, technocratic, and brusque, Helmut Schmidt frequently addressed the statist legacy of German political ideology explicitly, and his views were informed and straightforward: "the views of the nineteenth century" which posited "'the state' as an abstraction, as an active subject" and the source of society's "fundamental values," were simply outdated and wrong for the Federal Republic. Society's values, instead, came from society and not the state, and those values constituted not a "total" transcendental consensus, but rather a temporary "consensus on elementary basic values" among "individuals, communities, and groups of people." The nineteenth-century view of society as "tending toward anarchy" was consistent with the notion of a "totally regulated state, an authoritarian state, a dictatorship," but utterly inappropriate for the Federal Republic. Modern German "society" was the source of "fundamental values" for "people who work in and for the state," including "politicians, state ministers, the opposition, judges, and civil servants."[18]

Helmut Schmidt thus retained the distinction between state and society for the Federal Republic's political discourse, but that did not prevent the redefinition of the political role of German state officials. Instead of articulating the public interest themselves, they were now to act as transmission belts for the "fundamental values" coming out of West German society. At the same time, the political agency of Schmidt's state officials remained decidedly more pronounced than the political agency of citizens in German society. Schmidt's society was populated by the German bourgeois and not Brandt's ill-defined participatory *citoyen*. This is most clearly displayed in Schmidt's discussion of the social-democratic welfare state.

Schmidt argued that West German citizens had an obligation positively to acknowledge the unprecedented economic well-being and political stability of the postwar Federal Republic. Critical of the youth to whom Brandt frequently promised more democracy and more participation, Schmidt chastised those among them who took the welfare-state successes of the Federal Republic "for granted." He argued, "We have in the majority of the people the consciousness of participating in the achievements [*Ergebniße*] of economic growth and political decisions. For that reason, "the citizens … overwhelmingly identify with our state."[19] "Participating in the achievements" was not, however, the language of participating in the achieving, so to speak, that began to appear in the Federal Republic in the 1960s and was given voice by Willy Brandt and others. German state actors deserved support, Schmidt argued, because they delivered the goods to citizens in German society. According to Schmidt, state actors "constantly work so that it is possible for every citizen to be able to identify with this state, so that every citizen has the opportunity to develop freely in this state, to experience prosperity, and to identify with the state. We must take care so that no wide gulf develops between the citizenry and the state. The state must maintain a concern for the needs and interests of the citizens in order for the citizens to identify with it."[20]

Though Schmidt rejected the "wide gulf" of nineteenth-century German statism, he did not reject the substantive differentiation of a state acting for German society. State agents were to act upon the values that society provided them, and citizens were to judge the material and political results of that action and give or withhold their "identification" with the state in return. Schmidt's reception of nineteenth-century German statism was thus critical of the absolutism that denied the German citizenry any positive political role whatsoever, but the political role he defined for citizens was participatory only in the sense of being the source of fundamental political values, on the one hand, and judges of the performance of state actors, on the other. Helmut Schmidt's understanding of the Radicals Decree was similarly pragmatic. He never budged from the simple position he stated in 1975: the substance of the Decree had been in German civil service law "for decades," and "no one may be a civil servant who does not guarantee that he will intervene on behalf of the free democratic basic order at all times."[21] Schmidt saw the Decree as involving a tradeoff between "liberality" and "security": security was to be provided by state civil servants to allow citizens to live in liberality.[22] Schmidt's position was thus unproblematically consistent with the Federal Republic's institutionalized militant democracy. In contrast to Brandt's soul-searching over the Decree, Schmidt impatiently stated that he wished the Decree and all related legislative proposals would be "filed away," to permit "the principles of the civil service" to function, as "they have very well up until now."[23] The problem with the Radicals Decree for Helmut Schmidt was, in short, the Decree itself.

Helmut Schmidt's understanding of the German state in the 1970s as a welfare-producing service institution was shared by many of his Social Democratic colleagues.[24] Party Executive Board member Hans Koschnick summed up the party's position on the state with, "We give the state an active role in fixing society's problems." Those problems, in the era of *Modell Deutschland* in Western Europe, were primarily economic in nature.[25] But Koschnick warned that, "we must be aware of any form of statist thinking and acting," and that the state had "no value in itself apart from its connections to society."[26] Other party leaders dismissed the "state of the nineteenth century" as a "pre-constitutional" relic of "bureaucrats bearing state authority."[27] The SPD's social-welfare redefinition of state agency called for the provision of "public services" as "unbureaucratically" as possible, and that, according to one party member, was linked to the construction of "democracy" in the Federal Republic.[28] Peter von Oertzen argued in 1974 that "democracy cannot be realized only from above by the activity of the state ... [but] this realization is also simply not possible without the state institution."[29]

Social Democratic "democracy" in the 1970s thereby contained a central role for the state in the Federal Republic, in two senses: first, state institutions were to provide welfare-state and public services in a way that allowed citizens positively to identify with the state; second, the state was to continue to perform its traditional political function of providing "order" (or "security") to the non-self-regulating realm of German society, though not in an "absolutist" manner. West German "democracy" for the SPD in the 1970s thus differed significantly from the open-ended participatory rule by citizens that Willy Brandt's rhetoric periodically entreated. As Kurt Sontheimer has suggested, "Germans"—and we might add, Social Democrats among them—tended still in the 1960s and early 1970s to "go about democracy as an affair of the state."[30] Such an observation must be contextualized, however, by the postwar West German construct of militant democracy, discussed above, that ideally posited an institutional protection of democracy from its "enemies," not the protection of an absolutist regime from democrats.

The SPD's understanding of the state in the Federal Republic's militant democracy in the 1970s hinged on the party's understanding of the German citizen, but in a complicated manner. Politically, the SPD's citizen did not differ much from militant democracy's depiction of the ordinary German citizen as political victim or political perpetrator, needing protection from the forces of subversion in German society or posing a threat as a force of subversion. Ironically, the SPD's civil servant, however, closely resembled what Willy Brandt attempted to conceptualize as an activist West German citoyen. The SPD's civil servant was neither to be the absolutist German policy-making bureaucrat of the nineteenth century, nor the neutral public administrator that the Americans and British had tried to foist on the Federal Republic. The civil servant in the Federal Republic's militant democracy was to be, instead, the participatory citizen, but only within the "rational" membership environment of the state civil service. When the SPD issued its so-called Final Report on the Radicals Decree in 1978, the party argued that state civil servants owed "loyalty to the constitution" and needed to be in "agreement with the fundamental principles of the state." That meant, according to the Report, that the SPD "wants active citizens in the civil service."[31] The "rational" political members in the Federal Republic's political community in the 1970s were to be participatory citizens who embodied the requisite political loyalty to the Federal Republic's free democratic basic order at all times. Karl Liedtke stated in parliamentary debate in 1975 the SPD's full agreement with the opposition, that only active defenders of the free democratic basic order, and not "neutral administrators," should be allowed into the professional civil service.[32] At the party congress that year in Mannheim, it was decided: "For the realization of the basic order of our free democratic constitutional social state, independent and self-conscious democrats will be more than ever necessary in the civil service of the future— people who have the capacity for political judgment and who not only have political convictions, but also who act on them."[33]

In 1978, the party Executive Board called for civil servants who were "courageous" and "actively supported the free democratic basic order."[34] The SPD's call for activist citizens, so to speak, for the Federal Republic's state civil service was quite consistent with what the party saw as the Prussian "traditional principles" of the institution referred to in Article 33 of the Basic Law. In the Final Report, Hans Koschnick wrote, "the SPD wants to change nothing about the existing norms of civil service law," including the "principle of 'guaranteeing public security and order' appearing in the Prussian General Code of 1794." Koschnick argued, "We occasionally have retained not only concepts, but also the content [of those concepts] from the pre-constitutional era. In the civil service that has become clear with the concept of the duty of loyalty [*Treuepflicht*]."[35] Social Democrats in the Federal Republic thus wanted politically loyal civil servants whose role was partly defined by the Prussian General Code, but who were "courageous," "self-conscious," and had the "political convictions" to preserve the Federal Republic's free democratic basic order.

These Prussian images of order and security were probably not attractive to mobilized young West Germans who had entered the party in droves since 1969 and taken to heart Willy Brandt's and Gustav Heinemann's flowing rhetoric of participatory democracy. Yet the only organized politically viable home for mobilized leftist activists in the Federal Republic in the 1970s was the SPD, which housed the Young Socialists, or Jusos. To the great consternation of the SPD, one of the Jusos's main preoccupations in the 1970s was the Radicals Decree. The Jusos's congress in 1973 made the "Demand to Lift the So-Called Minister-Presidents' Decree" one of its four main discussion topics.[36] At their congress a year later they explicitly called for lifting what they termed the "anti-democratic

Berufsverbote," or professional proscription, mandated by the Radicals Decree.[37] The Jusos criticized the SPD as "state-fixated" and "silencing"dissent. They rejected the "precedence of the loyalty oath of the civil servant over [the citizens'] party privilege" as inappropriate for late twentieth-century West German politics.[38] To the profound dismay of the SPD leadership, they also participated in DKP-organized "anti-Berufsverbot" initiatives and suggested open political cooperation with the Communist Party, thereby violating the strict domestic "demarcation decree," or Abgrenzungsbeschluß, issued by the SPD leadership in 1971.[39]

This anti-Communist demarcation would have been easier for the SPD to uphold in the debate over the Radicals Decree if the party had been willing explicitly to list, as Adenauer had in 1950, specific organizations and political parties in which membership would automatically disqualify a person for the civil service. The party's rationale for not listing these parties and organizations, particularly the DKP, and insisting on the "single-case" test for civil service applicants, rested, in part, on the value of defeating political opponents at the ballot box and not via a constitutional banning—which the SPD thought the CDU/CSU would demand for the DKP if any such list were to appear. It also rested on the SPD's concern for the fate of its Ostpolitik, which many saw as hinging on placating Brezhnev at least to the extent of not formally banning the DKP.[40] Boxed in like this, the SPD engaged in a tortured effort to distinguish *Verfassungsfeindlichkeit*, or a not-unconstitutional enemy-like hostility to the constitution, from *Verfassungswidrigkeit*, or unconstitutionality, which was determined by a ruling of the Federal Constitutional Court. In the process, to the further distress of the Social Democratic leadership, the problematic effort of Nazi-era legal theorist Carl Schmitt to distinguish domestic political *Feinde*, or enemies, from political *Freunde*, or friends, was recalled.[41]

Though the nineteenth-century German statist logic of political membership was perhaps no longer fully appropriate for West Germany's Social Democrats by the end of the 1970s, the party's struggle over the Radicals Decree in this period indicated an inability, at the time, to offer a coherent alternative. In 1973 the party had cautiously called for "more precision" for the Decree, but it held that a positive "belief in" (*Bekenntnis*) and active support for the free democratic basic order at all times was required of all state employees. At this time it also characterized its support for the "single case test" as consistent with a "spirit of liberality."[42] The next year saw the SPD's legislative effort to codify the single-case test and thereby, according to the party, "discard" the Radicals Decree, but that was put on hold until 1975, in anticipation of an ultimately disappointing Federal Constitutional Court decision on the Decree that allowed almost all participants in the debate to claim victory. In the meantime, the CDU/CSU had floated their own alternative to the single-case test in the Bundesrat, which they controlled, with their preferred membership criterion. By 1976, gridlock had set in, and the legislative effort to amend the Decree had completely failed.[43] The SPD then decided to go it alone and announced a set of principles for the SPD/F.D.P. federal government and SPD-controlled Länder that it claimed would "invalidate" the original 1972 Decree. These included an initial assumption of political loyalty for all candidates for the civil service unless mitigating evidence existed. But again, this action was regarded by many as too little and too late, and even then it was not implemented in all SPD-controlled Länder.[44]

Hans Koschnick's Final Report for the party appearing at the end of 1978 informed a new set of federal guidelines in early 1979. But those guidelines only reiterated the single-case test and the end of the "automatic check" with the Office for the Protection of the Constitution for applicants. They did not include Koschnick's recommendation to focus only on the behavior, and not the beliefs, of candidates and to differentiate the security risks of various civil service positions. The SPD thus managed to change the status quo only marginally, despite the party leadership's rhetoric to the contrary.[45] In the next two years, the SPD explored the possibility of incorporating Koschnick's suggestions of focusing only on behavior and differentiating the institution's security risks.[46] A legislative bill to incorporate these proposals appeared in the Bundestag in 1982 and was passed and sent on to the CDU/CSU-controlled Bundesrat, where it was defeated on October 8, eight days after Helmut Schmidt's federal SPD-F.D.P. coalition fell to Helmut Kohl and the CDU/CSU.[47] At the time, Hans Koschnick, warned that a "fear psychosis" gripped the Federal Republic, and "the defense of the constitution which is to guarantee the free political activity of our citizens has degenerated to a negative ideology of defending the state of yesteryear and to a depoliticization of especially our younger citizens."[48] Thus ended the SPD's bitter odyssey with the Radicals Decree and with it the party's divisive public struggle to come to terms with the "appropriateness" of Germany's statist logic of political membership for the Federal

Republic in the 1970s. On this issue, their colleagues in the CDU/CSU had a much less conflicted experience.

The CDU/CSU

In the Federal Republic, the CDU, or *Christlich Demokratische Union* and its Bavarian affiliate, the CSU, or *Christlich Soziale Union*, constituted the prototypical postwar "catch-all" political party, a relatively nonideological body whose raison d'être was to attract voters from a broad swath of the political spectrum, present competent candidates for parliamentary office, and pragmatically govern.[49] The CDU/CSU's tremendous success in that role, which landed them in the federal government between 1949 and 1969, proceeded with the consolidation of the West German party-state.[50] The party's unambivalent pro-Western foreign policy, vigilant domestic security policy agenda, and free-market economic program had proven very successful with the West German electorate. By 1969, the CDU/CSU and its supporters had grown so accustomed to the party governing in the Federal Republic that many of its supporters equated the party to the German state itself.[51] As a result, the CDU/CSU suffered the formation of the SPD/FDP federal coalition in 1969 with a mixture of outrage and disbelief, treating it as an "institutional accident" (*Betriebsunfall*) that needed fixing as quickly as possible.[52] Some saw the party's sudden identity crisis in 1969 as a "government without ministers," or an "impeded governing party" (*verhinderte Regierungspartei*), as indicative of a short and still-weak parliamentary tradition that tended to view parliamentary opposition as uncomfortably akin to opposition to the state.[53]

Indeed, Germany's nineteenth-century statist discourse was not absent from the CDU/CSU's founding, when the party eschewed the title of "party," or *Partei*, for "union," or *Union*, which reflected, according to Geoffrey Pridham, "a traditional German aversion to party political divisiveness."[54] The paradigmatic catch-all party of the CDU/CSU that helped to consolidate the West German party-state thus insisted on a nonparty formal identity as they strove to overcome Germany's statist political legacy. The CDU/CSU's identity crisis in 1969 was abetted by the SPD's rhetoric of democracy "just beginning" in the Federal Republic in 1969 with what they called a *Machtwechsel*, or regime change.[55] The Social Democrats' vigorous and flexible "new Ostpolitik" pursued immediately upon taking office gave further pause to the Union parties: the SPD had shed its Marxist trappings only in 1959; it was now moving very rapidly down a foreign policy road that smacked of appeasing the Communists; and it had just opened its ranks to street activists and the "critical youth" of the 1960s. Cold War anti-communism combined with a lingering nineteenth-century German statist discourse to allow the CDU/CSU to view the SPD as an interloping societal actor illegitimately displacing the one and only legitimate *Staatspartei*, or state-party, of the West German party-state.

Relative to the SPD, the Union parties had a relatively easy time of sorting out their inheritance of the German statist tradition. While the traditional German state was largely rejected by the SPD, the value-laden and order-producing state rooted in nineteenth-century German ideology was unambiguously endorsed by the CDU/CSU. Helmut Kohl argued that a "state without authority is in the long run incapable of fulfilling its tasks." But a "state with authority," he argued, was "exactly the opposite of an authoritarian state, for only a state with authority can be a lawful and liberal state."[56] Richard von Weizsäcker similarly articulated a concept of the state distinguished from both the *Obrigkeitsstaat*, which he characterized as a "system of domination by the few," and its "opposite," which he derisively called a "technical service-providing entity." Neither the Obrigkeitsstaat, portrayed as "the realm of God realized" and an *Über-ich*, nor the Social Democratic state, which produced, according to Weizsäcker's colleague, Friedrich Vogel, "insecurity, unhappiness, and fear" in the Federal Republic, was appropriate.[57] The proper German state, according to Weizsäcker, had a "philosophical-political representation" and was endowed with "responsibilities and duties to guarantee ethical norms" and "prevent chaos."[58] Kohl similarly stated at a party congress in 1976 that the state needed to be "capable of action ... not only for material ends, but also spiritually and ideally," and for that the state could not be "neutral," but rather had to serve as a repository of "ethical norms and values."[59] The vertical differentiation between an ordering state and an anarchic civil society was thus upheld, as well as the idea of the state as a source of political morality and ethical norms.

At the same time, the Union parties saw the German state as performing a crucial functional role in the postwar Federal Republic. Rejecting what he called the "state negativism" prevalent in the Federal Republic in the early 1970s, the parliamentarian Alfred Dregger called on the traditional ordering function of the German state to counter what he regarded as the SPD's misplaced focus on society.[60] In 1974, he argued that in order for "law and order" and "domestic peace" to be maintained, "society cannot replace the state … we need not only social policy but also state policy in this country."[61] Helmut Kohl concurred: "we have recently had the state continually silenced in favor of society, with many dreaming of the societalization of the state." Kohl argued that there still existed a legitimate "longing in our society for a state that is a secure state … that maintains moral stature … and that does not allow everything."[62] The Union parties thus attempted to differentiate their functional "political" state from the "regulatory" and "increasingly bureaucratized" state of the SPD.[63] Contrary also to the state of Anglo-American liberalism, the German state, according to the CSU leader, Franz-Josef Strauss, was not "an enemy of freedom … it must be a guarantor, a savior, and a protector of freedom."[64] For the role of "guarantor" and "protector" to be fulfilled, politically loyal civil servants upholding the free democratic basic order were required.

Helmut Kohl saw the civil service as controlling the "levers of power of the state and politics," and that required people employed in the institution to "act decisively and courageously to protect the state and society from the enemies of the state."[65] The German state's role of protecting a non-self-regulating German society—a staple of the nineteenth-century statist logic of political membership—was unambivalently adopted by the CDU/CSU in this period. In order to protect society, the state itself needed to be protected from "enemies" of the political order. In 1976, the CDU campaigned that the "free state must defend itself against its enemies in order to protect the freedom of its citizens."[66] In other words, for the German state to protect German society, it needed to be protected from the potentially politically unreliable source of its own employees—German society. For the CDU/CSU, it was thus an unproblematic "matter of course" that the civil servant's duty of loyalty as a state actor took precedence over any rights he or she might have as a citizen in German society.[67] Hence, a civil servant's loyalty could not be demonstrated by the "mere expression of loyalty to a constitution," or by a "formally correct, disinterested, cool, and internally distant demeanor."[68] Required was a more substantial "constant willingness to intercede on behalf of the state and freedom"; an ability to remain immune from "psycho-social poisoning" and develop a "state consciousness"; an avoidance of participation in a "left- or right-radical party or organization"; and a readiness "consciously and decisively to intervene on behalf of our constitution."[69] Similarly, these intense requirements of political loyalty for a state civil servant were not differentiable according to the security risk of the employee's position. It was "unbelievably naïve—if not worse," the CDU/CSU held, to think that a "machinist at a water plant, an engineer at an electric power station, or a worker at a radio station"—all state employees—should be allowed to be "an enemy of the free democratic basic order."[70]

This image of West German society held by the CDU/CSU in this period was informed by the party's perception of Weimar as "pulverized between two radicalisms" and "delivered to its enemies."[71] West German society in the 1970s was similarly threatened by what Franz-Josef Strauss saw in 1978 as "at least" 50,000 "enemies of our democratic order on the march through our institutions," which added up to "more domestic enemies in our country than ever before."[72] These included "radical parties and groups" who "abused" their civil and political liberties, "enemies of the state," "political criminals" and their "intellectual assistants," "anarchists," "system-changers," "opponents of democracy," "Marxists," "Communists," and "chaotics," among others.[73] Vulnerable West German citizens required the protection of a strong state to defend against such threats. At the CDU convention in 1979, a motion passed that asserted the "right" of citizens in the Federal Republic to have politically loyal state civil servants.[74] Dangerous citizens should be allowed to function in the "normal economy," Strauss held, but not in the civil service, and for that they should be appreciative, for "in Communist societies they would be jailed in mental institutions, prisons, and concentration camps."[75]

Relative to the SPD, the CDU/CSU benefited enormously in the debate over the Radicals Decree from a virtual lack of internal party conflict.[76] Throughout the 1970s, the Union parties argued that since the Decree did not alter West German civil service law, and it was unanimously agreed upon in 1972 by the federal chancellor and the eleven Länder minister-presidents, there was no reason to amend the Decree in any significant manner. The CDU/CSU used their majority in the Bundesrat successfully to block all federal legislative initiatives to do so. Substantively, the CDU/CSU interpreted the Decree, at least until 1979, as mandating the so-called membership criterion for entrance into the civil service and not the single-case test supported by the SPD and F.D.P. The membership criterion held that if a candidate were a member of an organization "hostile" to the constitution (though not determined to be "unconstitutional" by the Federal Constitutional Court), the candidate would be automatically disqualified for civil service employment.

From the beginning of the debate over the Radicals Decree, the CDU/CSU regarded West German Communist Party (DKP) membership as categorically inconsistent with civil service employment: "Offering the guarantee [that the civil servant will intervene on behalf of the free democratic basic order] means that there may not be the slightest doubt about the constitutional loyalty of the candidate. Such doubt exists, however, with a DKP member."[77] While holding to the membership criterion, the CDU/CSU received support from the Federal Constitutional Court's long-anticipated 1975 decision on the Radicals Decree that called party membership "one part" of what mattered for a civil service applicant. The CDU/CSU accused the SPD and F.D.P. of creating a climate of *Gesinnungsschnüffelei*, or snooping into beliefs, with their single-case test, and that was more consistent with a "police state" than with the free democratic basic order.[78] The Union parties thereby turned the tables on the federal coalition and suggested that its "nonobjective" single-case test criterion, and not the Decree as such, produced fear and anxiety in the West German citizenry.[79]

The CDU/CSU's more substantive concern in this debate, however, was less the political mood of the country than the West German state's capacity to defend against what the parties saw as threats to the free democratic basic order.[80] That concern informed the Union parties' rejection of the SPD's call, in 1978, to end the "automatic check" with the Office for the Protection of the Constitution for all civil service candidates. Max Streibl of the CSU argued that this would usher in a "decisive stage in extremist marching plans" in the Federal Republic by allowing "political extremists" a staging area in the civil service.[81] Without the automatic check with security authorities, the state was forced to "play dumb."[82] The CDU/CSU thereby clung to the statist logic of political membership that the Federal Republic had inherited from the nineteenth century and institutionalized in its militant democracy. In the process, the state/society vertical dichotomization was unproblematically retained in party discourse, as was the politically protective role assignment for state civil servants, as well as the characterization of German society as politically vulnerable or dangerous. In short, an updated German statism remained a largely appropriate political discourse for the CDU/CSU in the 1970s.

The F.D.P.

The small liberal Free Democratic Party in the Federal Republic
governed in a federal coalition with the SPD between 1969 and
1982, when it broke with the SPD and formed a new government
with the CDU/CSU. The F.D.P. was founded in 1946, rejecting both
the state interventionism and confessionalism of the CDU/CSU.
And while German liberalism first appeared in the nineteenth century, liberal ideology has never informed party politics in Germany as powerfully as working class, nationalist, confessional, or
big business interests. That has not prevented the F.D.P., however,
from serving as the crucial "pivot" between the two main parties
in the Federal Republic's party system with its roughly 10 percent
of the national vote, and securing a presence in the federal government in all but seven years of the Republic's existence.[83] The
Free Democrats' centrist ideology in the 1970s was informed by the
nineteenth-century German liberal idea of individual freedom.
That idea was not the "negative liberty" of Anglo-American liberalism that regarded the state, as such, as an impediment to freedom. German liberalism saw impediments to freedom as lying
rather in political pathologies that a properly ordered German
state could remedy. Impediments to freedom included political
arbitrariness on the part of state actors and the threat of anarchy on
the part of ordinary citizens in German society. It was particularly
the latter impediment, in the form of "enemies" of the free democratic basic order that preoccupied Free Democrats after the political mobilization of West German society in the 1960s.

Hans-Dietrich Genscher, F.D.P. interior minister in the early
1970s, understood the German state as having primarily a "free-
dom-securing and freedom-promoting function" for individual
citizens. He argued that the state's institutionalization in the police, border guards, and the military was "not a necessary evil,
but rather the guarantor of our constitutional order." The state
protected, he argued, "personal freedom" and "life, health, and
personal property."[84] Genscher's colleagues in parliament argued that only a "falsely-understood logic of the state [*Staatsräson*]" posited a "constant conflict between the logic of the state
and citizens' rights."[85] Genscher's successor in the Interior Ministry, Werner Maihofer, was confronted by the noted French Ger-
manist, Alfred Grosser, who criticized the Federal Republic as
more concerned about defending the free democratic basic order
through the state and less about defending freedoms from the

state. Maihofer responded: "Defense of the basic order through the state and defense of the basic freedoms against the state are not values that cancel each other out—entirely the opposite!"[86] At the same time, the F.D.P. periodically invoked a discourse in the 1970s that resembled the Bureaukratiekritik of the Prussian Vormärz. Not just "enemies" of the political order residing in society, but an improperly functioning state, could also impede individual freedom. During the Radicals Decree debate the party worried about the poor "reputation" of the West German state in the eyes of many West German citizens."[87] The properly functioning state of the F.D.P. protected citizens' liberty from the "enemies" of the free democratic basic order and did so in an expert and respect-inspiring manner. That liberty was to be utilized, in turn, less for political projects like the "democratization" of state and society as held by the SPD, or for what Genscher dismissed as seeking the "'higher' good of the community," than for the private pursuit of a freely defined self-interest.[88]

The F.D.P.'s understanding of the German state in this period remained founded on the nineteenth-century dichotomization of state and society. Contrary to the CDU/CSU, however, the F.D.P. asserted that the state of this dichotomization served only pragmatically to "guarantee freedom and security" in society and was not itself a repository of "ethical norms and values."[89] It was thus simple for the Free Democrats in this period concretely to understand the institutional embodiment of the German state as the professional civil service. The state civil service was to protect German citizens in society who were pursuing their own self-interests, and that function could be performed, according to the F.D.P., only "if the state remained itself free of opponents of freedom." This allowed Genscher to view the Radicals Decree in the early 1970s as a means to "maintain the freedom of the individual [in society] under all circumstances." Genscher argued that freedom in society entailed the right of ordinary citizens to "oppose the constitution," and while opposition to the constitution was allowed to be "represented in elections, it could not appear in the civil service." In the civil service, the "common interest" had to be placed above "group or individual interest."[90]

With this view of the civil service, the F.D.P. shared with other parties the firm conviction that the professional civil service was not to be a politically neutral institution. Consistent with the construct of "militant democracy," the role of the F.D.P.'s state was actively to defend the free democratic basic order. Genscher argued

that the "fundamental principle of the militant democracy" provided "justification for the requirement that members of the civil
service be fighters for the free democratic basic order"; he concluded, "duty and the civil servant's position are basically the
same."[91] But Genscher also held that the "concept of freedom also
has a secure place in the professional civil service. The civil servant
should also freely represent views not shared by his superior. He
should do that without having to fear that he will suffer professional discrimination." Genscher thus differentiated loyalty to the
free democratic basic order from incidental party-political prefer-
ences that a civil servant might have. The Free Democrats advocated freedom for the latter as long as it was compatible with the
former. When Genscher stated, "We in no way want party-political
indifferent civil servants," he was saying that the freedom to support a political party, which none of the Federal Republic's political
parties wanted to deny to civil servants, had to remain consistent
with the civil servant's over-arching duty positively to uphold the
free democratic basic order at all times.[92] The duty of loyalty,
according to Maihofer, was "not simply performance for the state,
but activity for our citizens."[93] Adopting the old discourse of German statism, Maihofer's Free Democratic successor in the Interior
Ministry, Gerhart Baum, argued that the West German civil service
was "centrally responsible" for why "today we live in one of the
most free states [*Staatswesen*] in the world." For Baum, the professional civil service "carries [*trägt*] this Republic" with its "objec-
tivity, neutrality [in the performance of tasks], lack of self-interest,
and political loyalty."[94]

The logically sustainable distinction between a freedom for civil
servants constrained by regime loyalty, on the one hand, and a relatively unconstrained freedom for ordinary citizens, on the other,
became increasingly difficult for the F.D.P. to uphold in the second
half of the 1970s. Burkhard Hirsch's statement that "the wide band
of tolerance of our constitution … finds its borders where it concerns the maintenance of our state's capacities to function and act"
became difficult to operationalize.[95] The difficulty for the F.D.P. was
to define the borders of political tolerance clearly and pragmatically. F.D.P. parliamentarian Friedrich Wendig unproblematically
traced the protective "rational" membership logic of his party's
position on civil servants' political loyalty up to the point of implementing that logic in specific cases. Wendig argued that a deep
"inner" tie of the state civil servant to the free democratic basic
order was necessary and a "value-neutral loyalty" was inadequate.

He also agreed that "behavior" occurring "outside of professional obligations" and "including wide areas of personal life" was relevant, as was the "holding of certain beliefs." But Wendig would not continue beyond that point, stating that he "will not judge" which beliefs those are.[96]

By the end of the decade, the F.D.P.'s position that West German civil servants were not also citizens with guaranteed personal political and civil freedoms was fraying. Torsten Wolfgramm brought a study to the attention of his liberal colleagues in 1979 that concluded the Decree had created a "climate of fear and insecurity" in the Federal Republic and had "damaged the professional and private lives" of individual civil service applicants.[97] Yet the F.D.P.'s concept of the West German citizen as a political actor remained rather undeveloped, and intentionally so. The citizen in F.D.P. discourse was little more than a repository of civil and political liberties concerned more with private than with public affairs. Genscher's Lockeian citizen focused on "life, health, and personal property" and explicitly was not expected to "serve the common good."[98] The citizen's role, according to Genscher, was to "stand behind" and "trust" state civil servants as long as civil servants were properly fulfilling their duty.[99] Interior Minister Gerhard Baum even identified the "self-consciousness of this democracy" as "the attitude the citizens have toward the security officials of this state."[100] All else being equal, Baum saw the political role of the ordinary West German citizen as "identify[ing] with our state."[101] Here the F.D.P. was not arguing that citizens had a positive imperative to act politically; it was, instead, suggesting that ordinary citizens were primarily privately motivated. The F.D.P. thus continued to find the dichotomization of state and society meaningful in the 1970s, but the dichotomy's traditional verticality—locating the protective state above a vulnerable and/or dangerous society— was traded for a horizontal division of labor: state civil servants protected society's freedoms; free citizens in society engaged in private, e.g., economic, activity for the benefit of the entire community. For the F.D.P., the dependent relationship between these actors was mutual. The state was to maintain the order required by society to engage freely in private activity that would meet the needs of the community.[102]

The battle over the Radicals Decree in this period that so split the SPD also preoccupied the F.D.P., but less intensively. Left-liberals, including the party's youth organization, the Judos, demanded the fundamental amendment or repeal of the Decree, while moderates struggled to maintain its essential elements and calm the furor that had erupted around it. In the autumn of 1973, the Federal Executive Board of the F.D.P. issued a ten-point platform on the Decree. It called for keeping "opponents of the free democratic order" out of the state civil service, making more uniform the implementation of the Decree throughout the Federal Republic, basing all proceedings on the single-case test and not the membership criterion, and waiting for a decision by the Federal Constitutional Court to clarify the proper relationship between the party privilege and the loyalty duty of the civil servant.[103] But Martin Bangemann, a later head of the party, broke ranks with his colleagues at this time and argued that the Decree was unconstitutional.[104]

Substantive movement in the party's interpretation of the Decree first came in the summer of 1976, when Helga Schuchardt called for a differentiation in political demands on state employees according to both the level of employment and the security risk of each individual position.[105] The F.D.P. endorsed the differentiation at their autumn convention, thereby supporting a functional alternative to the nineteenth-century view of the state as a "unified" institution confronting a politically dangerous and/or vulnerable society. The F.D.P. did not dismiss the state function of protection; it only required the political loyalty of civil servants if they were "fulfilling sovereign functions" and/or working in a "security-sensitive field.[106] At the same time, the party reiterated that it stood firm in its "defense of the civil service against constitutional enemies."[107] This functionalism was developed at the party's 1977 convention, when it called for transforming the West German state into an "administration situated nearer to citizens" and from an "order-providing" institution to a "service-providing administration."[108] At that convention, the F.D.P. also rejected the "automatic check" with security officials for every civil service candidate and criticized the "climate of insecurity" that the Decree had produced in the Federal Republic.[109]

After the political and social mobilization of the 1960s in the Federal Republic, the small F.D.P., home to German liberalism, thus found itself rather tentatively coexisting between the SPD, which unclearly articulated a political role for German society, and the CDU/CSU, which endorsed a strong political role for the traditional German state. The F.D.P. endorsed the nineteenth-century distinction between state and society in this period, but it reconceptualized the political actors in those realms as more horizontally distributed along a division of labor than vertically located in a sovereign value-laden institution standing above ordinary citizens in society. For the F.D.P., state actors protected the freedoms of German citizens, and German citizens engaged in private activities devoted to their "life, health, and personal property." This was revealed in the party's positions on the Radicals Decree, which envisioned a protective and functional German state of politically loyal civil servants that made possible the experience of freedom for citizens in German society. The F.D.P.'s concern for the positive loyalty of West Germany's "rational" political members in the 1970s nonetheless revealed a significant debt to Germany's nineteenth-century statist logic of political membership.

Intellectual Debate and German Statism in the 1970s

The Federal Republic was the site of a vigorous political debate among the intelligentsia after the mobilization of the 1960s. Politically engaged intellectuals and academics began to flex their critical muscles and address the Federal Republic's institutional arrangement and discursive political inheritance from the past. One of the most interesting such exercises occurred in 1978, when the social theorist Jürgen Habermas circulated a letter among some fifty intellectuals and academics that requested essays for the one-thousandth volume of the imprint *edition suhrkamp* for the Suhrkamp Verlag. Suhrkamp had decided to follow the example of the de Gruyter publishing house that had, in 1931, commissioned Karl Jaspers to publish *Die geistige Situation der Zeit*, or *The Spiritual Situation of the Age*, as the one-thousandth volume of their Göschen imprint. Habermas refused to produce a "general theory of the present epoch" himself and instead invited the "observations" of a number of critical voices to comment on the "spiritual situation of the age," three decades after the Federal Republic's founding.[110] These people had their "identity formed only after the end of the war,... have exercised a certain intellectual influence in the Federal Republic,... stand committed to the traditions against which a German regime established itself in 1933," and as "pensive," were generally "removed equally from certainty and uncertainty" in the Federal Republic in the 1970s.[111]

The essays Habermas collected addressed both structural features of modern Western states, like capital accumulation and legitimation, and the more specific German "geistige Situation" at the end of the 1970s. Claus Offe found a "political-moral, aesthetic hedonism" in German citizens that was expressed not only in material consumerism, but also in the avid exercise of civil and political liberties. Both forms of hedonism, he argued, contributed to the West German state's legitimation in the 1970s, and each thus posed a challenge to the ability of the German state to maintain that status.[112] Wolf-Dieter Narr similarly saw a "superpowerful Leviathan demanding constant demonstrations of respect in both word and deed," and that was arrayed against an increasingly informed, relatively wealthy, and rights- and expectations-laden modern mass society.[113] That German state, according to Klaus von Beyme, had historically developed uncoupled from parliamentarism, and that had left the state with a "high degree of administrative independence" and capable of producing "policy mistakes" like the Radicals Decree.[114] Further contextualizing the German state, Hans Mommsen suggested that the Federal Republic's institutions were "informed by an historical burden ... grounded in traditional authoritarian forms of behavior and thought patterns."[115] Albrecht Wellmer identified one such historical thought pattern with the claim that in Germany, including the Federal Republic in the 1970s, "obedience and discipline—even state-organized terror—have always been viewed with less suspicion than the critical questioning of decayed orders and authorities."[116] That explained why, according to Ulrich Preuss, the concept of "tolerance" was so central in the political discourse of the modern Federal Republic. The concept derived, he argued, "from the conceptual world of the pre-constitutional state," where a beneficent but authoritarian institution "tolerated" an illegitimate "opposition." The pervasiveness of "tolerance" in a democratic political discourse suggested to Preuss a "system of legality ... transformed into an order of loyalty regulated by consensus."[117]

These "observations" thus found, on the one hand, a modern West German state laden with structural and specific ideological attributes that put it in tension with a mobilized mass public. They found, on the other, a West German public increasingly hedonistic, both politically and socially, and responsible for legitimating the West German state. A rights-laden and politicized mass public in the Federal Republic was increasingly rejecting obedience to the "Leviathan" and the mere "tolerance" of their oppositional politics. The "spiritual situation of the age" in the Federal Republic at the end of the 1970s was thus, according to these critical intellectuals, largely inhospitable to a statist logic of political membership that elevated "rational" political actors above ordinary German citizens.

But these authors did not abstractly valorize the political-emancipatory potential of ordinary citizens in German society, even after the 1960s. On the one hand, Narr and Wellmer criticized German society's historical "readiness to conform" that survived in the Federal Republic in a "political-institutional 'culture' based on the acquiescence as opposed to the participation of the citizens."[118] Hans Mommsen similarly wrote that even after the mobilization of the 1960s, too many West Germans continued to prefer the "regulation" of their lives by the German state bureaucracy.[119] On the other hand, Martin Walser warned of the German "Volk," which had thus far historically proven to be, at best, "stupid" and apolitical.[120] Dieter Wellershoff soberly located himself against the "forced politicization of everyday life" of the Nazi period, and the "count-me-out" generation of the immediate postwar era. Rejecting these options, Wellershoff stated, "I far prefer this privatization of life. Even though I know that important problems should only be solved collectively, I still do not want to be commanded to march and assemble." Beyond these choices Wellershoff wrote, "I want to participate ... with a skeptical and yet hopeful feeling for the unceasing, enduring historical change upon which we must depend," and that must mean more than the "ceremonial" act of casting a "single and statistically insignificant vote on election day."[121] Support for a citizenship of political moderation was also provided by Iring Fetscher's critique of the lack of "common sense, tolerance, and moderation" in some leftists in the Federal Republic in the 1970s. He preferred the much-maligned "superficial tolerance" of Anglo-American liberalism to "a fascinating bloody intolerance whose darkness typically is mistaken for 'deepness.'"[122] Jürgen Habermas similarly chastised the "ghettos of dogmatism or alternative lifestyles" developed by some of the 1960s activists in the Federal Republic, and the "active self-removal from the political public sphere" of others. He found that a "battlefront mentality ... has taken hold of the remnants of the protest movement and led them along complementary paths to irrelevance, be it the path to party Communism and neo-Stalinism or the path to the counterculture. Both have led equally to isolation."[123] Narr also attacked 1960s activists who "stew in the juice of their own irrelevant subjectivity and who, at best, can express themselves in irrational outbursts."[124]

At the end of the 1970s, Habermas's observers, though many of them had been leftist activists in the 1960s, thus remained sanguine about the political value of the mobilization of German society in this period. For most, a very cautious optimism was warranted, not least because of German society's historical unfamiliarity with the practice and discourse of democratic politics. Some found the citizens' initiatives and social movements in the late 1970s to be encouraging evidence of a growing "critical engagement and participatory partisanship in the public sector" that involved West German citizens beginning to understand themselves as rightfully "taking" instead of being "given" justice in West German society.[125] These observers saw the Federal Republic's "natural" political members entering a new, politically more reflective, and thus hopeful phase at the end of the 1970s.

In 1973, Kurt Sontheimer and Wilhelm Bleek contributed a quite different volume to the political-intellectual debate in the Federal Republic after the mobilization of the 1960s. In a book titled *Abschied vom Berufsbeamtentum?*, or *Farewell to the Civil Service?*, Sontheimer and Bleek assessed not the "spiritual" situation of the Federal Republic, but rather the role of the West German institution in the 1970s that the state "spirit" was said to inhabit in nineteenth-century Prussian political discourse—the Federal Republic's professional civil service. Sontheimer and Bleek's volume was a draft of a minority report to a study commissioned by the federal government in 1972 to investigate the reform of the West German civil service. The commission was assigned to develop a "plan for a modern civil service" by defining the "place and tasks of the civil service in today's state and society."[126] The commission's majority final report advocated the "most consistent possible implementation of existing law" and some "looking over" of "concepts in the law"; but apart from introducing a differentiated political loyalty demand commensurate with the security risks of particular state employees, it was "not necessary" to alter the "traditional principles of the professional civil service" that dated at least back to the nineteenth century and informed Article 33 of the Federal Republic's Basic Law.[127] Sontheimer and Bleek disagreed, arguing "strongly against a conception of the civil service in which the traditional German professional civil service, including its ideology, would remain conserved and privileged."[128] For that conception of the civil service to disappear, the nineteenth-century notion of "an autonomous state sphere" existing on a "heightened moral plane" relative to society, "embodying the common good" and "maintaining public security and order" would have to be exorcised from the Federal Republic's political discourse. While "traditionalist," "outmoded," and "superseded long ago" by reality, according to the authors, these ideas were not yet dead in the Federal Republic.[129]

Sontheimer and Bleek rejected not only the nineteenth-century traditional vertical dichotomy of state and society that located a hortatory politics in the former and anarchy in the latter, but also the modern version of that dichotomy positing the state professional civil service as the "constant factor" and "disinterested representative of the whole" next to a society of changing and interested political actors. Sontheimer and Bleek argued that a more accurate view of these entities was to see them as "two aspects of the life situation [*Lebenszusammenhang*] of *one* social community [*Gemeinschaft*], the 'essence' of which cannot be divided up." While the state was "necessarily a unified entity relative to the diversity and multiplicity of the other arena of social existence," that was not a "compelling reason to regard the public function that the state exercises as of higher value than the privately designated functions of a society."[130] Sontheimer and Bleek thus acknowledged the different functions of the main actors in the social community, but that differentiation was neither hierarchical nor informed by a moral-political attribution of a greater significance for "rational" West German political members. Civil servants merely occupied a different location "in the necessary division of labor in a society." Civil servants, according to Sontheimer and Bleek, were to "cooperate" with citizens in a "dynamic process" to allow the "best possible realization of the common good." That cooperation was not even contingent on the civil servant's "sense of devotion, loyalty, or self-sacrifice."[131]

Sontheimer and Bleek's reformulated role for the West German civil servant was not, however, joined by a significantly reformulated role for the West German citizen. The authors explicitly rejected any notion of a Rousseauian popular sovereignty as anachronistic and "inadequate" for a modern industrial society.[132] They thereby weighed in—not unlike Habermas's observers—with significant doubts about the rhetoric that accompanied the West German political mobilization of the 1960s. Rather like the F.D.P., Sontheimer and Bleek referred repeatedly to West German citizens less as political actors than as "the totality of taxpayers," "customers" who expect service, and workers with "functions in production or social service provision."[133] At the same time, the authors warned, "where the citizen is banished only to the role of customer ... the readiness for political engagement, on which the survival of democracy depends, has a tendency to atrophy."[134]

The solution for Sontheimer and Bleek was to ensure that political participation by the citizenry was functional for society's political development. Unlike Willy Brandt's open-ended call for "more democracy" in the early 1970s, Sontheimer and Bleek much more conservatively argued, "democratization in the sense of participation of those concerned is to be encouraged where it can be expected that the functional purpose of the institution can be optimally secured by means of the responsible inclusion of those concerned."[135] While such social-science-speak broke with the cautious optimism harbored by Habermas's observers, it was also not nineteenth-century German statism's categorical reduction of citizens to a "lower" realm of dangerous self-interest seeking in a nonpolitical society.

Sontheimer and Bleek's call for civil service reform in the Federal Republic entailed the transcendence of the state/society dichotomization in German politics, but both the means and the end of that transcendence were quite different from what was advocated by many 1960s political activists. The mobilized participants in the Federal Republic's "revolution" of the 1960s were generally less interested in the functional and system-stabilizing citizen behavior called for by Sontheimer and Bleek than in a more open-ended promise of more democracy in the Federal Republic. Habermas's observers were also critical of the excesses of the 1960s mobilization, but they ultimately welcomed the awakening of the West German citizenry in this period. Sontheimer and Bleek instead advocated a division of society's labor to be performed by service-providing civil servants, on the one hand, and moderate and responsible West German citizens, on the other.

The 1970s in the Federal Republic did not see only critiques of West Germany's statist political inheritance. A number of conservative writers in this period attempted to defend the traditional dichotomization of state and society and its attendant role assignments as still appropriate for West German democracy. The legal scholar Walter Leisner was one of the most eloquent advocates of this position, publishing a series of monographs warning against the dangers of democratic "anarchy" in the Federal Republic. What other intellectuals welcomed as a revolutionary awakening of political consciousness in the country in the 1960s, Leisner saw as a dangerous overpoliticization of a citizenry ill-equipped to maintain order. Leisner criticized what he called the efforts of "Marxist legal theory" to transcend the state/society dichotomization and engage in a "continuous ratification of the actual situation"—

thereby initiating a "complete retreat from the idea of law."[136] Instead, an "authoritative" state distinct from society must draw the boundaries of individual political freedom: "The larger the realm of freedom, the more necessary and higher its boundaries must be drawn. To avoid slipping into anarchy, the realm of freedom must always be relative to the strength and severity of the state intervention to limit this same freedom."[137]

The German state, according to Leisner, had experienced various historical incarnations: in the Wilhelmine era, it was the "patriarchal notables" of the civil service; in Weimar, it was political parties "confronting the people as rulers"; and in the Federal Republic, it was a "Chancellor democracy" controlling "pure parliamentarism."[138] Each of these preserved an instance of the German state—both institutionally and ideologically—that was separate from the citizenry in German society. That separation served not only the needs of system stability, in Leisner's view, but also the historical desire of the German public, still present in the 1970s, to be governed by German state institutions existing above German society.[139] In contrast to the many other commentators in the Federal Republic in the 1970s who posited the transcendence of the state/society dichotomy for West German politics, Leisner argued that the realms of state and society were "closely related" in a democracy like the Federal Republic's, but clearly not completely collapsed into each other.

The democratic state had to act, he wrote, "in the name of the people" and not "in the name of the monarch," and that made the state/society dichotomy very different in the Federal Republic from what it was in nineteenth-century Germany. Indeed, the dichotomy was profoundly changed in the Federal Republic by parliament, the "peak" of democratic authority, which allowed "anarchy to flow daily into the state."[140] To counter the societal anarchy flowing into the state through the parliament, however, state institutions needed to be strengthened: "No other state form needs so urgently the steadfastness and strength of the police and the courts as free parliamentary democracy—and it is increasingly diluting that strength, because of its own fundamental principles, into mildness if not weakness."[141] Recalling Carl Schmitt, the institutional culprit for Leisner was a parliament beset by "ecstatic vibrations," characterized by a "war of all against all" and a "jungle of commissions and party fractions ... where daggers are carried under garments."[142] Fortunately for the Federal Republic, in Leisner's view, the West German citizenry generally in the 1970s continued to understand democracy as a government of "representation by notables," which was expressed in the citizens' preference for "Chancellor democracy." That statist understanding of democracy injected a particularly useful "monarchical element" into the Federal Republic. Unfortunately, in Leisner's view, exactly that statist understanding of democracy retained a rather large "distance" between the state and its citizens, and as a result, "anarchy can more easily develop [in the Federal Republic] than elsewhere."[143]

The statist logic of political membership, according to Walter Leisner, was thus fortunately not yet dead in the Federal Republic in the late 1970s, either institutionally or ideologically. A hybridized "chancellor democracy" helped protect against the excesses of parliamentary governance, but even more crucial institutionally for defending against societal anarchy was, in Leisner's view, the Federal Republic's professional state civil service. Challenged by parliament's "maximal integration of society into the realm of the state," however mediated by "chancellor democracy," West Germany had to rely upon the "steadfastness and competence" of the "firm great entity [*die feste Grosse*]" of the state civil service. "Calm masters of technocracy," the Federal Republic's civil servants, Leisner wrote, were "outstanding instruments" who "orient themselves to the work to which they are dedicated for their entire lives." They eschewed the "endless discussion" of parliament and served as the "cement into which the entire trust mechanism of an electoral democracy is attached." As the "one constant factor," the "bulwark against anarchy," and the "center of genuine authority," the existing professional civil service was institutionally an "unalterable requirement" for the Federal Republic.[144] The civil service was not to become the plaything of democratizing reformers. The bureaucracy's "internal discipline," "hierarchical command structure," and differentiation from the "unconventional, creative, and innovative deal-making" of society had to be assiduously maintained.

Furthermore, to treat citizens like "customers," as suggested by Sontheimer and Bleek, was to violate the state's "requirements of abstract authority."[145] Part of that authority was built on the "rational" political membership requirements that the West German civil service had inherited from the nineteenth century. For Leisner, the very concept of the German civil servant entailed political loyalty, and, as such, it was impossible to conceive of loyalty as something external to and required of state employees.[146] This served not only the needs of the civil service, but also enhanced the relationship between the civil service and the West German citizenry. Because "democracy was fundamentally a state form of decriminalization," and its "enemies" were treated, unfortunately, according to Leisner, as citizens, the role of the civil service was to "lead citizens to freedom" by example—by embodying a political loyalty to the regime that was a "heightened form of normal obedience owed by all citizens."[147] The relationship one might typically expect to find in a democratic regime was thus reversed: civil servants were less the servants of a democratic public than democratic citizens were incomplete civil servants. Leisner's normative positions, which were essentially consistent with Germany's nineteenth-century statist logic of political membership, were also, Leisner believed, shared by the vast majority of West German's citizens at the end of the 1970s. West Germany's citizens, Leisner was confident, continued to harbor "old ideas about representation by notables."[148]

Conclusion

This chapter has presented a brief discussion of political party and intellectual discourse in the Federal Republic at the end of the 1970s. It focused on the relative consistency of that discourse with Germany's nineteenth-century statist logic of political membership. It discovered that German statism had become an explicit object of political and intellectual contention in the Federal Republic in the1970s. The political mobilization of West German society in the 1960s had produced among West German political and intellectual elites a series of calls to reject, reform, and defend the statist logic of political membership. Most of the voices in that debate at least questioned the appropriateness of this logic for the modern Federal Republic, though some strove to rescue the state/society dichotomy for West Germany and along with it a hortatory "rational" political membership based on adequate political loyalty. From the broader perspective of political discourse transformation, however, it was clear by the end of the 1970s that Germany's nineteenth-century statist logic of political membership was by no means hegemonic, or even very powerful, as a positive political discourse. The unsettling of German statism in this period was accompanied by abstract challenges to it, in the form of calls for "more democracy," and by abstract defenses of it, in the form of calls for a "strong state." Such abstractness revealed the slow, contradictory, and emotional process by which this fundamental shift in Germany's political discourse was taking place. To continue the account of that shift in the Federal Republic, we turn now to the Greens and their very conscious attempt in the mid-1980s radically to alter the surviving statist content of West Germany's political discourse.

Notes

1. Ronald Inglehart, *Culture Shift in Advanced Industrial Society* (Princeton: Princeton University Press, 1990), 3–14.
2. Ronald Inglehart, *The Silent Revolution: Changing Values and Political Styles among Western Publics* (Princeton: Princeton University Press, 1977), 3; Kenneth Dyson, "West Germany: The Search for a Rationalist Consensus," in *Policy Styles in Western Europe*, ed. Jeremy Richardson (London: George Allen and Unwin, 1982), 17; Philip Blair, "Law and Politics in Germany," *Political Studies* 26, no. 3 (1978): 348; M. Rainer Lepsius, "Institutional Structures and Political Culture," in *Party Government and Political Culture in West Germany*, ed. H. Döring and G. Smith (New York: St. Martin's Press, 1982), 124.
3. Manfred G. Schmidt, *CDU und SPD an der Regierung: Ein Vergleich ihrer Politik in den Ländern* (Frankfurt: Campus Verlag, 1980), 116–24.
4. Willy Brandt, "Rede auf dem außerordentlichen Parteitag der SPD: Politische Aufgaben nach der Halbzeit, 18. November 1971," *Reden und Interviews* (Bonn: Presse- und Informationsamt der Bundesregierung, 1973), 2: 82–84.
5. Willy Brandt, "Rede vor der Belegschaftsversammlung der Bayerischen Motorenwerken in München am 21. März 1972," *Reden und Interviews*, 2: 166; Willy Brandt, "Rede auf der Zentralen Maifeier des DGB in Dortmund, 1. Mai 1972," *Reden und Interviews*, 2: 228.
6. Willy Brandt, "Regierungserklärung, 18. Januar 1973," *Reden und Interviews*, 2: 536.
7. Willy Brandt, "Rede in Dortmund auf dem außerordentlichen Parteitag der SPD: 'Bilanz und Ausblick sozialliberaler Regierungsverantwortung,' am 12. Oktober 1972," *Reden und Interviews*, 2: 432–34.
8. Ibid., 434.
9. Willy Brandt, "Rede in München vor der Belegschaftsversammlung der Bayerischen Motorenwerke zur Sozialpolitik," *Reden und Interviews*, 2: 116; "Interview mit der 'Westfälischen Rundschau' zur inneren Sicherheit," *Reden und Interviews*, 2: 188.
10. Willy Brandt, "Das Grundgesetz verwirklichen—Deutsche Politik und sozialdemokratische Grundsätze," *Parteitag der Sozialdemokratischen Partei Deutschland vom 10. bis 14. April 1973, Protokoll der Verhandlungen* (Bonn: 1973), 79.
11. Willy Brandt, "Rechenschaftsbericht: Rede vom 11. November 1975," in *... auf der Zinne der Partei ...: Parteitagsreden 1960 bis 1983*, ed. Werner Krause and Wolfgang Gröf (Berlin/Bonn: Verlag J. H. W. Dietz Nachf., 1984), 254.

12. Willy Brandt and Helmut Schmidt, *Deutschland 1976—Zwei Sozialdemokraten im Gespräch* (Reinbek bei Hamburg: Rowohlt Taschenbuch Verlag, 1976), 49–50.

13. *SPD Pressemitteilungen und Informationen 76*, no. 300 (1976); "No. 41: Protokoll über die Sitzung des Parteivorstandes am 31. Mai 1976," *Sitzungen der Parteivorstandes [SPD] Protokolle, 1976* (Bonn-Bad Godesberg: Friedrich-Ebert-Stiftung, 1976), 3; Papers of Willy Brandt, "Extremisten (1) Korrespondenz—Ausl. Parteien," Bonn-Bad Godesberg: Friedrich-Ebert-Stiftung; Letter from Willy Brandt to Professor H. Poschlegel, 31 August 1976, in Papers of Willy Brandt, "Extremisten (4) Einzelfälle/2 (25–40)," Bonn-Bad Godesberg: Friedrich-Ebert-Stiftung.

14. "No. 42, Protokoll über die Sitzung des Parteivorstandes am 13. Oktober1977," *Sitzungen der Parteivorstandes [SPD] Protokolle, 1977* (Bonn-Bad Godesberg: Friedrich-Ebert-Stiftung, 1977), 8–9; Der Deutsche Beirat und Sekretariat des 3. Internationalen Russell-Tribunals, ed., *3. Internationales Russell-Tribunal: Zur Situation der Menschenrechte in der Bundesrepublik Deutschland: Dokumente, Verhandlungen, Ergebnisse* (Berlin: Rotbuch Verlag, 1978) vol. 1; Letter of Klaus-Henning Rosen (Brandt's personal assistant) to Christopher Farley, Director of the Bertrand Russell Peace Foundation, 10 July 1978, in Papers of Willy Brandt, "Russell-Tribunal," Bonn-Bad Godesberg: Friedrich-Ebert-Stiftung.

15. "No. 42: Protokoll über die Sitzung des Parteivorstandes am 26. Juni 1978," *Sitzungen der Parteivorstandes [SPD] Protokolle, 1978* (Bonn-Bad Godesberg: Friedrich-Ebert-Stiftung, 1978), 5.

16. Letter of Hans-Ulrich Klose to Willy Brandt, 29 September 1978, in Papers of Willy Brandt, "Extremisten (5) Korrespondenz—Bundesbehörden, Länder," Bonn-Bad Godesberg: Friedrich-Ebert-Stiftung.

17. Text of speech to Bundestag on 26 November 1980, in Papers of Willy Brandt, "Extremisten (30) Allgemeines, Korrespondenz, Presse, ab Okt. 1980 – Dez. 1982 (folgt Bd. 32)," Bonn-Bad Godesberg: Friedrich-Ebert-Stiftung.

18. Helmut Schmidt, "'Grundwerte in Staat und Gesellschaft,' Ansprache vor der Katholischen Akademie in Hamburg am 23.5.1976," *Bulletin*, 1976, no. 62: 582–84.

19. Helmut Schmidt, "Erklärung des Bundeskanzlers zur inneren Sicherheit über Rundfunke- und Fernsehanstalten am 5.3.1975," *Bulletin*, 1975, no. 31: 302.

20. Helmut Schmidt, "'Freiheit und Ordnung': Bundestagsdebatte über innere Sicherheit nach der Entführung Peter Lorenz, 155. Sitzung des 7. Bundestages am 13.3.1975," *Das Parlament*, 22 March 1975.

21. "Interview des Bundeskanzlers Helmut Schmidt für die 'Frankfurter Rundschau,' Ausgabe vom 4.7.1975," *Bulletin*, 1975, no. 89: 850.

22. Helmut Schmidt, "'Eindrucksvolle Erfolge der Sicherheitsbehörden,' 160. Sitzung des 8. Bundestages am 20. Juni 1979," *Das Parlament*, 30 June 1979.

23. Brandt and Schmidt, *Deutschland 1976*, 48.

24. Heino Kaack and Reinhold Roth, eds., *Parteien-Jahrbuch 1976: Dokumentation und Analyse der Entwicklung des Parteiensystems der Bundesrepublik Deutschland in Bundestagswahljahr 1976* (Meisenheim am Glan: Verlag Anton Hain, 1979), 357.

25. Hans Koschnick, *SPD Parteitag Berlin '79, 3.-7. Dezember 1979, Protokoll und Verhandlungen* (Bonn: n.d.), 1: 205.

26. Ibid.

27. Hans-Jochen Vogel, "'Die Handlungsfähigkeit bewahren!' 213. Sitzung des 7. Bundestages am 16.1.1976," *Das Parlament*, 31 Janaury 1976; notes of Hans

Koschnick in Papers of Willy Brandt, "Extremisten (17) Ausarbeitung Schluß-
bericht," Bonn-Bad Godesberg: Friedrich-Ebert-Stiftung.

28. Kaack and Roth, *Parteien-Jahrbuch 1976*, 357.
29. "No. 40: Protokoll über die Sitzung des Parteienvorstandes am 18.1.1974,"
Sitzungen der [SPD] Parteivorstandes Protokolle, 1974 (Bonn-Bad Godesberg:
Friedrich-Ebert-Stiftung, 1974), 42–43.
30. Kurt Sontheimer, *The Government and Politics of West Germany* (London: Hutchinson University Library, 1972), 144.
31. The notes and drafts of the "Final Report" on the Radicals Decree are contained in Papers of Willy Brandt, "Extremisten (17) Ausarbeitung, Schluß-
bericht," Bonn-Bad Godesberg: Friedrich-Ebert-Stiftung.
32. Karl Liedtke, "'Wehrhafte Demokratie,' 197. Sitzung des 7. Bundestages am
24. Oktober 1975," *Das Parlament*, 8 November 1975.
33. *Jahrbuch der Sozialdemokratischen Partei Deutschlands, 1975–1977* (Bonn-Bad
Godesberg: Neuer Vorwärts Verlag, 1977), 505.
34. "No. 42: Protokoll über die Sitzung des Parteivorstandes am 7./8. Dezember
1978," *Sitzungen der Parteivorstandes [SPD] Protokolle, 1978* (Bonn-Bad Godesberg: Friedrich-Ebert-Stiftung, 1978), 6.
35. Hans Koschnick, ed., *Der Abschied vom Extremistenbeschluß* (Bonn: Verlag
Neuer Gesellschaft, 1979), 14; Koschnick, *SPD Parteitag Berlin '79*, 1: 208–09.
36. Franz Osterroth and Dieter Schuster, *Chronik der deutschen Sozialdemokratie*,
2nd ed., vol. 3, *Nach dem Zweiten Weltkrieg* (Berlin: Verlag J. H. W. Dietz
Nachf., 1978), 576.
37. Ibid., 612.
38. Ibid., 756–58, 765–79; *SPD Jungsozialisten Pressemitteilung*, 19 March 1974, 1–2.
39. "No. 39: Protokoll über die Sitzung des Parteivorstandes am 16. März
1973," *Sitzungen der [SPD] Parteivorstandes Protokolle, 1973* (Bonn-Bad Godesberg: Friedrich-Ebert-Stiftung, 1973), 5–6; "No. 40: Protokoll über die
Sitzung des Parteivorstandes am 8. März 1974," *Sitzungen der [SPD] Parteivorstandes Protokolle, 1974* (Bonn-Bad Godesberg: Friedrich-Ebert-Stiftung,
1974), 158–59; "No. 40: Protokoll über die Sitzung des Parteivorstandes am
1. April 1974," *Sitzungen der [SPD] Parteivorstandes Protokolle, 1974* (Bonn-Bad
Godesberg: Friedrich-Ebert-Stiftung, 1974), 3; Osterroth and Schuster,
Chronik, 3: 638, 760–65.
40. Willy Brandt, "*… wir sind nicht zu Helden geboren …*": Ein Gespräch über
Deutschland mit Birgit Kraatz (Zürich: Diogenes Verlag, 1986), 132.
41. On this protracted internal SPD debate, see Karl Liedtke, "'Bewährungs-
probe für die Parteien,' 132. Sitzung des 7. Bundestages am 15.11.1974," *Das
Parlament*, 30 November 1974; and Hugo Brandt, "'Für das Engagement der
Bürger,' 138. Sitzung des 8. Bundestages am 15.2.1979," *Das Parlament*, 24
February 1979.
42. *Parteitag der Sozialdemokratischen Partei Deutschlands, vom 10. bis 14. April 1973,
Stadthalle Hannover*, vol. 1, *Protokoll der Verhandlungen*, 79 (Bonn: 1973), 123–24,
911–12; *Jahrbuch der Sozialdemokratischen Partei Deutschlands, 1973–1975* (Bonn-
Bad Godesberg: Neuer Vorwärts Verlag, 1975), 428, 466.
43. *Jahrbuch, 1973–1975*, 442; "No. 1061: Protokoll der Fraktionssitzung am
Dienstag, 12.11.1974," *Fraktionssitzungsprotokolle [SPD], VII, 8. Oktober 1974–
17. Dezember 1975* (Bonn-Bad Godesberg: Friedrich-Ebert-Stiftung, 1975), 11;
"Kurzprotokoll über die Sitzung des Parteivorstandes am 27.6.1975,"
Sitzungen des [SPD] Parteivorstandes Protokolle, 1975 (Bonn-Bad Godesberg:

Friedrich-Ebert-Stiftung, 1975), 9; Gerard Braunthal, *Political Loyalty and Public Service in West Germany: The 1972 Decree against Radicals and Its Consequences* (Amherst: The University of Massachusetts Press, 1990), 58–65.

44. Osterroth and Schuster, *Chronik*, 3: 693; *Jahrbuch der Sozialdemokratischen Partei Deutschlands, 1975–1977*, 505–07; *Parteitag der Sozialdemokratischen Partei Deutschlands vom 15. bis 19. November 1977* (Bonn: 1977), 112, 129–30, 248, 330–33, 666.

45. Koschnick, ed., *Der Abschied vom Extremistenbeschluß*; Papers of Willy Brandt, "Extremisten (13) Bestandsaufnahme (Material) (II)," Bonn-Bad Godesberg: Friedrich-Ebert-Stiftung; "Grundsätze für die Prüfung der Verfassungstreue vom 17. Januar 1979," *Bulletin*, 1979, no. 6:45–47.

46. *SPD Parteitag Berlin '79*, 139; *Jahrbuch der Sozialdemokratischen Partei Deutschlands, 1979–1981* (Bonn-Bad Godesberg: Vorwärts Verlag, 1981), 473.

47. *Jahrbuch der Sozialdemokratischen Partei Deutschlands, 1982–1983* (Bonn-Bad Godesberg: Neuer Vorwärts Verlag, 1984), 67.

48. Hans Koschnick, "'Ablehnung wirkt sich verhängnisvoll aus,' 431. Sitzung des Bundesrates am 20. Februar 1976," *Das Parlament*, 16 March 1976.

49. Peter Haungs, "Die CDU: Prototyp einer Volkspartei," in *Parteien in der Bundesrepublik Deutschland*, ed. Heinrich Oberreuter and Alf Mintzel (Munich: Olzog, 1990), 158–98.

50. Kenneth H. F. Dyson, *Party, State, and Bureaucracy in Western Germany* (Beverly Hills: Sage Publications, 1977). For reasons of convenience, the CDU and CSU will be referred to as the CDU/CSU.

51. Wolfgang Jäger, "Die Innenpolitik der sozial-liberalen Koalition, 1969–1974," in Karl Dietrich Bracher, Wolfgang Jäger, and Werner Link, *Geschichte der Bundesrepublik*, vol. 5/I, *Republik im Wandel, 1969–1974: Die Ära Brandt* (Stuttgart: Deutsche Verlagsanstalt, 1986), 77.

52. Geoffrey Pridham, *Christian Democracy in Western Germany: The CDU/CSU in Government and Opposition, 1945–1976* (London: Croom Helm, 1977), 191.

53. Jäger, "Innenpolitik," 10.

54. Pridham, *Christian Democracy*, 191.

55. Kurt Sontheimer, *Die verunsicherte Republik: Die Bundesrepublik nach 30 Jahren* (Munich: R. Piper Verlag, 1979), 29.

56. Bernd Conrad, "Kohl pladiert für einen starken Staat," *Die Welt*, 22 November 1974.

57. Friedrich Vogel, "'Gegen die Feinde der Demokratie,' 188. Sitzung des 6. Bundestages am 7. Juni 1972," *Das Parlament*, 24 June 1972; *30. Bundesparteitag der Christlich Demokratischen Union Deutschlands, Niederschrift, Hamburg, 2.-5. November 1981* (Bonn: n.d.), 380.

58. Richard von Weizsäcker, *20. Bundesparteitag der Christlich Demokratischen Union Deutschlands, Niederschrift, Wiesbaden, 9.-11. Oktober 1972* (Bonn: n.d.), 77–78.

59. *24. Bundesparteitag der Christlich Demokratischen Union Deutschlands, Niederschrift, Hannover, 24.-26. Mai 1976* (Bonn: n.d.), 36.

60. Alfred Dregger, "Selbstaufgabe der Demokratie?" *Die Politische Meinung*, 1982, January-February, 25.

61. Alfred Dregger, "'Bilanz nach 25 Jahren: Bestand und Auftrag unserer Verfassung,' 79. Sitzung des 7. Bundestages am 14. Februar 1974," *Das Parlament*, 23 February 1974.

62. Conrad, "Kohl pladiert für einen starken Staat."

63. *30. Bundesparteitag der Christlich Demokratischen Union Deutschlands, Niederschrift, Hamburg, 2.-5. November 1981* (Bonn: n.d.), 380.
64. Franz-Josef Strauss, "'Recht zu kritischer Stellungnahme,' 155. Sitzung des 7. Bundestages am 13. März 1975," *Das Parlament*, 22 March 1975.
65. *21. Bundesparteitag der Christlich Demokratischen Union Deutschlands, Niederschrift, Bonn, 12. Juni 1973* (Bonn: n.d.), 105; Helmut Kohl, "'Bonn wird nicht Weimar!' 155. Sitzung des 7. Bundestages am 13. März 1975," *Das Parlament*, 22 March 1975.
66. *24. Bundesparteitag der Christlich Demokratischen Union Deutschlands, Niederschrift, Hannover, 24.-26. Mai 1976* (Bonn: n.d.), 121.
67. Franz-Josef Strauss, "Die Sache mit dem 'Radikalenerlaß,'" *Bunte* 25, 10 June 1976.
68. Alfred Dregger, "'Für eine starke Demokratie,' 241. Sitzung des 7. Bundestages am 12. Mai 1976," *Das Parlament*, 26 June 1976; Alfred Siedl, "Keine Verfassungsfeinde in den öffentlichen Dienst," *Bayerische Staatsregierung Bulletin*, 1 December 1976.
69. Helmut Kohl, "Bonn wird nicht Weimar!"; Dregger, "Für eine starke Demokratie"; Karl Carstens, "Der Rechtsstaat muß sich wehren," *Die Zeit*, 7 September 1973; Helmut Kohl, "Wachsam bleiben!" *Deutschland-Union-Dienst* 29, no. 101 (1975); Alfred Dregger, "'Nur ein starker Staat gibt Schutz,' 155. Sitzung des 7. Bundestages am 13. März 1975," *Das Parlament*, 22 March 1975.
70. Heinz Eyrich, *CDU/CSU Fraktion im Deutschen Bundestag, Pressedienst*, 11 May 1978.
71. Alfred Dregger, "'Bilanz nach 25 Jahren: Bestand und Auftrag unserer Verfassung,' 79. Sitzung des 7. Bundestages am 14. Februar 1974," *Das Parlament*, 23 February 1974; *26. Bundesparteitag der Christlich Demokratischen Union Deutschlands, Niederschrift, Ludwigshafen, 23.-25. Oktober 1978* (Bonn: n.d.), 34–36.
72. Franz-Josef Strauss, "Parteitag 1978 der CSU in München," *Das Parlament*, 25 June 1978; Helmut Kohl, "Streitfall: Der Radikalenbeschluß oder wer darf Beamter werden?" *BPA-Nachrichtenabt.*, Ref. II R I, ZDF, 19 September 1978.
73. Gerhard Stoltenberg, "Streitfall: Der Radikalenbeschluß oder wer darf Beamter werden?" *BPA-Nachrichtenabt.*, Ref. II R I, ZDF, 19 September 1978; Richard Jäger, "'Den Bürger vor Gavoven schützen,' 168. Sitzung des 6. Bundestages am 2. Februar 1972," *Das Parlament*, 12 February 1972; Friedrich Vogel, "'Gegen die Feinde der Demokratie,' 188. Sitzung des 6. Bundestages am 7. Juni 1972," *Das Parlament*, 24 June 1972; Oskar Schneider, "'Die Würde des Meschens schützen!' 188. Sitzung des 6. Bundestages am 7. Juni 1972," *Das Parlament*, 24 June 1972; Alfred Probst, *CSU Presse-Mitteilungen*, 1974, no. 30.
74. *27. Bundesparteitag der Christlich Demokratischen Union Deutschlands, Niederschrift, Kiel, 25.-27. März 1979* (Bonn: n.d.), 280.
75. Franz-Josef Strauss, "Zum sog. Extremistenbeschluß für den öffentlichen Dienst und zum Wehrdienst," *BPA-Nachrichtenabt.*, Ref. II R3, DFS, 17 September 1980.
76. Schmidt, *CDU und SPD an der Regierung*, 121–22.
77. Richard Stücklen, *CSU Presse-Mitteilungen, Nachrichten aus der CSU-Landesgruppe im Deutschen Bundestag*, 1973, no. 198: 1–2.
78. Jäger, "Die Innenpolitik der sozial-liberalen Koalition," 85.
79. *24. Bundesparteitag der Christlich Demokratischen Union Deutschlands, Niederschrift, Hannover, 24.-26. Mai 1976* (Bonn: n.d.), 204–05.

80. "Verfassungsfeinde im öffentlichen Dienst," *UiD-Dokumentation*, 1976, no. 17.
81. "Bayern will Regelfrage bei Einstellungen noch ausweiten," *Frankfurter Rundschau*, 6 December 1978.
82. Hans Klein, "'Eine verantwortungslose Politik,'" 138. Sitzung des 8. Bundestages am 15. Februar 1979," *Das Parlament*, 24 February 1979.
83. Dennis L. Bark and David R. Gress, *A History of West Germany*, vol. 1, *From Shadow to Substance, 1945–1963* (Oxford: Basil Blackwell Ltd., 1989), 103–04; Gordon Smith, "The 'Model' West German Party System," *The Federal Republic of Germany at Forty*, ed. Peter Merkl (New York: New York University Press, 1989), 253–58; Christian Søe, "'Not Without Us!' The F.D.P.'s Survival, Position, and Influence," *The Federal Republic of Germany at Forty*, ed. Merkl, 313–19.
84. Hans-Dietrich Genscher, "'Der Gewalt den Kampf angesagt,'" 188. Sitzung des 6. Bundestages am 7.6.1972," *Das Parlament*, 24 June 1972.
85. Friedrich Wendig, "'Politische Moralisten nicht schon Phantasten,'" 197. Sitzung des 7. Bundestages am 24. Oktober 1975," *Das Parlament*, 8 November 1975.
86. Werner Maihofer, "'Im Dienste der menschlichen Freiheit,'" 197. Sitzung des 7. Bundestages am 24. Oktober 1975," *Das Parlament*, 8 November 1975.
87. Wolfgang Mischnick, "Dem Rechtsstaat droht auch von den eiferner Gefahr," *fdk Tagesdienst: Pressedienst der Bundestagsfraktion der F.D.P.*, 1976, no. 143: 1.
88. Hans-Dietrich Genscher, "'Die Zukunft des öffentlichen Dienstes,' bei der Gewerkschaftstag der Gewerkschaft Deutscher Bundesbeamten und -anwärter im Deutschen Beamtenbund am 10. Oktober 1973," *Bulletin*, 1973, no. 107: 1067.
89. Werner Maihofer, "'Öffentlicher Dienst—für die Bürger, für die Gesellschaft,' 9. Deutschen Beamtentag des DGB am 20. Februar 1975," *Bulletin*, 1975, no. 23: 228.
90. Genscher, "Der Gewalt den Kampf," 1–3; Genscher, "Die Zukunft," 1067; Genscher, "'Grundfragen des Beamtentums im freiheitlichen Rechtsstaat,' Bundesvertretertag 1972 des Deutschen Beamtentums am 6. November 1972," *Bulletin*, 1972, no. 156: 1868; Hans-Dietrich Genscher, "'Funktion und Bedeutung des öffentlichen Dienstes in der modernen Industriegesellschaft,' 15. Beamtenpolitischer Arbeitstagung der Deutschen Beamtenbundes am 8. Januar 1973," *Bulletin*, 1973, no. 3: 22.
91. Hans-Dietrich Genscher, "'Aufgaben des öffentlichen Dienstes im demokratischen Rechtsstaat,' 16. Beamtenpolitischen Arbeitstagung des Deutschen Beamtenbundes am 10. Januar 1974," *Bulletin*, 1974, no. 4: 30–33.
92. Ibid., 33.
93. Maihofer, "'Öffentlicher Dienst,'" 228.
94. Gerhart Baum, "'Bedeutung und Verantwortung des öffentlichen Dienstes,' Bundesvertretung 1979 des Deutschen Beamtenbundes am 15. November 1979," *Bulletin*, 1979, no. 141: 1295–99.
95. Burkhard Hirsch, "'Grundübereinstimmung aller Demokraten notwendig,' 155. Sitzung des 7. Bundestages, 13. März 1975," *Das Parlament*, 22 March 1975.
96. Wendig, "'Fraktion unterstützt Regierungsentwurf,' 132. Sitzung des 7. Bundestages, am 15. November 1974," *Das Parlament*, 30 November 1974; Wendig, "'Politische Moralisten nicht schon Phantasten,'" 4.
97. Torsten Wolfgramm, "'Oppositionsantrag geht ins Leere,' 160. Sitzung des 8. Bundestages am 20. Juni 1979," *Das Parlament*, 30 June 1979.

98. Genscher, "Die Zukunft," 1067.
99. Genscher, "Grundfragen des Beamtentums," 1867–68.
100. Gerhard Baum, "'Aufgaben der inneren Sicherheit und des Verfassungsschutzes,' Bundeskriminalamt und Bundesamt für Verfassungsschutz, 26. Juni 1978," *Bulletin*, 1978, no. 71: 675.
101. Gerhard Baum, "Gemeinsame Verantwortung bei der Verbrechensbekämpfung,' 23. Oktober 1978," *Bulletin*, 1978, no. 121: 1129.
102. Lothar Krall, "'Mitwirkung des Bürgers,' 188. Sitzung des 6. Bundestages am 7. Juni 1972," *Das Parlament*, 24 June 1972.
103. "Antrag 15: Betr.: Beschlüße der Ministerpräsidenten," *23. Ordentliche Bundesparteitag der F.D.P. vom 2. bis 4. Oktober 1972* (n.p., n.d.).
104. "FR Interview: Martin Bangemann, 'Erlaß ist rechtlich ein Nichts,'" *Frankfurter Rundschau*, 10 August 1973.
105. Helga Schuchardt, "Zu Fragen der Auslandskritik am Extremistenerlaß," *BPA-Abt. Nachrichten*, SFB, 12 June 1976.
106. "Beschlüße des Frankfurter Bundesparteitages, 1976," in *Das Programm der Liberalen: Zehn Jahre Programmarbeit der F.D.P.*, ed. Günter Verheugen (Baden-Baden: Nomos Verlagsgesellschaft, 1980), 258–60.
107. Andreas von Schoeler, "Wider die Einschränkung der freien politischen Auseinandersetzung," *fdk Tagesdienst: Pressedienst der Bundestagsfraktion der F.D.P.*, 1976, no. 676: 2.
108. "Bürger, Staat, Demokratie," *F.D.P. Die Liberalen, Kieler Thesen, Beschloßen auf dem 28. Ordentlichen Bundesparteitag der F.D.P. vom 6. bis 8. November 1977 in Kiel* (Bonn: Liberal-Verlag, n.d.), 57.
109. Ibid.
110. Jürgen Habermas, "Introduction," in *Observations on "The Spiritual Situation of the Age,"* ed. Jürgen Habermas (Cambridge: The MIT Press, 1985), 1–2. The MIT Press's translations of these essays will be used whenever possible. Not all of the essays that appeared in the German-language two-volume *Stichworte zur "Geistigen Situation der Zeit,"* vol. 1, *Nation und Republik*, and vol. 2, *Politik und Kultur* (Frankfurt: Suhrkamp Verlag, 1979), however, appeared in the one-volume English-language version. For convenience, the English-language volume will be cited as *"O"* and the two German-language volumes as *"S1"* and *"S2."*
111. Habermas, "Introduction," 2–3.
112. Claus Offe, "Ungovernability: On the Renaissance of Conservative Theories of Crisis," *O*, 77–85; Albrecht Wellmer, "Terrorism and the Critique of Society," *O*, 295–301; Ulrich Preuss, "Political Concepts of Order in Mass Society," *O*, 95–99.
113. Wolf-Dieter Narr, "Toward a Society of Conditioned Reflexes," *O*, 38.
114. Klaus von Beyme, "Der Neo-Korporatismus und die Politik des begrenzten Pluralism in der Bundesrepublik," *S1*, 237–42, 262.
115. Hans Mommsen, "Die Last der Vergangenheit," *S1*, 183.
116. Wellmer, "Terrorism," 288, 300, 302.
117. Preuss, "Political Concepts," 99, 110–12.
118. Narr, "Toward a Society," 44–45; Wellmer, "Terrorism," 302.
119. Mommsen, "Die Last der Vergangenheit," 207.
120. Martin Walser, "Händedruck mit Gespenstern," *S1*, 47.
121. Dieter Wellershoff, "Germany—A State of Flux," *O*, 356, 368.
122. Iring Fetscher, "Die Suche nach der nationalen Identität," *S1*, 115.

123. Habermas, "Introduction," 7–9.
124. Narr, "Toward a Society," 54.
125. Mommsen, "Die Last der Vergangenheit," 184; Narr, "Toward a Society," 61; Wellershoff, "Germany—A State of Flux," 108; Preuss, "Political Concepts," 118–19.
126. Kurt Sontheimer and Wilhelm Bleek, *Abschied vom Berufsbeamtentum? Perspektiven einer Reform des öffentlichen Dienstes in der Bundesrepublik Deutschland* (Hamburg: Hoffmann und Campe, 1973); Willi Thiele, *Die Entwicklung des Deutschen Berufs-Beamtentums: Preußen als Ausgangspunkt moderner Beamtentums* (Herford: Maximilian Verlag, 1981), 89.
127. Studienkommission für die Reform des öffentlichen Dienstrechts, *Bericht der Kommission* (Baden-Baden: Nomos Verlagsgesellschaft, 1973), 12: 163–66.
128. Sontheimer and Bleek, *Abschied vom Berufsbeamtentum?* 8–9.
129. Ibid., 8, 15–19, 28–29, 47, 49, 73, 85, 87.
130. Ibid., 17, 20–24, 28–34, 47–48 [Sontheimer and Bleek's italics].
131. Ibid., 51–52, 60, 102–06.
132. Ibid., 56.
133. Ibid., 40, 51–52.
134. Ibid., 76.
135. Ibid., 63.
136. Walter Leisner, *Demokratie: Selbstzerstörung einer Staatsform?* (Berlin: Duncker & Humblot, 1979), 23–24.
137. Ibid., 75.
138. Ibid., 26–27, 38.
139. Ibid., 28–29.
140. Walter Leisner, *Die demokratische Anarchie: Verlust der Ordnung als Staatsprinzip?* (Berlin: Duncker & Humblot, 1981), 220; Leisner, *Demokratie*, 74.
141. Leisner, *Demokratie*, 72.
142. Leisner, *Demokratie*, 128; Leisner, *Die demokratische Anarchie*, 215.
143. Leisner, *Demokratie*, 29, 39; Leisner, *Die demokratische Anarchie*, 210.
144. Leisner, *Demokratie*, 83, 122, 124–28, 135; Leisner, *Die demokratische Anarchie*, 221–23.
145. Leisner, *Demokratie*, 119–23; Leisner, *Die demokratische Anarchie*,125–26.
146. Leisner, *Demokratie*, 128.
147. Ibid., 77, 87, 122, 130.
148. Ibid., 28–29.

Five

THE TENSIONS ENDEMIC TO AN ALTERNATIVE POLITICS IN A STATIST CONTEXT

The West German Greens Between
State and Society

The fracturing of political discourse in the Federal Republic of Germany in the 1970s and early 1980s was not unique among Western industrial states. So-called anti-politics movements—demanding such things as radical democratic reform, equality, environmental protection, disarmament, and the protection of civil liberties—appeared in this period throughout Western Europe.[1] Social scientists producing the "new social movement" literature in the 1970s and early 1980s linked the rise of these phenomena to structural variables connected to the economic, social, and political modernization of Western industrial society. Alain Touraine, one of the foremost social movement theorists in this period, identified seven theoretically and historically distinct phases of social movement development, and he characterized the stage at the end of the 1970s as antitechnocratic and antistatist.[2] This more theoretically inclined new social movement literature was joined by cross-national survey-research studies in the 1970s and early 1980s that identified significant changes in the attitudes of Western publics. Almond and Verba revisited the sites of their classic 1963 civil culture study and found a growing convergence along the dimension of "civic"—as opposed to "subject"—competence among their cases.[3] Ronald Inglehart similarly found a broad generational reorientation of Western publics toward "postmaterialism," a value complex emphasizing "quality of life" issues over the traditional postwar economistic concerns of employment, wages, and inflation.[4] Both the theoretical and survey-research literatures tended to regard the Federal Republic—implicitly or explicitly—as unproblematically comparable to, and typical of, other Western industrial societies in the 1970s and early 1980s.

For scholars of German political development, however, especially of twentieth-century Germany, such an unreflective comparability, even if implicit, often gives pause. The pause is generated infrequently by methodological unsophistication, or by a vague ill will toward "Germans" or "Germany," or by some steadfast commitment to the incomparable "uniqueness" of the political development.[5] Frequently that pause is the result of an historical sensitivity to the uniqueness of the Nazi Holocaust not only in the history of state-sponsored genocide, but also in the history of modern European politics.[6] Because of the Holocaust, in 1949 the Federal Republic began its political development at a very different place from any other European state. Exactly what place that was depends upon what is being addressed. German political development was "burdened" by a past in 1949 that forced political institutions and political actors—including the German citizenry—to come to terms with the Holocaust, but in very different ways. The process of coming to terms with Nazi Germany for the Federal Republic's political institutions was, as argued above, mediated by the postwar construct of militant democracy and elite consciousness of the political-institutional "mistakes" of Weimar. That process for the political beliefs and attitudes of the Federal Republic's citizens, in contrast, did not enjoy the same relatively straightforward mediation.

Whether or not German mass political attitudes actually brought Hitler to power in 1933, Lepsius has argued that until the early 1980s, all survey research of mass political attitudes in the Federal Republic was either informed by, or informed, widespread international questions about the "democratic reliability" of West Germany's mass political culture.[7] Even by explicitly ignoring the Federal Republic's unique political-developmental starting point in 1949 as "burdened" by the Holocaust, survey-research studies of political attitudes in the Federal Republic could not control how those studies might be used and interpreted. By the early 1980s, however, survey-research scholars thought they could finally put the "democratic reliability" issue for the Federal Republic's mass political attitudes to rest. In addition to the studies cited above, an important English-language monograph appearing in 1981 explicitly announced in its title a "Germany Transformed" by a "new politics" that brought the Federal Republic's mass political attitudes unambivalently in line with the mass political attitudes of other Western European states.[8] By the early 1980s, therefore, political discourse appeared to be fracturing and in the process of being redefined in the Federal Republic in a manner that, on the one hand, the theoretical new social movement literature suggested was completely disconnected from any particular historical legacy, and that, on the other, the mass attitudinal survey-research literature suggested was now no longer "burdened" by mass "democratic unreliability." The "normalization" of mass German politics was thus apparently achieved by the early 1980s.

While the argument of this book does not reject that conclusion as such (depending on what is meant by "normalcy"), it also does not find it, or the question that generated the finding, interesting for the present discussion. In its attempt to trace the rise—and, since the 1960s—the demise of German statism as an appropriate logic of political membership, this book locates itself between the somewhat overdetermined theoretical new social movement literature, which tells us too much (that the Federal Republic's development is simply a case in the developmental schema of advanced industrial societies), and the somewhat underdetermined survey-research literature, which tells us too little (that the Federal Republic had become by the 1980s—if it was not before—like other advanced industrial societies). The book attempts to do that in this chapter by discussing the political ideology of the West German Greens in the 1980s and investigating the complex debt that ideology owed to the nineteenth-century German statist political discourse the Greens were so consciously and intensively attempting to transcend. In the process, we both eschew the troubling "normalcy" benchmark against which to measure the Federal Republic's relative political "performance" and avoid positing some deep and unchanging German political-cultural "uniqueness."

The cross-national accounts of the "Green phenomenon" in Western Europe in the 1980s are legion, typically springing from the premises that both the substantive interest (ecology) and the mode of interest intermediation (a social movement) of the Green phenomenon are generally understandable from within a cross-national account of the modernization of Western industrial society, the development of advanced capitalism, and the inadequate integrative success of postwar catch-all political parties. The focus of this chapter will be somewhat different. Instead of addressing the substantive issue complexes discussed by the Greens in the 1980s, or the alternative mode of interest intermediation they represented, it will argue that Green ideology in the Federal Republic in the mid-1980s offered a substantially coherent challenge to the statist logic of political membership, though in a complicated and contradictory way. Green political ideology both abstractly rejected and ironically incorporated elements of the statist logic of political membership that it so strongly sought to transcend. This argument does not entail the claim that the West German Greens in the mid-1980s were somehow completely unique relative to Green parties in France or Belgium. The argument, rather, is that the development of Green ideology in West Germany in this period reflected the development of the particular history of German political discourse since the early nineteenth century—in particular, the inheritance and conflict over Germany's statist logic of political membership. While the statist ideology of German political membership that informed the West German Greens in this period does not mediate the ideology of the environmental Agalev and Ecolo parties in Belgium, or the Ecologist or Green parties in France, other particular logics of political membership, with their own history and discourses, most certainly do.

Jürgen Habermas has provided a useful metaphor for understanding the West German Green ideological debt to the past in the mid-1980s. Echoing some of his colleagues in the *Observations* volume discussed in the previous chapter, Habermas commented on the intolerance of parts of the Green project in the Federal Republic in this period: "The closing in of the ghetto only mirrors, after all, the process of closing out."[9] While many Greens would argue in the early 1980s, especially after the appearance of their party in the Bundestag in 1983, that their "ghettoization" was over, the effects of this process of exclusion from the highly institutionalized political context of the Federal Republic in the early postwar years, part of which was produced by the functioning of militant democracy, left a deep imprint on early Green ideology. On the one hand, Greens "closed in" in the mid-1980s and reflected in significant ways the intolerance of those who had previously closed them out of institutionalized West German politics; on the other hand, Greens "closed in" and attempted—frequently very abstractly—to reject all that they perceived their former "ghettoiz-ers" (conflated as the West German political "system") to represent, including the intolerance which produced their own isolation.[10] In each instance, Green ideology and practice were deeply informed by the specific ideological and institutional context of postwar West German politics—and not only by a generic postmodern opposition to "the priority given to economic growth in public policy-making, an overly bureaucratized welfare state, and restric-tions placed on participation which confine policy making to the elites of well-organized interest groups and parties."[11] A good part of the West German context in which the Greens articulated their program was determined by the Federal Republic's ambivalent inheritance of Germany's statist ideological legacy. Green political ideology in the mid-1980s both abstractly rejected and abstractly incorporated significant elements of the traditional German statist logic of political membership. While the Greens set out to create nothing less than a new political discourse in the Federal Repub-lic, Green ideology in the mid-1980s bore a pervasive imprint of the old German statism that it sought to transcend.

Positive Reflections of the Statist Logic of Political Membership

Turning first to the positive ideological debt that the Greens owed to past German statist political discourse, it must first be stressed that the Greens were not authoritarian opponents of the West Ger-man liberal democratic political order in the mid-1980s. The im-agery of an all-powerful authoritarian "Eco-State" periodically attributed to the Greens in the 1980s revealed more about the lack of political imagination of Green detractors than what the party in any significant sense advocated. The goal of this section is to indi-cate the extent to which Green political ideology in the mid-1980s remained rather naturally hostage to the ideological and institu-tional context from which it sprang. If, as Wolf-Dieter Narr claimed in a discussion of the Greens, "the system" was inside of all polit-ical participants in the Federal Republic, the effort will be made to indicate how much and what part of that "system" was inside its best organized opponents in this period.[12]

The rejection of traditional Marxist class analysis by the new social movements in Western Europe in the 1970s and early 1980s left protest politics in the region groping for general categories to define both themselves and the objects of their mobilization. In the late 1970s, for example, the Federal Organization of Environmentalist Citizens' Initiatives in West Germany cited economic inequality, destruction of the environment, social injustice, and the growing dependence of individuals on the state as "existential indicators" of the "life-threatening system."[13] By the mid-1980s, some Green radical "fundamentalists" (in contrast to their more moderate "realist" colleagues) similarly forsook any meaningfully differentiated appraisal of the West German political system and its components, frequently lumping together the SPD and the CDU, and those catch-all parties with some vague construct of the West German state.[14] In a significant way, this undifferentiated hypostatization of political actors and institutions reflected not just the immaturity of a political oppositional project, but also an old German statist political tradition that had historically left German political actors struggling to conceptualize, as well as to act as, a force of responsible and legitimate political opposition.

German statism dichotomized the state, as a site of hortatory political action, above society, as a realm of system-threatening anarchy and self-interest. As we saw, the Weimar theorist Carl Schmitt's definition of the domestic political opponent as a *Feind* or an "enemy" that occupied the realm of society considerably narrowed the population of legitimate political actors.[15] Reflections of this statist membership ideology appeared also in the 1960s and 1970s in the Federal Republic, when West German political elites vilified broad sections of the West German activist youth and alternative culture as "terrorist sympathizers," *Verfassungsfeinde* (enemies of the constitution), and *Systemgegner* (opponents of the system) threatening the stability of the free democratic basic order. Closed out of West German politics and socialized in the hot-house state-of-siege atmosphere in the Federal Republic in the late 1960s and 1970s, many Greens agreed with Rudolf Bahro's assessment that the Federal Republic's "life-destroying structure" would lead either to fundamental social transformation or to civil war.[16] Regarding themselves in the 1970s as opponents not *in* the West German political system, but rather enemies *of* it, many West German Greens in the 1980s vilified and indicted with the same intensity and generality that was previously directed against them.

This undifferentiated and extreme conceptualization of the political opponent in Green ideology in the mid-1980s was joined by a similar tendency to equate politics with morality. The assertion that the Greens "reintroduced morality" into West German politics in the early 1980s was not only exemplified by the spectacle of Green parliamentarian Otto Schily skewering Chancellor Kohl in the *Bundestag* during the so-called Flick Affair in 1985.[17] Reflecting a broader concern than for the morals of elected politicians, the Greens adopted a discourse in the mid-1980s that eschewed claims of narrow individual, group, or class interest, and appealed to such universalistic concerns as species survival, social justice, and ecological balance. They thereby invoked the German statist tradition of conceptualizing politics generally, and especially the role of political leadership, as a source of collective public morality for German society. The Greens' rejection of an amoral "instrumental rationality" thus reflected not only a negative appraisal of the dynamics of advanced capitalism, but also the German statist tradition of a political elite providing a substantive public morality for German society. As a "state-society," according to Kenneth Dyson, the Federal Republic has inherited the tendency to view an "abstract, impersonal state as an entity or personality above and distinct from both government and governed,... as an object of universal service and respect ... and as the source of a distinct public morality."[18] While the *Basisdemokratie* (grassroots democracy) concept in Green ideology in the mid-1980s was at odds with the image of a moral teacher "above" society, especially if that teacher were the bureaucratic state, moralism was present in the Greens' fundamentalist portrayal of its parliamentary group as representing, in contrast to the parties of the West German party-state, a "principle of life," a "politics of love" and salvation," and a "political spirituality." In discussions of Green strategy and the Greens' place in history, Petra Kelly and Rudolf Bahro frequently invoked Christian imagery in their calls for the Greens to remain a "teaching party."[19] While different political actors and different substantive ends were at work in Green moralism relative to those of traditional German statism, the Greens' notion of politics as a hortatory and didactic invocation of substantive solutions was a constituent part of Germany's statist logic of political membership.

Complementing Green moralism in the mid-1980s were the Greens' particular difficulties with political conflict. In 1969, Ralf Dahrendorf rather broadly concluded: "Wherever opposing interests meet in German society, there is a tendency to seek authoritative and substantive rather than tentative and formal solutions. Many institutions in German society have been and are still set up in such a way as to imply that somebody or some group of people is 'the most objective authority in the world,' and is therefore capable of finding ultimate solutions for all issues and conflicts. In this manner, conflict is not regulated, but 'solved.'"[20] Green experiences at early party congresses would suggest an opposing "tendency" to what Dahrendorf observed for West German society as a whole in the late 1960s, as would polling data in the mid-1980s that suggested diminished support for Dahrendorf's generalization, especially among the Green constituency of younger West German voters.[21] Moreover, in the mid-1980s the party seemed to have effectively institutionalized the conflict that Germans allegedly avoided by establishing Basisdemokratie to foster internal decision making and to ensure easy access to all party officials.

The Greens' federal program read, "Grassroots democracy [Basisdemokratie] means putting decentralized, direct democracy into practice. We assume that the views of the grassroots [*die Basis*] have priority in principle."[22] But the apparent institutionalization of conflict via Basisdemokratie must be regarded in light of the principle of consensualism to which the Greens also held. Introduced in the early 1980s for the functioning of the Basisdemokratie, consensualism was offered as an alternative to majority rule, but it was an alternative quite consistent with the German statist tradition of "solving" conflict in the Greens' case—here not by deferring to a higher authority for answers, but rather by calling for the full, if perhaps uneasy, participation and agreement of all persons affected. As Alternative List member Martin Jänicke pointed out, the consensus principle does indeed counter the argument that "majority is majority," but it does so by assuming that issues for collective decision making lack legitimately opposing perspectives, or it forces such issues to be limited to the most mundane and least controversial—which certainly did not describe the Greens' agenda in the mid-1980s.[23] Basisdemokratische consensualism thus challenged the statist tradition of hankering after authoritative answers determined by a political elite. But it preserved the nonpluralistic tradition of hankering after authoritative answers, only now those determined by the Basis.

The Greens' conceptualization of political opposition, their moralism, and their ambivalence about political conflict were related to their critique of West German party politics in the mid-1980s. Neither observers nor activists in this period could agree on whether to identify the Greens as a political party or as a social movement. On the one hand, the Greens appeared to be a political party with a platform, fielding candidates in competitive elections, and, after 1983, working within the Bundestag for the realization of at least some of their goals. On the other hand, many Greens insisted that they constituted a social movement, arguing that the Green parliamentary fraction was merely a *Spielbein* (auxiliary leg) relative to the *Standbein* (leg to stand on) of the social movement.[24] Electoral politics for the social movement Greens was more a means to educate the West German public than to win political power. The identity of the Greens in the mid-1980s was one of the primary differences separating Green "realists" from Green "fundamentalists." Realists argued for the Greens becoming a fairly standard political party, though with a distinctive platform and organizational structure, while fundamentalists, among them Petra Kelly, argued that the Greens were an "anti-party party."

This fundamentalist critique of political parties in the Federal Republic shared significant characteristics with the traditional anti-party animus of German statism. Of course, the critique of party politics in the 1970s and early 1980s was not solely a West German affair. Catch-all political parties were losing ground all over Western Europe in this period.[25] In the Federal Republic, like elsewhere, young activists left the postwar Volksparteien in droves, especially the SPD, in the wake of dashed hopes for significant domestic political reform. Present in the Federal Republic, however, was a lingering ideological tradition of statist anti-partyism that was first articulated, as we saw, in the nineteenth-century Vormärz. That tradition was less about dashed hopes than about an institutional critique of political parties as problematic societal loci of conflict, disorder, and narrow particularism.

The Greens were not immune to what Wolf-Dieter Narr called the "old German attitude" of not respecting political parties.[26] That attitude located parties in the realm of society, doing the "dirty business"—as Bismarck referred to it—of parliamentary politics, ideologically located beneath the *überparteiliche* (above parties) universalism of the German state.[27] This "old attitude" resonated with groups as diverse as the Nazis in the early 1930s, who identified themselves first as a political and social movement and then as a party; the CDU/CSU in the Federal Republic, who identified themselves not as parties but as "unions"; and the Greens, who in their founding in 1980, eschewed "party" in their official name and adopted simply *Die Grünen*. Anti-partyism continued to hold considerable mass appeal in West Germany in the mid-1980s. Political parties in this period were accorded "trust" by 40 percent of the entire West German public and by only 18 percent of Green identifiers. That compared with a 59 percent/30 percent respective trust level for West German courts, a 62 percent/32 percent trust level for the police, and a 56 percent/20 percent trust level for the West German army.[28] These were rather remarkable findings given that the 1968 student generation, having had a unique experience with the West German police, formed the backbone of Green support in the early 1980s. The Greens' embodiment of traditional anti-partyism did not, however, include an ideological elevation of, or a leading role for, the German state relative to German society. It entailed instead an elevation of, or a leading role for, the Greens relative to other political parties in the Federal Republic. In the early 1980s a popular slogan portrayed the Greens as neither left nor right, but "in front." The überparteiliche attraction was also revealed in part of an early Green program: "As against the one-dimensional politics of increased production, we represent a total concept."[29] The universalistic "total concept" of the German state was familiar to traditional German political discourse.

We turn finally to what might be called the corporatization of Green parliamentarians in the mid-1980s, a process conducted according to principles the Greens identified as democratic, but that nonetheless positively reflected the statist logic of political membership the Federal Republic inherited. Thus far, this study has argued that the statist logic of political membership consolidating in mid-nineteenth-century Prussia and challenged but surviving in the short-lived Weimar Republic, had political loyalty as a positively determinable individual attribute as a main membership criterion. The centrality of this "rational" form of political membership was fundamentally challenged only in the Federal Republic, where an institutional arrangement provided at least an ambivalent rejection of this logic, but where a profound social mobilization and "revolution" beginning in the 1960s led to the unraveling of German statism as a hegemonic discourse of political membership. The 1970s battle over the Radicals Decree, with its insistence on the certain political loyalty of state employees in the Federal Republic, was both a major event for the systematic challenge of German statism in West Germany and a formative experience for many people who got involved with the Greens at the end of the decade.[30]

The subsequent Green challenge to the West German statist logic of membership in the mid-1980s was complicated, as is now being argued, but nonetheless profound, suggesting that the Greens would be particularly sensitive to anything resembling a "rational" logic of political membership that turned on a demonstrable and positive political loyalty. Indeed, Greens pointed to the Radicals Decree, which appeared when Willy Brandt was chancellor and was somewhat modified, but never repealed, during Helmut Schmidt's tenure, as one of the major causes of the SPD losing support among young West German voters in the 1970s.[31] Yet two of the main pillars of Green political ideology in the mid-1980s—Basisdemokratie, already discussed, and the imperative mandate, treated below—introduced practices within the Greens that significantly resembled parts of the Radicals Decree and the statist logic of political membership that informed it. In intent, Basisdemokratie and the imperative mandate were strong participatory-democratic concepts that located political power and responsibility not in the state or any other institution, but rather in the *Basis*, in the ordinary citizenry who constituted the Green membership. In effect, however, these concepts left Green parliamentarians and other leaders in an instrumentalized position strikingly similar to that faced by the "rational" West German civil servant, appearing in the Radicals Decree and in over a century of German civil service law.

At the Greens' national assembly in early 1983 it was decided that, "The Greens in the Bundestag are bound by the decisions of the national delegates' assembly and the national steering committee. Contravention of these decisions constitutes one reason for expulsion from the Bundestag group."[32] Critics argued that this mandate violated Article 38 of the Basic Law, which stated—in its own anti-party way—that parliamentarians were "representatives of the entire people" and not of a particular party. Reminiscent of critiques of the Radicals Decree in the 1970s, some Green parliamentarians complained of feeling a sense of "permanent political responsibility" that made them accountable at all times, and not just during work hours. Green responses to these criticisms ranged from a rejection of the nineteenth-century liberalism that held inviolate the individual conscience of representatives, to an assertion that other parties in the Federal Republic functionally engaged in the same practices, to the claim that if the individual Green parliamentarian willingly resigned his or her position— consistent with the call for a rotation of members of parliament— the free will of the parliamentarian was maintained.[33]

The Green program of 1980 read: "The core of the organizational concept concerns the continuous control of all office holders, elected representatives and institutions through the supporter base (open-access meetings; limited duration of terms of office) and the right to replace office holders at any time, both to ensure that the party organization and the process of policy formulation are clear to all and in order to prevent a detachment of party officials and parliamentarians from their grassroots [*Basis*]."[34] The "rational" nature of the Green parliamentary mandate in the mid-1980s thus turned on a political loyalty that resembled the "rational" nature of the civil service appointment appearing in the Radicals Decree and historical German civil service law. Green parliamentarians were allowed to act only in accordance with the vaguely defined will of the Basis, just as some critics argued German state civil servants were allowed to act—and think—only in accordance with the vaguely defined "idea" of the German state, or, in the Federal Republic, the free democratic basic order. The political membership gatekeeper shifted from "above" (the state) to "below" (the Basis), but "rational" gatekeeping based on a requisite political loyalty was maintained.

Negative Reflections of the Statist Logic of Political Membership

These mostly unconscious (and some might suggest fortuitous) positive reflections of German statism in Green political ideology in the mid-1980s were joined by more direct confrontational rejections of traditional Green statism. But here it will also be suggested that the direct criticisms of German statism within Green ideology also negatively incorporated significant elements of that old logic of political membership. This "abstract" Green negation of German statism mirrored in some ways the very object it was attempting to negate. This is clearly evident in the Greens' abstract identification of West German society as a genuine political realm to replace the false political realm of the West German state. In 1976, political scientist Kurt Sontheimer criticized West German leftism for treating "'society' as an all-encompassing category, almost as a universal concept [*Allerweltsbegriff*]. Differences between public and private are flattened and their total interconnection posited."[35] The tendency to consider "society" in this way, and to understand politics as what occurs in West German society and not in the West German state, as German statism would have it, informed Green political ideology in the mid-1980s. Although switching the normative values of the hierarchical dichotomy of state and society, Green ideology retained and accorded importance to this dichotomous conceptual pairing that has informed German politics since the beginning of the nineteenth century. Green anti-statist "societal-ism" in this period consisted of a rejection of West German parties as Staatsparteien, or state parties; a rejection of the state bureaucracy as anti-democratic, hierarchical, and incapable of solving the existential environmental and security crises besetting the Federal Republic; and a rejection of "militant democracy" as a statist mechanism for protecting West German society "from above" with a strong state and not "from below," by mobilizing the active participation of a democratic public.

It has been argued that Green anti-partyism shared significant characteristics with the German statist tradition of denigrating parliamentarism and party politics. Here we shall alternatively consider the extent to which Green anti-partyism was more negatively driven by a diffuse anti-statism—an anti-statism mediated by a particular Green interpretation of the West German postwar Parteienstaat (party-state). Perceived as being "closed out" of party politics in the Federal Republic at least since the years of the so-called Grand Coalition between the SPD and CDU/CSU (1966–1969), Green supporters identified the Federal Republic's catch-all political parties in the mid-1980s as upholders of a statist status quo. Green activist Jutta Ditfurth argued that fundamental reform in the Federal Republic was blocked by the entrenched Parteien-staat, an institution she regarded less as a democratic alternative to the authoritarian state of Germany's past than as an institutional mechanism for marginalizing popular initiatives emanating outside of the orbit of the SPD and CDU/CSU.[36]

The Green critique of these parties as state, and not societal, institutions had some coherence given the tradition in West Germany of referring to parties possessing the requisite political responsibility for governing as "*staatserhaltende*," or "state-maintaining." The too-easy identification of catch-all parties as organs not of parliamentary governance and opposition, but rather as institutions of a unified West German state, was also rooted in the years of the Grand Coalition, during which time mobilized leftist students, intellectuals, and academics loosely organized themselves into an "extra-parliamentary opposition" against the SPD-CDU/CSU coalition. The broad project of these activists, according to Dieter Wellershoff, was to "construct a new, critical public sphere" in the Federal Republic.[37] Their primary target was the SPD, which gave its support to the Emergency Legislation in this period and thereby established in the minds of many a direct link between a strong state executive and the only viable party of political reform. The "extra-parliamentary opposition," in which many future Greens were active, saw a nominally socialist party casting its lot with a conservative Christian party in an attempt to secure for the West German state the extraordinary legal means to contain and discipline West German society.[38] When the SPD became the dominant federal coalition partner with the F.D.P. in 1969, some activists had their hopes raised only to be dashed by the issuance of the Radicals Decree in 1972. The replacement of Willy Brandt by the more technocratic Helmut Schmidt in 1974 helped further to move many leftists out of the SPD. The subsequent SPD/F.D.P. coalition with Schmidt at the helm was characterized by Green member Joschka Fischer in the early 1980s as a "de facto all-party coalition." This coalition presided over a misnamed *Modell Deutschland* that, according to Fischer, sanctioned a systematic "state repression of West German society."[39] Other Greens similarly viewed the SPD as a "bureaucratic quasi-state apparatus" engaging at best in a "statist reformism" of West German society "from above."[40] When the F.D.P. scuttled its alliance with the SPD in 1982 and joined the CDU/CSU to form a new federal government, Green leader Petra Kelly rejected the change as insignificant and claimed that a functional "all-party coalition" continued to govern West Germany.[41]

The antistatist critique of the Federal Republic's catch-all parties was thus rooted not only in the Greens' perception of these parties as institutional allies of the German state in the repression of popular political opposition, but also in the Greens' rather abstract critique of the traditional German logic of political membership that located hortatory politics in the state realm. Instead of viewing the Federal Republic's political parties as agents of particularism (as we saw above), here Greens rejected those parties as agents of a false universalism and then substituted society as the location of an alternative and genuine public sphere. In both cases, Green oppositional political discourse in the mid-1980s was suffused with the traditional statist logic of political membership that, in Habermas's metaphor, had for so long "closed out" their critical political participation.

The Greens' critique of the bureaucratic state in the mid-1980s was also heavily informed by their explicit critique of traditional German statism. While some so-called value-conservatives extended Green anti-statism to call specifically for the dismantling of the West German welfare state in the name of individualism, the main Green position on the bureaucracy in this period was a more general rejection of the institution as the dominant political actor in the Federal Republic. Greens rejected the bureaucracy, however, with a counter-ideology that continued to invoke the institutional logic of statism that they ultimately wanted to transcend. Jutta Ditfurth warned her moderate Green colleagues of the "dialectic between structures and individuals" in politics. Those who would advocate leaving the West German state as it was, or merely replacing its personnel, would ultimately sanction a "state repression of society's power potential." For it was wrong, she argued, to suggest that "'below' there is irrationality and incompetence while 'above' people are more in control."[42]

Yet Green calls for civil disobedience, passive protest, "self-administration," the communalization of political power, making hierarchy "fluid," and locating decision making at the "bottom" or "from below" were all reflexively predicated on the existence of a centralized bureaucratic power to disobey and protest against, on the existence of a "rigid" structure at the "top" to resist.[43] The Green vision of plebiscitary democracy in the mid-1980s was less a positive alternative or full transcendence of the German statist logic of political membership than it was its abstract negation. Abstract in the sense of partial and beholden to the object of its critique, the Green democratic alternative to the bureaucratic state tradition was strongly criticized by other West German party elites who saw in the Green position not only "unrealism," but also a throwback to the dangerous plebiscitary elements of the Weimar constitution.[44] Viewed contextually, however, the Green demand in the mid-1980s for alternative and more directly democratic modes of decision making for the Federal Republic revealed an explicit and powerful challenge to the German statist tradition of viewing politics as a state activity engaged in by expert decision makers.

As with the Green critique of the bureaucratic state in the mid-1980s, Green anti-statism in this period also informed a critique of the postwar Federal Republic's understanding of democracy. The Green alternative to that democracy—conceptualized in the Federal Republic's political and legal commentary as a militant democracy—was a Basisdemokratie, or grassroots democracy. Greens and other critical voices in the Federal Republic, especially during the Radicals Decree controversy of the 1970s, tended to regard the construct of streitbare Demokratie as a "statist" democracy practiced "from above." The Green alternative, in contrast, was a "societalist" democracy to be practiced "from below." As discussed, streitbare Demokratie was a somewhat difficult concept both for West Germans to define and for others to understand. It referred more to a political order than to a political process. Looking backward to Weimar as a negative referent, West Germany's "democracy," it was argued, was required to defend itself against all domestic attacks on its fundamental values. Those values included, as articulated in the Federal Constitutional Court decision in 1956 banning the Communist Party of Germany (KPD), a respect for human rights and democratic sovereignty.[45] Such values were threatened, it was held, not only by political parties, but also by politically unreliable, or insufficiently loyal, West German citizens—especially those seeking public employment as state civil servants in the Federal Republic after the 1972 Radicals Decree.

The Federal Republic's streitbare Demokratie was thus a political order empowered to protect itself from all domestic political forces, be they political organizations or individuals, who "misused" their democratic constitutional rights, and thereby became Verfassungsfeinde, or enemies of the constitution, in an effort to subvert or overthrow the West German political order.[46] As a political order, and not a process, guarded by institutions of the state —the courts and the civil service—and not mobilized citizens, streitbare Demokratie was frequently criticized in this period as a nominal "democracy from above" protecting against potentially disloyal West German citizens acting "from below." Peter Mayer-Tasch characterized the citizens' initiatives of the late 1970s as elevating "the citizen" relative to "this or that political group." "On a very wide scale," according to Mayer-Tasch, "the achievements of the representatives [in West Germany] were put under the looking glass by the represented, and the citizens prepared for battle with their political leaders."[47] It was indeed "democracy as an affair of the state" that many Greens in the mid-1980s saw constituting the West German democracy they rejected.[48]

Thomas Schmid and Ernst Hoplitschek denounced streitbare Demokratie as democracy "from above" that was instituted in the Federal Republic to thwart popular politics "from below."[49] Others understood democracy in the Federal Republic as rendering any form of civil unrest in the country equivalent to "a fundamental opposition to the political system," or worse, to "verfassungsfeindliche" activity and the "criminalization" of any significant alternative politics in the Federal Republic.[50] The streitbare Demokratie in the Federal Republic thus left democracy in the mid-1980s, according to a Green critique, "hollow-cheeked," "deficient," and functioning by the "rule of elected elites."[51] As an alternative to what they understood as the statist democracy of streitbare Demokratie, the Greens offered Basisdemokratie. That entailed, according to Green activist Jutta Ditfurth, creating an "alternative societal power" to confront the statist democracy of the current Federal Republic.[52] Indeed, it is possible to characterize large parts of the Green project in the mid-1980s as promoting a "societalism" to counter the statist logic of appropriateness that had informed German political ideology for nearly two centuries. That "societalism" negated traditional German statism with a "politics of the concrete" and rejected the traditional view that the "concrete" did not concern the universalistic German state and was thus pre- or antipolitical. The Greens promoted a "societal emancipation," in the words of one activist, where politics "from below" would replace the failed politics "from above."[53] It also presented Basisdemokratie as *"betroffenendemokratisch,"* an odd word meant to contrast with a democracy of removed expert decision makers who did not feel the pinch of their own decision making. Joachim Müller elaborated that the "decisive entity" in the Federal Republic had to become the "community," where "consciousness is formed ... where conflicts arise, and ... [where] human beings are really affected."[54]

This abstract adoption of society as a political realm in the Green's Basisdemokratie, in short, was heavily, if negatively indebted to the traditional statist conceptualization of society as antipolitical. Green Basisdemokratie was envisaged as a democracy "from below" to challenge West Germany's current democracy "from above." This spatial imagery so dominated Green thinking in this period that Herbert Gruhl's founding of the *Grüne Aktion Zukunft*, or Green Action Future, was dismissed by many Greens as an act "from above."[55] Green activist Joschka Fischer similarly argued that even with a Green federal chancellor, democracy "from below" would be the order of the day.[56] At the same time, the historical importance of this Green ideological shift from "state" to "society" and from "above" to "below" for German political discourse cannot be minimized. Wolf-Dieter Narr welcomed these political innovations connected to Basisdemokratie as "profoundly un-German."[57] But they were also profoundly German, in the sense that the Green ideological alternative in the mid-1980s partly represented a shift within a political discourse, and not out of a political discourse, that had dominated German political thinking since the early nineteenth century. The abstract switching of the normative values of the old hierarchical dichotomy of German statism to make "society" the "new public sphere" in the Federal Republic revealed more about what the Greens were attempting to replace than a carefully constructed political alternative.

Conclusion

This chapter has argued that the Green political challenge in the Federal Republic in the mid-1980s was importantly informed by the statist logic of political membership that dominated German politics for almost two centuries. While the Greens offered a relatively systematic critique of German statism, the lingering power of that tradition in the Federal Republic, as well as the relative immaturity of the Green movement in this period, combined to leave Green politics in the mid-1980s ideologically hostage to the statism that it sought ultimately to transcend. Statism dominated the Green position in West Germany in two ways: positively, in the sense that Greens consciously or unconsciously employed several traditional statist images in both their critique of West German politics and their alternative political vision; and negatively, in the sense that the Green political alternative in the mid-1980s centrally included the primary hierarchical axes of German statism—state and society—and reflexively transposed the respective normative values of that dichotomy, i.e., society became the realm of "genuine" politics and the state became the realm of illegitimate domination. This two-fold debt to Germany's ideological past was neither a permanent feature of Green politics, as is evident since the mid-1980s, nor something like a fundamental flaw in Green political ideology. It is perhaps best understood as a temporal stage in the protracted effort to transcend this two-centuries-old powerful and functional means of thinking about the proper organization of institutional political life in Germany and the role that ordinary citizens play in that. The Greens built on the student protests of the 1960s, the citizens' initiatives and anti-*Berufsverbot* campaigns of the 1970s, and the women's, environmental, and peace movements of the early 1980s. Throughout these "revolutionary" mobilizations of citizens in the Federal Republic, the struggle to articulate a concept of politics that, as Wolf-Dieter Narr suggested, was "not focused on the state, but rather on the interests of citizens," was evident.[58]

As has been argued throughout this book, such a task is terribly difficult, for it requires citizens not only to reject a familiar logic of membership that assigns roles and tasks to institutions and individuals in a political community, but also to replace that logic with another—important especially in the Federal Republic's highly "rationalistic" policy environment that demands a consistent *Konzept* prior to acting.[59] In the midst of the rejection of one such logic of political membership, it can appear that no clearly transcendent alternative is available and a return to the familiar, history-laden, yet increasingly inappropriate—in terms both of the complexity of the institutional context and the normative appraisal of the citizenry—political ideology retains considerable appeal. Logics of political membership are not the malleable and easily replaceable phenomena of which some rational-choice institutional theories suggest politics consists. Confronting German statism's long-standing tradition of viewing politics as an activity of experts located "above" ordinary citizens was a complicated historical process that involved borrowing categories and normative values from old traditions in the effort to articulate new alternatives. The protracted nature of the process of shedding an old and adopting a new logic of political membership can allow particular political events to reinvigorate old and familiar political discourses.

One such complex of events, during which it would appear, on the face of it, German statism would not be reinvigorated, was the utterly unexpected collapse of the Berlin Wall in 1989 and the unification of the two German states in 1990. Green activist Joschka Fischer mightily attempted to write an early and alternative Germany history of the events of the autumn of 1989: "For the first time since the bloody end of the 1848 revolution, the concept of 'the people' [*das Volk*] in German political discourse has a good and respectable sound. It sounds like democracy, freedom, and human rights, and not like nationalism, the authoritarian state, goose-stepping, and war."[60] Fischer's enthusiasm was shared by many. Here was the successful political revolution that Germany had never had. Here was Germany's chance to experience the historical process of winning democracy for itself and not only as imposed by defeat in world war. Here were proud East German citizens standing up to Communist state authorities to declare, "*Wir sind das Volk,*" or "we are the people." Here was the abrupt end of the German statist tradition, and the beginning of another, a tradition of robust German citizenship. Here was the participatory-democratic Greens' historical chance to help redefine the nature of German politics.

The political headiness of the autumn of 1989 and early spring of 1990 led some political actors, like Fischer, briefly to forget the power of the discursive political legacy of German statism in the Federal Republic.[61] As we shall now see, by March 1990, it was clear that the process of unifying the two German states did not spell the end of German statist political discourse. Indeed, the German statist logic of political membership was skillfully deployed by conservative party elites in the Federal Republic to create the dominant discursive context for German unification in October 1990. That context intentionally rejected discourse of popular revolution that both East and West German political activists, including Joschka Fischer, attempted to will into existence at the end of 1989. The Greens, instead of successfully redefining the discourse of German politics on the occasion of the collapse of East Germany, were utterly marginalized. In the first free united federal German election in December 1990, the Western German Greens, for the first time since they entered parliament in 1983, failed to surpass the 5 percent hurdle for representation in the Bundestag.

Notes

1. Suzanne Berger, "Politics and Anti-Politics in Western Europe in the Seventies," *Daedalus* 108, no. 2 (1979): 27–50; Herbert Kitschelt, *The Logics of Party Formation: Ecological Politics in Belgium and West Germany* (Ithaca: Cornell University Press, 1989), 75–97.
2. Alain Touraine, *The Voice and the Eye* (Cambridge: Cambridge University Press, 1981), chapter 1; see also Alberto Melucci, "The New Social Movements: A Theoretical Approach," *Social Science Information* 19, no. 2 (1980): 199–226; Jost Halfmann, "Soziale Bewegungen und Staat," *Soziale Welt*, 1984, no. 3:294–312.
3. Gabriel Almond and Sidney Verba, eds., *The Civic Culture Revisited* (Boston: Little, Brown, 1980).
4. Ronald Inglehart, *The Silent Revolution: Changing Styles among Western Publics* (Princeton: Princeton University Press, 1977); Ronald Inglehart, "New Perspectives on Political Change," *Comparative Political Studies* 17, no. 4 (1984): 485–532.
5. See Kitschelt, *The Logics of Party Formation*, 91, note 25.
6. Charles S. Maier, *The Unmasterable Past: History, Holocaust, and German National Identity* (Cambridge: Harvard University Press, 1988).
7. M. Rainer Lepsius, "Institutional Structures and Political Culture," in *Party Government and Political Culture in Western Germany*, ed. Herbert Döring and Gordon Smith (New York: St. Martin's Press, 1982), 116.

8. Kendall L. Baker, Russell J. Dalton, and Kai Hildebrandt, *Germany Transformed: Political Culture and the New Politics* (Cambridge: Harvard University Press, 1981), 136–59.

9. Jürgen Habermas, "Introduction," in *Observations on the "Spiritual Situation of the Age,"* ed. Habermas (Cambridge: The MIT Press, 1984), 10.

10. See Hans Mommsen, "The Burden of the Past," in *Observations*, ed. Habermas, 272; for a critical Green perspective on the "closing in" of the party after the May 1985 election, see Thomas Hoof and Martin Pannen, "Teile der Partei sind verliebt ins Getto," *Grüner Basis-Dienst*, 1985, no. 4: 18–20; and Lukas Beckmann, "Tendenzielle Gettoisierung," *Grüner Basis-Dienst*, 1985, no. 4: 21–22.

11. Kitschelt, *The Logics of Party Formation*, 9.

12. Wolf-Dieter Narr, "Andere Partei oder eine neue Form der Politik?" in *Die Grünen: Regierungspartner von Morgen?* ed. Jörg R. Mettke (Hamburg: Rowohlt Taschenbuch Verlag, 1982), 246.

13. Gerd Langguth, *Der Grüne Faktor: Von Bewegung zur Partei?* (Osnabrück: Verlag A. Fromm, 1984), 20.

14. Thomas Schmid and Ernst Hoplitschek, "Auf dem Weg zur Volkspartei: Ökolibertäre Thesen zur Entwicklung der Demokratie," in *SPD und Grüne: Das neue Bündnis?* ed. Wolfram Bickerich (Hamburg: Rowohlt Taschenbuch Verlag, 1985), 81.

15. See discussion above in Chapter Two.

16. Rudolf Bahro, "Hinein oder hinaus? Die Position der Fundamentalisten," in *SPD und Grüne*, ed. Bickerich, 67.

17. Fritjof Capra and Charlene Spretnak, *Green Politics: The Global Promise* (New York: E.P. Dutton, 1984), 160.

18. Kenneth H. F. Dyson, *The State Tradition in Western Europe: The Study of an Idea and an Institution* (New York: Oxford University Press, 1980), 51.

19. Bahro, "Hinein oder hinaus?" 56; Petra K. Kelly, "Keine sozialdemokratischen Inhalte mit grünem Anstrich," in *SPD und Grüne*, ed. Bickerich, 156; Jörg Mettke and Hans-Dieter Degler, "'Wir müssen die Etablierten entblössen wo wir können': *Spiegel*-Gespräch mit der Bundesvorsitzenden der Grünen, Petra K. Kelly," in *Die Grünen*, ed. Mettke, 32.

20. Ralf Dahrendorf, *Society and Democracy in Germany* (Garden City: Doubleday and Company, 1969), 131; see also Nevil Johnson, *State and Government in the Federal Republic of Germany: The Executive at Work*, 2nd ed. (Oxford: Pergamon Press, 1983), 19.

21. Langguth, *Der Grüne Faktor*, 29; Wilhelm P. Bürklin, "Greens: Ecology and the New Left," in *West German Politics in the Mid-Eighties: Crisis and Continuity*, ed. J. G. Peter Wallach and George K. Romoser (New York: Praeger Publishers, 1985), 204–06; Ferdinand Müller-Rommel, "Die Grünen in Lichte von neuesten Ergebnissen der Wahlforschung," in *Grüne Politik*, ed. Thomas Kluge (Frankfurt: Fischer Taschenbuch Verlag, 1984), 141.

22. "Document 1: Federal Programme, 1980, Preamble," in *The Greens in West Germany: Organisation and Policy Making*, ed. Eva Kolinsky (Oxford: Berg Publishers, 1989), 242.

23. Martin Jänicke, "Parlamentarische Entwarnungseffeckte? Zur Ortsbestimmung der Alternativbewegung," in *Die Grünen*, ed. Mettke, 81.

24. See "Die Niederlage traf uns nicht unvorbereitet: Stellungnahme des Landesvorstandes der Grünen Nordrhein-Westfalen," *Grüner Basis-Dienst*, 1985, no. 4:14–17.

25. Berger, "Politics and Anti-Politics in Western Europe," 27–50.
26. Narr, "Andere Partei oder eine neue Form," 261.
27. Dyson, *The State Tradition*, 207–08.
28. Langguth, *Der Grüne Faktor*, 56.
29. Capra and Spretnak, *Green Politics*, 16; Jörg Mettke, "'Auf beiden Flügeln in die Höhe': Grüne, Bunte und Alternative zwischen Parlament und Straße," in *Die Grünen*, ed. Mettke, 14.
30. Author interview with Antje Vollmer, Green member of the German Bundestag, 2 March 1988; author interview with Regula Bott, Green member of the German Bundestag, 4 March 1988.
31. Joschka Fischer, "Identität in Gefahr!" in *Grüne Politik*, ed. Kluge, 32.
32. Quoted in Langguth, *Der Grüne Faktor*, 82–83.
33. Friedhelm Hase, "Die Grünen im Rechtsstaat: Basis-, repräsentative und pluralistische Demokratie," in *Grüne Politik*, ed. Kluge, 145–48; Jänicke, "Paliamentarische Entwarnungseffeckte?" 77.
34. "Document 1: Federal Programme, 1980," 242.
35. Kurt Sontheimer, "Die Bundesrepublik aus dier Perspektive linker Theorie," *Aus Politik und Zeitgeschichte, Beilage zur Wochenzeitung Das Parlament*, 1976, no. 6: 10.
36. Jutta Ditfurth, "Radikal und phantasievoll gesellschaftliche Gegenmacht organisieren! Skizzen einer radikalökologischen Position," in *Grüne Politik*, ed. Kluge, 62–63.
37. Dieter Wellershoff, "Germany—A State of Flux," in *Observations*, ed. Habermas, 358.
38. Gerard Braunthal, *The West German Social Democrats: 1969–1982* (Boulder: Westview Press, 1983), 102–03, 191.
39. Fischer, "Identität in Gefahr!" 26–27.
40. Horst Mewes, "The West German Green Party," *New German Critique*, no. 28, (1983): 81.
41. Kelly, "Keine sozialdemokratischen Inhalte," 28.
42. Ditfurth, "Radikal und phantasievoll gesellschaftliche Gegenmacht organisieren!" 58, 65.
43. Mettke and Degler, "Wir müssen die Etablierten entblössen," 29–30; Thomas Schmid, "Plädoyer für einen reformistischen Anarchismus," in *Grüne Politik*, ed. Kluge, 76.
44. Johannes Rau, "Nährboden für rechtsauthoritäre Kräfte," in *Die Grünen*, ed. Mettke, 190–91.
45. "Urteil des Bundesverfassungsgerichts vom 23. Oktober 1956," in *Freiheitliche demokratische Grundordnung*, ed. Erhard Denninger (Frankfurt: Suhrkamp Verlag, 1977), 1: 114.
46. Eckart Bulla, "Die Lehre von der streitbaren Demokratie: Versuch einer kritischen Analyse unter besonderer Berücksichtigung der Rechtssprechung des Bundesverfassungsgerichts," *Archiv des öffentlichen Rechts*, no. 98, (1973): 341.
47. Peter Cornelius Mayer-Tasch, *Die Bürgerinitiativbewegung* (Reinbek bei Hamburg: Rowohlt Taschenbuch Verlag, 1976), 12–15.
48. Kurt Sontheimer, *The Government and Politics of West Germany* (London: Hutchinson University Library, 1972), 135, 144, 195.
49. Schmid and Hoplitschek, "Auf dem Weg zur Volkspartei," 83–84.
50. Hase, "Die Grünen im Rechtsstaat," 142–144; Fischer, "Identität in Gefahr!" 29; Ditfurth, "Radikal und phantasievoll gesellschaftliche Gegenmacht organisieren!" 65; see also Mommsen, "The Burden of the Past," 269.

51. Fischer, "Identität in Gefahr!" 29; Schmid and Hoplitschek, "Auf dem Weg zur Volkspartei," 86.

52. Ditfurth, "Radikal und phantasievoll gesellschaftliche Gegenmacht organ isieren!" 61–65.

53. Jänicke, "Parlamentarische Entwarnungseffekte?" 80; Karl Kerschgens, "Gratwanderung zwischen zwei Verlockungen," in *SPD und Grüne*, ed. Bickerich, 120.

54. Cited in Capra and Spretnak, *Green Politics*, 100–01; Schmid and Hoplitschek, "Auf dem Weg zur Volkspartei," 86.

55. Langguth, *Der grüne Faktor!* 23–24.

56. Fischer, "Identität in Gefahr," 32.

57. Narr, "Andere Partei oder eine neue Form," 269.

58. Ibid., 270.

59. Kenneth H. F. Dyson, "West Germany: The Search for a Rationalist Consensus," in *Policy Styles in Western Europe*, ed. Jeremy Richardson, (London: George Allen & Unwin, 1982), 17–46.

60. Quoted in Roger de Weck, "Im besten Sinne deutsch," *Die Zeit*, 1 December 1989.

61. This is not a reference to critics like Günter Grass, who warned of the dangers of German unification for the rest of the world in *Two States—One Nation?* (New York: Harcourt Brace Jovanovich, 1990).

Six

THE DISCOURSE OF
GERMAN UNIFICATION
Between Statist Reassurance and
Societalist Risk

B etween October and December of 1989, the Berlin Wall fell, a
popular mobilization of GDR citizens demanded German unification, the Communist regime in that state collapsed from within,
and the Federal Republic's *Deutschlandpolitik*, or inter-German
policy, was completely upended.[1] With these events, what had
been a basically consensual and consistent inter-German policy
practiced by successive West German governments for two decades became a much grittier inter-German politics fought out for
the most part on the West German party-political battlefield.[2] At
stake were the existential questions of postwar German politics:
how and when German unification? Because of the collapse of the
GDR and the federal election schedule in the Federal Republic,
that question came to be posed electorally—in both the East and
the West. Yet the East's first (and last) free and fair federal election,
held in March 1990, was primarily a Western party-political battle.
The heavy participation of West German party elites on GDR soil
and the election's outcome (75 percent support for FRG-oriented
parties) appreciably speeded up a unification process that many
observers, German and non-German, thought premature. These
events also determined that the December 1990 election for the
Federal Republic would be an "all-German" contest.

A frenzied agenda was thus set for West German party elites in early 1990. They were forced to mount a political campaign that addressed the task of unifying the two German states—a "work of the century," as one politician put it—but that also made sense to two very disparate electorates. To "form the political will" of the people at this time, as Article 21 of the Basic Law mandated for the Federal Republic's political parties, elites scrambled to find an "appropriate" political discourse for German unification that spoke to the political imaginations, if not to all of the stark realities, of the two German electorates. A period of near revolutionary crisis found Western German party elites "borrowing language," in Karl Marx's words, from the nineteenth-century German political ideology of statism.[3] This chapter will argue that Germany's traditional statist logic of political membership—though, as argued above, trampled on and battered by both deed and word in the Federal Republic since the 1960s—still resonated well enough to be analytically and normatively useful among modern German elites and citizens in this unanticipated, unprecedented, and, for German politics, existential context of state unification in 1989 and 1990.

This argument must be considered in light of the long and troubled history of the nineteenth-century state/society dichotomization of German politics. Briefly to recapitulate, that dichotomization was verticalized with an assignment of hortatory politics to the realm of the state, populated primarily by civil servants, and a lower or antipolitical identity assigned to society, populated by ordinary citizens and their "partial" political parties and interest organizations. The Federal Republic's institutional reception of this tradition, as we saw, was articulated in the positive construct of the Parteienstaat, or party-state (in contrast to the negative connotation attached to that construct in the Weimar Republic), that endeavored to transform the identity of political parties from lower societal actors of dubious political legitimacy to the commanding heights of state political authority. Hence the formal institutional role of political parties in the Federal Republic was founded on a reworking of this state/society vertical dichotomy. This book has thus far argued, however, that remnants of that dichotomization and the meanings attached to its terms continued to appear and resonate in the Federal Republic's political debate through the 1980s.[4] This chapter will further argue that the statist logic of political membership was not only present in the German unification debate of 1989 and 1990, but because of that debate's literally existential importance for German politics, the power of

German statism actually increased in intensity for West German political elites.

The Federal Republic's institutional arrangement marked a watershed with respect to Germany's traditional statist logic of political membership. Conscious efforts were made during the founding of the Republic to elevate the role of political parties to the commanding heights of political power. Developments in the 1950s and 1960s in West Germany seemed to secure a predominant role for these institutions that German statism had dismissed as particularistic, conflictual, and incapable of genuine politics. At the same time, the construction of a new institutional role did not automatically entail the destruction of the nineteenth-century logic of political membership that had been more or less appropriate for the German public for well over a century. Indeed, given the breadth and depth of the statist logic of political membership that had survived the Weimar Republic, it would be surprising if some of its features were not to survive the Federal Republic's institutional efforts to bury it. In the 1970s and 1980s, many observers found—and certainly not all critically—an assimilation of specifically "statist" elements into the activities and identities of West German parties in the country's extraordinarily successful Parteienstaat. West Germany's parties were "heirs to state norms," "institutional reference points of the state," and "bearers" of the German state; and that facilitated the "accommodation" of state and society and not their complete dissolution as relevant frames of reference.[5]

In other words, the Federal Republic's political parties had adopted identities and roles still informed by the statist tradition that the Basic Law's political-institutional arrangement had essentially rejected. Rejecting an institutional arrangement was not the same as rejecting every element of an extraordinarily rich, successful, and flexible political logic of membership. Political parties in the Federal Republic benefited from, and were partly consolidated in the postwar era by, linking themselves to a tradition of political discourse that was familiar to many constituencies and serviceable for both democratic reconstruction and democratic governance. It was to that traditional discourse that party elites turned, especially the CDU/CSU, when, in 1989 and 1990, the very meaning of "Federal Republic of Germany" was transforming. This chapter will argue that the vertical state/society segmentation of Germany's statist logic of political membership appeared as a powerful identifier for institutions and particular policies in the

German unification debate of 1989 and 1990. The vagaries of what Helmut Kohl called political "fortune" in this period forced elites frequently to respond in an ad hoc but not random manner to the political challenges appearing before them. Those elites frequently improvised and relied on what seemed an "appropriate" political discourse instead of detailed party programs crafted over the years. That entailed falling back on familiar, though not simply deployed, political categories and normative positions that almost two centuries of German political discourse had bequeathed.

The Unification Debate

Despite the deep convulsions occurring in the GDR in the early autumn of 1989, the Federal Republic's political parties were clearly shocked by the fall of the Berlin Wall on that infamous date in German history, 9 November. The Social Democrat Willy Brandt stated that things would never again be as they had been, and he called for caution. The party leadership of the CDU/CSU, F.D.P., and SPD all similarly warned against the party-politicization of the "historical developments" in the GDR.[6] This "above-party" consensus lasted only until Helmut Kohl made his first foray as an "all-German statesman" on 27 November, with his ten-point plan for a new Deutschlandpolitik. While some observers impatiently wondered when Kohl would respond to the developments in the GDR, the announcement of his plan not only belied his reactive image but also inspired concern that he wanted to direct events according to his own personal and party agenda. SPD leader Hans-Jochen Vogel and parliamentarian Karsten Voigt nonetheless immediately praised Kohl's initiative, which included a call for a "federation" of the two states and ultimately "unity," as largely consistent with their own party's views. The CDU/CSU welcomed this Social Democratic support, but warned the SPD, particularly its likely chancellor candidate for the upcoming election, Oskar Lafontaine, to avoid "polemics" in this delicate context.[7]

A party-political critique of Kohl's plan nonetheless erupted the next day from all corners. The Greens rejected the plan outright, hoping for a "third way" for the GDR—consistent with Joschka Fischer's early version of the events in East Germany as constituting, finally, a genuine revolution on German soil. The leader of the F.D.P., the federal coalition partner with the CDU/CSU, complained bitterly that neither his party nor Hans-Dietrich

Genscher, the F.D.P. foreign minister, had even been consulted prior to Kohl's speech. The SPD parliamentary party, in turn, rebuffed the initial praise of Vogel, and Voigt and refused to support Kohl's ten points. In this flurry of response, the opposition in the Federal Republic did raise some substantive issues, like Kohl not mentioning the Polish border question; but much of the SPD's concern had more to do with process and party profile. As one SPD parliamentarian asked, "where is our own Deutschlandpolitik signature?"[8] In this first post-Wall party skirmish, Kohl thus appeared as a classic statist political actor taking the initiative, rising above and bypassing parliament, and warning of party polemics interfering with statesmanship. The SPD, in contrast, initially acknowledged the statist value of avoiding party politics, confirmed by its leaders' support for Kohl's plan, but then immediately launched an attack less about substance than about procedure and the need to differentiate party profile. Subsequently joined by internal party bickering and uncoordinated attacks on the government's plan, the SPD's response essentially followed the script for a party located in the pejorative societal realm of Germany's statist logic of political membership.

By December, internal party conflict in the SPD intensified as some in the party were criticized for supporting Kohl's plan. Oskar Lafontaine took up the party's critique and dismissed Kohl's policy as a "major diplomatic failure" that would create mistrust in the GDR, in Europe, in the United States, and in the Soviet Union; that would endanger the GDR's economy; and that would exacerbate social tensions in the Federal Republic.[9] Whether or not Lafontaine may have been correct in some of his concerns, the point here is that Lafontaine's stance on unification from the very beginning, including the discourse he used to articulate it, fitted in to a statist logic of political membership that located him—and much of his party—in a "societal" realm that many Germans regarded as the wrong location for such a monumental task. Lafontaine's nearly indefatigable pessimism about virtually every aspect of the unification process noted obstacles and dangers at every turn. He insisted on addressing only what he called "practical" societal problems like costs, housing, economic collapse, and taxes. Lafontaine even argued in early December (unconvincingly to his own party) that "the [East German] people should stay over there." Digging up an obscure law from 1950, he suggested making it illegal for GDR citizens to enter the Federal Republic unless they had previously secured employment and housing.[10] Following the statist script, the CDU/CSU, in contrast, rejected what it called Lafontaine's "party-political complaints and know-it-all attitude" that did not appreciate the more important—and universalistic—needs of freedom and human dignity of the GDR citizenry.[11] The CDU/ CSU could not realistically have asked for a better opponent to highlight their own statist "moral sense of mission" and "high-minded view of politics" than Lafontaine. The conservatives presented him as a "populist" irresponsibly pandering to the economic self-interests of West German citizens, thus improperly casting the unification debate on a "lower" discursive plane than where they believed it belonged.[12]

Lafontaine's message was rooted, however, in the SPD's anti-statist political ideology of the early 1970s, when Willy Brandt promised an agenda of domestic political reform with "more democracy" and more citizen participation—in short, more "society" and less "state" in the discourse of traditional German statism. The anti-statist strain in West German politics in the 1970s, still tied negatively to German statism, was considerably enhanced, as we saw in the previous chapter, when the Greens appeared in the Federal Republic in the early 1980s. Similarly, in the unification debate, Lafontaine eschewed talk of "nation" and "state" and instead focused on "society's" concerns in both Germanys: jobs, housing, social security, taxes, social justice, equity, the rights of women, and environmental protection. Lafontaine saw the statism that was rejected by two decades of SPD ideology and by the Green alternative in the Federal Republic as clearly and problematically located in the CDU/CSU: in Kohl's "go-it-alone" approach at home and abroad, in the CDU/CSU's flirtation with nationalism and its prevarication on the Polish border question, and, generally, in the heady idealism attending many of the CDU/CSU's early Deutschlandpolitik pronouncements. At the SPD's party program convention in December 1989, which was moved to Berlin at the last minute, Lafontaine argued, "we have never understood the idea of unity as an abstract idea of the state, but rather as a coming together and working together of the people."[13]

Unfortunately for the SPD in this debate, its "societalist" message on unification was joined in December by a quite visible internal party bickering over appropriate policy, and that was also consistent with the traditional German statist identity of political parties as fractious agents of narrow particularism. This was joined, through the end of the year, by the SPD's dispirited campaign to convince Helmut Kohl to allow the Social Democrats to participate in the formulation of unification policy. By then, Vogel had turned his initial praise for Kohl's plan into pathos-laden complaints about the chancellor's "distance" and "rejection" of SPD overtures. Though the Social Democrats tried to charge Kohl with "dilettantism," an epithet that had stuck in the past, the SPD as the party of the "new Ostpolitik" twenty years earlier now found itself lacking a unified position and, apparently, an organizing concept, for a Deutschlandpolitik over which it had no appreciable influence.[14] The SPD was unwillingly and unwittingly resembling the party that nineteenth-century German statism had warned against.

Against this backdrop, the CDU/CSU had little difficulty representing itself "above" party conflict and particularism. Kohl's ten points were quickly made irrelevant by developments in the GDR, but they nonetheless created a "patriotic aura" around him. His go-it-alone strategy vis-à-vis foreign allies was welcomed by CDU parliamentary leader Alfred Dregger, who thanked Kohl for first informing "the elected representatives of the German people" of his plan; and Kohl's role as "visionary" national statesman had not (yet, at least) raised the taboo specter of German expansionism.[15] Indeed, the Greens' charge of "nationalist rumblings" within the CDU did not stick. Kohl's patriotism in this debate rejected what Kohl himself called the "crude slogans of the local bar," and endorsed "acts of human assistance for our countrymen."[16] Kohl's deeds may have been few in this period, but what he did he enveloped in a political discourse that was deeply familiar and subjectively "appropriate" for millions of Germans who remained willing to see unification in 1990 as a project for a German statesman "above" political parties who acted on ideal and moral imperatives and not concerns about material welfare.

By January 1990, internal party conflict within the SPD had died down somewhat and the party had agreed to support the goal of German unification, though the CDU continued to mock the SPD with comments like "with Willy Brandt and Oskar Lafontaine for and against German unity."[17] Kohl also made sure that SPD support for unification opened the gate neither for policy participation nor for receiving much information about its formulation. The SPD, in its desire to participate in talks about future FRG-GDR relations, remained in the uncomfortable position of repeatedly appealing to and being ignored by Kohl. Egon Bahr lashed out at Kohl's go-it-alone approach as "deeply unwise and contradictory to the style of our democracy" and contrasted it with the SPD's effort to inform Rainer Barzel, CDU head during Brandt's tenure, of the Brandt government's Ostpolitik.[18] Kohl's approach, however, was consistent with and benefited from a lingering statist logic of political appropriateness. In this context, Kohl's refusal to collaborate with other political parties was not a liability, and Vogel's repeated demands for the formation of a parliamentary committee to plan the unification process could too easily be framed as the meddling of a particularistic "societal" actor unable and/or unwilling to appreciate the universalistic dimensions of the task.

As the March 1990 election in the GDR approached, Willy Brandt pleaded not to foist the "bad habits" and "indecencies" of the Federal Republic's electioneering onto the "electorally virgin" GDR. Defamatory rhetoric nonetheless flowed from all corners as the Federal Republic's political parties virtually flooded the electoral landscape of the GDR.[19] The Union parties accused the SPD of being "socialistic," politically "unreliable," using scare tactics to attract GDR voters, and paying only lip service to the goal of German unification. It dismissed distinctions between the SPD's "democratic socialism" and what failed in the GDR as mere "words of intellectuals."[20] Lafontaine was called a "Deutschlandpolitik deserter" of the "German fatherland" who "once more left Germans in the lurch" as he vacationed in "southern regions" (referring to Lafontaine's vacation in Tyrol). Vicious images of Willy Brandt's role in the underground during the Second World War, cultivated by the CDU in the 1960s, were thereby resuscitated. Brandt's own image, however, had shifted by this time and become much more benign within the CDU/CSU. But that was not to be allowed to benefit the SPD. The Union parties instead located the traditional German state/society dichotomy right within the SPD in an effort to characterize the party as riven with contradiction: "Here Willy Brandt for the German soul; there Oskar Lafontaine for the Federal German stomach."[21]

For its part, the SPD attacked Kohl for treating unification as though it were his "private affair" and likened the Federal Republic's experience with the policy so far as "sailing in stormy waters on the chancellor's private yacht." It also claimed that the CDU was hiding the real costs of unification from voters, especially West Germans. The image of Kohl the independent statesman was thereby recast by the SPD to Kohl the private man, in society, keeping secrets about finances from the German public.[22] At the same time, the SPD's continual stress on the high costs of unification was framed by the CDU/CSU as "cynical," materialistic, and the product of party minds unable to appreciate the universalistic values of national unity and political freedom. Kohl stated, "In such a situation, more is at stake than economics. Everyone must rather provide a clear and unequivocal signal of hope and encouragement to the people of the GDR."[23] This rejection of the "practical" did not, however, render Kohl vulnerable on the national question.

As one observer wrote, "Kohl made space for the German national idea. At the same time he has fused that to a harmless patriotism à la Kohl, to a new German movement without corners and edges which now works to his benefit."[24] In early March, however, the Poland border question allowed Kohl's critics briefly to turn the tables on the chancellor, and the SPD hammered on Kohl's "absurd talk" about "*Mitteldeutschland*" and his questioning of the eastern borders of the future united Germany. However painful for many to endure, Kohl momentarily appears to have neutralized the far right with his prevarication on this issue, and he probably relented early enough not to cause lasting damage. No matter how the SPD tried—with considerable justification—to make this international scandal a liability for the CDU, criticism of Kohl's "absurd talk" did not resonate broadly with the German public. Instead, the Social Democrats at this time suffered more from their own dire warnings in the spring of 1990 of the "coming hard times in the Federal Republic and the GDR," burdensome new taxes, and the need to scrap the Basic Law for an entirely new constitution. In March, Lafontaine seemed not only to reject unification, he also led a party that appeared mired in a "societal" realm where Germany's problems could only be experienced, but not fixed. For the East German election scheduled for 18 March, this was not an easy message to sell, particularly as the CDU/CSU was trumpeting the "security" and "reliability" of the "*Königsweg*," or "royal path"—itself suggestive statist imagery—of newly formed East German Länder acceding to the already wealthy, intact, and liberal-democratic Federal Republic via Article 23 of the Basic Law.[25]

The route to German unification became the defining issue of the March GDR election campaign, and it pitted an arguably "statist" proposal against a "societalist" one. Article 23 of the constitution, supported by the CDU/CSU and the F.D.P., left the Basic Law intact and created five new Länder by means of parliamentary accession. Article 146, supported by the SPD and the Greens, called for a constituent assembly, a new draft constitution, and a ratification by the entire German citizenry. Article 23 called for action by existing Parteienstaat elites, while Article 146 invited the direct sovereign participation of ordinary citizens in the founding of a new German constitutional order. The massive victory of the CDU/ CSU-affiliated "Alliance for Germany" in the GDR on 18 March was a de facto victory for Article 23 and Kohl's policy, represented as the quickest, elite-led, most predictable route to German state unification. The CDU/CSU was considerably emboldened by the unforeseen election victory; the SPD was surprised and dejected, but Oskar Lafontaine was not deterred. In late March, he once more derided Kohl for treating unification as his own private "toy" and then again stressed the economic and social dangers of the unification process. He reiterated that unification was "not primarily a national-state" phenomenon, but rather concerned the "well-being of the people," the "unification of society," and "social justice."[26] Indeed it did, but at stake were also ideas about freedom, self-determination, and national unity. Lafontaine's fear of statist imagery, and Kohl's easy embrace of it, not only led to two very different party messages on German unification, but also to the relative electoral benefit of the CDU/CSU in 1990.

In April, the SPD was still locked out of any meaningful unification policy role, and the party complained of not even receiving information about the government's aims. The party continued to criticize Kohl's "one-man-show," calling it a holdover from a nineteenth-century *Kabinettspolitik*, or royal court politics, and argued that parliament had not been adequately informed about the forthcoming monetary, economic, and social union scheduled for July, or about the true costs of unification.[27] The CDU/CSU met this charge not by denying it, but by arguing that "elements and certain parts of the [first state] treaty should not now be debated in public." While secrecy may have been justified by the treaty's currency conversion ratios, the CDU/CSU's response nicely reproduced the state/society dichotomy of Germany's traditional logic of political membership: CDU/CSU state actors made policy in a realm above a bickering societal SPD stuck in parliament. The SPD's Jochen Vogel contributed to this spatial imagery by complaining that the chancellor was quickening the speed of unification "over the heads of the people in both German states."[28] While the SPD could perhaps have counted in other periods on this striking a critical chord with large parts of the German public, it seems not to have resonated very broadly in this debate.

By May, however, the SPD's electoral victory in Lower Saxony changed the party constellation of the Bundesrat, the federal upper house of parliament; and that meant the SPD could no longer be ignored by the Kohl government. The CDU/CSU finally allowed the creation of a parliamentary committee called "German Unity," which the SPD had been demanding since November 1989. The SPD was grateful for the chance to participate, but the government's new dependence on the SPD-controlled Bundesrat did not prevent the Union parties from characterizing the Social Democrats' positions in this period as imbued with "untenable, unspeakable, and pure party-political polemics" that created "unrest," "chaos," and "fear." CDU parliamentary leader, Volker Rühe, acknowledged that the SPD "now carries more responsibility … for constructive cooperation in this historical phase of German politics," but he warned, "now is not the time for tactical games!"[29] In response, the SPD rather sheepishly stated that it would not use its majority in the Bundesrat to block government policy, and the party announced, "we want to cooperate."[30] At the end of May, however, Klaus von Dohnanyi, an SPD Executive Board member, openly criticized his party's chancellor candidate and berated the SPD for the "unclarity of its positions that undeniably made difficult any common action with the chancellor."[31] The SPD's "societalism," in other words, was not merely a structural function of the party's confinement to parliament. The party under Lafontaine had difficulty regarding the project of German unification as having much symbolic or ideational value at all.

In the summer of 1990, the CDU/CSU continued to portray itself as "the party of German unity," the party of "German patriots and Europeans," and the "party of national consensus" that had, "from the beginning, acted dutifully and conscientiously." The CDU/CSU contrasted this universalistic statist self-identification with what they saw as the SPD's lower societalist "politics of pure opportunism," "egoism," "strategy of highlighting only the risk of failure," "incapability of accepting national responsibility," and inability to view unification "also as a question of the heart as well as the mind." CDU leader Volker Rühe concluded that the SPD had no "concept" for unification, and—consistent with the Federal Republic's statist-inspired highly rationalistic policy style—"one who has no concept cannot discuss the major questions of our time."[32] The SPD tried to counter this by noting that their party's support for unification was not a question of "whether" but "how," and that it would decide in a "timely" manner (within three weeks) on how to vote on the economic and monetary union treaty in parliament. But even as the SPD tried to redefine its image as a unification player, Lafontaine continued to remind both East and West Germans to ask the questions, "what about my apartment?" and "what about my job?" Lafontaine once more differentiated what he saw as Kohl's understanding of German unification as a project of "state unity" from his own understanding of the "unity of living standards."[33] Kohl's preference for statist universalistic imagery to identify his and his party's project of German unification was well accommodated by Lafontaine's own preference for a societalist imagery of distribution and self-interest.

As the December 1990 federal election approached, Social Democrats portrayed Helmut Kohl as an "arrogant" dilettante whose go-it-alone strategy and rejection of what they now referred to as an "above-party cooperation" had "divided the nation" and produced unnecessary hardship for all German citizens. The SPD mounted this attack from its slightly more visible position as a participant in the "German Unity" parliamentary committee that was discussing the second state unification treaty. That participation gave the SPD greater opportunity to trumpet its "societalist" concerns about unemployment, environmental degradation, social tensions, infrastructural decay, pensions, and "two societies with different wages, pensions, and social services" under "one state." Lafontaine even called for that "one state," which had not yet been unified, to be superseded. Two weeks before unification, he argued that the "national-state" idea was an anachronism and that the unified German state should be seen as "provisional."[34] In light of developments in the European Union, Lafontaine's comments no doubt had some validity, but their timing was of questionable appropriateness for a political community that was about to be at least formally reunited after forty tragic years of division.

The CDU/CSU, in contrast, announced in early September that the "work of the century," the two unification treaties that it had produced with only minor SPD input at the end, had won the support of over 90 percent of the Bundestag and unanimous support in the Bundesrat. Wolfgang Schäuble, CDU Interior Minister who was most responsible for the treaties, rebutted the SPD's concerns in the Bundestag with the statement that German unification in 1990 was "not a question of costs," but of "investment in the common future of our fatherland."[35] Though "fatherland" rolled off Union lips rather easily, this language suggested not the darkness of an expansionistic nationalism but rather positive statist values like common purpose, collaboration, and the public interest. As 3 October approached, Kohl in any case kept his fuzzy nationalism from acquiring sharper edges by suggesting that true "patriotism" was European and conciliatory and "had as little to do with nationalistic egoism as national forgetfulness."[36] German patriotism in 1990 was portrayed by the CDU as a hortatory, statist, and universalistic nationalism accommodating even of European integration, not one mired in societalist "egoism" or subversive agendas to forget the past horrors of Nazism.

On the day before German unification, on 2 October 1990, the statist logic of political membership that had so profoundly informed this debate—but typically by creating implicit discursive boundaries and not by suggesting the debate's actual words—was explicitly invoked by both the Christian Democrats and the Social Democrats. A press service linked to the SPD critically wrote, "The spirit of Kohl sways above Germany ... [above] worries and fears of people in the GDR.... It is almost as though the world-spirit has descended to earth in the person of the chancellor."[37] On television that day, Helmut Kohl accommodated the SPD's imagery: "the political idea of the state as such is not evil, only equating it with the absolute truth is [as had occurred in the GDR]." Twenty minutes before midnight, Kohl also reassured all Germans that within five years the economic problems of the GDR that the SPD had so emphasized in this debate would be solved.[38] On the question of the actual costs of German unification, neither Kohl's possible ignorance or deception, nor Lafontaine's possible prescience or uninformed pessimism, was the issue for this argument. It was, rather, that each actor and their respective political parties adopted political roles and discourses that were perfectly consistent with Germany's traditional statist logic of political membership. Each actor believed that his role was not only preferable to the other, but also that it resonated more deeply with the German public in 1989 and 1990.

Kohl attached himself and the CDU/CSU to the traditional German idea of a state above and responsibly acting for society in a manner that embodied the public interest. That could be caricatured but not demolished by the SPD as it attempted to link Kohl and his party to a discreditable (and itself caricatured) Hegelian "world-spirit" incarnate. Lafontaine, in contrast, complained on television forty minutes before midnight that unification had gone too quickly, though he was reassured—and thought the German public would similarly be reassured—that the unified German state was, in any case, only a "transitional institution" (*Übergang*) to a united states of Europe.[39] On 3 October, while others celebrated

German unity, Lafontaine explained once more that the "concept of unity" held by the CDU/CSU and F.D.P. "was too strongly fixated on state unity and therefore overlooked what happened in society."[40] Lafontaine thus attached himself and his party to a revisionist hortatory definition of German society—one that had been articulated by parts of the SPD since the late 1960s and more fully by the Greens in the 1980s. Unlike the German society's traditional nineteenth-century identity as conflictual, particularistic, and incapable of producing a genuine political will, it had now become, according to this revised definition, the realm of genuine politics inhabited by legitimately political German citizens.

The role of the German citizen in the unification debate was, however, somewhat more complicated than that suggested by the attachments of the CDU/CSU to a still viable German statism, and the attachments of the SPD to a revisionist, and, since the 1960s, invigorated "societalism." Helmut Kohl's statism could not simply denigrate the German citizen, in either the West or the East, to the nineteenth-century role of a dangerous antipolitical actor requiring containment by a strong bureaucratic state. Preventing Kohl and his party from unproblematically articulating such a negative view of the German citizen—had they wanted to in the first place—were a number of institutional and political-cultural realities in West and East Germany. First, the political-institutional arrangement of the Federal Republic, according to Article 20 of the Basic Law, located the source of political power ultimately in a citizenry mediated by political parties. Second, the attitudinal "revolution" of the West German citizenry in the 1960s and 1970s had created a "Germany transformed" by a "new politics" of empowerment and participation. Third, and most important here, the events that occurred on the streets of the GDR in the autumn of 1989 seemed to belie, as Fischer had suggested, the historically negative image of the German "Volk." Indeed, in the course of the Federal Republic's party-political debate over unification in 1989 and 1990, a revised image of the German citizen, breaking with the tradition of viewing "the people" as dangerous and ultimately antipolitical actors, appeared briefly, unevenly, and in a complicated manner.

The "colonization" of the East German political landscape by West German political parties in the run-up to the March 1990 election in the GDR is indisputable.[41] The most important issue driving that election was the path to unification. As noted above, the CDU/CSU and F.D.P. supported the route of Article 23, which mandated the accession of reconstituted East German Länder to the existing Federal Republic; while Article 146, supported by the SPD and the Greens, offered a reconstitution of the Federal Republic itself, scrapping the Basic Law, a new constituent assembly, and the popular ratification of a democratic German constitution. The first route was preservative of the "provisional" Federal Republic; the second route was creative of a new expressly legitimated German democratic constitutional order. According to the old statist logic of political membership, the first would be consistent with a statist reliance on political expertise "from above," while the second would dangerously empower ordinary German citizens to construct a political order "from below." Though the spring election in the GDR was to create the first legitimate government in East German history, the Western CDU treated the election as a referendum on the substantive value of the Federal Republic and its institutions—not only as Germany's "best" regime ever, but as a model parliamentary democracy for the rest of the world. On 8 March, Helmut Kohl argued that the Basic Law was the "best constitution in the history of the Germans ... [and one] that has made us a respected member of the community of nation-states, and Germans in the GDR know that as well." Kohl's colleague Volker Rühe argued that the choice of the CDU-backed "Alliance for Germany" in the election meant a choice for Article 23, which would bring the East German citizenry a "constitutional and legal political, economic, and social order that is a model for the world."[42] At stake in this election, then, were regimes and international political respect, not just party platforms.

A resounding electoral triumph for the CDU-backed Alliance for Germany (48 percent of the vote, as opposed to 22 percent for the SPD) was taken by all to mean victory for Article 23 as the route of unification. That electoral outcome, in turn, was taken to mean a popular legitimation of the Federal Republic and its institutions. The impressive level of participation in this East German electoral contest (93 percent turnout) that was dominated by West German party organizations appeared to ratify the West German Parteienstaat. The implicit endorsement of the West German Parteienstaat by East German voters helped, symbolically, to transform the Bonn Republic from a provisional postwar accommodation into an internationally respectable model political regime. For Kohl and many other West German politicians, the spring election in the GDR had less to do with the German Mark and consumption, or even with the chance for East German citizens freely to create their own government, than with the virtues of the Federal Republic's political system, undiluted by any of the changes that Article 146 might have wrought. The election's outcome could be read as providing a popular legitimation of the Bonn Republic that, given the context of the Federal Republic's founding, West German citizens had never been asked, or able, to supply.

As noted above, the West German Green leader, Joschka Fischer, posited in November 1989 the image of the East German citizen as a revolutionary hero rising up and successfully toppling an illegitimate, authoritarian, and repressive regime. But even Fischer wanted to appropriate this image for German history and not merely for the GDR: "the [word] 'people' in German political discourse," he argued, "has a good and respectable sound … like democracy, freedom, and human rights, and not like nationalism, authoritarian state, goose-stepping, and war."[43] In the autumn of 1989, West German Greens and other leftists in both the Federal Republic and East Germany encouraged "revolutionary" East German citizens to build democracy in the GDR "from below." Some in the East, like activist Bärbel Bohley, preferred that the Wall remain in order to facilitate an orderly construction of a genuine socialism. She complained after the Wall fell on 9 November, "The [East German] people are crazy, and the [East German] government has lost its mind."[44] Other West German parties in this period, however, particularly the CDU, spoke only very cautiously of "political developments" in the East that would lead ultimately to "self-determination." For the CDU/CSU prior to the GDR's March election, any discussion of revolutionary citizens rising up to throw off an illegitimate regime, even in East Germany, could be argued as giving voice to Article 146 as the path to German unification—not the "*Königsweg*" of Article 23, as Kohl called it, but rather the revolutionary citizens' path of a new constituent assembly and a new constitutional order.

Yet after the March election results in the GDR demonstrated that the East German citizenry would not follow Fischer's, let alone Bohley's, script of regime construction "from below," Western German political elites from across the party landscape, including the CDU/CSU, began to describe just how "revolutionary" the East German citizens had been in the autumn of 1989. This was now allowed by the end of March because it was clear that the West German Parteienstaat had performed in East Germany what the Basic Law had mandated it to do for the Federal Republic: to "form the political will of the people" and thereby undercut the plebiscitary excesses (and dangers of German citizens acting as sovereign political actors) widely regarded in the Federal Republic as having helped to doom the Weimar Republic. By that time, the "revolutionary" GDR and the "revolutionary" East German citizenry could safely be celebrated by the Federal Republic's Parteienstaat elites as historical phenomena that posed no future challenges to the Federal Republic's institutionalized political order.

Bundestag president Rita Süssmuth, for example, pointedly referred to the peaceful, nonviolent "revolution" in the GDR as a successful "test of democratic maturity," evidently referring to the "maturity" of German, and not only GDR, citizens. Helmut Kohl similarly asserted after the election that the GDR population had "overthrown" a dictatorship.[45] As the October unification approached, the imagery of German citizen as heroic actor appeared with ever-greater frequency. The SPD thanked the "people in the GDR who began the unification process with a peaceful revolution," while the CDU's Wolfgang Schäuble, the architect of the unification treaties, lauded the "first peaceful revolution on German territory."[46] But the most stirring tribute to the new German citizen was provided by West German foreign minister, Hans-Dietrich Genscher, in an open letter: "This was the first successful emancipatory revolution in our history. It was a peaceful revolution, which gave it particular historical value. It not only brought freedom to 17 million people; it brought all Germans unity and the respect of the world ... In these months our people have demonstrated their political maturity. Levelheaded responsibility determined our actions, not nationalistic exuberance. The world has answered with respect and high regard."[47]

In other words, developments in the GDR allowed a revisionist image of the German citizen at least to appear, if not take root, as an *historical* freedom fighter able to bring down an authoritarian and illegitimate regime from below, but not, at the same time, to threaten the institutional status quo of the Federal Republic. This image challenged German statism's derogatory image of the citizen, but not in the open-ended activist manner of the SPD in the 1960s and 1970s, or of the Greens in the 1980s. The revised image of the German citizen as heroic and revolutionary was immediately historicized and consigned to the GDR—a German regime that was about to disappear. The imagery suggested a German citizen who had undergone a political maturation process that had culminated in 1989 and was now to function within the political institutions of the Federal Republic that had been freely chosen—and thereby legitimized—by the East German citizenry in the March election. As an historical figure, the participatory revolutionary German citizen thus did not threaten the Federal Republic's political institutional framework. West Germany's Parteienstaat, in fact, was now even more securely in the saddle than ever—it had been popularly legitimized by the East Germans' choice in their first free election, or so West German political elites could believe.

Conclusion

The statist logic of political membership that consolidated in early nineteenth-century German political discourse survived in the Federal Republic intact enough to allow political party elites in the Federal Republic to deploy it, in a complicated and sometimes contradictory manner, to frame issues and positions during the unification debate of 1989 and 1990. While not the only discursive tool available to political actors during the unification debate, Germany's traditional statist logic, with its contested terms and normative values, lent itself particularly well to the efforts of the two major parties, the CDU/CSU and the SPD, to articulate their positions on this literally existential question of German politics. In the process, these political actors embodied the somewhat ambivalent identities of postwar German catch-all parties in the postwar German Parteienstaat. The parties neither functioned entirely within, nor contributed to a discourse that defined, "state" and "society" as hermetically sealed spatial realms that could not be bridged, as Hegel and traditional German political ideology suggested; nor did they regard "state" and "society" and their attendant institutions and values completely meaningless as the result of German democratization, as some modern observers of German politics had asserted.

Instead, the statist logic of political membership was useful to the Federal Republic's political parties for intensifying programmatic distinctions between them and their opponents, particular in this totally unforeseen political context. It made party positions not just horizontally differentiable on a left-right scale, but also vertically distinguishable according to "statist" and "societalist" spatial characteristics, though in a contested manner: "state" connoted (mainly to the CDU/CSU) the public good, consensus, and rational problem solving, but also (mainly to the SPD) anti-democratic idealism that failed to comprehend the concrete needs of real citizens; "society" connoted (mainly to the SPD) practical concerns of ordinary people, citizen participation, and self government, but also (mainly to the CDU/CSU) conflictual self- and partial-interest maximization. The identity of the German citizen in this debate was even more complicated, as we saw. The "statist" unreliable citizen was exchanged for the "societalist" participatory citizen over the course of the unification debate even by the CDU/CSU and F.D.P., but only after the societalist participatory citizen was consigned to an historical, if only very recently historical, location (the GDR) to which a backwards but not forward reference could be made.

To an outsider, particularly one steeped in the Anglo-American liberal tradition, these nearly acrobatic deployments of the categories and values of this statist logic of appropriateness appear much more complicated than they did to the political actors using them. Lacking detailed plans for responding specifically to the events that suddenly upended German politics-as-usual in November 1989, West Germany's political parties and their constituents turned to this old, familiar, and latently appropriate statist ideological inheritance in the attempt to make sense of, and issue policy alternatives for, the complicated events that engulfed them. Though, as we saw, the statist logic of appropriateness was battered in the Federal Republic by an only partly congenial political-institutional framework—and in the late-1960s through the 1980s more seriously by an oppositional and sometimes directly challenging anti-statist political discourse—the German statist logic of political membership had nonetheless survived to be put to work during the German unification debate of 1989 and 1990. This survival did not amount to a full resuscitation of a largely discredited nineteenth-century political ideology, but it did indicate that reports in the late 1980s of statism's complete demise in Germany were exaggerated.

Notes

1. Though many volumes have appeared on various aspects of the German unification process, the best English-language (now translated into German) descriptive account remains Konrad Jarausch, *The Rush to German Unity* (New York: Oxford University Press, 1994). For an English-language account of the East German perspective on the events of the autumn of 1989, see Dirk Philipsen, *We Were the People: Voices from East Germany's Revolutionary Autumn of 1989* (Durham: Duke University Press, 1993).
2. See A. James McAdams, "Revisiting *Ostpolitik* in the 1990s," *German Politics and Society*, no. 30, (1993): 49–60.
3. Karl Marx, "The Eighteenth Brumaire of Louis Bonaparte," in Karl Marx and Friedrich Engels, *Selected Works* (Moscow: Progress Publishers, 1973) 1: 398.
4. Heinrich Oberreuter, "Politische Parteien: Stellung und Funktion im Verfassungssystem der Bundesrepublik," in *Parteien in der Bundesrepublik Deutschland*, ed. Oberreuter and Alf Mintzel (Munich: Olzog Verlag, 1990), 15–16; Klaus von Beyme, *Das politische System der Bundesrepublik Deutschland nach der Vereinigung* (Munich: Piper Verlag, 1991), 138–52.
5. Kenneth Dyson, "Party Government and Party State," in *Party Government and Political Culture*, ed. Döring and Smith, 88–90; Nevil Johnson, "Parties and the Conditions of Political Leadership," in *Party Government and Political Culture*, ed. Döring and Smith, 160.
6. *BPA-Nachrichtenabt.*, Ref. II 5, 11 November 1989, Brandt, 1110–16; *CDU/CSU Fraktion im Deutschen Bundestag*, Pressedienst, 14 November 1989; *DPA*, no. 776, 28 November 1989.
7. *CDU/CSU Fraktion im Deutschen Bundestag*, Pressedienst, 28 November 1989.
8. *Die Grünen im Bundestag*, Pressedienst, no. 998, 30 November 1989; *BPA-Nachrichtenabt.*, Ref. II 5, 30 November 1989, Lambsdorff, 1130–33; "Die SPD auf der Suche nach der verlorenen Handschrift," *Frankfurter Rundschau*, 30 November 1989.
9. "Die SPD wurde von Kohl 'kalt erwischt,'" *Stuttgarter Nachrichten*, 1 December 1989; *Presseservice der SPD*, no. 745, 3 December 1989.
10. "Die deutsche Einheit entzweit die SPD," *Stuttgarter Nachrichten*, 9 December 1989; "SPD will baldige 'Konföderation' als Vorstufe einer Einigung," *Frankfurter Allgemeine Zeitung*, 12 December 1989.
11. *Pressemitteilung der CDU*, 4 December 1989.
12. "Das Bonner Spiel um die Volksseele," *Süddeutsche Zeitung*, 6 December 1989.
13. *Protokoll vom Programm-Parteitag Berlin 18.-20.12.1989* (Bonn, 1989).
14. "Farthmann: Die SPD ist in die Defensive geraten," *Westfälische Rundschau*, 6 December 1989; "Das Bonner Spiel um die Volksseele," *Süddeutsche Zeitung*, 6 December 1989; "Vom Bundeskanzler kamen nur Signale der Ablehnung," *General-Anzeiger*, 16 December 1989; "Vogel: Kohl geht es nur um die eigene Partei," *Bonner Rundschau*, 6 December 1989.
15. "Sie kennen nur noch Deutsche," *Der Spiegel*, no. 52, 25 December 1989; *CDU/CSU Fraktion im Deutschen Bundestag*, Pressedienst, 5 December 1989; "Kohl bezeichnet deutsche Einheit als eine 'Vision,'" *Frankfurter Rundschau*, 12 December 1989.
16. *Pressemitteilung der CDU*, 11 December 1989; "Kooperation statt Anschluß," *Die Grünen*, Pressedienst, no. 188, 19 December 1989.

17. *Die SPD im Deutschen Bundestag*, no. 76, 16 January 1990; *Deutschland-Union-Dienst* 44, no. 15, 22 January 1990.

18. *ppp* 41, no. 8, 11 January 1990.

19. *Presseservice der SPD*, 27 March 1990.

20. *CDU/CSU Fraktion im Deutschen Bundestag*, Pressedienst, 16 January 1990.

21. *Union-Medienbeobachter*, 3 February 1990; *Deutschland-Union-Dienst* 44, no. 33, 15 February 1990; *UiD*, July 1990; *CDU/CSU Fraktion im Deutschen Bundestag*, Pressedienst, 14 February 1990; "Waigel: SPD schürt Angst and macht Bocksprünge," *Die Welt*, 17 February 1990.

22. *Presseservice der SPD*, no. 66, 9 February 1990; "Der Bundeskanzler macht die Einheit im Alleingang," *Stuttgarter Nachrichten*, 13 February 1990; "SPD: Kosten der Einheit nennen," *Frankfurter Rundschau*, 14 February 1990; *DPA*, no. 405, 23 February 1990.

23. *CDU/CSU Fraktion im Deutschen Bundestag*, Pressedienst, 14 February 1990.

24. "Wer zahlt, hat auch das Sagen," *Die Zeit*, 16 February 1990.

25. *Die SPD im Deutschen Bundestag*, no. 473, 3 March 1990; "Die Eile hat Methode," *Die Abendzeitung*, 5 March 1990; *DPA*, no. 113, 14 March 1990; "Lafontaines Handschrift prägt Leitlinien der SPD," *Westfälische Rundschau*, 8 March 1990; "Der Königsweg zur Einheit," *Frankfurter Allgemeine Zeitung*, 6 March 1990.

26. *Presseservice der SPD*, 27 March 1990.

27. *Die SPD im Deutschen Bundestag*, no. 767, 4 April 1990; *Presseservice der SPD*, no. 170, 23 April 1990.

28. *Pressemitteilung*, Presse- und Informationsamt der Bundesregierung, no. 153, 18 April 1990; *Die SPD im Deutschen Bundestag*, no. 955, 6 May 1990.

29. *Pressemitteilung*, Presse- und Informationsamt der Bundesregierung, no. 200, 16 May 1990; *Pressemitteilung CDU*, 16 May 1990.

30. "SPD weist Vorwurf der Angstkampagne zurück," *Kölner Stadtanzeiger*, 15 May 1990.

31. "Es gibt keine Wahl," *Der Spiegel*, no. 22, 28 May 1990.

32. *UiD*, no. 20, 21 June 1990; "Das traurige Spiel der Genossen," *Bayernkurier*, 7 July 1990.

33. *Die SPD im Deutschen Bundestag*, no. 1221, 1 June 1990; *BPA-Nachrichtenabt.* Ref. II A 5, 23 July 1990, Lafontaine, 0720–2; "Im Herbst wird Helmut Kohls Glanz verblassen," *Süddeutsche Zeitung*, 26 July 1990; *Die SPD im Deutschen Bundestag*, no. 1221, 1 June 1990; "Zusammenstellung der Forderungen der SPD," *Arbeitsgruppe "Deutsche Einheit" der SPD-Bundestagsfraktion*, 13 June 1990, mimeo.

34. *Die SPD im Deutschen Bundestag*, no. 1643, 11 August 1990; *Presseservice der SPD*, no. 348, 13 August 1990; *Die SPD im Deutschen Bundestag*, no. 1820, 5 September 1990; Letter of Brigitte Schulte, MdB, to SPD, 21 September 1990, mimeo; *DPA*, no. 732, 4 September 1990; Hans-Ulrich Klose, "Die deutsche Einheit zum Guten der Menschen gestalten," *Hamburger Kurs*, 1990, no. 4; "Lafontaine: Nationalstaat überholt," *Süddeutsche Zeitung*, 18 September 1990.

35. "Jede Seite beansprucht den Sieg für sich," *Süddeutsche Zeitung*, 1 September 1990; Deutscher Bundestag, ed. *Auf dem Weg zur deutschen Einheit*, vol. 5, *Deutschlandpolitische Debatten im Deutschen Bundestag vom 5. bis zum 20. September 1990 mit Beratungen der Volkskammer der DDR zu dem Vertrag über die Herstellung der Einheit Deutschlands* (Bonn: Deutscher Bundestag, 1990), 21.

36. "Patriot und Europäer im Geiste Adenauers," *Deutschland Magazin*, September 1990.

37. *ppp* 41, no. 189, 2 October 1990.

38. *Bulletin*, no. 118, 5 October 1990; *BPA-Nachrichtenabt.*, Ref. II A 5, 4 October 1990, Kohl, 1002–05.

39. *BPA-Nachrichtenabt.*, Ref. II A 5, 4 October 1990, Lafontaine, 1002–12.

40. "SPD ist für viele bares Geld," *Hamburger Morgenpost*, 5 October 1990.

41. Daniel Hamilton, "After the Revolution: The New Political Landscape in East Germany," *German Issues*, no. 7, (1990): 17–18.

42. "'Der Königsweg zur Einheit,'" *Frankfurter Allgemeine Zeitung*, 6 March 1990; Deutscher Bundestag, ed., *Auf dem Weg zur deutschen Einheit*, vol. 1, *Deutschlandpolitische Debatten im Deutschen Bundestag vom 28. November 1989 bis zum 8. März 1990* (Bonn: Deutscher Bundestag, 1990), 751.

43. Quoted in Roger de Weck, "Im besten Sinne deutsch," *Die Zeit*, 1 December 1989.

44. Quoted in Hamilton, "After the Revolution," 12.

45. "Die friedliche Revolution als demokratische Reifeprüfung," *Die Welt*, 19 March 1990; *Bulletin*, no. 86, 3 July 1990.

46. *Die SPD im Deutschen Bundestag*, no. 1717, 23 August 1990; *Der Bundeminister des Innern teilt mit*, 31 August 1990.

47. *Der Bundesminister des Auswärtigen informiert*, no. 1197, 28 September 1990.

Seven

UNIFED GERMANY AND THE NEW POLITICS OF "RATIONAL" MEMBERSHIP

Civil Service and Naturalization Policy in the 1990s

The unforeseen unification of the two postwar German states in 1990 forced German policymakers to find a discursive means by which to cast this dramatic political event. The previous chapter argued that Germany's traditional statist logic of political membership significantly informed the unification debate as a latently appropriate political discourse. German statism's categories and normative values—with its hierarchical differentiation of state and society, its hortatory role for state actors above the derogatory role of ordinary citizens in society, and its accompanying reliance on a positive political loyalty checked from above—remained discursively familiar and useful enough to German party elites and voters to help make sense of the tumultuous political events they were experiencing in 1989 and 1990. But it is important to remember how extraordinary this particular debate was. If there was ever a time for symbolic speech to flood German political discourse, it was during the unification debate of 1989 and 1990. Political debate does not get more extraordinary than one in which the literal boundaries of the political community are at issue. Thus to argue that the logic of German statism appeared in the German unification debate is not to assert a general appropriateness of German statism for typical German political debate in the early 1990s. Indeed, the German statism of the unification debate had survived decades of critique and dismissal of its relevance for politics in the postwar Federal Republic. An institutional arrangement in 1949 challenged it with the elevation of political parties to the commanding heights of political activity; political reformers in the SPD in the late 1960s and 1970s rejected it with abstract calls for "more democracy"; and the West German Greens in the 1980s attempted to replace it with an explicitly anti-statist Basisdemokratie. By the 1990s, there were few, if any, overt defenders of the statist logic of political membership in the Federal Republic. We now turn to two more typical—compared to unification—policy debates in the early 1990s in which German statism had historically loomed large. Each concerned rational political membership in the Federal Republic, and neither, as we shall now see, was dominated by the discourse of German statism.

Two rational membership policy questions forced themselves on to the Federal Republic's political agenda in the early 1990s: first, civil service policy for post-unification Germany, in particular, the question of what to do with the former state employees of the GDR; and second, naturalization policy for a post-Cold War Federal Republic, in particular, what to do with long-term legal alien residents in the country, as well as *Aussiedler*, or ethnonational German settlers from East-Central Europe. Each of these policy debates addressed what it had meant, and what it might mean, to be a "rational" member of the German political community in the early 1990s. The first addressed membership in the form of entering the German civil service; the second addressed it in the form of acquiring German citizenship. Historically, each had been significantly and in parallel fashion informed by the German statist logic of political membership and its concern for demonstrable political loyalty.

While the types of membership at issue in these debates differed immensely—the state civil service, on the one hand, and naturalized citizenship, on the other—each involved the acquisition of a nonnatural or "rational" status that no one held in the Federal Republic as a birthright. Civil servants in the Federal Republic were, like naturalized citizens, made and not born. Moreover, the acquisition of a "rational" political status involves candidates striving to meet the particular qualifications for membership that a political community has deemed appropriate. When a political community reserves a discretionary right to determine the adequacy of a candidacy, it is preventing the acquisition of rational political membership as a consequence of fulfilling certain minimum conditions.

In German statism, adequate political loyalty had functioned as a requirement for rational political membership beyond the fulfillment of certain minimum conditions. Political loyalty had historically been the prime political object of the German state's discretionary power over granting rational political membership. But as we shall now see, in the early 1990s the political loyalty requirement for rational membership in the Federal Republic—and hence the discursive power of German statism—diminished markedly for civil service employment and virtually disappeared for naturalization. The German state's discretionary power over the acquisition of rational political membership status was being replaced by an objective power to grant or withhold that status according to more universalistic and certifiable criteria.

Civil Service Policy in Post-Unification Germany

In the 1970s and 1980s, as we saw, studies of postmaterialism and new social movements often treated the Federal Republic as one comparative case within the cluster of advanced Western industrial states. The previous chapter discussed some of the problems that entailed. In the early 1990s, as we shall now see, studies of institutional policy sometimes treated the Federal Republic as one comparative case within the cluster of East-Central European former Communist states. This chapter will discuss some of the obvious problems associated with that approach. One such policy literature addressed the question of what post-Communist successor regimes—unified Germany among them—chose to do with state bureaucrats from the old regimes. Two hypotheses, with very different causal sequences and policy outcomes, were generated from within this latter comparative venture. But when applied to the unified Federal Republic as the successor regime to the GDR, neither could find much support. Neither adequately incorporated the fact of the Federal Republic's political modernity and institutional stability relative to other successor states in East-Central Europe, nor the specific German struggle over the politics of membership that the Federal Republic had been experiencing since the 1960s.

One accounting of the regime crises, breakdowns, and transitions in East-Central Europe in 1989–1990 focused on the timing and intensity of these phenomena. Informed by a Gerschenkronian emphasis on sequencing, Grzegorz Ekiert argued that three clusters of cases could be identified: the "negotiated openings" of Poland and Hungary that prompted long-term gradual transition between the old and new power holders; the "rapid political mobilizations" of Czechoslovakia and East Germany that led first to significant concessions but quickly to entirely new regimes; and the "full-blown revolution" of Romania that violently overthrew the old regime and forced new political actors into power.[1] Related studies more specifically considered elite replacement in the states of the region and treated the speed and intensity of regime crisis and breakdown as independent variables determining the readiness to "cleanse" old elites and bureaucracies.[2] The more prolonged and gradual the crisis/breakdown/transition, the less desire to "cleanse" and the greater willingness to accommodate holdovers from the old regime; the more intensive and abrupt the crisis/breakdown/transition, the greater desire to "cleanse" and the less willingness to accommodate old power holders. In other words, Czechoslovakia and East Germany should have a strong impulse to "cleanse" old elites, and Poland and Hungary should not.

This hypothesis directly conflicted with a second and more familiar view of bureaucracy and elite replacement. Max Weber's work on the modern state rejected the society-centered foundation of the above argument and pointed instead to what he called the "objective indispensability of once-existing bureaucratic apparatuses" for modern states generally, and especially for those undergoing massive political and social transformation. The "technical superiority" of bureaucratic organization, based on expert training, functional specialization, and virtuosity in the mastery of tasks, prevented transforming societies from succumbing to anarchy: "A rationally ordered officialdom continues to function smoothly after the enemy has occupied the territory; he merely needs to change the top officials. It continues to operate because it is to the vital interest of everyone concerned, including above all the enemy."[3] Contrary to the society-centered timing/intensity hypothesis, Weber's state-centered perspective suggested that the "escape-proof" nature of bureaucracy in the modern world promoted successor-regime accommodation with most old functionaries. Successor regimes in East-Central Europe that inherited from their predecessors anything approaching a rationally organized bureaucracy with competent officials should thus be inclined to accommodate and not "cleanse" those officials.

Applied to the Federal Republic immediately after unification, however, neither the society-centered mobilization hypothesis nor the Weberian state-centered competence hypothesis could adequately account for the German civil service policy that appeared. Each was too unidimensional and abstract to incorporate the German statist logic of rational political membership that so dominated—positively and negatively—German political discourse since the mid-nineteenth century. Powerful, but ultimately partial, institutional and societal forces were isolated in each. The timing/intensity society-centered hypothesis overvalued a vengeful popular political will and undervalued the imperatives of bureaucratic organization for determining willingness to "cleanse" state actors from the old regime. It thereby underestimated the popular political value of a service-providing modern bureaucratic state, regardless of the politics of its personnel, particularly in times of dire social need and uncertainty. Conversely, the technocratic state-centered Weberian hypothesis overvalued the structural imperative of bureaucratic organization and undervalued the importance of political will in a society. Popular political will in this policy area can take the form not only of a revenge-laden demand for post-revolutionary justice, but also as popular support for—or familiarity with—a political logic of membership.[4] Bringing these perspectives together, Graham Wilson observed that in the short term, both modern bureaucrats and citizens valued the services of bureaucracy too strongly not, respectively, to conform politically and preserve the institution in a new regime. In the long term, however, modern bureaucracies themselves responded as dependent variables to major societal transformations.[5] Specifically for the Federal Republic, the societal transformation of the discourse of political membership occurring since the 1960s forced civil service policy in the early 1990s to become a dependent variable.

If the role of "reference societies" was important for East-Central European states experiencing the transformations of 1989–1990, it was absolutely defining for the events in East Germany.[6] GDR exposure to the Federal Republic had increased over the years from a trickle of elderly Eastern visitors to the West, to Western television blanketing all but one small area of East Germany and vast numbers of East Germans traveling to the West on holiday. No other citizens in East-Central Europe could look to an enormously successful parliamentary-democratic market system and imagine they were seeing their countrymen and women—which they formally were, according to West Germany's legal definition of East Germans as citizens of the Federal Republic. By early 1990 the question of "whether German unification" had become "when and how unification." The how part included the "transformation of the 'stateness' of the GDR"—the personnel, structure, responsibilities, and raison d'être of the ex-GDR state administration.[7]

As a "reference society," however, the Federal Republic offered the GDR a "reference institution" on this question: the professional state civil service, which, as we have seen, was one of the oldest, most hallowed, and robust institutions in the history of German politics. Nevertheless, the GDR's first (and last) freely elected government, coming to power after the March 1990 election, explicitly rejected the Federal Republic's professional civil service and its "traditional principles" located in Article 33 of the Basic Law.[8] This East German anti-statist rejection of Germany's civil service tradition, however, was quickly rendered politically meaningless. The overwhelming victory in that election of the "Alliance for Germany" effectively put the German state professional civil service in the GDR's future, regardless of the immediate will of the newly elected East German government. As the compressed treaty-drafting phase of the unification process ensued, it became clear that the "accession choice" for unification championed by the "Alliance for Germany" was to entail the wholesale adoption of standing political, legal, economic, and social institutions in the Federal Republic by the GDR, including the West German professional civil service and its "traditional principles."

The Unification Treaty signed in August 1990, which followed the Monetary, Economic, and Social Union Treaty signed in May, dealt with unified Germany's future legal and institutional environments. The fifth section of the Unification Treaty addressed the "legal relationship in the public service [öffentlicher Dienst]" and posited the introduction of the German professional civil service and its "traditional principles" into the former GDR. It stated, "the implementation of public tasks (sovereign-legal power in the sense of Article 33, Section 4, Basic Law), is to be taken over by civil servants [Beamten] as soon as possible."[9] According to Article 33, every German was equally eligible for any position in the public service according to aptitude, qualifications, and professional achievements; no one was to suffer any disadvantage by reason of adherence or nonadherence to a denomination or ideology; the exercise of sovereign state authority was to be entrusted to members of the public service who stood in a service and loyalty relationship as defined by public law; and civil service law was to be regulated with due respect to the traditional principles of the professional civil service.[10] The Unification Treaty's appendixes indicated that state employees of the GDR were initially to remain in their positions unless employed in institutions not taken over by the Federal Republic; the latter would receive 70 percent of their most recent income while they searched for positions elsewhere (for six months for those under fifty years, for nine months for those fifty and older); the former, who initially retained employment in the Federal Republic, could nonetheless be dismissed in a "regular" manner for "lack of technical qualifications or personal aptitude [*Eignung*]" or because their services were no longer needed in the institution taken over; "extraordinary dismissal" was allowed if the former East German state employee had "violated the principles of humanity or the rule of law [*Rechtsstaatlichkeit*]" as established by international treaties in 1948 and 1966, or if the employee had been "active in the former Ministry of State Security or Office of National Security"—each of which was deemed to make state employment in the unified Federal Republic "unreasonable"; and ex-GDR state employees who remained could be appointed to civil service (Beamte) positions in the Federal Republic "on probation" for a period of two to three years, during which time opportunities for further education were to be pursued in order to "demonstrate competence."[11]

On the face of it, these treaty and constitutional provisions making up post-unification Germany's civil service policy supported neither the society-centered timing/intensity → "cleansing" hypothesis, nor that of a state-centered technical imperative → accommodation. First, neither policy outcome was chosen in its simple form. With regard to "cleansing," *Stasi* employees and human rights violators were banned, but not top officials or SED (Communist Party) members as such. With regard to accommodation, GDR state employees were to be retained and retrained if possible, but technical skills alone were not the sole criterion for determining future employment. Second, neither of the causal sequences posited by these hypotheses matched what occurred in either the GDR or the Federal Republic at this time. A popular uprising calling for the heads of officials of the old regime did not galvanize in the GDR, nor did a concerted argument to retain the bureaucratic "experts" of the old Communist state. Instead, both state-centered and society-centered perspectives did enter into this policy debate in 1990, but with decidedly Western German inflections: the state-centered perspective turned less on the Weberian concern for expertise (though that did appear) than on the particular institution of the traditional German civil service; the society-centered perspective turned less on post-revolutionary vindictive demands of East German citizens (though those were discussed) than on the perceived political and fiscal needs of the Federal Republic.

The Federal Republic's retention of skilled—or skilled enough and trainable—ex-GDR state employees in an "accession civil service" with exceptional probationary rules partly embodied Weber's imperative to accommodate state actors from the old regime. Gerhard Lehmbruch cautiously suggested that amidst all of the pathologies of the GDR cadre administration, some basic "competence expectations" had to exist simply to have kept the institution from collapse.[12] But those expectations were apparently exceedingly low when they existed at all. Among participants in this debate, the SPD and a public service union (the ÖTV—Public Service and Transport Workers Union) were closest to supporting the state-centered Weberian competence argument for what to do with ex-GDR state employees. Yet their position was directed not toward the specific competencies that these employees may have embodied, but rather toward their vision of the bureaucratic institution that the ex-GDR needed for the future. That, according to the SPD and ÖTV was not the Federal Republic's civil service with its "traditional principles," but rather a functional, efficient, modernized, effective, and service-providing institution that could address unified Germany's needs at the end of the twentieth century.[13] By implication though not explicit recommendation, if ex-GDR state employees could function in such a modernized institution, there was no reason not to retain them. This reformist focus of the SPD and the ÖTV reached back to civil service reform efforts in the Federal Republic in the 1970s. The SPD and ÖTV endorsed a modernized Weberian civil service minus what they rejected as the "predemocratic relics" of the German "authoritarian state," in particular the tripartite division of the institution and the political loyalty demands on officials.[14] While not explicitly endorsing the retention of ex-GDR state employees, the SPD and ÖTV also did not recommend a political "cleansing."

In contrast, center-right participants in this debate, including the federal governing coalition (CDU/CSU and F.D.P.) and the DBB (the German Federation of Civil Servants), explicitly did reject a Weberian accommodationist position. Contributing to the perception that the Federal Republic, like the former Czechoslovakia, chose a radical "cleansing" of the elites from the old regime, the Union parties and the DBB argued that the future German civil service had to be functionally efficient, but they unambiguously rejected this criterion as the raison d'être for the institution as a whole or for addressing the specific question of what to do with ex-GDR state employees.[15] An Interior Ministry official asserted that the probationary status for ex-GDR employees was informed by concerns "not only about professional competence," but also about the employees' loyalty toward the Federal Republic's "free democratic basic order."[16] One observer identified the target of these dual concerns as the "politicized incompetence" of ex-GDR state employees.[17] But this side of the debate also rejected Karl-Dietrich Bracher's call for an across-the-board political "cleansing" of the former employees. For the federal government and the DBB, an "accession civil service" of ex-GDR officials was acceptable, but only if it, as the Federal Republic's regular civil service institution had historically, combined both competence and political loyalty imperatives for its personnel.[18] In short, a state-centered institutionalism did inform the policy debate over ex-GDR state employees, but not as a Weberian technical competence → accommodation hypothesis would have it.

To the extent that a Weberian bureaucracy was supported by reformers in the Federal Republic in this debate (and since the 1970s), it focused instead on institutional imperatives and not the need to accommodate former East German technically competent state employees. In turn, to the extent that the political loyalty of state civil servants retained salience for center-right policy participants, it was an invocation of an old German civil service tradition that, by the early 1990s, was not appropriate enough to endorse a blanket "cleansing" of all ex-GDR state employees. Post-unification German civil service policy in this period was thus informed by a political institutionalism that incorporated distinctly German inflections of both the state-centered and society-centered hypotheses.

The political side of this institutionalism, which this study has identified as a statist logic of political membership, has, as we have seen, very deep roots in the German tradition. While this book has argued that a statist logic of political membership consolidated in Vormärz Prussia, others have gone back as far as tenth-century feudal law to root the "traditional principles" of the professional civil service that appear in the Federal Republic's constitution.[19] The German civil service thereby became an institutional embodiment of what Hobsbawm called "sets of practices, normally governed by rules ... which seek to inculcate certain values and norms of behaviour ... which automatically impl[y] continuity with the past."[20] That distinctly German past, which historically marked state civil servants as "rational" members of the German political community on the basis of a reliable political loyalty checked "from above," went way beyond what Weber termed "loyalty" to the "functional purposes" of bureaucracy.[21] The check on the political loyalty of civil servants in the Federal Republic entailed the demand of the Radicals Decree in 1972, for instance, that West German state civil servants uphold the "free democratic basic order" at all times, including nonwork hours. The broadside attacks on the Radicals Decree and its loyalty demands that appeared in the 1970s and early 1980s managed to invalidate neither the "traditional principles" for the German civil service nor the political loyalty requirement for state employees. While the Unification Treaty, in turn, did nothing explicitly to invalidate those principles and the loyalty requirement, societal transformations in West Germany during the previous two decades had a tremendous impact on what those principles were to mean in the early 1990s and what kind of policy they rationalized.

The statist logic of political membership that had informed German civil service policy since the middle of the nineteenth century still had a few—at least rhetorical—defenders in this period. In the autumn of 1989, CDU interior minister Wolfgang Schäuble, preaching to the choir, told the DBB that "the professional civil service is part of our stateness." The institution and its "traditional principles" were not, according the Schäuble, "relics of the authoritarian state," but rather the "guarantee of our constitutional law state."[22] Schäuble's party colleagues later asserted that the civil service was necessary for "successfully resolv[ing]" problems accompanying unification, and historically "ha[d] guaranteed our citizens an obligation to the common good, free of party-political pressures"; "Germans in the GDR," the CDU concluded, "have the same right to that guarantee." CDU politician Rita Süssmuth similarly warned of "chaos" if the institution were abandoned. The DBB, for its part, reiterated that the traditional loyalty requirement for civil servants guaranteed that they "would always be there for citizens."[23]

This nearly ritualistic rhetoric drew on decades of invoking Germany's traditional statist logic of political membership. By the late 1980s, however, that logic had lost much of its original compulsion for a large section of the West German public. Not only had it been confronted in the 1960s, 1970s, and 1980s with a broadly mobilized

West German criticism of statist "authoritarianism," but in the midst of unification discussions in the early 1990s, the CDU/CSU-F.D.P. federal government was itself throwing the appropriateness of statist discourse into doubt by advocating the privatization of the postal and railway services. The horrors of which Communist postal and railway officials were said to be capable in some of the debates over the Radicals Decree in the 1970s were apparently no longer a threat. With the railway and postal service in private hands, the political loyalty concerns attending rational political membership in these sectors would have no place to be articulated. Ironically, the anti-statist SPD was pushed into a back-handed defense of the public nature of these institutions.[24] Even more ironically, Social Democrats at this time called on the "traditional principles" of the civil service in a dispute over how to get West German officials to participate in an "elite transfer" to the GDR on temporary assignment. The CDU-led federal government provided monetary and promotion incentives to Western state employees to get them to move, while the SPD argued that if the duty and loyalty demands of the "traditional principles" meant anything, they meant that civil servants should willingly go where needed, and without the promise of better pay and/or promotion.[25] Generally, however, the Social Democrats clung to their long-standing critique of the traditional institution, which was reiterated in the new party program appearing at the end of 1989 that called for "an efficient administration close to citizens" that was "free from the traditions of the authoritarian state," that allowed the right to strike, and whose "demands for constitutional loyalty were interpreted from within the liberal [*freiheitliche*] spirit of the Basic Law."[26] This was joined by Engholm's statement in 1991 that civil service "modernization," which had been on the SPD's agenda since the early 1970s, did not mean dissolution of the institution, but it also did not mean its expansion.

In short, if there were state-centered forces at work in the response the Federal Republic gave to the question of what to do with ex-GDR state employees in unified Germany, they were not informed by a simple Weberian concern for the indispensability of administrative competence. The institutionalism that did appear in this debate was somewhat tenuously linked, rhetorically, to the deeply rooted statist logic of German political membership. In this debate, that statism was no longer one coherent and consistently defended political discourse. Familiar conservative defenses of it were mixed with interloping suggestions for privatization and market incentives. Familiar critiques of it were, in turn, laced with need-provision defenses of the welfare state and calls for a "liberal constitutional loyalty" for its personnel. By the early 1990s, the traditional self-contained statist logic of German political membership that had for a century-and-one-half determined the "rational" construction of the German civil service had irretrievably lost its discursive hegemony in the Federal Republic. German political elites were no longer able, or willing, to seal off what traditional German statism had historically defined as "lower" societal factors affecting this policy area.

At the same time, the societal factors influencing the Federal Republic's response to this question were not Eastern German in origin. The society-centered timing/intensity → "cleansing" hypothesis suggested that the GDR, like Czechoslovakia, experienced an internal, rapid, intense, and politicizing societal "implosion" in 1989 and 1990 that resulted in a "cleansing" or "negative elite recruitment" of old GDR state employees in unified Germany. We have seen so far that these studies had the policy wrong: an across-the-board society-centered "cleansing" was not the policy chosen in Germany. They also had the causal sequence wrong: a state-centered German "political" institutionalism helped determine the policy outcome in the Federal Republic. We turn now to the specific societal factors at work in this policy area. The society-centered timing/intensity → "cleansing" hypothesis attributed political participation to a mobilized GDR citizenry that successfully demanded "from below" and received an age-old form of "revolutionary justice." It was suggested that elites of the old regime were hated by the masses and had to be swept out of office and replaced by politically reliable adherents of the new. This hypothesis reversed the Weberian competence-before-loyalty imperative and emphasized the political legitimation demands of a "meta-democratic movement of collective identity that swept through East-Central Europe in 1989–1990."[27]

In the Unification Treaty, only Stasi employees and identifiable human rights violators were categorically denied state employment in the unified Federal Republic. Neither previous state employment in the GDR nor SED (Communist Party) membership as such disqualified old GDR state elites for the state of the unified Federal Republic. This relative liberality contrasted sharply with both Czechoslovakia's "lustration" law, which disqualified old-regime Czech state employees from state employment in the new regime for five years, and West Germany's Radicals Decree, which was frequently interpreted in the 1970s and 1980s to render West German Communist Party (DKP) membership sufficient to disqualify a candidate for civil service employment.[28] Nonetheless, if the society-centered hypothesis is stretched, purging Stasi employees and human rights violators might represent a type of political "cleansing." For these particular East Germans, technical competence was clearly subsidiary to political reliability. Yet for the "cleansing" hypothesis to hold, this purge must have been undertaken in response to the demands of a mobilized East German citizenry calling for the heads of Stasi employees and human rights violators. The brief occupation of the Stasi headquarters by demonstrators in East Berlin in January 1990 might have been a storming of the Bastille. But this incident was immediately clouded by suspicions of Stasi action by *agents provocateurs* attempting to destroy self-incriminating files.[29] In any case, the event did not acquire the mythic status of a revolutionary act that many West and East German activists were clamoring to provide.

An arguably better and ideologically very different indicator of East German post-Wall popular sentiment would be the electoral outcome of the March 1990 election, a contest in which six different parties and electoral groupings (including the indigenous former SED [renamed the PDS] and the citizens' initiative "Alliance '90") participated. The election was decisively won by the Western-CDU-oriented "Alliance for Germany," a grouping that made no secret about its desire for quick unification via Article 23 of the Basic Law. As discussed in the last chapter, the election result mandated a quick and direct accession of the GDR to the Federal Republic, without either an assembly to write a new constitution or a popular referendum on any aspect of the unification process. Therefore, any East German demand to "cleanse" GDR state employees would have to be mainly channeled through West German political elites who, by the March election results, were essentially given license—which was readily accepted—to draw up the terms of unification.[30]

West German political elites, as it turns out, were not very concerned about the political consequences for East Germans of leaving ex-GDR state employees in place. A Social Democrat worried that promoting former East German border controllers (alleged, but not proven, to be part of a Stasi unit) to civil service status in the Federal Republic would "run up against a lack of understanding and outrage among the population of the new [East German] Länder."[31] The CDU similarly expressed concern about the "trust" that former East Germans would have for the civil service in unified Germany. But for neither the SPD nor the CDU were these defining positions. The CDU's "trust" concern was, in any case, related less to possible East German memories of the abuses of East German state employees than to the question of whether new employees in the unified Germany could demonstrate the requisite positive readiness to "intervene on behalf of [former West Germany's] free democratic basic order." This was a political concern held by West German officials, not the East German public untutored in the Federal Republic's "free democratic basic order."[32] But the primary "societal" force driving West German debate on this question was hardly political at all, in the sense of a demand for revenge from below or for positive loyalty tested from above. Both the SPD and the CDU/CSU argued instead for a "modernized," "effective," "efficient" and "service-providing" unified German institution that could promote the equalization of living conditions between East and West German citizens "in the economy, culture, science, and education."[33]

In keeping with this pragmatism, and in contrast to the more politicized demands of the 1970s in the Federal Republic, neither government nor opposition supported the politically informed "membership" criterion to determine the political fit of ex-GDR state employees for the Federal Republic.[34] In the 1970s battle over the Radicals Decree, the "membership" criterion—steadfastly endorsed by the CDU/CSU but not the SPD (which clung to the "single-case test" or an evaluation of what they called the "whole" candidate)—led in some instances to the automatic exclusion of West German Communist Party members from civil service employment. In the early 1990s, former SED (East German Communist Party) members were not similarly excluded. Indeed, Interior Minister Schäuble explicitly rejected what he called a "new de-Nazification" for the ex-GDR, suggesting that the "forty-year regime of injustice" in the GDR made it difficult to differentiate victim from perpetrator. Instead, he magnanimously asked East German state employees to inspect their own consciences to decide if they belonged in the Federal Republic's civil service. In the Radicals Decree debate of the 1970s and 1980s, nothing of the sort was conceivable from the Union side. Clearly, the goal here was not a "cleansing" of the ranks of ex-GDR state employees in the name of a society-supported East German "political justice." It was, rather, the creation of a functional civil service and what Schäuble called an "internal reconciliation and new beginning" in the former GDR.[35] To return to Wilson, however, a society-centered politics *did* figure powerfully in this debate, but it addressed more the needs of the Western Federal Republic than needs specific to the former GDR. The societal determinants of post-unification civil service policy included West German concerns about European integration, West German desires not to reprise the loyalty oath controversy of the 1970s, and West German worries about financing the professional civil service in the 1990s.

Article 48 of the EEC Treaty stated that any member-state citizen could exercise any trade or occupation within the European Community (Union) on the same terms as those applied to nationals of the host country, including most state employment positions.[36] During German unification, it was hard to remember that this was a divisive issue in the Federal Republic at the end of the 1980s. The CDU argued that the EC had to "retain room for member states responsibly to determine the structures of their national administrations in keeping with their own traditions." The F.D.P. similarly argued that neither European integration nor German unification provided sufficient reason to change the "constitution-anchored structure of our civil service."[37] Some civil service experts in the CDU, however, advocated a "loosening" of German civil service law to allow non-German Europeans to become Beamten as long as other European states opened their institutions to Germans.[38] In other words, the "traditional principles" of the civil service were not to be removed; but their traditional meaning was to be altered. The political loyalty of civil servants in Germany still mattered, but the CDU claimed—contrary to their utterances in the 1970s about the Federal Republic's special justification for requiring the positive political loyalty of its civil servants—that "all EC states are committed to the common values of a free and democratic constitutional-law state."

At the same time, concern was expressed about the "flood of applicants from southern Europe with no academic training." By implication, if "southern Europeans" could "flood" the Federal Republic with applicants for civil service positions, why should not ex-GDR state employees—who were "ethnically" German and many of whom were "victims" of the GDR's "*Unrechtsregime*," or regime of injustice—be allowed the same?[39] The CDU's liberal answer to the question of what to do with ex-GDR state employees in unified Germany was thus encouraged by West German "societal" concerns about European integration. For its part, the SPD saw Article 48 of the EEC Treaty as contradicting German civil service law and argued that the Beamten status be retained, but drastically narrowed. The party argued that relegating Beamten to only a few "core" areas would broadly depoliticize the institution and mark a decisive break with Germany's "authoritarian state" tradition.[40] The SPD thus deployed the rationale of Germany's functioning as a good European Community member to call for removing the political loyalty stakes for hiring all but a handful of the Federal Republic's public sector workers. That meant lower political stakes not only for West Germans and Italians, but also for ex-GDR state employees. While the CDU redefined the "traditional principles" of the German civil service in this debate and the SPD asserted they were anachronistic, both were able to do this in the name of German participation in European integration. An accommodation of most ex-GDR state employees was therefore justifiable.

A second West German societal concern driving this policy debate was the fear of reliving the protracted debate over the Radicals Decree. Were that battle to repeat itself in the early 1990s, the CDU/CSU would be cast as supporting relatively restrictive measures for ensuring the political loyalty of prospective civil servants, and the SPD would support generally more liberal measures. In fact, the CDU/CSU did reiterate in the early 1990s some of the old 1970s arguments about the indispensability of the professional civil service for "guaranteeing" and "protecting" the "free democratic basic order." But as noted above, they also reversed their 1970s Radicals Decree position and endorsed the single-case test for ex-GDR state employees in the early 1990s. This relatively accommodationist position adopted for East Germans was taken as the CDU/CSU oversaw, in 1990 and 1991, what many viewed as the final dismantling of the 1972 Radicals Decree in CDU/CSU-governed Länder.[41] The SPD smarted most severely from the prospect of reprising the Radicals Decree controversy of the 1970s. In 1989, party leader Hans-Jochen Vogel claimed that the decree had damaged the "psychological climate of the Republic ... The Social Democrats got rid of this decree, piece by piece, in every Land that it governed. But the memory of this mistaken decision is still very painful today."[42] In the unification debate, the SPD labeled the Decree a "political absurdity" and a mistaken "instrument of the Cold War"; that, with the collapse of East Germany, removed all rationale for it or similar provisions.[43] The party supported with the CDU/CSU the single-case test for civil servants in the newly unified state. This convergence of the two main political parties on more liberality may have been consistent with the needs of ex-GDR citizens, but not by definition or intention. The overriding societal concern of both of these parties was to avoid repeating the West German Radicals Decree debacle of the 1970s and early 1980s.

The final societal concern constraining the Federal Republic's response to ex-GDR state employees in unified Germany was fiscal in nature. Walking a fine line between a call for fundamentally reforming the institution and alienating the powerful DBB, the CDU/CSU had, by the late 1980s, grown wary of the fiscal consequences of increasing the size of the professional civil service—with its provisions for lifetime tenure, insurance, and noncontributory pension systems. In January 1989, eleven months before the fall of the Wall, the CDU interior minister endorsed the need for "flexibility" in civil service salaries, "individual performance incentives," and the use of new technologies to promote competitiveness.[44] During the unification debate, the Union parties continued along these lines—on the one hand, reassuring the DBB with periodic calls for the preservation and even expansion of the institution, but, on the other, telling the DBB in 1991 that "promises for concrete measures in the areas of benefits and salaries would be frivolous" and that the "size of the civil service must be further reduced in the next few years."[45]

Indirectly, but unmistakably, the CDU/CSU was giving notice that money did matter for this institution. This was nowhere better illustrated than in the Union parties' support for the privatization of the postal service and the railway, which, for purposes here, was a clear indicator of the breakdown of the appropriateness of the statist logic of political membership among conservatives in the Federal Republic. While the CDU/CSU along with the F.D.P. was thereby willing to send a significant part of the professional civil service into the realm of "society," the Social Democrats, themselves acknowledging the high costs of the institution, nonetheless argued that a social welfare state was still necessary for providing services to all citizens equally. The SPD was concerned to find the "organizational form for the state that can in the future provide service better for a modern and more democratic society."[46] This fiscal constraint, again, was certainly not incommensurate with the "societal" needs of the ex-GDR citizenry. Yet its genesis rested not in East German societal demands, but rather in West German society's fiscal capacity to extend the institution to the new Länder.

For Germany, then, we find each general hypothesis explaining the response of successor regimes to the question of what to do with the bureaucratic elites of the old regime to be wanting. A Weberian state-centered "competence" institutionalism was supported by the Federal Republic's initial retention of ex-GDR state employees whose offices survived unification; but that hypothesis could account neither for the development of the "single-case test" to determine a candidate's competence, which included both technical and (relatively liberal) political loyalty criteria, nor for the categorical proscriptions against hiring ex-Stasi employees and human rights violators. In turn, a society-centered political mobilization hypothesis which predicted a wholesale "cleansing" of ex-GDR state employees clearly misstated the case; the society-centered concerns that did enter this policy debate were not those of the ex-GDR, but rather West German concerns about European integration, West German concerns about a failed policy initiative in the 1970s, and West German Marks. Missing from each of these hypotheses is an accounting of the fate of a distinctly German political discourse that had defined state actors as necessary and politically loyal protectors of an inherently anarchic German society since the mid-nineteenth century and that was now dissolving as inappropriate for German political debate generally. Traces of that logic of membership still appeared in this policy arena in the early 1990s—especially for Stasi members and human rights violators—but that logic was being replaced by a counter-discourse of functionalism, efficiency, European integration, fiscal responsibility, and, not least, a legitimate political role for ordinary German citizens.

Naturalization Policy in Post-Unification Germany

The acquisition of "rational" membership status within the German statist logic of appropriateness has historically involved the demand positively to demonstrate to membership gatekeepers a reliable political loyalty. We now turn to naturalization policy in the Federal Republic of German in the early 1990s. Regardless of the massive functional differences in the political roles of civil servants and naturalized citizens, the German statist logic of political membership had historically required of each candidate for these rational membership statuses a positive and demonstrable—to discretionary state actors—political loyalty. We just discovered that civil service policy, the classic statist policy arena in German politics, was informed in this period by nothing more than traces of this historically powerful but now fading logic of political membership. We shall now find that two significant reforms of naturalization law in the Federal Republic similarly registered the demise of this statist logic of membership.

The horror of xenophobic violence after unification in 1990—with Hoyerswerda, Rostock, Mölln, and Solingen becoming short-hand for thousands of acts of right-wing violence perpetrated against foreigners—left politicians and activists in the Federal Republic desperately searching for policy solutions.[47] Two main responses to these events surfaced in the early 1990s. As conservatives defined "too many foreigners" to be the problem, the solution advocated and adopted by the German federal government in the early spring of 1993 was considerably to tighten the country's constitutionally guaranteed right to asylum.[48] As liberals and leftists alternatively defined Germany's citizenship law to be the problem—based on the principle of jus sanguinis, or the law of blood descent—calls for a liberalization of Germany's restrictive practices were advanced. In response to the xenophobic violence, reformers demanded changes in both citizenship and naturalization law, arguing that easing the requirements for achieving German citizenship status would improve the lives of foreigners in Germany, reduce violence against "outsiders," and contribute to making Germany a more tolerant and multicultural society.[49] Historically, the main objection to liberalizing the Federal Republic's citizenship law had been linked to its identity as "not a country of immigration" and—frequently added—"not a country of naturalization."

Supporters of the status quo rejected the reformers' idea of "merely transforming foreigners into [German] citizens." Drawing on Germany's ethnocultural-national definition of citizenship, reform opponents cited the myriad difficulties surrounding the ability and willingness of foreigners to integrate and assimilate themselves to German social, cultural, and political life.[50] Reformers responded that this objection put undue emphasis on very questionable attributions of the inherent differences between foreigners and Germans and on the purported inability of foreigners to adapt to "German" life. Reformers in the Federal Republic argued that it was German law that needed changing, that ethnocultural criteria were anachronistic for defining membership in a community, and that the hurdles to acquiring "rational" political membership in the form of naturalized citizenship in the Federal

Republic were unreasonably high. The Federal Republic's somewhat problematic definition of "natural" political membership by means of jus sanguinis, or the law of blood descent was historically relevant for, but not the specific criterion of membership at stake in, these calls to reform naturalization law. Without German blood in the veins but with a will to become naturalized, a person had to satisfy other criteria to be awarded "rational" membership in the Federal Republic. Until the reforms in the early 1990s, the criteria in the Federal Republic for acquiring naturalized citizenship status were strict, difficult to meet, and significantly political in nature. One of the main political requirements for such membership was the positive demonstration of a reliable—and not just legal—political loyalty to the Federal Republic's free democratic basic order.

Max Weber's account of citizenship stressed the nonvoluntary "legitimate domination" of "compulsory members" of an institutionalized political community.[51] If Weber's state management perspective had any relevance anywhere in the 1990s, it was in the geographical area of Western Europe. As states in Europe began to sort out the consequences of the end of the Cold War, the problem of managing who was, was not, and might become a citizen of these wealthy industrialized democracies acquired immense significance.[52] Rogers Brubaker's comparison of German and French immigration thus treated modern citizenship in this era as an instrument to effect "exclusion," "inclusion," "separation," "differentiation," "closure," and "restriction."[53] Tomas Hammar similarly referred to states acting as "controller, regulator or gatekeeper" with their citizenship laws.[54] The institution of citizenship can thus be viewed, though not exclusively, as a sorting mechanism for modern nation-states to determine who is "in" and who is "out," especially in periods of large-scale migration and attempted migration. "Insiders" are legally differentiable from "outsiders" horizontally, in the sense that citizen and noncitizen are exclusive classes of rights- and duties-bearing persons. Noncitizens of one nation-state are virtually always citizens of another, and the wall that separates these two classes is, from a global nation-state perspective, legally separating level territory—regardless of the views of particular migrating individuals. For the recent reform of naturalization law in the Federal Republic, it was this differentiation—the horizontal distinction between German citizens and non-Germans—that was most relevant.

In the late 1980s, the potential differentiation among types of "foreigner" in the Federal Republic acquired relevance as local voting rights were advocated by Social Democrats in Schleswig-Holstein and Hamburg for long-term foreign residents. But the Federal Constitutional Court's unanimous decision in October 1990 to prohibit the extension of local voting rights to non-Germans—in the name of a "uniform foundation of democratic legitimation"—effectively rendered "non-German" the most relevant political status of all foreigners living in the Federal Republic.[55] "Who is German?" as opposed to "what kind of foreigner?" was the operative question in the debate over naturalization. Conservatives suggested limiting the number of "non-Germans" in the Federal Republic, thereby removing non-German persons targeted by xenophobia; liberal and leftist reformers, in contrast, advocated making the acquisition of the status "German" easier, thereby limiting the non-German status targeted by xenophobia.

The formal "region of equality" that constituted the "natural" status of German citizenship has been delineated since 1913 by the principle of jus sanguinis.[56] This principle holds that citizenship status was transmitted genealogically, by the "blood" of a person's biological father or (since 1974) mother. Location of birth, the fact that is relevant for the principle of jus soli, was meaningless for "natural" German citizenship. Prior to 1913, the contradictory blood and territory bases of jus sanguinis and jus soli respectively were combined in German citizenship law. In nineteenth-century Germany, a joining of these two principles was possible within a "state-national" citizenship law: "Prolonged residence in the territory no longer [as it had in Prussia prior to 1842] sufficed to acquire citizenship. Prolonged absence from the territory, however, still occasioned the loss of citizenship."[57] Foreigners living within Germany's borders acquired no right to citizenship, while Germans living abroad could be (after ten years) transformed into "outsiders" to the German community by their chosen place of residence.

This "state-national" understanding of German citizenship prior to 1913 was a political understanding. Its pivot was loyalty, or the purported intensity of the tie between an individual citizen and the modern nation-state. According to Brubaker, "from a state-national point of view ... descent creates a more substantial community than the 'accidental fact' of birthplace. Descent binds the individual more closely to the destiny of the state; and the strength of the ties between state and citizen is a central concern in the age of the nation-state, particularly at the historical moment of the nation at arms."[58] A genealogical transmission of citizenship provided a deeper and more reliable tie to the German nation-state than the accidental physical location of birth, but the genealogical basis of loyalty to the German community could be ruptured by extended periods of residence abroad, and that justified removing a person's natural citizenship status. The loyalty tie between German citizens and the German nation-state was thus potentially but not universally variable, dependent for Germans (but not non-Germans) on the choice of domicile. The "state national" understanding of natural citizenship thus understood extended residence outside of the nation-state as producing political unreliability. Extended German residence in the nation-state by non-Germans, however, did not at the same time produce the binding ties of loyalty required for rational political membership. Prior to 1913, for "ethnic non-Germans," genealogy alone, and not birthplace, residence, or political will implied insufficient loyalty to the German nation-state. Similarly, for "ethnic Germans," genealogy and residence, but not birthplace or political will, were taken to indicate loyal ties to the nation-state.

After 1913, an ethnonational adjustment to the state-national understanding of German citizenship meant that loyalty lost its legal relevance for the retention, though not attribution or acquisition, of German citizenship. That occurred by removing the domicile modification of jus sanguinis that had previously allowed the loss of German citizenship for extended periods of residence abroad. The new law even allowed the reacquisition of German citizenship by those who had lost it under the old.[59] With the removal of all traces of residence considerations from the law, "ethnic Germans" joined "ethnic non-Germans" in having "natural" citizenship attribution and retention be controlled solely by descent. This formal "de-statification" of German citizenship, by which political membership ties were reconceptualized as unalterable bonds to an ethnonational German community, meant that political loyalty was no longer regarded as variable for "ethnic Germans" regardless of residence. For "ethnic non-Germans," the assumption of nonloyalty—regardless of residence, place of birth, or political belief and actions—remained unchanged. The citizenship law of 1913 permitted naturalization, or the acquisition of a "rational" membership status in the German Reich, but that required a candidate positively to demonstrate to state officials that he or she had "led a life of irreproachable [*unbescholtenen*] conduct" and did not "endanger the well-being of the Reich."[60] In any case, no "ethnic non-German" had a right to naturalization with the 1913 law. Bureaucratic discretion, turning partly on loyalty concerns, remained the means for naturalized citizenship acquisition.

This shift to an ethnonational understanding of German citizenship in 1913 occurred in a politicized context not unlike that of the Federal Republic after the end of the Cold War in 1989. By the early twentieth century, Germany had become an economic magnet for immigrants, especially Poles, working in heavy industry, mining, and commercial agriculture.[61] As migration increased, the Pan-German League's concern for the "preservation of German *Volkstum*," or German nationality, enveloped virtually all of Wilhelmine Germany's political parties as they supported the retention (and requisition) of German citizenship for foreign-domiciled *"Auslandsdeutsche,"* or German residing abroad.[62] The presence of over a million foreigners working in the Reich encouraged German lawmakers to view the potential political falling-away of ethnic German residents living abroad with much less disfavor. The ethnocultural threat of the alleged *"Drang nach Westen,"* or push to the West, of Slavs and Jews to Germany's "flourishing economy" and "free institutions" was to be met, according to the Reich Interior Ministry, by the promotion of *Deutschtum*, or Germanness, both in Germany and abroad, wherever "ethnic Germans" and their blood descendents resided.[63]

Gone was the "state-national" concern for the lapsed political loyalty of Germans who had left the fatherland. The only valid legal differentiation now was the ethnonational horizontal one between definitionally loyal "ethnic Germans," on the one hand, and definitionally nonloyal "ethnic non-Germans," on the other, regardless of domicile. Jus soli, or the principle attributing "natural" citizenship on the basis of place of birth, was left completely out of the government policy debate in 1913. For conservatives, the principle of jus soli implied a problematic territory-based assimilation (the territory of birth and not the territory of residence), and not the preferred descent-based immediate loyalty, to "Germanness" as a means to acquire "natural" membership status. Conservatives in 1913 saw the former as both undesirable and impossible: undesirable given Germany's "front-line" status facing the East; and impossible because the "accident" of the location of birth could never, it was held, equal the blood-tie to the German ethnonational community.[64]

The ethnonational rendition of pure jus sanguinis in 1913 thus turned on the definition of "ethnic German." After the Second World War, "ethnic Germans" included not only Germans inhabiting the

Federal Republic, but also Germans carrying a GDR passport, who were officially treated as citizens of the Federal Republic, and "ethnic Germans" who resided outside of the combined territory of the FRG and the GDR. Officially, this last group was to include only those who qualified as postwar *"Vertriebene,"* or "expellees," from Eastern Europe and the former USSR because of their German "ethnicity." A combination of Cold War policy and the powerful political clout of the organization of expellees in the Federal Republic, however, led authorities to "consider virtually all ethnic German immigrants from Eastern Europe and the Soviet Union as *Vertriebene,* without inquiring into the actual circumstances of their emigration."[65] The government's *Sonderprogramm Aussiedler,* or Special Program for Ethnic-German Immigrants, in 1988 provided these "ethnic Germans" with German citizenship and complete legal equality with Germans in the Federal Republic. The political loyalty assumptions that underlay jus sanguinis thus labeled ethnocultural "Germans" who had never set foot in the Federal Republic, knew nothing of its political and social system, and spoke no German as categorically "loyal" to the free democratic basic order. The large number of "ethnic German" migrants to the Federal Republic (nearly 1,200,000 between 1988 and 1991) after the collapse of Communism combined with the absurdity of this assumption to lead to a slight tightening of the treatment of "ethnic German" Aussiedler in 1991, including more stringent application procedures, some demonstration of connection to German "culture," and limitations on freedom of settlement once in the Federal Republic.[66] The operative principle for citizenship in the Federal Republic remained, however, jus sanguinis and its accompanying definitional assumption of loyal ties to the German nation among "ethnic Germans," regardless of domicile. For "ethnic non-Germans" seeking naturalization, the obverse definitional assumption of nonloyalty provided a significant hurdle to acquiring a naturalized "rational" German citizenship.

During the 1980s, foreigners became "Germans" at an average annual rate of less than one-tenth of what occurred in France, with its combination of jus soli and jus sanguinis. Controlling for France's attribution of citizenship in response to birth location and subsequent residence—which Germany did not allow—German naturalization was still roughly one-sixth of that of France's in the same period.[67] These figures suggested a rather high wall that naturalization applicants had to scale in the Federal Republic. Part, but not all, of that height was constructed, until the reforms of

1991 and 1993, by the rigorous formal demands made by the German state on the political beliefs and actions of naturalization applicants. Because the principle of pure jus sanguinis made irrelevant a person's country of birth or residence, long-term residents in the Federal Republic, including even second- and third-generation "ethnic non-Germans" who had never visited the country of their formal citizenship, were forced positively to demonstrate a number of extraordinary characteristics to qualify for naturalized German citizenship. These were characteristics not legally required of lifetime "ethnic Germans" of the Federal Republic, ex-East-German *Übersiedler*, or "ethnic German" Aussiedler from Eastern Europe and the ex-USSR at least until 1991.[68]

Most generally, these characteristics were captured in what was referred to as a "positive attitude toward German culture." Specifically, these included a long period of permanent residence and adequate accommodation in the Federal Republic; a good reputation; the capability to make a living for self and dependents without reliance on welfare; spoken and written German-language fluency; a "voluntary attachment" to Germany; a basic knowledge of Germany's political and social structures; no criminal record; and a positive commitment to the Federal Republic's "free democratic basic order."[69] The strong political ties to the ethnonational community that were assumed to be in place among "ethnic Germans" had to be positively demonstrated by "ethnic non-Germans" seeking the "rational" membership status of naturalized citizenship in the Federal Republic, regardless of their length of residence in the Federal Republic. Naturalization remained discretionary, controlled by state authorities whose job it was to determine the public interest in naturalizing any particular applicant. No private legal right to naturalization existed among "ethnic non-Germans," regardless of place of birth or residence.

While natural citizenship status was of course nonpoliticized for "ethnic Germans" in the Federal Republic during this period—for them there existed the legal assumption of a "realm of equality" without the need for a positive demonstration of political loyalty—for non-Germans seeking naturalization, citizenship law was politicized by the effects of the Federal Republic's lingering retention of the state/society dichotomy in the 1970s and 1980s. That dichotomy helped drive the German state's preoccupation with internal security and the potential political threat that foreigners posed. In the early 1980s, concerns for the "undivided loyalty" of German citizens and the "German nation's right to protect its own culture" drove the CDU/CSU to reject a liberalization of German naturalization policy.[70] Regular official reports in the Federal Republic on the criminality of foreigners in this period were consistent with the traditional dichotomization of hortatory state political actors "above" a society of unreliable citizens—or, even more problematic in this case, foreign residents.[71] The political stakes of West German naturalization reform in the 1980s turned directly on "militant democracy's" concern for political loyalty. The SPD stressed the need for foreigners in the Federal Republic to be provided assimilationist opportunities like education that would allow them to "earn" the "trust to respect democratic politics and eschew extremism." The CDU/CSU, in contrast, stressed integration and posited the desire of many foreigners to return to their countries of origin. According to Peter O'Brien, "both parties claim to protect pluralist democracy by excluding a large contingent of potentially antidemocratic voters [foreigners] from the political process."[72]

But liberal pluralist democracy was not the only issue at stake in this debate. In naturalization policy in this period, as well as with civil service policy, the old German statist logic of political membership was being invoked. That logic registered a deep concern for the state's ability to protect German society, or, in the Federal Republic, the "free democratic basic order." The concern in the 1980s to "protect" German democracy from the political threat of foreigners on German soil replicated West German civil service policy's concern to "protect" the "free democratic basic order" from dangerous West German citizens. Indeed, an Administrative Appeals Court judge in Baden-Württemberg argued: "To my mind, it is perfectly reasonable to require loyalty to the basic principles of the constitution as long as a clear distinction is made between fundamental constitutional principles and the existing political regime ... Political activities in emigrant organizations are usually taken as evidence against a permanent attachment to Germany. Activities in extremist or radical organizations justify, in general, the conclusion that the applicant is not committed to the democratic order of the Federal Republic."[73] The requirement to demonstrate a heightened positive political loyalty—and not mere political legality, required of "ethnic German," "natural" members of the political community—revealed the implicit assumption of positive attachment to the German ethnonation that accompanied the principle of pure jus sanguinis in the Federal Republic. That requirement was articulated in language nearly identical to that used in the 1970s to rationalize the exclusion of certain applicants, especially members of the Communist Party, from the "rational" political membership arena of the West German civil service. In this debate over naturalization, descent was at least implicitly held to create a more significant political tie to the German community than the "accidental" location of a person's birth or even lengthy domicile. If an "ethnic non-German" therefore desired naturalization, he or she had to demonstrate to a state official an extraordinary positive political tie to Germany and its institutions in order to remove a definitionally nonloyal status he or she harbored as an "outsider," regardless of possible domicile in the Federal Republic for decades.

Reformers in the Federal Republic responded by arguing that xenophobia and ethnocultural discrimination could be diminished if the wall between "insiders" and "outsiders" the German political community were substantially lowered. That is, if citizenship status were made less difficult to obtain—via "natural" attribution and "rational" acquisition—fewer "foreigners" would exist in Germany, and an officially sanctioned definition of "otherness" would end. If jus sanguinis were modified for the "natural" attribution of citizenship, and the demand for an extraordinary political loyalty were removed or lessened for the "rational" acquisition of naturalized status, political membership in the Federal Republic would become more universalized and more inhabitants would formally occupy a "region of legal equality." According to Jürgen Fijalkowski, "a modernized understanding of citizenship and nation ... could be based only on the rejection of an ethnonational understanding of citizenship. It would represent a turn toward an understanding of nation as a self-governing society formed by heterogeneous citizens. The nation of common ethnic descent would be transformed into a post-national society characterized by the will of citizens to live together under the common law of constitutional democracy irrespective of race, gender, ethnicity, descent, origin, social group, religion, and political thinking, looking to the future rather than to the past."[74] The new Aliens Law that took effect in January 1991, did not alter jus sanguinis for attributing "natural" citizenship, but it did significantly change some of the necessary, if not sufficient, criteria that a naturalization applicant had to meet to acquire "rational" membership in the Federal Republic.[75]

Most important, the 1991 reform granted a *Regelanspruch auf Einbürgerung*, or a typical eligibility for naturalization, to foreigners who had renounced their previous citizenship and met a number of formal conditions. For foreigners between the ages of sixteen and twenty-three, those included legal residence in the Federal Republic for eight years, school attendance for six years, and no criminal convictions. For foreigners over the age of twenty-three they included legal residence for fifteen years, no criminal convictions, and a means of maintenance for the applicant and his or her dependents that did not include welfare and unemployment assistance.[76] Gone was the explicit demand to demonstrate an extraordinary—at least relative to "ethnic Germans"—attachment and "positive attitude toward German culture." Remaining in the 1991 law was, however, a continued reliance on bureaucratic discretion, or *Ermessen der zuständigen Behörden*, for determining the public interest in granting German citizenship to any particular naturalization applicant. While that was to be granted typically, or *in der Regel*, these "eligible" foreigners possessed no automatic right to German citizenship. The Aliens Law of 1991 thus in no way changed German citizenship law, which continued to be based on the principle of pure jus sanguinis. It also did not affect the definition of the Federal Republic as "not an immigrant country." And it finally did not reverse federal government policy, in force since October 1982, to strive for the "integration" but not the "assimilation" of foreigners.

The government minister in charge of the affairs of foreigners defined the government policy of "integration" as a "peaceful coexistence between people of different origins."[77] The continued validity of pure jus sanguinis for "natural" membership attribution suggested that "origins"—or genealogical descent—continued to matter for defining membership in the German political community. "Peaceful coexistence" among "insiders" and "outsiders" within Germany's national-state borders, and not the assimilation of foreigners, was all that the German government formally declared was desirable. Cutting across these remnants of an ethnonational understanding of German membership, however, was the reform's stipulation of a Regelanspruch for German naturalization according to mainly domicile-based criteria. Gone was the political demand for a positive demonstration of an attachment to "Germanness." For adult foreigners, then, "peaceful coexistence" among "ethnic Germans" for fifteen years produced an "eligibility" for naturalization *in der Regel*. The odd juxtaposition of "peaceful coexistence" and "eligibility" for naturalization was an artifact of a government able to tackle and willing to liberalize the determinants of the "rational" acquisition of German membership but not its "natural" attribution, which still occurred according to the principle of jus sanguinis.

By the end of 1992, however, policymakers in the Federal Republic had agreed to amend the 1991 provision of a typical legal eligibility, or Regelanspruch, for naturalization, to a legal right, or *Rechtsanspruch*, to naturalization for persons meeting the formal, mainly domicile-related, requirements.[78] Coming into force in 1993, this amendment was not trivial. It appeared in a nation-state with an ethnonational tradition of defining "natural" citizenship according to jus sanguinis and "rational" naturalization as an extraordinary process available only to those who are able positively to demonstrate a deep loyal attachment to "German culture" and its political institutionalization. In the former context, as long as naturalization remained a matter defined by the public interest and not by private right, and as long as government policy continued to identify the Federal Republic as "not a country of immigration" striving for the "integration" but not "assimilation" of foreigners, bureaucratic discretion could very easily continue to make naturalization, even for those legally eligible, arduous and extraordinary. With the 1993 amendment granting a legal right to naturalization, however, bureaucratic discretion disappeared and Germany's naturalization policy was significantly depoliticized. Reinstituting Germany's pre-1913 concern for choice of domicile—but this time for "ethnic non-Germans" living in Germany and not for "ethnic Germans" living outside of the country—the 1993 law gave long-term foreign residents of Germany the right relatively unproblematically to acquire German citizenship. That status would not flow automatically, by "natural" attribution, but persons meeting other formal and universalistic requirements could legally claim it. This state-national reform of German membership now meant that state boundaries mattered for "ethnic non-German" foreigners who chose to live legally inside the borders of the Federal Republic for a lengthy period and who formally applied for naturalization.

The introduction of *jus domicilii*, or law of domicile, for "rational" membership in the Federal Republic did not alter pure jus sanguinis for "natural" political membership. But it marked a clear liberalization and universalization of German citizenship law. It also marked the increasing anachronism of German statism, with its central role of political loyalty, as an appropriate logic for defining political membership in the Federal Republic. Though naturalization remained relatively arduous in the Federal Republic after 1993, it no longer involved a positive demonstration of heightened—relative to "ethnic Germans"—political loyalty. The reforms of 1991 and 1993 at least sanctioned if they did not create a society of more heterogeneous citizens in the Federal Republic. All political parties in the early 1990s, including the most reluctant CDU/CSU, recognized the undesirability of having vast numbers of legal foreign residents living in the Federal Republic.[79] After the murderous violence against foreigners, especially in 1991 and 1992, hundreds of thousands of Germans from all parties, interest groups, and religious denominations protested in candle-light marches against intolerance and the mistreatment of foreigners on German soil. Though the 1993 law still required fifteen years of "integration" before the status of citizenship became a legal right, it—like Germany's more pragmatic civil service personnel policy for ex-GDR state employees—marked a considerable shift away from the historical politicization and segmentation of political membership in Germany that was based on a positive political loyalty vetted "from above."

Conclusion

Shifts in the Federal Republic's political culture beginning in the 1960s left an increasing number of German citizens rejecting German statism as an inappropriate logic of political membership. That logic, which was latently appropriate for the German debate in 1989 and 1990, succumbed to a more pragmatic and universalistic understanding of the nature of German political membership in policy debates the early 1990s. In this chapter, two policy areas in which "rational" political membership in the German community was clearly at stake—civil service policy and naturalization policy—revealed that a concern for political loyalty, which had historically been overarching in these policy areas, had either completely disappeared (in the case of naturalization) or been substantially watered down (in the case of civil service policy). At the same time, jus sanguinis continued to define "natural" citizenship in the Federal Republic, and the "traditional principles of the professional civil service" were not struck from the Federal Republic's Basic Law. But the removal, or substantial reduction, of required political loyalty to enter these areas of rational political membership signaled that the statist barrier to the gradual development of a more heterogeneous, multicultural, and horizontally differentiated public sphere in the Federal Republic had been considerably lowered. Both the pragmatic liberalization of civil service policy and the residence modification of naturalization law reduced the political stakes for the acquisition of a rational membership status in the German political community and thereby reduced the relevance of loyalty politics in the Federal Republic generally.

As ordinary German citizens began in the 1960s to demonstrate a will and a competence to engage in a meaningful, successful, and creative "politics of the first person," not only did the extraordinary political demands on professional German civil servants decrease in sensibility, but similar demands placed on foreigners applying to become naturalized German citizens grew anachronistic as well. This process in the Federal Republic since the 1960s has been eminently political and its progress slow and uneven. But with the demise of the vertical segmentation of German public life and the creation of a vibrant and active democratic horizontal differentiation among different kinds of "Germans" that this process promises, the political legitimacy of German citizens will increasingly displace that of German state civil servants in Germany's new political logic of membership. Xenophobia and intolerance of the "other"—people once marginalized not only ethnoculturally but also politically in statism's "lower" realm of society—are also likely to lessen in a political landscape whose discursive axes have become more horizontal and less vertical.

Notes

1. Grzegorz Ekiert, "Democratization Processes in East Central Europe: A Theoretical Reconsideration," *British Journal of Political Science* 21, no. 3 (1991): 287.
2. George J. Szablowski and Hans-Ulrich Derlien, "East European Transitions, Elites, Bureaucracies, and the European Community," *Governance* 6, no. 3 (1993): 304–324; Klaus von Beyme, "Regime Transition and Recruitment of Elites in Eastern Europe," *Governance* 6, no. 3 (1993): 409–25.
3. Max Weber, "Bureaucracy," *Economy and Society*, 2 vols., ed. Guenther Roth and Claus Wittich (Berkeley: University of California Press, 1978), 2: 973, 988–89.
4. Claus Offe, "'Crises of Crisis Management': Elements of a Political Crisis Theory," *Contradictions of the Welfare State* (Cambridge: The MIT Press, 1984), 35–64.
5. Graham K. Wilson, "Counter-Elites and Bureaucracies," *Governance* 6, no. 3 (1993): 435.

6. Giuseppe DiPalma, "Legitimation from the Top to Civil Society: Politico-Cultural Change in Eastern Europe," *World Politics* 44 (1991): 64; Beyme, "Regime Transition and Recruitment of Elites," 416.

7. Klaus König, "Bureaucratic Integration by Elite Transfer: The Case of the Former GDR," *Governance* 6, no. 3 (1993): 88–89.

8. Walter Leisner, "Verfassungsreform des öffentlichen Dienstrechts?" *Aus Politik und Zeitgeschichte, Beilage zur Wochenzeitung Das Parlament* 1991, no. 49: 33; Franz Kroppenstedt, "Der öffentliche Dienst der Zukunft," *Zeitschrift für Beamtenrecht*, 1990, no. 7: 198.

9. *Texte zur Deutschlandpolitik*, ed., Bundesministerium für innerdeutsche Beziehungen (Bonn: Deutscher Bundesverlag, 1991), series 3, vol. 8b-1990, 7–17.

10. *Das Grundgesetz für die Bundesrepublik Deutschland*, Article 33, Sections 1–5.

11. *Texte zur Deutschlandpolitik*, 458–62.

12. Gerhard Lehmbruch, "Die deutsche Vereinigung: Strukturen und Strategien," *Politische Vierteljahresschrift* 32, no. 4 (1991): 596.

13. "Öffentliche Dienst so klein und effektiv wie möglich machen," *Süddeutsche Zeitung*, 6 July 1991; "Berufsbeamte falsch am Platz," *Berliner Zeitung*, 24 August 1991; *ÖTV Pressedienst* 41, no. 37 (1990).

14. Peter Katzenstein, *Policy and Politics in West Germany: The Growth of a Semisovereign State* (Philadelphia: Temple University Press, 1987), 260–66.

15. *CDU/CSU Fraktion im Deutschen Bundestag*, no. 543, 8 January 1991; "Der Beamte—ein auslaufendes Modell?" *Kölner Stadtanzeiger*, 8 November 1991.

16. *Der Bundesminister des Innern teilt mit:* "Ansprache von Staatssekretär Franz Kroppenstedt," 8 January 1991; Heinz Schmitz, "Schonzeit für Staatsdiener," *Handelsblatt*, 18 September 1990; *CSU Pressemitteilung*, no. 193, 22 May 1990.

17. König, "Bureaucratic Integration by Elite Transfer," 386–89.

18. Karl-Dietrich Bracher, "Vierzig Jahre Diktatur (SED Unrecht)—Herausforderung an den Rechtsstaat," *Recht und Politik* 27, no. 3 (1991): 139.

19. Anke Warbeck, "Die hergebrachten Grundsätze des Berufsbeamtentums im Wandel der Zeiten und ihre Bedeutung," *Recht im Amt* 37, no. 6 (1990): 296.

20. Eric Hobsbawm, "Introduction: Inventing Traditions," in Hobsbawm and Terence Ranger, eds., *The Invention of Tradition* (Cambridge: Cambridge University Press, 1983), 1, 9–10.

21. Weber, "Bureaucracy," 959 [Weber's italics].

22. *DPA*, no. 767, 29 November 1989; *Deutschland-Union-Dienst* 43, no. 147, 3 August 1989.

23. *CDU/CSU Fraktion im Deutschen Bundestag*, 8 November 1991; *CDU/CSU Fraktion im Deutschen Bundestag*, 7 May 1990; "Der Beamte—ein auslaufendes Modell?" *Kölner Stadtanzeiger*, 8 November 1991; "Aufbau Ost als Meisterstück des deutschen Beamtentums," *Frankfurter Rundschau*, 11 November 1991.

24. "Momper gibt SED-Beamten Chance," *Wirtschaftswoche*, 31 August 1990; "SPD will die Sonderzulagen für Beamte in der DDR stoppen," *Die Tageszeitung*, 17 September 1990.

25. *Sozialdemokratischer Pressedienst* 46, no. 144, 31 July 1991; "Ersatzlose Abschaffung des Berufsbeamtentums nicht in Frage," *Bonner Behörden Spiegel*, October 1991; "Bonn kommentiert," *Staatszeitung*, 8 April 1991; "Staatsdiener sind nicht anders," *Saarbrücker Zeitung*, 3 July 1991; "Lohn nach Rückkehr," *Frankfurter Allgemeine Zeitung*, 7 May 1991.

26. *Grundsatzprogramm der Sozialdemokratischen Partei Deutschlands* (Bonn: 1989), 49.

27. DiPalma, "Legitimation from the Top to Civil Society," 55 (note 20), 63–78.

28. Szablowski and Derlien, "East European Transitions," 312.
29. Uwe Thaysen, *Der Runde Tisch. Oder: Wo blieb das Volk?* (Opladen: Westdeutscher Verlag, 1990), 73–82.
30. William E. Paterson and Gordon Smith, "German Unity," in *Developments in German Politics*, ed. Smith, Paterson, Peter H. Merkl, and Stephen Padgett (Durham: Duke University Press, 1992), 26.
31. *Die SPD im Deutschen Bundestag*, no. 618, 13 March 1991.
32. *Der Bundesminister des Innern teilt mit.*
33. "Ersatzlose Abschaffung des Berufsbeamtentums nicht in Frage," *Bonner Behörden Spiegel*, October 1991; "Berufsbeamtentum falsch am Platz," *Berliner Zeitung*, 24 August 1991; *CDU/CSU Fraktion im Deutschen Bundestag*, no. 484, 26 November 1990.
34. *Der Bundesminister des Innern teilt mit.*
35. *Der Bundesminister des Innern teilt mit; Deutschland-Union-Dienst* 45, no. 182, 29 October 1991; "Stasi im Staatsdienst," *Der Spiegel*, 5 March 1990.
36. Emil Kirchner, "The Federal Republic of Germany in the European Community," in *The Federal Republic of Germany at Forty*, ed. Peter H. Merkl (New York: New York University Press, 1989), 428; T. Hitiris, *European Community Economics* (New York: St. Martin's Press, 1991), 251–71.
37. *CDU/CSU Fraktion im Deutschen Bundestag*, no. 543, 8 January 1991; *F.D.P.-Bundestagsfraktion informiert*, no. 620, 28 May 1990.
38. *CDU/CSU Fraktion im Deutschen Bundestag*, 8 January 1991; *CDU/CSU Fraktion im Deutschen Bundestag* August 13, 1991; *CDU/CSU Fraktion im Deutschen Bundestag* November 8, 1991; *Der Bundesminister des Innern teilt mit; DPA*, no. 935, 28 October 1991; *Bayrische Staatsregierung Bulletin*, no. 20, 2 October 1990.
39. *CDU/CSU Fraktion im Deutschen Bundestag*, 13 August 1991; *Der Bundesminister des Innern teilt mit.*
40. *Grundsatzprogramm der Sozialdemokratischen Partei Deutschlands*, 36; *ppp* 40, no. 7, 10 January 1989; *Sozialdemokratischer Pressedienst*, no. 144, 31 July 1991.
41. "Diskussion um Radikalenerlaß neu entbrannt," *Stuttgarter Zeitung*, 4 July 1990.
42. *Presseservice der SPD*, no. 656, 18 October 1989.
43. "Kritik am Radikalenerlaß," *Stuttgarter Nachrichten*, 13 July 1990; "Hetzjagd auf unbescholtene Genossen," *Süddeutsche Zeitung*, 10 November 1990.
44. *Der Bundesmininster des Innern teilt mit: Rede von Bundesinnenminister Dr. Friedrich Zimmermann*, 10 January 1989, 20–21; *DDP*, no. 205, 10 January 1989.
45. "Zu viel Beschäftigte beim Staat," *Stuttgarter Nachrichten*, 11 January 1991; *DPA*, no. 935, 28 October 1991; *Deutschland-Union-Dienst* 45, no. 182, 29 October 1991.
46. *Sozialdemokratischer Pressedienst*, no. 144, 31 July 1991.
47. See Karsten Schröder and Hermann Horstkotte, "Foreigners in Germany," *Sozial-Report* 2 (1993): 1–6.
48. "Erklärung des Bundeskanzlers zu den Ausschreitungen in Rostock," *Bulletin*, no. 90, 29 August 1992, 860; Dieter Roth, "*Volksparteien* in Crisis? The Electoral Successes of the Extreme Right in Context," *German Politics* 2, no. 1 (1993): 12–15; Alan Watson, *Focus on Germany: Dangers from the Right?* (Washington, D.C.: Edition Q, Inc., 1993), 8; Sam Blay and Andreas Zimmermann, "Recent Changes in German Refugee Law: A Critical Assessment," *The American Journal of International Law* 88, no. 2 (1994): 361–78; Hermann Kurthen, "Germany at the Crossroads: National Identity and the Challenges of Immigration," *International Migration Review* 29, no. 4, (1995): 924–29.

49. Kay Hailbronner, "Citizenship and Nationhood in Germany," in *Immigration and the Politics of Citizenship in Europe and North America*, ed. William Rogers Brubaker (Lanham, MD: University Press of America, 1989), 72.

50. Ibid., 77–79.

51. Max Weber, "Political Communities," in *Economy and Society*, 2 vols., ed. Guenther Roth and Claus Wittich (Berkeley: University of California Press, 1978), 2: 901ff.

52. William J. Serow et al., eds., *Handbook on International Migration* (New York: Greenwood Press, 1990), 1–5.

53. Rogers Brubaker, *Citizenship and Nationhood in France and Germany* (Cambridge: Harvard University Press, 1992), ix-xi.

54. Tomas Hammar, *Democracy and the Nation-State: Aliens, Denizens, and Citizens in a World of International Migration* (Aldershot: Avebury, 1990), 29.

55. Fritz Franz, "Wahlrecht, ZAR-Rechtsprechung," *Zeitschrift für Ausländerrecht und Ausländerpolitik*, 1991, no. 1: 40–43; Barbara Marshall, "German Migration Policies," in *Developments in German Politics*, ed. Gordon Smith, et al., 250–51.

56. "Reichs- und Staatsangehörigkeitsgesetz, vom 22. Juli 1913, No. 4263," *Reichs-Gesetzblatt*, 1913, no. 46: 583–84; "Bericht der Beauftragten der Bundesregierung für die Belange der Ausländer über die Lage der Ausländer in der Bundesrepublik Deutschland, 1993," *Mitteilungen der Beauftragten der Bundesregierung für die Belange der Ausländer*, 1994, 84.

57. Brubaker, *Citizenship and Nationhood*, 115.

58. Ibid., 123.

59. Ibid., 115.

60. "Reichs- und Staatsangehörigkeitsgesetz, vom 22. Juli 1913, No. 4263, Sections 8–9," *Reichs-Gesetzblatt*, 1913, no. 46: 584–85.

61. Peter O'Brien, "German-Polish Migration: The Elusive Search for a German Nation-State," *International Migration Review* 26, no. 2 (1991): 379.

62. Brubaker, *Citizenship and Nationhood*, 16.

63. Ibid., 134, 136.

64. Ibid., 136–37.

65. Katzenstein, *Policy and Politics in West Germany*, 212–13; Brubaker, *Citizenship and Nationhood*, 206–07, note 19.

66. Marshall, "German Migration Policies," 256–57; James F. Hollifield, *Immigrants, Markets, and States: The Political Economy of Postwar Europe* (Cambridge: Harvard University Press, 1992), 35.

67. Brubaker, *Citizenship and Nationhood*, 82.

68. Jürgen Fijalkowski, *Aggressive Nationalism, Immigration Pressure, and Asylum Policy Disputes in Contemporary Germany*, Occasional Paper no. 9, ed. Hartmut Lehmann (Washington D.C.: German Historical Institute, 1993), 19.

69. Hailbronner, "Citizenship and Nationhood," 68–69; Kurthen, "Germany at the Crossroads," 932.

70. Laura M. Murray, "*Einwanderungsland Bundesrepublik Deutschland?* Explaining the Evolving Positions of German Political Parties on Citizenship Policy," *German Politics and Society*, no. 33, (1994): 28.

71. James Sperling, "(Im)migration and German Security in Post-Yalta Europe," *German Studies Review* 17, no. 3 (1994): 542.

72. Peter O'Brien, "The Civil Rights of West Germany's Migrants," *German Politics and Society*, no.19, (1990): 34–38.

73. Hailbronner, "Citizenship and Nationhood," 68–69.

74. Fijalkowski, *Aggressive Nationalism*, 26–27.
75. Marshall, "German Migration Policies," 251–52.
76. "Gesetz zur Neuregelung des Ausländerrechts vom 9. Juli 1990, Article 1, Sections 85–86," *Bundesgesetzblatt*, part 1, no. 34, 14 July 1990, 1375; Schröder and Horstkotte, "Foreigners in Germany," 4; "Bericht der Beauftragten der Bundesregierung," 84.
77. Schröder and Horstkotte, "Foreigners in Germany," 2–3.
78. "Gesetz zur Änderung asylverfahrens-, ausländer- und staatsangehörigkeitsrechtlicher Vorschriften vom 30. Juni 1993, Art. 2, No. 12–13," *Mitteilungen der Beauftragten der Bundesregierung für die Belange der Ausländer*, part 1, no. 33, 1 July 1993, 1072; "Bericht der Beauftragten der Bundesregierung," 85.
79. Murray, "*Einwanderungsland Bundesrepublik Deutschland?*" 23–56.

CONCLUSION

The Demise of German Statism and the Tensions of Democratic Political Membership

This study has traced the rise and demise of statist loyalty politics in Germany from the beginning of the nineteenth century to the end of the twentieth. It addressed a powerful logic of political membership that vertically segmented a German state of reliably loyal professional political actors above a German society of politically unreliable ordinary citizens or subjects. We first clarified the terms of the study by differentiating "natural" from "rational" political membership. Defining "rational" political membership as contingent on the intentional wills of applicants to, and gate-keeping members of, established political communities, we turned next to the concept of political loyalty. In the German political tradition, an adequate political loyalty had historically been required of successful applicants to "rational" venues of German political membership. Indeed, a required political loyalty, vetted "from above" by German state gatekeepers, had served as the main ideological requirement in Germany's statist logic of political membership since the nineteenth century. Moving from concerns of conceptualization, the study investigated three German historical episodes of political mobilization "from below." These episodes were the liberal political mobilization of the Prussian Vormärz, the workers' and soldiers' mobilization of the early Weimar years, and the leftist/student political mobilization beginning in the 1960s in the Federal Republic. To determine the relative appropriateness of German statism for these episodes of political mobilization, we considered the discourse used in these periods to sort German political actors into different venues of political membership.

The case of the Prussian Vormärz revealed the initial articulation and consolidation of the statist logic of membership in a context of significant political and social upheaval. In this period, Germany's first mass logic of political membership defined loyal service to the universalistic Geist of the Prussian state as hortatory political action relative to the particularistic strivings of mobilized subjects in Prussian society. Seventy years later, the Weimar Republic was founded during a revolutionary mobilization of soldiers and workers in the aftermath of war defeat. Periodic rhetorical overtures to republican virtues notwithstanding, Weimar's reluctant new political leaders, plucked from the opposition SPD and thrust unexpectedly into power, lacked anything resembling a distinctive republican political discourse to help them govern. In the process, they retained a tremendous respect tainted by intimidation for the professional civil service that they preserved virtually intact from the Wilhelmine era, and they harbored a tremendous fear of the anarchy represented by mobilized German workers and soldiers. In the early Weimar years, German statism thus remained a familiar, systematic, partly functional, and yet ultimately tragic political logic of membership for the Republic's hesitant new regime to adopt.

Germany's second experiment with democracy began once more in the wake of war defeat. The Federal Republic's new institutional arrangement in 1949, which elevated German political parties to the commanding heights of political authority, represented a conscious rejection of the normative values that nineteenth-century German statism had attached to key German political institutions. Despite this institutional rearrangement, the identities of West Germany's postwar civil service and new political parties nonetheless retained traces of the old hierarchical logic pitting a politically reliable German state (now including political parties) above a politically unreliable German society. Unlike the Weimar Republic thirty years earlier, however, the Federal Republic was about to experience a protracted decades-long confrontation with, and ultimately successful rejection of, the appropriateness of this logic for the practice of contemporary German politics. Mobilized West Germans began in the 1960s to "dare more democracy" and reform the Federal Republic's political institutions and political culture. Their targets included the venerated professional state civil service that the Federal Republic had anchored constitutionally with the Basic Law's codification of the institution's "traditional principles"— which some observers traced back to tenth-century feudal law.

They also included the Federal Republic's political parties of the Parteienstaat, challenged by citizens' initiatives in the 1970s and by the Greens, as an "anti-party" party, in the 1980s. At the end of the 1980s, the appropriateness of Germany's nineteenth-century statist logic of membership briefly rebounded. That discourse was found to be appropriate for the German unification debate by many—though certainly not all—political elites and German voters. At that time, CDU-led federal government attempted to speed up German unification, reassure East German citizens, and defeat the SPD in the federal election of 1990 by deploying familiar and reassuring, if generally anachronistic, statist imagery in this extraordinary political context. Less existential political debates in the early 1990s, however, indicated the extraordinary nature not just of German unification, but also of the political discourse party elites used to debate it. In civil service and naturalization policy—where required political loyalty for these "rational" venues of political membership had traditionally loomed large—German statism was revealed as a political discourse no longer fully appropriate. It was gradually being replaced by the expectation that political loyalty, or its equivalent, would authentically develop in people "from below," in an adequate amount, to permit their entrance into these rational membership venues.

Statist Loyalty and Its Alternatives

The demise of the statist logic of political membership in the Federal Republic in the mid-1990s did not signal the wholesale rejection of the relevance of political loyalty for German politics generally. The anti-statist political mobilization the Federal Republic had experienced since the 1960s targeted the top-down statist vetting of the political loyalty of individual applicants for venues of "rational" political membership. It did not target the idea of strong political attachment as such. It rejected a logic of political membership that vertically dichotomized a hortatory realm of loyal political action and belief above a realm of definitionally nonloyal political unreliability. And it alternatively offered the open-ended expectation that ordinary people in German society would authentically develop over time, through complex processes of socialization and adaptation, systemic political attachments that were genuine, but perhaps not suitably measured by political tests administered by German state actors from above. The demise of German statism thus left contemporary German politics more democratic and less alien to ordinary German citizens, but not at the same time less contentious, either substantively or procedurally.

Specifically, the demise of German statism left politics in the Federal Republic discursively contentious not only in a manner familiar to the practice of modern democratic politics generally, but also in a manner specific to a context that had just rejected the discursive appropriateness of German statism. Political discourse in the Federal Republic in the 1990s had to cope with the tension between the political participation of mobilized German citizens, on the one hand, and the political leadership of legitimate German political authorities, on the other—especially political party elites in the Parteienstaat. While the tension between citizen participation and political leadership is typical for modern democracy, it was made particularly taut in the Federal Republic in the 1990s by the recent demise of the appropriateness of German statism. German statism's understanding of the tension between citizen participation and political leadership had been to reduce it to a resolvable contradiction: the participation of narrow interest-seeking citizens or subjects in the lower realm of German society was to be contained by the leadership of vetted professional civil servants located in the hortatory political realm of the German state. With the demise of German statism, the transformation of a resolvable contradiction between citizens and leaders into an unresolvable tension left more than one German political observer in the 1990s lamenting the poor quality of political leadership in the Federal Republic— which not accidentally followed a widespread criticism of the poor quality of political citizenship, so to speak, in the Federal Republic in the 1980s.

As discussed above, the lingering survival of German statism in the 1980s left the Greens struggling to define a political program free of the statist discourse they so explicitly despised. That surviving statism also left the Greens susceptible to critiques that dismissed them, and political forces like them, as anarchistic and politically illegitimate actors located in the "lower" realm of German society. But with the general demise of this surviving statism in the 1990s, the ritualistic denigration of German citizens was traded for a not-yet-ritualistic, but definitely rhetorical, denigration of German political leaders, especially those found in political parties and especially Helmut Kohl.[1] Somewhat consistent with the imagery of German statism, political party elites came under fire in this period for their alleged leadership incompetence. This was particularly problematic because the citizens they might lead in the Federal Republic in the 1990s were much less politically threatening than they had been in the 1980s. The Greens, German society's most successful political force organized "from below," had discarded most of their plebiscitary trappings and become a functioning "realo" party with a nonrotating slate of leaders and a willingness to entertain almost all manner of coalitional options, including the CDU.[2] The normalization of representative politics in the Federal Republic in the 1990s focused attention on Germany's political representatives. No doubt the leadership critiques in this period had to do with the malaise of post-unification, but they were made discursively possible by a shift that now targeted the performance of political leaders and their capacity to lead a newly legitimized, but not solely legitimate, society of participating German citizens.

One of the most noteworthy critiques of political leadership in the Federal Republic in the 1990s came from the state's former federal president, Richard von Weizsäcker. In 1995, Weizsäcker, the "conscience" of the German nation, defined democracy as a constitutional order in which imperfect citizens constructed imperfect compromises from the clash of particular interests. Modern democracy thus desperately required, he argued, the presence of a politically informed and competent leadership by example.[3] In this speech, Weizsäcker reiterated arguments he had developed in 1992, when he attacked—in the process unleashing a major political controversy—what he saw as the incompetence, overdeveloped power, and ubiquitous presence of catch-all political parties and their leaders in the Federal Republic. Then he argued, "the German parliament hardly has a member who could, as an equal, discuss such an important and difficult topic as monetary policy with an expert from the Federal Bank, from academia, or from the state administration. The main aspect of the acquired profession of our politicians consists of supporting what the party wants in order to be nominated and attain a high position in the party list and then secure that position once there."[4] Lost in the process, Weizsäcker continued, was any appreciation of the "political will of the people." With the end of the Cold War, "the need for an orientation is only getting stronger." He asked, "do our party politicians have the ability to provide that?"[5] Weizsäcker was read by some in 1992 as rehashing the old German statist critique of parliament, political parties, and their respective members as "lower" and politically illegitimate societal actors. But here

Weizsäcker's critics were themselves caught in the old dichotomy that Weizsäcker was rejecting.

In Germany's nineteenth-century statist logic of political membership, German political leaders—primarily professional state bureaucrats—were assigned the role of providing not only the orientating political leadership Weizsäcker demanded, but also the political answers to questions that they more or less posed themselves. In the very best of times, these state actors came close to embodying German statism's ideal of educated, professional, politically loyal, and dutiful service to citizens and subjects located in German society. At other times, like in the late Prussian Vormärz, German liberals denounced individual state actors as inept, corrupt, ineffective, and self-interested. Weizsäcker's 1992 critique thus somewhat resembled the Bureaukratiekritik of the 1840s, but the target of his comments were power-hungry political parties and inept party politicians, not power-hungry and inept bureaucrats. Even more important, Weizsäcker's solution to the failures of political leadership in the Federal Republic in the 1990s —unlike that of the Bureaukratiekritik—was the further political empowerment of Germany's citizens. Weizsäcker's flowing endorsement of the Green party's struggle to maintain a productive tension between the responsibility of political leadership, on the one hand, and mass political mobilization, on the other, was not the statist solution of German liberals in the 1840s, or, even more oddly, of a Hegelian statism of which some of his critics in this debate accused him.[6] Weizsäcker's critique of party politicians in the 1990s was entirely consistent with the articulation and consolidation of a horizontal democratic logic of German political membership beginning to take root in Germany at the end of the twentieth century. The transition from statist political discourse to a democratic idea of belonging to and participating in a political community is a transition from a profoundly rationalistic and security-providing political logic to one that is open-ended and produces tentative and contentious outcomes. It is not a small transition. But it is one that bodes well for German democracy.

Notes

1. Erwin K. and Ute Scheuch, *Cliquen, Klüngel and Karrieren: Über den Verfall der politischen Parteien—eine Studie* (Reinbek bei Hamburg: Rowohlt, 1992).
2. E. Gene Frankland, "The Greens' Comeback in 1994: The Third Party of Germany," in *Germans Divided: The 1994 Bundestag Elections and the Evolution of the German Party System*, ed. Russell J. Dalton (Oxford: Berg, 1996), 85–108.
3. Richard von Weizsäcker, "The VII International Catalonia Prize," *Catalonia*, no. 44, (1996): 39–43.
4. Gunter Hofmann, ed., *Richard von Weizsäcker im Gespräch mit Gunter Hofmann und Werner A. Perger* (Frankfurt am Main: Eichborn Verlag, 1992), 150–51.
5. Ibid., 151.
6. Ibid., 173–75.

BIBLIOGRAPHY

Newspapers, unaffiliated press services, magazines:

Die Abendzeitung, Bayernkurier, Berliner Zeitung, Bonner Behörden Spiegel, Bonner Rundschau, DPA, Frankfurter Allgemeine Zeitung, Frankfurter Rundschau, General-Anzeiger, Hamburger Kurs, Hamburger Morgenpost, Kölner Stadtanzeiger, Das Parlament, ppp, Saarbrücker Zeitung, Der Spiegel, Staatszeitung, Stuttgarter Nachrichten, Süddeutsche Zeitung, Die Tageszeitung, Die Welt, Westfälische Rundschau, Wirtschaftswoche, Die Zeit.

Government publications, press services:

(Bundesregierung) Bulletin; BPA-Nachrichtenabteilung; Pressemitteilung, Presse- und Informationsamt der Bundesregierung; Der Bundesminister des Innern teilt mit; Der Bundesminister des Auswärtigen informiert; Bayrische Staatsregierung Bulletin; Reichs-Gesetzblatt; Mitteilungen der Beauftragten der Bundesregierung für die Belange der Ausländer; Bundesgesetzblatt.

Political party and interest group publications, documents, press services:

SPD: *Parteitag der Sozialdemokratischen Partei Deutschland—Protokoll der Verhandlungen 1973, 1977, 1979, 1989; Jahrbuch der Sozialdemokratischen Partei Deutschlands, 1973–1975, 1975–1977, 1979–1981, 1982–1983; Grundsatzprogramm der Sozialdemokratischen Partei Deutschlands, 1989; Sitzungen der [SPD] Parteivorstandes Protokolle, 1973, 1974, 1975, 1976, 1977, 1978* (meeting minutes, Friedrich-Ebert-Stiftung, Bonn-Bad Godesberg); *Fraktionssitzungsprotokolle [SPD], VII, 8. Oktober 1974—17. Dezember 1975* (meeting minutes, Friedrich-Ebert-Stiftung, Bonn-Bad Godesberg); *Collected Papers of Willy Brandt* (Friedrich-Ebert-Stiftung, Bonn-Bad Godesberg); *SPD Pressemitteilungen und Informationen; SPD Jungsozialisten Pressemitteilung; Presseservice der SPD; Die SPD im Deutschen Bundestag; Sozialdemokratischer Pressedienst.*
CDU/CSU: *Bundesparteitag der Christlich Demokratischen Union Deutschlands, Niederschrift, 1972, 1973, 1976, 1978, 1979, 1981; Deutschland-Union-Dienst; UiD-Dokumentation; Union-Medienbeobachter; CDU/CSU Fraktion im Deutschen Bundestag, Pressedienst; Pressemitteilung der CDU; CSU Presse-Mitteilungen, Nachrichten aus der CSU-Landesgruppe im Deutschen Bundestag; CSU Pressemitteilung.*
F.D.P.: *23. Ordentliche Bundesparteitag der F.D.P. vom 2. bis 4. Oktober 1972; F.D.P. Die Liberalen, Kieler Thesen, Beschloßen auf dem 28. Ordentlichen Bundesparteitag der F.D.P. vom 6. bis 8. November 1977; fdk Tagesdienst: Pressedienst der Bundestagsfraktion der F.D.P.*

Greens: *Grüner Basis-Dienst; Die Grünen im Bundestag, Pressedienst.*
ÖTV: *ÖTV Pressedienst.*

Books, articles:

Albertin, Lothar. "German Liberalism and the Foundation of the Weimar Republic: Missed Opportunity?" In *German Democracy and the Triumph of Hitler*, ed. Anthony Nicholls and Erich Matthais. London: George Allen and Unwin, 1971.
———. *Liberalismus und Demokratie am Anfang der Weimarer Republik.* Düsseldorf: Droste Verlag, 1972.
Almond, Gabriel, Scott Flanagan, and Robert Mundt, eds. *Crisis, Choice and Change: Historical Studies in Political Development.* Boston: Little, Brown, 1973.
Almond, Gabriel, and Sidney Verba, eds. *The Civic Culture Revisited.* Boston: Little, Brown, 1980.
Angermann, Erich. *Robert von Mohl: Leben und Werke, Ein altliberalen Staatsgelehrten.* Neuwied: Hermann Luchterhand Verlag, 1962.
———. "Germany's 'Peculiar Institution': The *Beamtentum*." In *Oceans Apart? Comparing Germany and the United States: Studies in Commemoration of the 150th Anniversary of the Birth of Carl Schurz*, ed. Erich Angermann and Marie-Luise Frings. Stuttgart: Klett-Cotta, 1981.
Arndt, Gottfried. "Zur Vereinbarkeit der Mitgliedschaft in nicht verfassungs-feindlichen Parteien und Vereinigungen mit Beschäftigung im öffentlichen Dienst." *Zeitschrift für Beamtenrecht*, 1974, no. 4: 121–28.
Ash, Timothy Garton. *In Europe's Name: Germany and the Divided Continent.* New York: Random House, 1993.
Bahro, Rudolf. "Hinein oder hinaus? Die Position der Fundamentalisten." In *SPD und Grüne: Das neue Bündnis?* ed. Wolfram Bickerich. Reinbek bei Hamburg: Rowohlt, 1985.
Baker, Kendall, Russell Dalton, and Kai Hildebrandt. *Germany Transformed: Political Culture and the New Politics.* Cambridge: Harvard University Press, 1981.
Balfour, Michael. *West Germany: A Contemporary History.* New York: St. Martin's Press, 1982.
Ball, Terence, James Farr, and Russell L. Hanson. "Editors' Introduction." In *Political Innovation and Conceptual Change*, ed. Terence Ball, James Farr, and Russell L. Hanson. Cambridge: Cambridge University Press, 1989.
Barbalet, J. M. *Citizenship: Rights, Struggle, and Class Inequality.* Minneapolis: University of Minnesota Press, 1988.
Baring, Arnulf. *Machtwechsel: Die Ära Brandt-Scheel.* Stuttgart: Deutsche Verlags-Anstalt, 1982.
Bark Dennis L., and David R. Gress. *A History of West Germany.* Vol. 1, *From Shadow to Substance, 1945–1960.* Oxford: Basil Blackwell, 1989.
Battis, Ulrich. "Rechtssprechung zur Radikalen-Frage." *Juristische Arbeitsblätter*, 1979, no. 2: 73–77.
Bendersky, Joseph. *Carl Schmitt: Theorist for the Reich.* Princeton: Princeton University Press, 1983.
Bendix, Reinhard. *Max Weber: An Intellectual Portrait.* Garden City: Doubleday, 1962.
———. *Nation-Building and Citizenship.* New York: John Wiley & Sons, 1967. Reprint, Berkeley: University of California Press, 1977.
Bendix, Reinhard, John Bendix, and Norman Furniss. "Reflections on Modern Western States and Civil Societies." *Research in Political Sociology* 3 (1987): 1–38.
Berdahl, Robert. *The Politics of the Prussian Nobility: The Development of a Conservative Ideology, 1770–1848.* Princeton: Princeton University Press, 1988.
Berger, Suzanne. "Politics and Anti-Politics in Western Europe in the Seventies." *Daedalus* 108, no. 2 (1979): 27–50.
Berghahn, Volker R., and Martin Kitchen, eds. *Germany in the Age of Total War.* London: Croom Helm, 1981.
Berner, Georg. "'Radikalenerlaß' und Rechtssprechung." *Politische Studien*, no. 233, (1977): 287–303.

Bessel, Richard, and E. J. Feuchtwanger, eds. *Social Change and Political Development in Weimar Germany*. London: Croom Helm, 1982.

Betz, Hans-Georg. *Radical Right-Wing Populism in Western Europe*. New York: St. Martin's Press, 1994.

Beyme, Klaus von. "Der Neo-Korporatismus und die Politik des begrenzten Pluralism in der Bundesrepublik." In *Stichworte zur "Geistigen Situation der Zeit."* Vol. 1, *Nation und Republik*, ed. Jürgen Habermas. Frankfurt am M.: Suhrkamp Verlag, 1979.

———. "Partei, Faktion." In *Geschichtliche Grundbegriffe: Historisches Lexikon zur politisch-sozialen Sprache in Deutschland*, ed. Werner Brunner, Werner Conze, and Reinhart Koselleck. Vol. 4, *Mi-Pre*. Stuttgart: Klett-Cotta, 1990.

———. *Das politische System der Bundesrepublik Deutschland nach der Vereinigung*. Munich: R. Piper Verlag, 1991.

———. "Regime Transition and Recruitment of Elites in Eastern Europe," *Governance* 6, no. 3 (1993): 409–25.

Bickerich, Wolfram, ed. *SPD und Grüne: Das neue Bündnis?* Reinbek bei Hamburg: Rowohlt, 1985.

Birtsch, Günter. "Gemäßigter Liberalismus und Grundrechte: Zur Traditionsbestimmtheit des deutschen Liberalismus von 1848–1849." In *Liberalismus in der Gesellschaft des deutschen Vormärz*, ed. Wolfgang Schieder. Göttingen: Vandenhoeck & Ruprecht, 1983.

Blackbourn, David, and Geoff Eley. *The Peculiarities of German History: Bourgeois Society and the Politics of Nineteenth-Century Germany*. Oxford: Oxford University Press, 1984.

Blair, Philip. "Law and Politics in Germany." *Political Studies* 26, no. 3 (1978): 348–362.

Blanke, Bernhard. "'Staatsräson' und demokratischen Rechtsstaat." *Leviathan*, 1975, no. 2: 153–69.

———. "Theorien zum Verhältnis von Staat und Gesellschaft zum Problem der Legitimation politischer Herrschaft in der bürgerlichen Gesellschaft." In *Kritik der Politischen Wissenschaft I: Analysen von Politik und Ökonomie in der bürgerlichen Gesellschaft*, ed. Bernhard Blanke, Ulrich Jürgens, and Hans Kastendick. Frankfurt: Campus Verlag, 1975.

Blasius, Dirk. "Bürgerliches Recht und bürgerliche Identität: Zu einem Problemzusammenhang in der deutschen Geschichte des 19. Jahrhunderts." In *Vom Staat des Ancien Regimes zum modernen Parteienstaat*, ed. Helmut Berding et al. Munich: R. Oldenburg Verlag, 1974.

Blay, Sam, and Andreas Zimmermann. "Recent Changes in German Refugee Law: A Critical Assessment." *The American Journal of International Law* 88, no. 2 (1994): 361–78.

Bloch, Herbert. *The Concept of Our Changing Loyalties: An Introductory Study into the Nature of the Social Individual*. New York: Columbia University Press, 1934.

Böckenförde, Ernst-Wolfgang. "Die Einheit von nationaler und konstitutioneller politische Bewegung im deutschen Frühliberalismus." In *Moderne deutsche Verfassungsgeschichte (1815–1918)*, ed. Ernst-Wolfgang Böckenförde. Cologne: Kiepenheuer & Witsch, 1972.

———, ed. *Moderne deutsche Verfassungsgeschichte (1815–1918)*. Cologne: Kiepenheuer & Witsch, 1972.

Bolaffi, Angelo. "Verfassungskrise und Sozialdemokratie. Hermann Heller und die Kritiker der Weimarer Verfassung am Vorabend der Krise der Republik." In *Staatslehre in der Weimarer Republik: Hermann Heller zu ehren*, ed. Christoph Müller und Ilse Staff. Frankfurt: Suhrkamp, 1985.

Bonham, Gary. "State Autonomy or Class Domination: Approaches to Administrative Politics in Wilhelmine Germany." *World Politics* 35, no. 4 (1983): 631–51.

Borgs-Maciejewski, Hermann. "Radikale im öffentlichen Dienst." *Aus Politik und Zeitgeschichte, Beilage zur Wochenzeitung Das Parlament*, 1973, no. 27: 3–22.

Böttcher, Reinhard. *Die politische Treuepflicht der Beamten und Soldaten und die Grundrechte der Kommunikation*. Berlin: Duncker & Humblot, 1967.

Bracher, Karl-Dietrich. *The German Dilemma: The Throes of Political Emancipation*. London: Weidenfeld & Nicholson, 1974.

———. *The German Dilemma: The Relationship of State and Democracy*. New York: Praeger, 1975.

————. "Democracy and the Power Vacuum: The Problem of the Party State during the Disintegration of the Weimar Republic." In *Germany in the Age of Total War*, ed. Volker R. Berghahn and Martin Kitchen. London: Croom Helm, 1981.

————. "Vierzig Jahre Diktatur (SED Unrecht)—Herausforderung an den Rechtsstaat." *Recht und Politik* 27, no. 3 (1991): 137–41.

Bramsted, E. K., and K. J. Melhuish, eds. *Western Liberalism*. London: Longman, 1978.

Brandt, Edmund, ed. *Die politische Treuepflicht: Rechtsquellen zur Geschichte des deutschen Berufsbeamtentums*. Karlsruhe: C. F. Müller Juristischer Verlag, 1976.

Brandt, Willy. *Reden und Interviews*. 2 vols. Bonn: Presse- und Informationsamt der Bundesregierung, 1971.

————. "Rechenschaftsbericht: Rede vom 11. November 1975." In *...auf der Zinne der Partei ...: Parteitagsreden 1960 bis 1983*, ed. Werner Krause and Wolfgang Gröf. Berlin/Bonn: Verlag J. H. W. Dietz Nachf., 1984.

————. "*...wir sind nicht zu Helden geboren...*": *Ein Gespräch über Deutschland mit Birgit Kraatz*. Zurich: Diogenes Verlag, 1986.

Brandt, Willy, and Helmut Schmidt. *Deutschland 1976—Zwei Sozialdemokraten im Gespräch*. Reinbek bei Hamburg: Rowohlt, 1976.

Braunthal, Gerard. *The West German Social Democrats: 1969–1982*. Boulder: Westview Press, 1983.

————. *Political Loyalty and Public Service in West Germany: The 1972 Decree against Radicals and Its Consequences*. Amherst: The University of Massachusetts Press, 1990.

Broszat, Martin. *The Hitler State: The Foundation and Development of the Internal Structure of the Third Reich*. London: Longman, 1981.

Brubaker, William Rogers. "Citizenship and Naturalization: Policies and Results." In *Immigration and the Politics of Citizenship in Europe and North America*, ed. William Rogers Brubaker. Lanham: University Press of America, 1989.

————, ed. *Immigration and the Politics of Citizenship in Europe and North America*. Lanham: University Press of America, 1989.

————. *Citizenship and Nationhood in France and Germany*. Cambridge: Harvard University Press, 1992.

Brunner, Werner, Werner Conze, and Reinhart Koselleck, eds. *Geschichtliche Grundbegriffe: Historisches Lexikon zur politisch-sozialen Sprache in Deutschland*, 6 vols. Stuttgart: Klett-Cotta, 1990.

Bulla, Eckhart. "Die Lehre von der streitbaren Demokratie: Versuch einer kritischen Analyse unter besonderer Berücksichtigung der Rechtssprechung des Bundesverfassungsgerichts." *Archiv des Öffentlichen Rechts* 98 (1973): 340–60.

Bundesministerium für innerdeutsche Beziehungen, ed. *Texte zur Deutschlandpolitik. Series 3, vol. 8b-1990*. Bonn: Deutscher Bundesverlag, 1991.

Burke, Kenneth. *A Grammar of Motives*. Berkeley: University of California Press, 1969.

Bürklin, Wilhlem P. "Greens: Ecology and the New Left." In *West German Politics in the Mid-Eighties: Crisis and Continuity*, ed. J. G. Peter Wallach and George K. Romoser. New York: Praeger Publishers, 1985.

Caplan, Jane. "'The Imaginary Universality of Particular Interests': The 'Tradition' of the Civil Service in German History." *Social History* 4, no. 2 (1979): 299–317.

————. *Government without Administration: State and Civil Service in Weimar and Nazi Germany*. Oxford: Oxford University Press, 1988.

Capra, Fritjof, and Charlene Spretnak. *Green Politics: The Global Promise*. New York: E.P. Dutton, 1984.

Carens, Joseph H. "Membership and Morality: Admission to Citizenship in Liberal Democratic States." In *Immigration and the Politics of Citizenship in Europe and North America*, ed. William Rogers Brubaker. Lanham: University Press of America, 1989.

Cecil, Andrew R. *Equality, Tolerance, and Loyalty: Virtues Serving the Common Purpose of Democracy*. Dallas: The University of Texas Press, 1990.

Conradt, David. "Changing German Political Culture." In *The Civic Culture Revisited*, ed. Gabriel Almond and Sidney Verba. Boston: Little, Brown, 1980.

Conze, Werner. "Ständegesellschaft und Staat." In *Geschichtliche Grundbegriffe: Historisches Lexikon zur politisch-sozialen Sprache in Deutschland*, ed. Werner Brunner, Werner Conze, and Reinhart Koselleck. Vol. 6, *St-Vert*. Stuttgart: Klett-Cotta, 1990.

Craig, Gordon. *Germany: 1866–1945*. New York: Oxford University Press, 1978.

Dahrendorf, Ralf. *Society and Democracy in Germany*. Garden City: Doubleday and Company, 1969.
Dalton, Russell J., ed. *Germans Divided: The 1994 Bundestag Elections and the Evolution of the German Party System*. Oxford: Berg, 1996.
Damkowski, Wulf. "Radikale im öffentlichen Dienst." *Recht im Amt*, 1976, no. 1:1–12.
Denninger, Erhard, ed. *Freiheitliche demokratische Grundordnung*. 2 vols. Frankfurt: Suhrkamp Verlag, 1977.
Der Deutsche Beirat und Sekretariat des 3. Internationalen Russell-Tribunals, ed. *3. Internationales Russell-Tribunal: Zur Situation der Menschenrechte in der Bundesrepublik Deutschland—Dokumente, Verhandlungen, Ergebnisse*. 2 vols. Berlin: Rotbuch Verlag, 1978.
Deutscher Bundestag, ed. *Auf dem Weg zur deutschen Einheit*. 5 vols. Bonn: Deutscher Bundestag, 1990.
DiPalma, Giuseppe. "Legitimation from the Top to Civil Society: Politico-Cultural Change in Eastern Europe." *World Politics* 44 (1991): 49–80.
Ditfurth, Jutta. "Radikal und phantasievoll gesellschaftliche Gegenmacht organisieren! Skizzen einer radikalökologischen Position." In *Grüne Politik: Der Stand der Auseinandersetzung*, ed. Thomas Kluge. Frankfurt am M.: Fischer, 1984.
Döring, Herbert, and Gordon Smith, eds. *Party Government and Political Culture in Western Germany*. New York: St. Martin's Press, 1982.
Dregger, Alfred. "Selbstaufgabe der Demokratie?" *Die Politische Meinung*, 1982, January–February.
Duve, Freimut, and Wolfgang Kopitzsch, eds. *Weimar ist kein Argument, oder Brachten Radikale im öffentlichen Dienst Hitler an die Macht?* Reinbek bei Hamburg: Rowohlt, 1976.
Dyson, Kenneth. *Party, State, and Bureaucracy in Western Germany*. Beverly Hills: Sage, 1977.
———. "The Ambiguous Politics of Western Germany: Politicization in 'State' Society." *European Journal of Political Research* 7 (1979): 375–96.
———. *The State Tradition in Western Europe: A Study of an Idea and Institution*. New York: Oxford University Press, 1980.
———. "Party Government and Party State." In *Party Government and Political Culture in Western Germany*, ed. Herbert Döring and Gordon Smith. New York: St. Martin's Press, 1982.
———. "West Germany: The Search for a Rationalist Consensus." In *Policy Styles in Western Europe*, ed. Jeremy Richardson. London: George Allen & Unwin, 1982.
Edelman, Murray. *The Symbolic Uses of Politics*. Urbana: University of Illinois Press, 1964.
Ekiert, Grzegorz. "Democratization Processes in East Central Europe: A Theoretical Reconsideration." *British Journal of Political Science* 21, no. 3 (1991): 285–313.
Elben, Wolfgang. *Das Problem der Kontinuität in der deutschen Revolution: Die Politik der Staatssekretäre und der militärischen Führung vom November 1918 bis Februar 1919*. Düsseldorf: Droste Verlag, 1965.
Eley, Geoff. *Reshaping the German Right: Radical Nationalism and Political Change after Bismarck*. New Haven: Yale University Press, 1980.
Ellwein, Thomas. *Das Regierungssytem der Bundesrepublik Deutschland*. 4th ed. Opladen: Westdeutscher Verlag, 1977.
Emerson, Rupert. *State and Sovereignty in Modern Germany*. New Haven: Yale University Press, 1928.
Entscheidungen des Bundesverfassungsgerichts. Vol. 39. Tübingen: J. C. B. Mohr, 1975.
Eschenburg, Theodor. *Die improvisierte Demokratie: Gesammelte Aufsätze zur Weimarer Republik*. Munich: R. Piper Verlag, 1963.
Eyck, Erich. *A History of the Weimar Republic*. 2 vols. New York: John Wiley & Sons, 1967.
Faber, Karl-Georg, "Strukturprobleme des deutschen Liberalismus im 19. Jahrhundert," *Der Staat* 14 (1975): 201–27.
Fenske, Hans. "Monarchisches Beamtentum und demokratischer Staat: Zum Problem der Bürokratie in der Weimarer Republik." In *Demokratie und Verwaltung: 25 Jahre Hochschule für Verwaltungswissenschaft Speyer*. Berlin: Duncker & Humblot, 1972.

Fetscher, Iring. "Die Suche nach der nationalen Identität." In *Stichworte zur "Geistigen Situation der Zeit."* Vol. 1, *Nation und Republik*, ed. Jürgen Habermas. Frankfurt am M.: Suhrkamp Verlag, 1979.

Fijalkowski, Jürgen. *Aggressive Nationalism, Immigration Pressure, and Asylum Policy Disputes in Contemporary Germany.* Occasional Paper no. 9, ed. Hartmut Lehmann. Washington D.C.: German Historical Institute, 1993.

Fischer, Joschka. "Identität in Gefahr!" In *Grüne Politik: Der Stand der Auseinandersetzung*, ed. Thomas Kluge. Frankfurt am M.: Fischer, 1984.

Fletcher, George P. *Loyalty: An Essay on the Morality of Relationships.* New York: Oxford University Press, 1993.

Frankland, E. Gene. "The Greens' Comeback in 1994: The Third Party of Germany." In *Germans Divided: The 1994 Bundestag Elections and the Evolution of the German Party System*, ed. Russell J. Dalton. Oxford: Berg, 1996.

Franz, Fritz. "Wahlrecht, ZAR-Rechtsprechung." *Zeitschrift für Ausländerrecht und Ausländerpolitik*, 1991, no. 1:40–43.

Frederking, Kurt. "Das außerdienstliche Verhalten des Beamten aus beamtenrechtlicher Sicht," *Die Polizei*, 1980, no. 2:60–61.

Freeman, Gary P. "Modes of Immigration Politics in Liberal Democratic States," *International Migration Review* 29, no. 4 (1995): 881–902.

Friedrich, Carl J. "Rebuilding the German Constitution, II," *American Political Science Review* 43, no. 4 (1949): 704–20.

Frisch, Peter. *Extremistenbeschluß.* Opladen: Heggen-Verlag, 1975.

Fromme, Friedrich Karl. "Das Grundgesetz und die Lehren von Weimar." In *Fünfzig Jahre deutsche Republik: Entstehung-Scheitern-Neubeginn*, ed. F. A. Krummacher. Frankfurt: Norddeutsche Verlagsanstalt O. Gödel, 1969.

Fuchs, Friedrich, and Eckhard Jesse, "Der Streit um die 'streitbare Demokratie': Zur Kontroverse um des Beschäftigung von Extremisten im öffentlichen Dienst." *Aus Politik und Zeitgeschichte: Beilage zur Wochenzeitung Das Parlament*, 1978, no. 3: 17–35.

Gall, Lothar, ed. *Liberalismus.* Cologne: Kiepenheuer & Witsch, 1976.

———. "Liberalismus und 'bürgerliche Gesellschaft': Zu Charakter und Entwicklung der liberalen Bewegung in Deutschland." In *Liberalismus*, ed. Lothar Gall. Cologne: Kiepenheuer & Witsch, 1976.

Gerlach, Johannes. *Radikalenfrage und Privatrecht: Zur politischen Freiheit in der Gesellschaft.* Tübingen: J. C. B. Mohr, 1978.

Gillis, John R. *The Prussian Bureaucracy in Crisis: 1840–1860.* Stanford: Stanford University Press, 1971.

Gollwitzer, Helmut. "Stellungnahme." *Wortlaut und Kritik der verfassungswidrigen Januarbeschlüße.* Cologne: Pahl-Rugenstein Verlag, 1972.

Grass, Günter. *Two States—One Nation?* New York: Harcourt Brace Jovanovich, 1990.

Greenfeld, Liah. *Nationalism: Five Roads to Modernity.* Cambridge: Harvard University Press, 1992.

Griewank, Karl. "Ursachen und Folgen des Scheiterns der deutschen Revolution von 1848." In *Moderne deutsche Verfassungsgeschichte (1815–1918)*, ed. Ernst-Wolfgang Böckenförde. Cologne: Kiepenheuer & Witsch, 1972.

Habermas, Jürgen. *Toward a Rational Society*, trans. Jeremy Shapiro. Boston: Beacon Press, 1970.

———, ed. *Stichworte zur "Geistigen Situation der Zeit."* 2 vols. Frankfurt: Suhrkamp Verlag, 1979.

———, ed. *Observations on "The Spiritual Situation of the Age."* Cambridge: The MIT Press, 1985.

Haffner, Sebastian. *Failure of a Revolution*, trans. Georg Rapp. New York: Library Press, 1973.

Hailbronner, Kay. "Citizenship and Nationhood in Germany." In *Immigration and the Politics of Citizenship in Europe and North America*, ed. William Rogers Brubaker. Lanham, MD: University Press of America, 1989.

Halfmann, Jost. "Soziale Bewegungen und Staat." *Soziale Welt*, 1984, no. 3:294–312.

Hamerow, Theodore. *Restoration, Revolution, and Reaction: Economics and Politics in Germany, 1815–1871.* Princeton: Princeton University Press, 1958.

————. "Die Wahlen zum Frankfurter Parlament." In *Moderne deutsche Verfassungs-geschichte (1815–1918)*, ed. Ernst-Wolfgang Böckenförde. Cologne: Kiepenheuer & Witsch, 1972.

Hamilton, Daniel. "After the Revolution: The New Political Landscape in East Germany." *German Issues*, 1990, no. 7: 1–53.

Hammar, Tomas. *Democracy and the Nation-State: Aliens, Denizens, and Citizens in a World of Internal Migration.* Aldershot: Avebury, 1990.

Hardtwig, Wolfgang. *Vormärz: Der monarchische Staat und das Bürgertum.* Munich: Deutscher Taschenbuch Verlag, 1985.

Hartung, Fritz, ed. *Staatsbildende Kräfte der Neuzeit: Gesammelte Aufsätze.* Berlin: Duncker & Humblot, 1961.

————. "Studien zur Geschichte der preußischen Verwaltung." In *Staatsbildende Kräfte der Neuzeit: Gesammelte Aufsätze*, ed. Fritz Hartung. Berlin: Duncker & Humblot, 1961.

Hase, Friedhelm. "Die Grünen im Rechtsstaat: Basis-, repräsentative und pluralistische Demokratie." In *Grüne Politik: Der Stand der Auseinandersetzung*, ed. Thomas Kluge. Frankfurt am M.: Fischer, 1984.

Hattenhauer, Hans. *Handbuch des öffentlichen Dienstes*, ed. Walter Wiese. Vol. 1, *Geschichte des Beamtentums.* Cologne: Carl Heymans Verlag, 1980.

Haungs, Peter. "Die CDU: Prototyp einer Volkspartei." In *Parteien in der Bundesrepublik Deutschland*, ed. Heinrich Oberreuter and Alf Mintzel. Munich: Olzog, 1990.

Hegel, G. W. F. *Philosophy of Right*, trans. T. M. Knox. London: Oxford University Press, 1967.

Heimeshoff, Erich. "Bemerkungen zur Extremisten-Problematik." *Deutsche Richterzeitung*, 1979, no. 3: 79–82.

Heinemann, Gustav. *Präsidiale Reden.* Frankfurt: Suhrkamp Verlag, 1975.

Heller, Hermann. *Gesammelten Schriften.* 3 vols. Leiden: A.W. Sijthoff, 1971.

Hennig, Eike. "Nationalismus, Sozialismus, und die 'Form aus Leben': Hermann Hellers politische Hoffnung auf soziale Integration und staatliche Einheit." In *Staatslehre in der Weimarer Republik: Hermann Heller zu ehren*, ed. Christoph Müller and Ilse Staff. Frankfurt: Suhrkamp, 1985.

Herf, Jeffrey. *Reactionary Modernism: Technology, Culture, and Politics in Weimar and the Third Reich.* New York: Cambridge University Press, 1984.

Herz, John. "Political Views of the West German Civil Service." In *West German Leadership and Foreign Policy*, ed. H. Speier and W. P. Davison. Evanston, Ill.: Row, Peterson, 1957.

Herzog, Roman. "Recht und Schutz des Einzelnens." *Die Politische Meinung*, no. 166, (1976): 7–13.

Hess, Jürgen C. "Wandlungen im Staatsverständnis des Linksliberalismus der Weimarer Republik 1930–1933." In *Wirtschaftskrise und liberale Demokratie: Das Ende der Weimarer Republik und die gegenwärtige Situation*, ed. Karl Holl. Göttingen: Vandenhoeck und Ruprecht, 1978.

Hildebrand, Klaus. *Geschichte der Bundesrepublik Deutschland*, eds. Karl Dietrich Bracher, Wolfgang Jäger, and Werner Link. Vol. 4, *Von Erhard zur Großen Koalition.* Stuttgart: Deutsche Verlags-Anstalt, 1984.

Hitiris, T. *European Community Economics.* New York: St. Martin's Press, 1991.

Hobsbawm, Eric. "Introduction: Inventing Traditions." In *The Invention of Tradition*, ed. Eric Hobsbawm and Terence Ranger. Cambridge: Cambridge University Press, 1983.

Hobsbawm, Eric, and Terence Ranger, eds. *The Invention of Tradition.* Cambridge: Cambridge University Press, 1983.

Hofmann, Gunter, ed. *Richard von Weizsäcker im Gespräch mit Gunter Hofmann und Werner A. Perger.* Frankfurt am Main: Eichborn Verlag, 1992.

Holl, Karl, ed. *Wirtschaftskrise und liberale Demokratie: Das Ende der Weimarer Republik und die gegenwärtige Situation.* Göttingen: Vandenhoeck und Ruprecht, 1978.

Hollifield, James F. *Immigrants, Markets, and States: The Political Economy of Postwar Europe.* Cambridge: Harvard University Press, 1992.

Hönes, Ernst-Rainer. "Beamte als Verfassungsfeinde? *Der Öffentliche Dienst*, 1972, no. 12: 221–28.

Huber, Ernst Rudolf, ed. *Nationalstaat und Verfassungsstaat*. Stuttgart: W. Kohlhammer Verlag, 1965.
————. "Zur Geschichte der politischen Polizei im 19. Jahrhundert." In *Nationalstaat und Verfassungsstaat*, ed. Ernst Rudolf Huber. Stuttgart: W. Kohlhammer Verlag, 1965.
————. *Deutsche Verfassungsgeschichte Seit 1789*. Vol. 2, *Der Kampf um Einheit und Freiheit 1830 bis 1850*. Stuttgart: W. Kohlhammer Verlag, 1968.
————, ed. *Dokumente zur deutschen Verfassungsgeschichte*. Vol. 1, *Deutsche Verfassungdokumente 1803–1850*. Stuttgart: W. Kohlhammer Verlag, 1978.
Inglehart, Ronald. *The Silent Revolution: Changing Styles among Western Publics*. Princeton: Princeton University Press, 1977.
————. "New Perspectives on Political Change." *Comparative Political Studies* 17, no. 4 (1984): 485–532.
————. *Culture Shift in Advanced Industrial Society*. Princeton: Princeton University Press, 1990.
Jacob, Herbert. *German Administration since Bismarck: Central Authority versus Local Planning*. New Haven: Yale University Press, 1963.
Jäger, Wolfgang. "Die Innenpolitik der sozial-liberalen Koalition, 1969–1974." In *Geschichte der Bundesrepublik*, ed. Karl Dietrich Bracher, Wolfgang Jäger, and Werner Link. Vol. 5/I, *Republik im Wandel, 1969–1974: Die Ära Brandt*. Stuttgart: Deutsche Verlagsanstalt, 1986.
Jänicke, Martin. "Parlamentarische Entwarnungseffeckte? Zur Ortsbestimmung der Alternativbewegung." In *Die Grünen: Regierungspartner von morgen?* ed. Jörg R. Mettke. Reinbek bei Hamburg: Rowohlt, 1982.
Janßen, Karl-Heinz. "Die ungewohlte Revolution." In *Fünfzig Jahre deutsche Republik: Entstehung-Scheitern-Neubeginn*, ed. F. A. Krummacher. Frankfurt: Norddeutsche Verlagsanstalt O. Gödel, 1969.
Jarausch, Konrad. *The Rush to German Unity*. New York: Oxford University Press, 1994.
Jasper, Gotthard. *Der Schutz der Republik: Studien zur staatlichen Sicherung der Demokratie in der Weimarer Republik*. Tübingen: J. C. B. Mohr, 1963.
————. "Wer schützt die Republik?" In *Weimar ist kein Argument, oder Brachten Radikale im öffentlichen Dienst Hitler an die Macht?* ed. Freimut Duve and Wolfgang Kopitzsch. Reinbek bei Hamburg: Rowohlt, 1976.
Jaspers, Karl. *Wohin treibt die Bundesrepublik?* 2nd ed. Munich: R. Piper Verlag, 1988.
Jeserich, Kurt G. A. "Die Entstehung des öffentlichen Dienstes, 1800–1871." In *Deutsche Verwaltungsgeschichte*, ed. K. Jeserich, H. Pohl, and G.C. von Unruh. Vol. 2, *Vom Reichsdeputationshauptschluß bis zur Auflösung des Deutschen Bundes*. Stuttgart: Deutsche Verlags-Anstalt, 1983.
Jeserich, Kurt G. A., Hans Pohl, and Georg-Christoph von Unruh, eds. *Deutsche Verwaltungsgeschichte*. Vol. 2, *Vom Reichsdeputationshauptschluß bis zur Auflösung des Deutschen Bundes*. Stuttgart: Deutsche Verlags-Anstalt, 1983.
Jesse, Eckhard. *Die Demokratie der Bundesrepublik Deutschland*. 7th ed. Berlin: Colloquium Verlag, 1986.
————. "Parteien in Deutschland." In *Parteien in der Bundesrepublik Deutschland*, ed. Heinrich Oberreuter and Alf Mintzel. Munich: Olzug, 1990.
Johnson, Nevil. "Parties and the Conditions of Political Leadership," In *Party Government and Political Culture in Western Germany*, ed. Herbert Döring and Gordon Smith. New York: St. Martin's Press, 1982.
————. *State and Government in the Federal Republic of Germany: The Executive at Work*. 2nd ed. Oxford: Pergamon Press, 1983.
Kaack, Heino, and Reinhold Roth, eds. *Parteien-Jahrbuch 1976: Dokumentation und Analyse der Entwicklung des Parteiensystems der Bundesrepublik Deutschland in Bundestagswahljahr 1976*. Meisenheim am Glan: Verlag Anton Hain, 1979.
Kant, Immanuel. *Groundwork of the Metaphysics of Morals*, trans. H. J. Patton. New York: Harper and Row, 1964.
Katzenstein, Peter. *Policy and Politics in West Germany: The Growth of a Semisovereign State*. Philadelphia: Temple University Press, 1987.
Kaufmann, Walter H. *Monarchism in the Weimar Republic*. New York: Bookman Associates, 1953.

Kelly, Petra K. "Keine sozialdemokratischen Inhalte mit grünem Anstrich." In *SPD und Grüne: Das neue Bündnis?* ed. Wolfram Bickerich. Reinbek bei Hamburg: Rowohlt, 1985.

Kennedy, Ellen. "Introduction." In Carl Schmitt, *The Crisis of Parliamentary Democracy.* Cambridge: The MIT Press, 1985.

Kielmansegg, Peter Graf. "Von der Notwendigkeit und den Schwierigkeiten streitbarer Demokratie." In *Verfassungsfeinde als Beamte?* ed. Wulf Schönbohm. Munich: Günter Olzog Verlag, 1979.

———. "The Basic Law—Response to the Past or Design for the Future?" In *Forty Years of the Grundgesetz,* Occasional Paper no. 1, ed. Hartmut Lehmann and Kenneth Ledford. Washington, D.C.: German Historical Institute, 1989.

Kirchheimer, Otto. "The Transformation of the Western European Party Systems." In *Political Parties and Political Development,* ed. Joseph LaPalombara and Myron Weiner. Princeton: Princeton University Press, 1966.

Kirchner, Emil. "The Federal Republic of Germany in the European Community." In *The Federal Republic of Germany at Forty,* ed. Peter H. Merkl. New York: New York University Press, 1989.

Kitschelt, Herbert. *The Logic of Party Formations.* Ithaca: Cornell University Press, 1989.

———. *The Radical Right in Western Europe.* Ann Arbor: The University of Michigan Press, 1995.

Kluge, Thomas, ed. *Grüne Politik: Der Stand der Auseinandersetzung.* Frankfurt am M.: Fischer, 1984.

Knight-Patterson, W. M. *Germany: From Defeat to Conquest, 1913–1933.* London: George Allen and Unwin, 1945.

Kolinsky, Eva, ed. *The Greens in West Germany: Organisation and Policy Making.* Oxford: Berg Publishers, 1989.

Komitee für Grundrechte und Demokratie, ed. *Ohne Zweifel für den Staat.* Reinbek bei Hamburg: Rowohlt, 1982.

Kommers, Donald P. *The Constitutional Jurisprudence of the Federal Republic of Germany.* Durham: Duke University Press, 1989.

König, Klaus. "Bureaucratic Integration by Elite Transfer: The Case of the Former GDR." *Governance* 6, no. 3 (1993): 386–96.

Konow, Karl-Otto. "Grenzen der schriftstellerischen Betätigung der Beamten." *Zeitschrift für Beamtenrecht,* 1972, no. 1: 47–50.

Koschnick, Hans, ed. *Der Abschied vom Extremistenbeschluß.* Bonn: Verlag Neuer Gesellschaft, 1979.

Koselleck, Reinhart. *Preußen zwischen Reform und Revolution: Allgemeines Landrechts, Verwaltung, und soziale Frage von 1791 bis 1848.* Stuttgart: Ernst Klett Verlag, 1967.

Kranzberg, Melvin, ed. *1848: A Turning Point.* Boston: D. C. Heath, 1959.

Krause, Werner, and Wolfgang Gröf, eds. *...auf der Zinne der Partei ...: Parteitagsreden 1960 bis 1983.* Berlin/Bonn: Verlag J. H. W. Dietz Nachf., 1984.

Kriele, Martin. "Der rechtliche Spielraum einer Liberalisierung der Einstellungspraxis im öffentlichen Dienst." *Neue Juristische Wochenschrift,* 1979, no. 1–2:1–8.

Kroppenstedt, Franz. "Der öffentliche Dienst der Zukunft." *Zeitschrift für Beamtenrecht,* 1990, no. 7: 197–99.

Krüger, Helmut. "Verzicht auf die Gewähr der Verfassungstreue?" *Zeitschrift für Rechtspolitik,* 1978, no. 12: 273–77.

Krummacher, F. A., ed. *Fünfzig Jahre deutsche Republik: Entstehung-Scheitern-Neubeginn.* Frankfurt: Norddeutsche Verlagsanstalt O. Gödel, 1969.

Kurthen, Hermann. "Germany at the Crossroads: National Identity and the Challenges of Immigration." *International Migration Review* 29, no. 4 (1995): 914–38.

Kutscha, Martin. *Verfassung und "streitbare Demokratie."* Cologne: Pahl-Rugenstein Verlag, 1979.

Kvistad, Gregg O. "Civil Liberties and German State Employees." *German Politics and Society,* 1990, no. 19: 14–26.

Lameyer, Johannes. *Streitbare Demokratie: Eine verfassungshermeneutische Untersuchung.* Berlin: Duncker & Humblot, 1978.

Langguth, Gerd. *Der Grüne Faktor: Von Bewegung zur Partei?* Osnabrück: Verlag A. Fromm, 1984.

LaPalombara, Joseph, and Myron Weiner, eds. *Political Parties and Political Development.* Princeton: Princeton University Press, 1966.

Lecheler, Helmut. "Die Treuepflicht des Beamten—Leerformel oder Zentrum der Beamtenpflichten?" *Zeitschrift für Beamtenrecht,* 1972, no. 8: 228–37.

Lehmbruch, Gerhard. "Die deutsche Vereinigung: Strukturen und Strategien." *Politische Vierteljahresschrift* 32, no. 4 (1991): 585–604.

Leisner, Walter. *Demokratie: Selbstzerstörung einer Staatsform?* Berlin: Duncker & Humblot, 1979.

———. *Die demokratische Anarchie: Verlust der Ordnung als Staatsprinzip?* Berlin: Duncker & Humblot, 1981.

———. "Verfassungsreform des öffentlichen Dienstrechts?" *Aus Politik und Zeitgeschichte, Beilage zur Wochenzeitung Das Parlament,* 1991, no. 49: 29–36.

Lepsius, M. Rainer. "Institutional Structures and Political Culture." In *Party Government and Political Culture in Western Germany,* ed. Herbert Döring and Gordon Smith. New York: St. Martin's Press, 1982.

Loewenstein, Karl. *Max Weber's Political Ideas in the Perspective of Our Time.* Amherst: The University of Massachusetts Press, 1966.

Ludz, Peter Christian. "Anarchie." In *Geschichtliche Grundbegriffe: Historisches Lexikon zur politisch-sozialen Sprache in Deutschland,* ed. Werner Brunner, Werner Conze, and Reinhart Koselleck. Vol. 1, *A-D.* Stuttgart: Klett-Cotta, 1990.

Luthardt, Wolfgang. "Staat, Demokratie, Arbeiterbewegung: Hermann Hellers Analysen im Kontext der zeitgenössischen sozialdemokratischen Diskussion." In *Staatslehre in der Weimarer Republik: Hermann Heller zu ehren,* ed. Christoph Müller and Ilse Staff. Frankfurt: Suhrkamp, 1985.

Maier, Charles S. *Recasting Bourgeois Europe: Stabilization in France, Germany and Italy in the Decade after World War I.* Princeton: Princeton University Press, 1975.

———. *The Unmasterable Past: History, Holocaust, and German National Identity.* Cambridge: Harvard University Press, 1988.

Maier, Hans. "Ältere deutsche Staatslehre und westliche politische Tradition." *Recht und Staat,* no. 321, (1966): 9–20.

Mandt, Hella. "Grenzen politischer Toleranz in der offenen Gesellschaft: Zum Verfassungsgrundsatz der streitbaren Demokratie." *Aus Politik und Zeitgeschichte, Beilage zur Wochenzeitung Das Parlament,* 1972, no. 1–2: 3–16.

March, James P., and Johan P. Olsen. *Rediscovering Institutions: The Organizational Basis of Politics.* New York: The Free Press, 1989.

Marshall, Barbara. "German Migration Policies." In *Developments in German Politics,* ed. Gordon Smith, William E. Paterson, Peter H. Merkl, and Stephen Padgett. Durham: Duke University Press, 1992.

Martin, Ernst. "Extremistenbeschluß und demokratische Verfassung." *Aus Politik und Zeitgeschichte, Beilage zur Wochenzeitung Das Parlament,* 1973, no. 50:3–27.

Marx, Karl. "Contribution to the Critique of Hegel's Philosophy of Law." In Karl Marx and Friedrich Engels, *Collected Works.* Vol. 3. New York: International Publishers, 1975.

———. "The Eighteenth Brumaire of Louis Bonaparte." In Karl Marx and Friedrich Engels, *Selected Works.* Vol. 1. Moscow: Progress Publishers, 1973.

Matz, Ulrich. "Extremisten im öffentlichen Dienst." *Die Öffentliche Verwaltung,* 1978, no. 13–14: 464–68.

Maurer, Hartmut. "Das Verbot politischen Parteien." *Archiv des Öffentlichen Rechts* 96 (1971): 203–07.

Mayer-Tasch, P. C. *Die Bürgerinitiativbewegung.* Reinbek bei Hamburg: Rowohlt, 1976.

McAdams, A. James. *Germany Divided: From the Wall to Reunification.* Princeton: Princeton University Press, 1993.

———. "Revisiting *Ostpolitik* in the 1990s." *German Politics and Society,* 1993, no. 30: 49–60.

Meinck, Jürgen. *Weimarer Staatslehre und Nationalsozialismus: Eine Studie zum Problem der Kontinuität im staatsrechtlichen Denken in Deutschland, 1928 bis 1936.* Frankfurt: Campus Verlag, 1978.

Melucci, Alberto. "The New Social Movements: A Theoretical Approach." *Social Science Information* 19, no. 2 (1980): 199–226.

Merkl, Peter H. *The Origin of the West German Republic.* New York: Oxford University Press, 1963.

———, ed. *The Federal Republic of Germany at Forty.* New York: New York University Press, 1989.

Mettke, Jörg. "'Auf beiden Flügeln in die Höhe': Grüne, Bunte und Alternative zwischen Parlament und Straße." In *Die Grünen: Regierungspartner von morgen?* ed. Jörg R. Mettke. Reinbek bei Hamburg: Rowohlt, 1982.

———, ed. *Die Grünen: Regierungspartner von morgen?* Reinbek bei Hamburg: Rowohlt, 1982.

Mettke, Jörg, and Hans-Dieter Degler. "'Wir müssen die Etablierten entblössen wo wir können': *Spiegel*-Gespräch mit der Bundesvorsitzenden der Grünen, Petra K. Kelly." In *Die Grünen: Regierungspartner von morgen?* ed. Jörg R. Mettke. Reinbek bei Hamburg: Rowohlt, 1982.

Mewes, Horst. "The West German Green Party." *New German Critique*, 1983, no. 28:51–85.

Miller, Susanne. "Die Entscheidung für die parlamentarische Demokratie." In *Fünfzig Jahre deutsche Republik: Entstehung-Scheitern-Neubeginn*, ed. F. A. Krummacher. Frankfurt: Norddeutsche Verlagsanstalt O. Gödel, 1969.

Mohl, Robert von. *Politische Schriften*, ed. Klaus von Beyme. Cologne: Westdeutscher Verlag, 1966.

Möller, Horst. *Weimar: Die unvollendete Demokratie.* Munich: Deutscher Taschenbuch Verlag, 1985.

Mommsen, Hans. "Die Last der Vergangenheit." In *Stichworte zur "Geistigen Situation der Zeit."* Vol. 1, *Nation und Republik*, ed. Jürgen Habermas. Frankfurt am M.: Suhrkamp Verlag, 1979.

———. "The Burden of the Past." In *Observations on "The Spiritual Situation of the Age,"* ed. Jürgen Habermas. Cambridge: The MIT Press, 1985.

Mommsen, Wolfgang. "The German Revolution 1918–1920: Political Revolution and Social Protest Movement." In *Social Change and Political Development in Weimar Germany*, ed. Richard Bessel and E. J. Feuchtwanger. London: Croom Helm, 1982.

———. *Max Weber and German Politics: 1890–1920*, trans. Michael S. Steinberg. Chicago: The University of Chicago Press, 1984.

Morsey, Rudolf. "Zur Beamtenpolitik des Reiches von Bismarck bis Brüning." In *Demokratie und Verwaltung: 25 Jahre Hochschule für Verwaltungswissenschaften Speyer.* Berlin: Duncker & Humblot, 1972.

Mosse, George L. *Germans and Jews: The Right, the Left, and the Search for a "Third Force" in Pre-Nazi Germany.* New York: Howard Fertig, 1970.

Müller, Christoph, and Ilse Staff, eds. *Staatslehre in der Weimarer Republik: Hermann Heller zu ehren.* Frankfurt: Suhrkamp, 1985.

Müller-Rommel, Ferdinand. "Die Grünen in Lichte von neuesten Ergebnissen der Wahlforschung." In *Grüne Politik*, ed. Thomas Kluge. Frankfurt: Fischer Taschenbuch Verlag, 1984.

Murray, Laura M. "*Einwanderungsland Bundesrepublik Deutschland?* Explaining the Evolving Positions of German Political Parties on Citizenship Policy." *German Politics and Society*, 1994, no. 33:23–56.

Narr, Wolf-Dieter. "Andere Partei oder eine neue Form der Politik?" In *Die Grünen: Regierungspartner von Morgen?* ed. Jörg Mettke. Reinbek bei Hamburg: Rowohlt, 1982.

———. "Toward a Society of Conditioned Reflexes." In *Observations on "The Spiritual Situation of the Age,"* ed. Jürgen Habermas. Cambridge: The MIT Press, 1985.

O'Brien, Peter. "The Civil Rights of West Germany's Migrants." *German Politics and Society*, 1990, no.19: 27–40.

———. "German-Polish Migration: The Elusive Search for a German Nation-State," *International Migration Review* 26, no. 2 (1991): 373–87.

Oberreuter, Heinrich. "Politische Parteien: Stellung und Funktion im Verfassungssystem der Bundesrepublik." In *Parteien in der Bundesrepublik Deutschland*, ed. Heinrich Oberreuter and Alf Mintzel. Munich: Olzog Verlag, 1990.

Oberreuter, Heinrich, and Alf Mintzel, eds. *Parteien in der Bundesrepublik Deutschland.* Munich: Olzog, 1990.

Offe, Claus. *Contradictions of the Welfare State*. Cambridge: The MIT Press, 1984.
———. "Ungovernability: On the Renaissance of Conservative Theories of Crisis." In *Observations on "The Spiritual Situation of the Age,"* ed. Jürgen Habermas. Cambridge: The MIT Press, 1985.
Olden, Rudolf. *The History of Liberty in Germany*. London: Victor Gollancz, 1946.
Orlow, Dietrich. *Weimar Prussia 1918–1925: The Unlikely Rock of Democracy*. Pittsburgh: University of Pittsburgh Press, 1986.
Osterroth, Franz, and Dieter Schuster. *Chronik der deutschen Sozialdemokratie*. 2nd ed. Vol. 3, *Nach dem Zweiten Weltkrieg*. Berlin: Verlag J. H. W. Dietz, Nachf., 1978.
Pasquino, Pasquale. "Politische Einheit, Demokratie und Pluralismus: Bemerkungen zu Carl Schmitt, Hermann Heller und Ernst Fraenkel." In *Staatslehre in der Weimarer Republik: Hermann Heller zu ehren*, ed. Christoph Müller und Ilse Staff. Frankfurt: Suhrkamp, 1985.
Paterson, William E., and Gordon Smith. "German Unity." In *Developments in German Politics*, ed. Gordon Smith, William E. Paterson, Peter H. Merkl, and Stephen Padgett. Durham: Duke University Press, 1992.
Philipsen, Dirk. *We Were the People: Voices from East Germany's Revolutionary Autumn of 1989*. Durham: Duke University Press, 1993.
Plümer, Egon. "Mitgliedschaft von Beamten und Beamtenanwärtern in verfassungsfeindlichen Parteien." *Neue Juristische Wochenschrift*, 1973, no. 1–2: 4–10.
Preuss, Ulrich. "Political Concepts of Order in Mass Society." In *Observations on "The Spiritual Situation of the Age,"* ed. Jürgen Habermas. Cambridge: The MIT Press, 1985.
Pridham, Geoffrey. *Christian Democracy in Western Germany: The CDU/CSU in Government and Opposition, 1945–1976*. London: Croom Helm, 1977.
Raiser, Ludwig. "Der 'Radikalen-Erlaß': Prüfstein eines demokratischen Rechtsstaates?" *Zeitschrift für Evangelische Ethik*, 1979, no. 2: 106–17.
Rammstedt, Otthein. "Zur Vermessung des Beamten." *Frankfurter Hefte*, 1975, no. 10: 4–6.
Rau, Johannes. "Nährboden für rechtsauthoritäre Kräfte." In *Die Grünen: Regierungspartner von morgen?* ed. Jörg R. Mettke. Reinbek bei Hamburg: Rowohlt, 1982.
Rejewski, Harold-Jürgen. *Die Pflicht zur politischen Treue im preußischen Beamtenrecht (1850–1918)*. Berlin: Duncker & Humblot, 1973.
Richardson, Jeremy, ed. *Policy Styles in Western Europe*. London: George Allen & Unwin, 1982.
Ridder, Helmut."'Berufsverbot'? Nein, Demokratieverbot." *Das Argument*, 1975, no. 7–8: 576–84.
Ridley, R., ed. *Government and Administration in Western Europe*. New York: St. Martin's Press, 1979.
Riedel, Manfred. "Gesellschaft, bürgerliche." In *Geschichtliche Grundbegriffe: Historisches Lexikon zur politisch-sozialen Sprache in Deutschland*, ed. Werner Brunner, Werner Conze, and Reinhart Koselleck. Vol. 2, *E-G*. Stuttgart: Klett-Cotta, 1990.
Rittberger, Volker. "Revolution and Pseudo-Democratization: The Formation of the Weimar Republic." In *Crisis, Choice and Change: Historical Studies in Political Development*, ed. Gabriel Almond, Scott Flanagan, and Robert Mundt. Boston: Little, Brown, 1973.
Ritter, Gerhard A., and Susanne Miller, eds. *Die deutsche Revolution, 1918–1919*. Frankfurt: Fischer, 1983.
Röhrich, Wilfried. *Die Demokratie des Westdeutschen: Geschichte und politisches Klima einer Republik*. Munich: Verlag C. H. Beck, 1988.
Rosenberg, Arthur. *A History of the German Republic*, trans. Ian F. D. Morrow and L. Marie Sieveking. London: Methuen and Co., 1936.
Rosenberg, Hans. *Bureaucracy, Aristocracy and Autocracy: The Prussian Experience, 1660–1815*. Boston: Beacon Press, 1966.
Ross, George. "After Maastricht: Hard Choices for Europe." *World Policy Journal* 9, no. 3 (1992): 487–513.
Roth, Dieter. "*Volksparteien* in Crisis? The Electoral Successes of the Extreme Right in Context," *German Politics* 2, no. 1 (1993): 1–20.
Royce, Josiah.*The Philosophy of Loyalty*. New York: Macmillan, 1924.

Runge, Wolfgang. *Politik und Beamtentum im Parteienstaat: Die Demokratisierung der politischen Beamten in Preußen zwischen 1918 und 1933*. Stuttgart: Ernst Klett Verlag, 1965.

———. "Die alte Oberklasse—die neue Beamtenschaft." In *Weimar ist kein Argument, oder Brachten Radikale im öffentlichen Dienst Hitler an die Macht?* ed. Freimut Duve and Wolfgang Kopitzsch. Reinbek bei Hamburg: Rowohlt, 1976.

Rürup, Reinhard. "Entwurf einer demokratischen Republik? Entstehung und Grundlagen der Weimarer Verfassung." In *Fünfzig Jahre deutsche Republik: Entstehung-Scheitern-Neubeginn*, ed. F. A. Krummacher. Frankfurt: Norddeutsche Verlagsanstalt O. Gödel, 1969.

Ryder, A. J. *The German Revolution of 1918: A Study of German Socialism in War and Revolt*. Cambridge: Cambridge University Press, 1967.

Schaar, John. *Legitimacy in the Modern State*. New Brunswick: Transaction Books, 1981.

Scheerbarth, Hans-Walter, and Heinz Höffken. *Beamtenrecht: Lehr- und Handbuch*. 3rd ed. Siegburg: Verlag Reckinger, 1979.

Scheuch, Erwin K., and Ute Scheuch. *Cliquen, Klüngel and Karrieren: Über den Verfall der politischen Parteien—eine Studie*. Reinbek bei Hamburg: Rowohlt, 1992.

Scheuner, Ulrich. "Der Rechtsstaat und die Soziale Verantwortung des Staates: Das wissenschaftliche Lebenswerk von Robert von Mohl." *Der Staat* 18 (1979): 1–30.

Schieder, Wolfgang, ed. *Liberalismus in der Gesellschaft des deutschen Vormärz*. Göttingen: Vandenhoeck & Ruprecht, 1983.

Schluchter, Wolfgang. "Hermann Heller: Ein wissenschaftliches und politisches Portrait." In *Staatslehre in der Weimarer Republik: Hermann Heller zu ehren*, ed. Christoph Müller and Ilse Staff. Frankfurt: Suhrkamp, 1985.

Schmid, Thomas. "Plädoyer für einen reformistischen Anarchismus." In *Grüne Politik: Der Stand der Auseinandersetzung*, ed. Thomas Kluge. Frankfurt am M.: Fischer, 1984.

Schmid, Thomas, and Ernst Hoplitschek. "Auf dem Weg zur Volkspartei: Ökolibertäre Thesen zur Entwicklung der Demokratie." In *SPD und Grüne: Das neue Bündnis?* ed. Wolfram Bickerich. Hamburg: Rowohlt Taschenbuch Verlag, 1985.

Schmidt, Manfred G. *CDU und SPD an der Regierung: Ein Vergleich ihrer Politik in den Ländern*. Frankfurt: Campus Verlag, 1980.

Schmitt, Carl. *The Crisis of Parliamentary Democracy*. Cambridge: The MIT Press, 1985.

———. *Political Theology: Four Chapters on the Concept of Sovereignty*. Cambridge: The MIT Press, 1985.

Schoeler, Andreas von. "Liberalismus und Extremismus." *Liberal*, 1978, no. 4: 272–89.

Schönbohm, Wulf, ed. *Verfassungsfeinde als Beamte?* Munich: Günter Olzog Verlag, 1979.

Schröder, Karsten, and Hermann Horstkotte. "Foreigners in Germany." *Sozial-Report* 2 (1993): 1–6.

Schuster, Rudolf, ed. *Deutsche Verfassungen*. Munich: Wilhelm Goldmann Verlag, 1978.

Schwab, George. *The Challenge of the Exception: An Introduction to the Political Ideas of Carl Schmitt between 1921 and 1936*. Berlin: Duncker & Humblot, 1970.

Serow, William J., et al., eds., *Handbook on International Migration*. New York: Greenwood Press, 1990.

Sheehan, James J. "Liberalism and Society in Germany, 1815–1848." *Journal of Modern History* 45, no. 4 (1973): 583–604.

———. *German Liberalism in the Nineteenth Century*. Chicago: University of Chicago Press, 1978.

Simon, Walter. *The Failure of the Prussian Reform Movement*. Ithaca: Cornell University Press, 1955.

Smith, Gordon. *Democracy in West Germany: Parties and Politics in the Federal Republic*. New York: Holmes and Meier, 1979.

———. "The 'Model' West German Party System." In *The Federal Republic of Germany at Forty*, ed. Peter Merkl. New York: New York University Press, 1989.

Smith, Gordon, William E. Paterson, Peter H. Merkl, and Stephen Padgett, eds. *Developments in German Politics*. Durham: Duke University Press, 1992.

Søe, Christian. "'Not without Us!' The F.D.P.'s Survival, Position, and Influence." In *The Federal Republic of Germany at Forty*, ed. Peter Merkl. New York: New York University Press, 1989.

Sontheimer, Kurt. *The Government and Politics of West Germany*. London: Hutchinson University Library, 1972.

———. "Die Bundesrepublik aus die Perspektive linker Theorie." *Aus Politik und Zeitgeschichte, Beilage zur Wochenzeitung Das Parlament*, 1976, no. 6: 3–21.

———. *Die verunsicherte Republik: Die Bundesrepublik nach 30 Jahren*. Munich: R. Piper Verlag, 1979.

———. "Einführung zur Neuausgabe, 1988." In Karl Jaspers, *Wohin treibt die Bundesrepublik?* 2nd ed. Munich: R. Piper Verlag, 1988.

Sontheimer, Kurt, and Wilhelm Bleek. *Abschied vom Berufsbeamtentum? Perspektiven einer Reform des öffentlichen Dienstes in der Bundesrepublik Deutschland*. Hamburg: Hoffmann und Campe, 1973.

Southern, David. "Germany." In *Government and Administration in Western Europe*, ed. R. Ridley. New York: St. Martin's Press, 1979.

Soysal, Yasemin Nuhoglu. *Limits of Citizenship: Migrants and Postnational Membership in Europe*. Chicago: The University of Chicago Press, 1994.

Speier, H., and W. P. Davison, eds. *West German Leadership and Foreign Policy*. Evanston, Ill.: Row, Peterson, 1957.

Sperling, James. "(Im)migration and German Security in Post-Yalta Europe." *German Studies Review* 17, no. 3 (1994): 537–57.

Staff, Ilse. "Staatslehre in der Weimarer Republik." In *Staatslehre in der Weimarer Republik: Hermann Heller zu ehren*, ed. Christoph Müller and Ilse Staff. Frankfurt: Suhrkamp, 1985.

Stern, Klaus. *Zur Verfassungstreue der Beamten*. Munich: Verlag Franz Vahlen, 1974.

———. *Das Staatsrecht der Bundesrepublik Deutschland*. Vol. 1. Munich: C. H. Beck'sche Verlagsbuchhandlung, 1977.

Sternberger, Dolf. "Demokratie der Furcht order Demokratie der Courage?" *Die Wandlung* 4, no.1 (1949): 3–18.

Stolleis, Michael. "Verwaltungslehre und Verwaltungswissenschaft, 1803–1866." In *Deutsche Verwaltungsgeschichte*, ed. Kurt G. A. Jeserich, Hans Pohl, and Georg-Christoph von Unruh. Vol. 2, *Vom Reichsdeputationshauptschluß bis zur Auflösung des Deutschen Bundes*. Stuttgart: Deutsche Verlags-Anstalt, 1983.

Strauss, Franz-Josef. "Die Sache mit dem 'Radikalenerlaß.'" *Bunte* 25, 10 June 1976.

Strothman, Dietrich. "Hitler's Aufstieg—'Versagen' der Demokraten?" In *Fünfzig Jahre deutsche Republik: Entstehung-Scheitern-Neubeginn*, ed. F. A. Krummacher. Frankfurt: Norddeutsche Verlagsanstalt O. Gödel, 1969.

Studienkommission für die Reform des öffentlichen Dienstrechts. *Bericht der Kommission*. Vol. 12. Baden-Baden: Nomos Verlagsgesellschaft, 1973.

Szablowski, George J., and Hans-Ulrich Derlien. "East European Transitions, Elites, Bureaucracies, and the European Community." *Governance* 6, no. 3 (1993): 304–24.

Taylor, A. J. P. "1848: The Year of German Liberalism." In *1848: A Turning Point*, ed. Melvin Kranzberg. Boston: D. C. Heath, 1959.

Thaysen, Uwe. *Der Runde Tisch. Oder: Wo blieb das Volk?* Opladen: Westdeutscher Verlag, 1990.

Thiele, Willi. *Die Entwicklung des Deutschen Berufs-Beamtentums: Preußen als Ausgangspunkt moderner Beamtentums*. Herford: Maximilian Verlag, 1981.

Touraine, Alain. *The Voice and the Eye*. Cambridge: Cambridge University Press, 1981.

Turner, Henry Ashby, Jr. *Germany from Partition to Unification*. New Haven: Yale University Press, 1992.

Ule, Carl Hermann. *Die Grundrechte: Handbuch der Theories und Praxis der Grundrechte*. Berlin: Duncker & Humblot, 1962.

Verheugen, Günter, ed. *Das Programm der Liberalen: Zehn Jahre Programmarbeit der F.D.P.* Baden-Baden: Nomos Verlagsgesellschaft, 1980.

Vierhaus, Rudolf. "Liberalismus, Beamtenstand und konstitutionelles System." In *Liberalismus in der Gesellschaft des deutschen Vormärz*, ed. Wolfgang Schieder. Göttingen: Vandenhoeck & Ruprecht, 1983.

Viet-Brause, Irmgard. "Partikularismus." In *Geschichtliche Grundbegriffe: Historisches Lexikon zur politisch-sozialen Sprache in Deutschland*, ed. Werner Brunner, Werner Conze, and Reinhart Koselleck. Vol. 4, *Mi-Pre*. Stuttgart: Klett-Cotta, 1990.

Wallach, J. G. Peter, and George K. Romoser, eds. *West German Politics in the Mid-Eighties: Crisis and Continuity.* New York: Praeger Publishers, 1985.

Walser, Martin. "Händedruck mit Gespenstern." In *Stichworte zur "Geistigen Situation der Zeit."* Vol. 1, *Nation und Republik,* ed. Jürgen Habermas. Frankfurt am M.: Suhrkamp Verlag, 1979.

Warbeck, Anke. "Die hergebrachten Grundsätze des Berufsbeamtentums im Wandel der Zeiten und ihre Bedeutung." *Recht im Amt* 37, no. 6 (1990): 292–303.

Watson, Alan. *Focus on Germany: Dangers from the Right?* Washington, D.C.: Edition Q, Inc., 1993.

Weber, Max. *Economy and Society,* eds. Guenter Roth and Claus Wittich. 2 vols. Berkeley: University of California Press, 1978.

Wehler, Hans-Ulrich. *The German Empire: 1871–1918.* Leamington Spa: Berg Publishers, 1985.

Weiss, Hans-Dietrich. "Die Verfassungstreuepflicht des Beamten im Spiegel der Rechtssprechung—eine Dokumentation zum 'Radikalen-Problem.'" *Zeitschrift für Beamtenrecht,* 1974, no. 3: 81–89.

Weizsäcker, Richard von. "The VII International Catalonia Prize." *Catalonia,* 1996, no. 44: 39–43.

Wellershoff, Dieter. "Germany—A State of Flux." In *Observations on "The Spiritual Situation of the Age,"* ed. Jürgen Habermas. Cambridge: The MIT Press, 1985.

Wellmer, Albrecht. "Terrorism and the Critique of Society." In *Observations on "The Spiritual Situation of the Age,"* ed. Jürgen Habermas. Cambridge: The MIT Press, 1985.

Wilson, Graham K. "Counter-Elites and Bureaucracies." *Governance* 6, no. 3 (1993): 426–37.

Wunder, Bernd. *Geschichte der Bürokratie in Deutschland.* Frankfurt am M.: Suhrkamp, 1986.

INDEX